Other Children, Other Languages
Issues in the Theory of Language Acquisition

Other Children, Other Languages
Issues in the Theory of Language Acquisition

Edited by

Yonata Levy
The Hebrew University, Israel

LEA LAWRENCE ERLBAUM ASSOCIATES, PUBLISHERS
1994 Hillsdale, New Jersey   Hove, UK

Lawrence Erlbaum Associates, Inc., Publishers
365 Broadway
Hillsdale, New Jersey 07642

Library of Congress Cataloging-in-Publication Data

Other children, other languages : issues in the theory of language
  acquisition / edited by Yonata Levy.
    p.   cm.
  Rev. papers of an international meeting held June 1991 in
Jerusalem, Israel, under the auspices of the Institute for Advanced
Studies of the Hebrew University.
  Includes bibliographical references and index.
  ISBN 0-8058-1330-6
  1. Language acquisition – Congresses. I. Levy, Yonata.
P118.088   1993
401'.93 – dc20   93-3936
                                                           CIP

Books published by Lawrence Erlbaum Associates are printed on acid-free
paper, and their bindings are chosen for strength and durability.

Printed in the United States of America
10 9 8 7 6 5 4 3 2 1

Contents

v

Preface

This volume is an outgrowth of one week in June of 1991, when the authors of the chapters met in Jerusalem, Israel, under the auspices of the Institute for Advanced Studies of the Hebrew University, to discuss the theoretical contributions of cross-linguistic and cross-populations studies to language acquisition. In addition to individual presentations, time was devoted to discussions of the specifics of the talks and to the general issues that they raised. Although the discussions do not appear in writing, they have deeply influenced the written versions of the papers that appear here.

We would like to take this opportunity to thank the Institute for Advanced Studies, the Faculty of Social Sciences, and the Department of Psychology of the Hebrew University, who made this international meeting possible. Their generous support and the beautiful Jerusalem setting made this week pleasurable as well as enlightening.

—*Yonata Levy*

CHAPTER ONE

Introduction

Yonata Levy
The Hebrew University
Jerusalem

This book presents cross-linguistic and cross-population studies of language acquisition. In the history of research in the area of language acquisition, there were times when such a book would have been controversial. But for over a decade research has moved away to typologically diverse languages and to clinically varied populations in an effort to arrive at a generalized model of language acquisition.

The logic behind cross-linguistic studies is straightforward. Assuming a universal core to language, a position that most current theories take, cross-linguistic studies are necessary in order to establish potential candidates for universal, as well as for language-specific features. This is true not only for claims concerning Universal Grammar (Hyams, chap. 2; Roeper & Seymour, chap. 10; Hoekstra, chap. 5) but also for approaches that argue for the primacy of conceptual distinctions in the early phases of language development (Schlesinger, chap. 4; Bloom, chap. 3), because the assumption that there is a universal core to language does not commit one as yet to what these universals might be. It does state, however, that human languages are similar in certain specific ways that crucially influence acquisition. This latter statement has to be tested in cross-linguistic contexts.

The logic behind the relevance of research in pathology to theories of normal acquisition is less direct. Pathologies may assume a multiplicity of forms, therefore one must decide on a general model within which they will be interpreted. The issue relates to congenital, or very early

1

pathologies, as well as to later, acquired ones. However, it is mostly early pathologies occurring at the preverbal stage that are most relevant to language development; we therefore concentrate on these.

A possible framework within which to think about the relevance of pathology to normal acquisition is provided by the notion of *plasticity*. Generally speaking, plasticity states that the immature, partially differentiated brain has means of compensating for some critical deficiencies.

But how should the notion of plasticity be interpreted? Is it the claim that the eventual outcome of acquisition in children with brain pathologies is equivalent to that in normal children? Let us refer to this interpretation as "weak" plasticity. Alternatively, plasticity can be understood as referring to the final outcome, as well as to the developmental course. If both these are similar to normal we have a case of "strong" plasticity.

If evidence from pathology favors "strong" plasticity, then it will be relevant to models of normal development in a simple, straightforward way: The status of data from pathology will be identical to that of data from normal children (Levy, Amir, & Shalev, 1992). Apart from being an empirical validation of the notion of plasticity—not a small contribution in itself—there is a further, unique methodological advantage to such data, namely, because delay and slowness are the hallmarks of pathology, a protracted period of acquisition may offer new opportunities for a separation of variables in the course of development.

However, if the evidence favors "weak" plasticity, then this would present serious conceptual difficulties for theories that assume the existence of innate constraints that have a crucial role in acquisition, such as the theory of Principles and Parameters (Chomsky, 1986). This is so because on the assumption of "weak" plasticity the child achieves an adequate knowledge of language through an atypical developmental course. If so, then in what sense are these innate constraints crucial for acquisition?

Notice, that it does not matter whether the hypothesized acquisitional course for which innate constraints are crucial, involves linguistic postulates and thus is domain-specific or if it is dependent on particular cognitive substructures, as for example, Schlesinger's theory of the origin of linguistic categories. "Weak" plasticity adversely affects the plausibility of both models since it means that the child can achieve mastery of language through a developmental route that is different from the hypothesized one.

There are three major classes of congenital pathologies for which the notion of plasticity is relevant.

1. First, consider deaf or blind children: If visual input is critical for language acquisition, if a brain that is deprived of visual input is different

in relevant ways from a brain that does receive pictorial information, then there cannot be "strong" plasticity. The reasoning is similar in the case of deaf children. If the modality in which language is cast, vocal versus manual signing, critically affects language development, then there cannot be "strong" plasticity. If, on the other hand, as most research to date shows, being deprived of visual input or having recourse to manual signing instead of voice does not affect the developmental course, the claim of "strong" plasticity is strengthened. I submit that in view of current research in which the line of argument is that sign languages are structurally equivalent to spoken languages (e.g., Bellugi & Studdert-Kennedy, 1980; Lillo-Martin, 1992; Newport & Meier, 1985), it is doubtful whether in the case of deafness one wants to invoke plasticity. However, language learning that proceeds in the absence of visual input, conceivably does call for reorganization.

2. The second group of subjects are children who have suffered a physical insult to the brain. Most relevant to language acquisition are cases that result in major left-hemisphere lesions. Plasticity presupposes that the redundancy of brain tissues is such that if an area of the brain is unable to subserve the function normally assigned to it, other brain areas will take over. In the case of language, one has to assume that there is enough "free" brain areas of the kind that is potentially capable of developing language. A normal developmental course in such children supports "strong" plasticity.

If empirical findings favor "weak" plasticity, this may mean that a deficient brain, for which reorganization is required, is indeed functionally different from the normal. As mentioned earlier, "weak" plasticity will create serious difficulties for theories that presuppose that the ultimate achievement of language knowledge is crucially affected by innate constraints.

A further, intriguing question concerns reorganization. Assuming the brain sets limitations on possible reorganizations and therefore on possible functional outcomes, what might those be? How is such a reorganization related to the normal course of development? Finally, are there different ways of reorganization or does reorganization result in functional commonalities regardless of the nature of the original pathology?

3. A third class of congenital pathologies includes those that result in global, diffuse pathology (such as occurs in Down syndrome or in autism). Plasticity in these cases may assume different forms, including, at least as a logical possibility, a shift in language localization. These children may begin by following the normal course of acquisition. Yet, such "strong" plasticity may nevertheless stop short of the final achievements of normal children as seems to be the case with Down syndrome children (Fowler, 1989).

Alternatively, such children may show "weak" plasticity, that is, good command of language despite a deviant developmental course. It is also possible that both learning and ultimate achievements will be generally "depressed."

What then is the relevance of studies of pathology to theories of acquisition? The reality of work in pathology has taught us that there are always many more possibilities than those outlined by any given theoretical model. Perhaps the way to proceed is to assume some version of a "double dissociation," familiar from cognitive neuropsychology. The minimal methodological requirement is the following: In the absence of a generalized model of acquisition, specific empirical predictions in the context of normal acquisition should be considered. These very same things are examined in cases of pathology. For example, assume that there are two phenomena, A and B, and they present a typical developmental picture in normals. In this case, double dissociation predicts that there will be cases in which A will be deficient yet B will be intact, and other cases in which B will be deficient while A will remain intact.

So, although we can firmly assert the crucial role of cross-linguistic studies in a generalized model of language acquisition, the question whether pathology will prove critical in the same sense remains primarily an empirical one.

A number of general issues recur in this book. They all relate to the major theoretical debate between *nativism* and *empiricism*. Given the current state of our empirical knowledge, one may look on this division as expressing acts of faith from which follow research agendas (Schlesinger, chap. 4). Nativism presupposes innate constraints and mechanisms that guide language acquisition, while empiricism is committed to showing how things develop out of observables. Consider the nature of early categories: Empiricist approaches to language acquisition tend to view early categories as derived from preexisting cognitive/semantic or social interactive notions. However, semantics seems necessary for bootstrapping the formal linguistic system even in some otherwise strictly nativist approaches to acquisition (Pinker, 1984). Notice that whereas semantic, cognitive, or social categorization seem meaningful and relevant to the world around us, abstract linguistic categories are devoid of content and specific to language. Still, all categorization is necessarily dependent on formal systematization.

Another question concerns modularity (Fodor, 1983). Within language acquisition this term has been mostly used to refer to domain specificity and thus is more frequently argued for among nativists. However, modularity is by no means logically entailed by nativism. Domain specificity is ruled out by the empiricist approaches to acquisition, such as those expressed in this volume, although in this case too, one may envisage empiricist approaches to acquisition that will be domain specific, for example, learning based on distributional analyses (Wolff, 1988). The concluding chapter to this book discusses the empirical contributions of data from pathology to the modularity thesis.

While empiricism cannot take off without assuming the existence of certain innate constraints, both within language and in other relevant domains, nativism must allow for development in certain areas. In some cases this involves developmental mechanisms that another discipline will have to explain (i.e., maturation), but there is also linguistic learning, such as must occur for language-specific properties. The differences between the empiricist and the nativist agendas seem to lie in the amount of work that innate constraints are allowed to do, the readiness with which one resorts to such a mechanism and the kind of constraints they purport to be—"obscure" formal parameters or "palatable" cognitive ones.

Hyams (chap. 2) provides a rebuttal of the major criticism that has been voiced against the theory of Principles and Parameters as a theory of acquisition. In her view, research should aim at an account of language acquisition that will have explanatory power. This is achieved when children's grammars are "possible" grammars, that is, intermediate stages en route to the mature grammar. In order to be "possible," children's grammars have to follow the principles of UG. Hyams responds to the charges that the data does not support instantaneous learning and that within UG there is no room for individual differences. She explains how partial learning may be accounted for and shows how principles of UG and core grammar in interaction with language-specific structures result in cross-linguistic differences.

Bloom (chap. 3) argues against the postulation of LAD as an intermediate level between grammar and cognition. He offers an account of the acquisition of the count/mass distinction in English, which assumes a direct mapping between the cognitive notion of individuals and the linguistic notion of count nouns. He further suggests that this notion accounts for facts relating to word learning. Bloom is a nativist who considers general cognitive constraints that map directly onto the linguistic system.

Schlesinger (chap. 4) sets the stage for the debate between empiricism and nativism. He views these as two competing research programs. For Schlesinger, empiricism is the only serious research program currently available. He introduces the process of semantic assimilation as a means of assuring a gradual expansion of semantic categories into corresponding syntactic categories. Clearly, this procedure does not presuppose modularity. He presents counter-arguments to some specific claims made by the theory of Principles and Parameters and concludes that there is no evidence in favor of nativism, nor are there conducive arguments against it.

Hoekstra (chap. 5) is concerned with the fact that child language lacks functional categories. He considers three types of explanations: (a) A parametric approach that assumes that the grammar of children is a "possible" grammar in the sense of Hyams; (b) the subgrammar approach, which is the assumption that at each given stage children have a partial knowledge of the adult grammar; (c) the approach that treats children's grammar as a system by itself rather than as part of UG. Hoekstra offers an analysis of functional categories in Dutch, which stays within the options offered by the principles of UG.

Pizzuto and Casseli (chap. 6) present data from the development of inflections in Italian, which serve to argue against the major tenets of the theory of Principles and Parameters (Chomsky, 1986). In her view the major prediction of this model, namely, that there is rule learning, cannot be reconciled with the thrust of the empirical findings that demonstrate gradual development. Pizzuto views language development as taking place in a cognitive framework within which there is frequent concurring of distributional, pragmatic, semantic, morphophonological, as well as cognitive factors, which together are responsible for the pace and sequence of grammatical development. This is argued in detail in relation to the development of the morphological system in Italian.

Berman's (chap. 7) views are in line with Pizzuto's. She argues that development is affected by a "confluence of cues." It is an interactive developmental approach assuming that development reflects morphological and syntactic complexity on the one hand, and the availability of rhetorical options in the language and typological centrality on the other. Berman discusses the development of Hebrew derivational and inflectional morphology, centering her argument specifically on the development of transitivity. She assumes a general developmental model that proceeds from unanalyzed forms to segregated small systems with rules and structures, to an integrated linguistic system. Thus, early phases will be similar across languages and later acquisitional stages will show more of language-specific differences.

Pye (chap. 8) discusses the variability that is found in the ways in which languages divide semantic domains. The example he studies in detail is the causative system in K'iche'. In this language, transitivity is marked morphologically and has an additional morphological paradigm for causatives. Pye finds that children learning K'iche' follow a unique developmental course for causatives. The fact that they differ from English speakers is interpreted by Pye as evidence for the centrality of the language typology as opposed to the universal structure of the semantic field.

Rispoli (chap. 9) examines the ways in which children learn grammatical relations. Viewed from the perspective of Relational Grammar, his cross-linguistic data afford the conclusion that the child constructs the adult system of grammatical relations by piecing together local, discrete subsystems. The result is a mosaic of relationships that fall together in language-specific ways. This, then, is an approach that views grammatical structure as strongly linked to semantic or pragmatic functions.

Linguistic theory as a data-generating device is the starting point of Roeper and Seymour (chap. 10). The acquisitional problem is seen not as that of knowing which sentences are grammatical but rather ruling out impossible interpretations. In the authors' view, detailed aspects of linguistic theory are relevant to the diagnosis of impairment. Children with deficits inform the general developmental theory, as well as provide insights into specific problems arising in pathology. To illustrate these points, barriers on short and long distance binding are studied in normal children and in one language-impaired child.

Gopnik (chap. 11) considers data from one, multigenerational family in which there is a very large number of dysphasics. Cases like this support the hypothesis that there may be an underlying genetic factor in dysphasia. Gopnik considers various explanations for the difficulties language-impaired people have with morphology. In her view, the data support a description of this deficit in terms of theoretically relevant grammatical distinctions. Dysphasia, under Gopnik's analysis, seems to support the modular view of language.

Tager-Flusberg (chap. 12) adopts the Specificity Hypothesis (Gopnik & Meltzoff, 1986) concerning the relationship between language and cognition, which asserts that the connections between the cognitive and the linguistic domains may be circumscribed and specific, rather than global. She studies the connections between a theory of mind and language deficiency in autism. The findings suggest a strong interdependence between theory of mind as a cognitive notion and its linguistic expression.

Levy (chap. 13) concludes the book. This chapter is an attempt to evaluate the empirical status of the modularity thesis, as viewed from the perspective of language acquisition. Special consideration is given to the studies of pathology, which have repeatedly argued for modularity. I question the interpretation of the evidence and suggest a different way to view these cases. As expected, we are left with more puzzles than answers but, hopefully, also with a clearer conception of the directions in which efforts should be expended.

REFERENCES

Bellugi, U., & Studdert-Kennedy, M. (Eds.) (1980). *Signed and spoken language: Biological constraints on linguistic form*. Weinheim: Verlag Chemie.

Chomsky, N. (1986). *Knowledge of language: Its nature, origin, and use*. New York: Prager.

Fodor, J. (1983). *The modularity of mind.* Cambridge, MA: MIT Press.

Fowler, A. (1989). Language acquisition in Down's syndrome children: Syntax and morphology. In D. Cicchetti & M. Beeghly (Eds.), *Down's syndrome: The developmental perspective.* New York: Cambridge University Press.

Gopnik, A., & Meltzoff, C. (1986). Relations between semantic and cognitive development in the one-word stage: The specificity hypothesis. *Child Development, 57,* 1040–1053.

Levy, Y., Amir, N., & Shalev, R. (1992). Linguistic development of a child with a congenital, localised L.H. lesion. *Cognitive Neuropsychology, 9*(1), 1–32.

Lilo-Martin, D. C. (1992). *Universal grammar and American sign language.* London: Kluwer.

Newport, E., & Meier, R. (1985). The acquisition of American sign language. In D. Slobin (Ed.), *The cross-linguistic study of language acquisition* (pp. 881–938). Hillsdale, NJ: Lawrence Erlbaum Associates.

Pinker, S. (1984). *Language learnability and language development.* Cambridge, MA: Harvard University Press.

Wolff, J. G. (1988). Learning syntax and meanings through optimization and distributional analysis. In Y. Levy, I. M. Schlesinger, & M. D. S. Braine, (Eds.), *Categories and processes in language acquisition* (pp. 179–216). Hillsdale, NJ: Lawrence Erlbaum Associates.

PART ONE

GENERAL THEORETICAL ISSUES

Nondiscreteness and Variation in Child Language: Implications for Principle and Parameter Models of Language Development

Nina Hyams
Department of Linguistics
UCLA

1. INTRODUCTION

Within the idealizations of linguistic theory, language acquisition is viewed as an "instantaneous" process (Chomsky, 1965). One abstracts away from the effects of maturation as well as issues related to the presentation of data. Actual acquisition is of course not instantaneous.[1] In normal development children progress through stages, they make errors (errors from the viewpoint of the adult language), and there are delays. The challenge for any developmental theory is to explain these stages, errors, and delays. It must specify those factors—learning, maturational, grammatical, and so forth—that extend the acquisition process beyond the idealized instant.

The purpose of this chapter is to explore the kinds of predictions that the principle-and-parameter (henceforth P&P) model (Chomsky, 1981) makes with respect to actual, real-time acquisition. I am concerned with two questions in particular: First, do such models predict *discrete stages* in the course of language development and thereby preclude "gradualness," and second, do P&P theories predict *universal stages*, that is, stages that are invariant across children and languages? I argue that whereas parameter models do indeed predict discrete changes in the child's

---

[1]But see Crain (1992), who proposed that actual development is very close to instantaneous, at least as regards principles of core grammar.

grammar—or to follow Chomsky's (1986) terminology, the child's I(nter-nalized)-language—this need not show up as discrete stages in the child's E(xternalized)-language. I further argue that the gradual, piecemeal kind of development that is often observed in children's language results from the staggered development of different modules of language and from interactions between the different modules. Thus, the appearance of "gradualness" is largely an effect of modularity.

I begin by laying out some of the basic assumptions of the P&P frame-work. In section 2, I turn to the issue of discreteness and in section 3 I consider the question of variation. I should note that it is not my in-tention to defend any particular parameter or any particular analysis. Rather, I am interested in the broader question of whether the P&P model has the right general character to provide an explanatory account of cer-tain fundamental aspects of actual language development. Finally, in sec-tion 4, I consider a couple of alternatives to the "standard" view of parameter setting and I show that these models are problematic in vari-ous respects.

2. PRINCIPLE-AND-PARAMETER THEORY: SOME BASIC ASSUMPTIONS

The central concern of linguistic theory is to explain how human beings come to acquire a system of linguistic knowledge the complexity, speci-ficity, and richness of which is vastly underdetermined by the available data. This is the so-called logical problem of language acquisition or what Chomsky sometimes referred to as "Plato's Problem" (Chomsky, 1986). Linguistic theory answers that we are innately endowed with a set of lin-guistic principles, Universal Grammar (UG), which interact with the in-put from a particular linguistic context to determine in each of us a particular adult grammar.

Within current conceptions, UG is a parametrized system (Chomsky, 1981, and references cited there). The parameters of UG express the limit-ed range of variation that exists across languages. Languages are either head first (VO) or head last (OV) (English vs. Japanese); pro-drop or non-pro-drop (Italian vs. German); verbs undergo syntactic movement or they do not (French vs. English); question words undergo syntactic movement or they do not (English vs. Chinese); anaphors are locally bound or they are not (English vs. Icelandic); and so on. The parameters of UG must be "fixed" by the child through experience. The P&P framework makes the implicit assumption, with respect to learning, that the fixing of parameters (and language development, more generally) is an "error-driven" process (Wexler & Culicover, 1980). Children progress from one developmental stage (read grammar) to the next when they encounter input data that are not analyzable by the current grammar.[2] This input is said to "trigger" a change from one state of linguistic knowledge to another state of linguistic knowledge. Given a finite number of parameters, each with a finite number of values (ideally, each parameter is binary), the transition is straightforward. If the child's parameter P is set at value x, then recalcitrant data will trigger a resetting to value y. Error-driven acquisition usually presupposes that in the child's grammar P is set to some "initial" or "default" (also referred to as the "unmarked" value; Wexler & Manzini, 1987).[3] This value may or may not be the correct value for a particular adult "target" language. Where it is incorrect, the input data will force a resetting to the correct value. A further assumption is that the child does not have access to negative evidence—information about the ill-formedness of certain strings—and thus parameters must be fixed on the basis of positive evidence.

Language development thus involves, among other things, fixing the parameters of UG at the values that are correct for a particular linguistic community. The system that results from the fixing of parameters is a "core grammar" (Chomsky, 1981), a central component of linguistic knowledge. Like the familiar "instantaneous acquisition," core grammar is an idealization insofar as what is actually represented in the mind of an individual goes beyond core grammar in various ways. The actual internalized knowledge is a core grammar plus a "periphery" of language-specific rules and constructions, lexical and marked properties, pragmatic rules, and much else.

Central to the P&P model is the modularity hypothesis, that is, the thesis that human language is an epiphenomenon that arises through the interaction of rules and principles in a number of distinct modules. There is modularity within the syntax proper. For example, "passives" are formed by the interaction of principles of case assignment, theta-role assignment, and Move alpha (cf. Baker, Johnson, & Roberts, 1989; Chomsky, 1981; Jaeggli, 1986; and not through a single transformational operation as in the standard theory; Chomsky, 1965). And there is modularity within the larger "language faculty," which contains (minimally) a syntax, a semantics, morphological and phonological components, a pragmatics, as well as a lexicon and language processor, and various other cognitive faculties that affect language. Thus, the P&P theory

---

[2]Equivalently, we may think of this as a parsing problem, that is, the child's parser (which incorporates a grammar) is unable to assign a well-formed representation to some input—a failed parse.

[3]But this assumption is not uncontroversial. See, for example, Valian (1990, 1992), who argued that children start out with *all* values of a parameter, and Verrips (in press). These proposals are discussed in section 4.

marked a radical shift away from a system of language-specific and construction-specific rules prevalent in earlier theories to general principles with parameters of variation.

Any linguistic theory imposes a particular conception of development and thus the theory must reckon with the facts of actual development insofar as these are apparent. Some have argued that the P&P model predicts *discrete stages* in language development and have criticized the model on these grounds because the "stages" of language acquisition appear to be nondiscrete. For example, Verrips (in press) claimed that "the fact that transitions [from one stage to the next, NMH] extend over a long period of time and that they appear to be gradual rather than sudden and complete poses a problem for the parametric approach." Similarly, Pizzuto and Caselli (1992) argued that parameter models preclude "gradual" or "partial" acquisition and thus fail to explain those cases where the child shows less than perfect mastery of some aspect of language. Others have argued that the P&P model predicts a *universal course* of development and thus fails to account for the cross-linguistic and individual variation we find during development (Bates & MacWhinney, 1987).[4] In the sections that follow I explore these issues and criticisms in more detail.

2.1. Nondiscreteness and Modularity

As typically conceived, parameter setting is a discrete operation. For example, the switch from a hypothesized default (+ pro-drop) setting to a (- pro-drop) setting (Hyams, 1986b) is discrete. Fixing the head parameter results in a language that is either head first or head final and not something in between, and so on. Focusing in, then, on the development of core grammar, we have a picture in which the child passes through a series of discrete stages, each corresponding to the fixing of a particular parameter (e.g., pro-drop, verb raising, head direction, etc.). But the picture just described is a highly idealized one; the child's language is not a pure reflection of parameter setting or core grammar. As noted, the system of knowledge that develops in the mind of an individual extends beyond core grammar in various ways. Alongside parameter setting the child must acquire all the peripheral properties of the language, language-specific rules and constructions, the lexicon, the discourse and pragmatic rules, and the marked and exceptional aspects of the language. If development in the different modules is staggered, either due to un-

---

[4]Bates and MacWhinney (1987) claimed that parameter-setting models predict "sudden and all-or-none decisions, carried out in a single specified order, with essentially no opportunity to turn back once a parameter is set" (p. 158).

even maturation or differences in availability or accessibility of input, we would have the appearance of partial or nondiscrete development. Also, one can imagine interactions between the various components, or even between two parameters, which would mask a discrete development and give rise to apparent gradualness (such cases are discussed later).

Consider, for example, the acquisition of "passives." Borer and Wexler (1987) argued that principles of A-chain formation (NP movement) mature at a relatively late point in development. However, the child knows the morphological properties associated with passives prior to the maturation of A-chain (the case and thematic properties of passive participle formation). As a result the child controls adjectival (lexical) passives earlier than verbal passives, which are derived via movement. According to Borer and Wexler, because actional verbs have semantic properties that make them better "adjectives" (e.g., the *torn* doll vs. *the *seen* doll), the child's first passives will be restricted to these verbs (see Maratsos, Fox, Becher, & Chalkley, 1985). We thus have the appearance of gradual acquisition (some verbs are passivized before others); the gradualness, however, is an artefact of uneven development of the different components that make up the "passive construction."

In addressing the question of whether the P&P model predicts discrete stages in language development it is useful to distinguish two senses of the word "language," which Chomsky (1986) referred to as I-language and E-language. *I(nternalized)-language* is the system of knowledge represented in the mind of an individual.[5] The I-language of the child is whatever system of knowledge is represented in the child's mind at some particular maturational point. *E(xternalized)-language*, on the other hand, refers to a set of actual or potential utterances. With respect to the child, E-language would be the set of utterances associated with a particular period of development. Most discussions of discreteness in language acquisition center around the apparent gradualness of transitions in the child's E-language, that is, changes in the set of utterances associated with different "stages" (cf. Bates & MacWhinney, 1987; Pizzuto & Caselli, 1992; Verrips, in press). Thus, null subject sentences do not disappear from the child's corpora in one fell swoop, just as the full range of passivized verbs do not appear at once. It is important to bear in mind, however, that the P&P theory is a theory of I-language and discreteness is a property associated with rules and principles. Thus, to the extent that the theory predicts discrete changes in development, it predicts them with respect to the child's I-language and such changes need not be per-

---

[5]I-language is what was previously referred to as the "grammar" and the term *grammar* is now reserved for the linguist's theory of the I-language. This eliminates the previous ambiguity associated with the term.

fectly reflected in the child's E-language. Viewed from a slightly different perspective, discreteness (like instantaneous acquisition) exists under idealized circumstances, circumstances in which the different modules of I-language develop at precisely the same rate and in complete isolation from one another. Such discreteness is not likely to show up in actual development, which involves interactions between the parameters of core grammar and rules, principles, lexical properties, and so forth outside the core, and in which the rate and manner of development in different components varies. We expect the child's E-language to reflect the interaction of these modules.

The section that follows explores the effects of modularity in language development in more detail, focusing in on the acquisition of binding (anaphora). We begin by outlining some of the different components that enter into binding.

2.2. Discreteness and Modularity: Binding as a Case in Point

As noted earlier, the P&P framework marked a shift away from construction-specific rules to general principles and parameters, a modularized system. Consider, for example, the properties of reflexive and non-reflexive pronouns. "Reflexivization," formerly a transformational rule deriving "himself" from "him" under a particular structural description (Lees & Klima, 1963), is now described by general principles of grammar that determine the structural domain within which an anaphor must be syntactically bound and a pronoun must be syntactically free—Principles A and B of the binding theory (Chomsky, 1981; we return to this later). There are, moreover, pragmatic principles that specify the contexts within which a pronoun may *corefer* with an antecedent, as distinct from being *bound* to an antecedent (Reinhart, 1983). Thus, coreference is possible between *her* and *Lucy* in (1a), though *her* is not c-commanded by *Lucy* and hence there is no binding relation between the two NPs.

(1) a. Most of *her* friends adore *Lucy*
    b. **John* loves *him*
    c. *John* loves *himself*

In (1b), in contrast, neither binding nor coreference is possible between *John* and *him*. Binding is ruled out by Condition B of the binding theory, which requires that pronouns be free from a local antecedent (i.e., within the same clause). Coreference is ruled out by a pragmatic principle that states roughly that coreference is blocked where a bound anaphora interpretation is possible (if the two sentences have the same meaning). Because the sentence in (1c) containing a bound anaphor is well-formed, the sentence in (1b), under a coreference construal, is blocked (Grodzinsky & Reinhart, 1993; Reinhart, 1983).

Languages exhibit a certain amount of variation with respect to binding domains. Thus, anaphors such as English *himself* or Icelandic *sjalfan sig* must be bound within a strictly local domain (i.e., the minimal clause containing the anaphor), whereas Icelandic *sig* (self) may take an antecedent from a higher clause under certain specific structural constraints. Thus, the Icelandic sentence in (2) is grammatical.

(2) *Jón* vildi ađ María rakadi *sig* á hverjum degi
   (John wanted that Maria shaved [subj.] himself everyday)
   'John wanted Maria to shave himself everyday'

Whether an anaphor is "local" or "long distance" is, on some accounts, determined by its morphological structure (Pica, 1987; Reinhart & Reuland, 1991). Thus, morphologically simple anaphors, such as Icelandic *sig*, are assumed to undergo head movement at the level of Logical Form (LF) (not overt syntactic movement), that is, they can "escape" the local clause by moving through the functional head positions, INFL and COMP, and thus find their antecedents in a higher clause. Morphologically complex anaphors, such as English *himself* and Icelandic *sjalfan sig* are NPs and not heads and hence cannot escape the local domain.

There are also lexical factors that affect binding relations. For example, Icelandic has two classes of verbs. When *sig* occurs with verbs of the *raka* (shave) class, as in (2), *sig* may take either a local or long distance antecedent. However, when *sig* occurs with verbs of the *gefa* (give) class, it must take the long distance antecedent (Hyams & Sigurjónsdóttir, 1990; Sigurjónsdóttir, 1993; Sigurjónsdóttir & Hyams, 1991). For example, the most natural interpretation of the sentence in (3) is with *Jón* as the antecedent to *ser*. (*Ser* is the dative form of *sig*.)

(3) Jón vildi ađ Pétur gæfi sér bók í jólagjöf

   'John wanted (subj) that Peter gave self (= John) a book for Christmas'

   'John wanted Peter to give self (= John) a book for Christmas'

Thus, the properties of anaphors in particular languages are determined by the interaction of several modules. Minimally, anaphoric relations involve the syntax, semantics, pragmatics, and the lexicon. Because the acquisition of anaphora involves development in many domains, it is not likely to be an all-or-none development. (What is the likelihood, after all, of all of the relevant principles developing at the same time?). Interestingly, such a discrete development of binding is more expected under a standard theory analysis in which reflexivization was captured by a single (albeit, complicated) rule.

In the following sections, we first look at three "case studies" in the acquisition of binding. It becomes apparent that cases of "gradual" or "partial" acquisition arise through the interactions of the different modules just discussed. In section 2.3 we discuss lexical development and its interaction with principles of grammar.

2.2.1. The Apparent Delay of Condition B. Let us first consider

the so-called developmental delay of Condition B. A number of researchers have shown that in comprehension tasks, children do significantly worse in interpreting sentences such as (4a) than sentences like (4b) (Chien & Wexler, 1991; Jacubowicz, 1984; Jacubowicz & Olsen, 1988; J. Koster & C. Koster, 1986; McDaniel, Cairns, & Hsu, 1990; Wexler & Chien, 1985).

(4) a. Pluto told Donald to wash him.
    b. Pluto told Donald to wash himself.

Specifically, in (4b) children as young as age 4;6 correctly interpret the local antecedent *Donald* as the antecedent to *himself*, in accordance with Principle A of the binding theory. Principle A requires that anaphors be locally bound. In contrast, the same children incorrectly allow *Donald* to serve as antecedent for the pronoun *him* in (4a), thereby violating Principle B of the binding theory, which requires that pronouns be locally free. As noted earlier, languages vary with respect to what constitutes a binding domain for binding; in English the domain is the minimal clause containing the reflexive or pronoun. In other languages the domain may be larger, for example, the minimal tensed clause (Johnson, 1984; Wexler & Manzini, 1987; Yang, 1983) Children must determine the binding domain for their specific language.[6]

---

[6]In this section, we discuss binding in terms of parameter setting, though strictly speaking, the binding theory may not be parameterized in the manner suggested by Wexler and Manzini (1987). Wexler and Manzini proposed, following Johnson (1984) and Yang (1984), that UG makes available a set of binding domains, the minimal clause containing a subject, the minimal tensed clause, minimal indicative clause, and so forth. Children choose the appropriate domain for their language. As noted earlier, however, Pica (1987) more recently proposed that the choice of binding domain for a particular language follows from the morphological properties of specific anaphors, and hence is not a parameter as such.

Though these different approaches to binding have important theoretical consequences, we ignore them for the purposes of this discussion. On either analysis, children must make a determination about some property of their language that would lead to a discrete

Prima facie, the experimental results pertaining to sentences such as (4a,b) lead to the conclusion that children know the binding domain for Principle A early on, but that they do not have similar knowledge of Principle B. However, Montalbetti and Wexler (1985), Wexler and Chien (1985), Chien and Wexler (1991), Grodzinsky and Reinhart (1993) argued that children do in fact know Principle B, which blocks *anaphoric binding* between *Donald* and *him* in (4a); what they do not know (Chien & Wexler, 1991), or fail to use due to processing limitations (Grodzinsky & Reinhart, 1993), is the pragmatic principle discussed previously, which bars *coreference* between these two NPs (Reinhart, 1983). Sentences such as (4a), which allow both binding and coreference, do not permit us to tease apart children's knowledge of Principle B from their knowledge of the pragmatic principle. However, it is easy to construct examples that do tease the two principles apart. Pronouns can *bind* to quantifiers, but they may not *corefer* with them because quantifiers are not referential. We can therefore use sentences containing quantifiers to unambiguously test children's knowledge of Principle B because in this instance the pragmatic principle does not apply.

Chien and Wexler (1991) carried out the relevant experiments. Their results show, in fact, that children do not allow the pronoun *him* to take *every bear* as antecedent in sentences such as that in (5), evidence that they have the appropriate binding domain for pronouns.

(5) Pluto told every bear to wash him.

Their acceptance of a local antecedent in sentences such as (4a) results from the fact that they are allowing *coreference* between the two NPs—an option not available in (5)—in violation of the pragmatic principle.[7]

If we simply took the results related to children's interpretation of sentences (4a) and (5) at face value, we would conclude that children sometimes know Principle B and sometimes do not. In other words, they had only partial or imperfect knowledge of the principle. A more fine-grained analysis shows, however, that the children know the appropriate binding domain for pronouns (evidenced by their performance on sentences

---

development with respect to binding (either by choosing a particular binding domain directly or by determining the morphological structure of a particular anaphor, from which the binding domain can be deduced). Also, both analyses present a highly modularized picture of the system of anaphora. Thus, it seems to us that couching the discussion in terms of parameter setting in no way violates the spirit of Pica's analysis, or other principle-based accounts, such as Reinhart and Reuland (1991), as they relate to acquisition and the issues of discreteness and modularity.

[7]There is further evidence involving children's interpretation of VP-ellipsis that supports this conclusion. See Thornton and Wexler (1991) for discussion.

with quantified antecedents), but their knowledge of this specific syntactic principle is obscured by their lack of knowledge (or inability to implement)—another principle belonging to a completely independent component, namely, pragmatics.[8]

2.2.2. Long Distance Reflexivization in Icelandic.

Consider a second example involving long distance reflexivization in Icelandic. As noted earlier, Icelandic has a "long distance" anaphor *sig*. When *sig* occurs in a subjunctive or infinitival clause, it may take a long distance antecedent, but not when it is contained in an indicative clause. We do not attempt to explain this property of Icelandic grammar here, but simply refer to it as the indicative constraint (cf. Sigurjónsdóttir, 1993; Sigurjónsdóttir & Hyams, 1991, for discussion). Thus, the sentence in (2) is grammatical in Icelandic with *Jón* as the antecedent to *sig*, though the sentence in (6) is not.

(6) **Jón* veit að Maria rakar *sig* a hverjum degi
    'John knows that Maria shave (ind.) himself everyday'

By about age 3;6, Icelandic children freely allow reflexives to take a long distance antecedent, which suggests that the binding domain for Icelandic *sig* is set at that point. However, at that age, long distance reflexivization is not appropriately restricted; children allow long distance reflexivization out of indicatives as well, as in (6). The indicative constraint emerges at around age 4;6. We hypothesize that this is the point at which Icelandic children sort out the morphological contrasts that mark subjunctive versus indicative versus infinitive. (This hypothesis is supported by the longitudinal data showing that children begin using subjunctive morphology at this point.) Thus, we propose that children need not learn the indicative constraint (which follows from general principles of grammar that make an indicative clause an opaque domain—the Tensed S condition of Chomsky, 1977), but that this innate constraint can emerge only after the child has identified the various mood/aspect/tense distinctions. At this point the child will correctly restrict the long-distance use of *sig* to nonindicative clauses.

The acquisition of long distance reflexivization in Icelandic happens in pieces, as is expected given the modularity of the system. First, *sig* is analyzed as a long-distance anaphor, that is, as undergoing head movement. As discussed in the next section, this presupposes a particular kind of morphological analysis. Next, the precise domain that *sig* can move

---

[8]See Chien and Wexler (1991) and Grodzinsky and Reinhart (1993) for detailed discussion of this issue.

out of is determined; that is, the indicative constraint emerges. This latter development depends on the child's lexical knowledge of how tense and mood distinctions are marked. Note that each grammatical development contributing to the phenomenon is discrete so the "gradualness" exists only with respect to the child's E-language and not with respect to I-language.

2.2.3. Long Distance Reflexivization in English. In a series of experiments designed to test the English-speaking child's knowledge of the binding principles, Chien and Wexler (1991) found that there was a marked tendency for the youngest children in their study to select a nonlocal antecedent for the reflexives *himself* and *herself*. Thus, in an act out task with sentences such as (7), children often chose *Kitty/Snoopy* as the antecedent to *herself/himself*.

(7) $\begin{Bmatrix} \text{Kitty} \\ \text{Snoopy} \end{Bmatrix}$ wants $\begin{Bmatrix} \text{Sarah} \\ \text{Adam} \end{Bmatrix}$ (child's name) to point to $\begin{Bmatrix} \text{herself} \\ \text{himself} \end{Bmatrix}$

Connell and Franks (1991) proposed that the long distance responses do not result from a lack of knowledge of the relevant binding principle (Principle A). Rather, they claim that the long distance responses are due to the fact that these children have failed to analyze the English anaphors as NPs. Recall that according to Pica (1987), anaphors that are heads, such as Icelandic *sig*, may escape the local clause and find a long-distance antecedent, whereas NP anaphors are clausebound. Thus, if English-speaking children fail to analyze the internal structure of anaphors such as *himself* and *herself* and analyze them instead as being morphologically simple, it will follow from general principles of grammar that these anaphors may take a long distance antecedent. The Connell and Franks hypothesis receives some interesting support from the fact that the children's performance on anaphors in the Chien and Wexler studies did not improve even where they were provided with a gender cue. Thus, in a sentence such as (8a), children were still likely to choose the long-distance antecedent, namely, *Kitty*, even though this did not match the gender of the anaphor. Interestingly, however, in a sentence such as (8b), which contained a pronoun, children were extremely sensitive to the gender of the pronoun and most often matched it to the same gender antecedent.

(8) a. Kitty wants Adam (child's name) to point to himself.
    b. Kitty wants Adam (child's name) to point to her.

If children are failing to segment the anaphor into a pronoun + self, the lack of attentiveness to gender would follow.

The morphological misanalysis hypothesis predicts that children who allow a long distance antecedent for the English anaphors will only allow the antecedent to be a subject and not an object. This is because on Pica's analysis the anaphor moves to INFL and is thus c-commanded by the subject, but not the object. Thus, only a subject can count as a proper antecedent for an anaphor that undergoes head movement. In contrast, an NP anaphor can take either a subject or object antecedent. Connell and Franks (1991) tested this hypothesis directly with a group of 10 children. Their results show a striking confirmation of the hypothesis. All five children who allowed long distance binding also allowed only a subject antecedent. Four of the remaining children had local binding only and they allowed either a subject or object to serve as antecedent. (We return to the issue of the individual differences later.) Thus, in the development of English anaphora we see that the effects of a syntactic principle, Principle A, is masked by development in a separate, morphological component.

In the aforementioned examples we have seen how principles of core grammar, specifically the binding principles, may interact with other modules (pragmatic, morphological, etc.) to give rise to the gradualness that often characterizes children's E-language. Shifting the focus to I-language, however, we see that the development of the relevant principles and parameters in each component is discrete. The next section discusses the lexicon.

2.3. Lexical Development

Within parameter theory, there is an important distinction between grammatical development and lexical development. While parameter setting is a discrete operation, the learning of particular morphemes and their associated syntactic, semantic, and phonological properties is expected to be piecemeal and gradual.[9] Thus, we do not expect that children will acquire all the verbs in a language in one fell swoop, or that they will acquire all the properties associated with a particular lexical item at the same time. The gradualness of lexical development extends to the learning of inflectional paradigms. Individual affixes must be learned and this learning depends on a number of semantic, syntactic, and phonological factors.

On many analyses there is an interesting interaction between principles and parameters and lexical development. Thus, Wexler and Manzini (1987) proposed a "lexical learning" approach to acquisition of binding. The binding principles are innate, but children must learn the individual

---

[9]The distinction between grammatical development and lexical learning has been discussed quite explicitly within the parameter-setting framework. (See, for example, Chien & Wexler, 1991; Hyams, 1988; Wexler & Manzini, 1987).

anaphors and pronouns in their language. For example, the English-speaking child must learn that *himself* is an anaphor. Having learned this lexical property, the anaphor is "plugged into" the appropriate principle (Principle A), effectively setting the principle into operation.

In Hyams (1986a) I proposed a model of the acquisition of inflection involving both parameter setting and lexical (affix) learning. I suggested a parameter of UG, the stem parameter, which attempts to describe a morphological difference between languages like English, in which a verb may surface as a bare stem—for example, *talk*—and languages like Italian, in which the verb must always bear an affix—for example, **parl* (from *parlare*, 'to speak'). The stem parameter is a well-formedness condition on word formation—a bare stem is/is not a well-formed word. With respect to acquisition, I claim that children "set" this parameter very early on, which is to say that they determine at a young age what constitutes a well-formed word in their language.[10]

The analysis makes two specific predictions for languages of the Italian type. First, Italian children will never produce verbs in their bare stem form (whereas English-speaking children, who, by hypothesis, learn inflection as a "marked" property of the language, will use bare stem forms). Second, children acquiring Italian will learn the inflectional affixes in their language earlier than English-speaking children (which is crucially not a direct deductive consequence of the stem parameter but related to it). This is because, given the Italian setting of the stem parameter, Italian children do not have the option of omitting inflectional elements. Thus, they are forced to a more rapid lexical development. Both these predictions are fully supported by the Italian acquisition data (Pizzuto & Caselli, 1992; chap. 6, this volume). First, Italian children do not produce bare stem forms. Second, the Italian children acquire the singular present-tense affixes (1,2,3 person singular) significantly earlier than English-speaking children acquire the third person singular—*s*.[11]

---

[10]The difference between Italian-like languages and English-like ones with respect to inflectional requirements seems to be an important grammatical difference between the two language types, one that is reflected not only in the differences in the acquisition of inflectional morphology in the two languages but also in the language of adult aphasics. As discussed in Grodzinsky (1990), Italian agrammatic aphasics do not drop inflection in the way that English-speaking aphasics do. The parameter analysis developed in Hyams (1986b) attempted to provide a unified account of this shared property of child language and aphasic language.

[11]Two of the Italian children reached criterion on these forms during Brown's Stage I, and one child in Stage III (age range 1;10–2;1), whereas the English children reached criterion for the third person -*s* at Stage IV, Stage V, or beyond (age range 2;4–3;10, or beyond). The development of plural forms could not be measured because the child failed to use plural subjects. See Pizzuto and Caselli's (1992) Table 9 and their discussion section. See also Hyams (1992b) for further discussion of the Pizzuto and Caselli results and the acquisition of Italian morphology.

The manner in which parameter-setting interacts with lexical development has been a source of some confusion, however. Thus, Pizzuto and Caselli (1992; chap. 6, this volume) claimed that the stem parameter account also predicts that "Italian children will master all verb inflections . . . and that they do so more or less immediately, at the same time as, or shortly after they begin to produce verbs" (1992; p. 506). In fact, the stem parameter account makes no such prediction. As noted earlier, the setting of the stem parameter entails only that the child know a specific condition on word formation. It does not predict instantaneous and simultaneous acquisition across several inflectional paradigms. The fact that Italian children acquire inflectional morphology gradually—for example, singular forms preceding plural forms and present-tense affixes developing prior to past-tense morphology—is entirely consistent with the view of lexical development proposed with the P&P framework.

Pizzuto and Caselli expressed what is perhaps a common misunderstanding about parameter models—that the course of acquisition is determined *solely* by the setting of parameters and hence all of the observable properties of early child language should be accounted for within the parameters of core grammar.[12] However, as discussed previously, the P&P model stresses the modular and interactive nature of language development—exactly the opposite view. We argue here, in fact, that it is precisely the interaction of parameter setting with other aspects of linguistic knowledge (e.g., morphological, lexical, pragmatic) that gives rise to the appearance of "partial" or "gradual" acquisition that we observe in the child's language.

In the next section we turn to the issue of variation.

3. VARIATION WITHIN A
PARAMETER-SETTING MODEL

3.1. Cross-linguistic Variation

Another criticism of the P&P model is that it predicts a *unique* or *universal* sequence in development and hence precludes both cross-linguistic variation and variation among individual children. For example, Bates and MacWhinney (1987) claimed to "present cross-linguistic evidence

---

[12]Pizzuto and Casselli (1992) stated that their data "do not seem to support a parameter-setting account of language acquisition, in which a limited set of innate 'principles' or 'parameters' univocally [sic] determine acquisition" (p. 47). The notion that within P&P models all aspects of acquisition are determined solely by parameter setting is also implicit in much of the discussion in Bates and MacWhinney (1987), to be discussed later.

to suggest that languages vary not only in their end point (as parameter models would predict) but also in the initial hypotheses that children hold about their grammar. The evidence indicates that the sequence of 'parameter testing' is apparently not universal" (p. 158). The implication, which is made explicit elsewhere in their chapter, is that parameter theory predicts that the sequence *should* be universal. In this section, we show that this notion of "universality" is not only misconceived, but runs directly counter to the spirit of the P&P model, which is to describe variation within principled limits—both the variation exhibited by adult languages and that shown within the course of development. In what follows we discuss word order variation in the early grammars of German, Italian, English, Spanish, and Irish. We will see how differences in word order follow directly from the interaction of various parameters.

As a point of departure, consider the early grammars of English, Italian, and German. These three child languages share the property of having phonologically unrealized subjects (as do all child languages). In Hyams (1983, 1986b) I argued that this is due to an initial setting of the null subject parameter under which null subjects are licensed. The parameter will have to be reset in English and German, but not in Italian. In other respects the three languages are quite different. English word order is strictly subject-verb-object (SVO), whereas in Italian postverbal subjects predominate in the earliest stages, giving rise to a verb-object-subject (VOS) order. In German, in contrast, we find both SVO and SOV orders, with verb final patterns predominating (Clahsen, 1986, 1991).

German is a verb-second (V2) language, which is to say, a language in which tensed verbs in root clauses raise to functional head positions (INFL and then COMP under standard analyses). Thus, the verb ends up in C while the SPEC-CP position is occupied by the subject or other XP, as illustrated in (9). (Irrelevant details omitted.) In (9) and all subsequent diagrams, *t* is a "trace" and indicates the position from which the coindexed element has moved. Thus, Hans$_j$ has moved from SPEC IP position, for example.

(9)

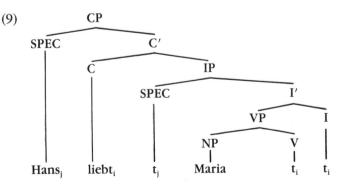

As has been extensively documented, German children set the verb raising parameter very early (Clahsen, 1991; Hyams, 1992a; Meisel & Müller, 1992; Poeppel & Wexler, 1993; Weissenborn and Verrips, 1992; Wexler, 1991). They distinguish between finite and nonfinite verbs; they raise finite forms to a functional head position resulting in (S)VO order, whereas nonfinite forms remain in sentence final position, allowing the basic (S)OV order to surface.[13] Thus, although 2-year-old German- and English-speaking children have the same setting along the null subject parameter (null subjects are possible), they differ with respect to the verb raising parameter; German children raise verbs, English children do not. The difference obviously arises from differences in the input languages; German children see evidence of verb raising in the input—for example, different word orders in main and subordinate clauses—and no such evidence is forthcoming in English. Verbs also raise in Italian (and other Romance languages), though only as high as INFL. We return to this later.

The variation in the position of subjects that we see in English and Italian children is due to a different parameter. Within current grammatical theory, subjects are assumed to be base-generated within the VP and then raised to the external subject position (Kitagawa, 1986; Koopman & Sportiche, 1991), as illustrated in (10). In (10) and in all subsequent tree diagrams, irrelevant details are omitted.

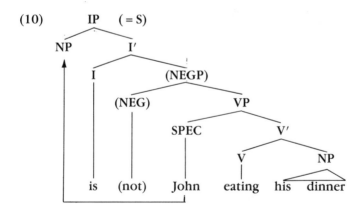

There are parametric options associated with VP-internal subjects. First,

---

[13]There is disagreement over whether children raise the verb only as far as INFL (Clahsen, 1991; Meisel & Müller, 1992) in the early stages or whether they raise all the way up to C (Hyams, 1992a; Deprez & Pierce, 1993; Weissenborn & Verrips, 1992). This issue is irrelevant to our present concerns.

the internal subject position, the SPEC(ifier) of VP on some accounts, may be to the left or right of V'. Second, subject raising may be obligatory or optional.[14] In English, SPEC-VP is on the left (as illustrated in 10, and the subject must raise from the VP-internal position to the external subject position ([NP,S]). That subject raising is required is evidenced by the fact that in noninterrogative sentences subjects are always to the left of negation, as in (11).

(11) a. John is not eating his dinner
     b. *Not John is eating his dinner
     c. *Not is John eating his dinner
     d. *Is not John eating his dinner

In Italian, on the other hand, SPEC-VP is to the right of V' as in (12), and subject raising is optional. If the subject raises to the external subject position, indicated by the arrow in (12), it appears preverbally; if the subject remains within the VP, it appears postverbally.

(12)

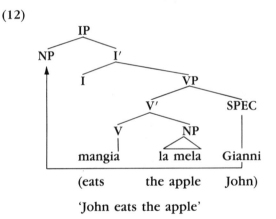

'John eats the apple'

Interestingly, Spanish, a language typologically quite close to Italian, differs from Italian with respect to the base position of the subject. SPEC-VP is to the left of V' in Spanish (Belletti, personal communication, 1992) and the subject may raise to the external subject position,

---

[14]The optionality or obligatoriness of subject raising need not be stipulated, but rather derives from the different ways in which nominative case is assigned, whether via SPEC-head agreement or government. See Koopman and Sportiche (1991) for details and Deprez and Pierce (1992) for an extension of the theory to child language.

as in English. Both structures result in an SVO word order, illustrated in (13).

(13)

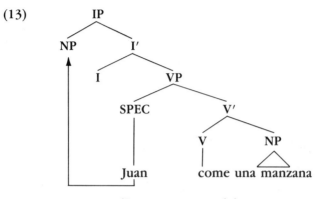

'Juan eats an apple'

Postverbal subjects are possible in Spanish and Italian. In Spanish, however, postverbal subjects occur when the verb raises to I and the subject remains inside the VP, as in (14).[15]

(14)

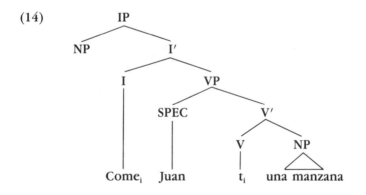

In other languages—for example, Irish—the subject does not raise at all (Koopman & Sportiche, 1991). Irish is underlying SVO; SPEC VP is to the left of V'. The verb raises to I while the subject remains within VP producing a derived VSO order, as in (15).[16]

---

[15]Verbs in Italian also undergo raising to I. This movement does not affect the relative order of the subject and verb, as should be clear from the diagram in (12).

[16]One construction in which the verb does not raise in Irish is the verbal noun construction. This is discussed further in the text.

(15)

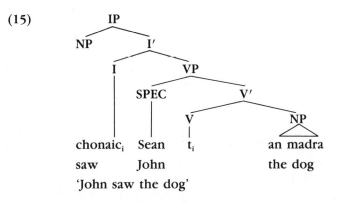

'John saw the dog'

The VP-internal subject hypothesis has direct implications for development. Because the VP-internal subject is the "basic," nonderived position and because subject raising does not occur in all languages, we might expect the early grammar *not* to have subject raising. Irish would then represent the "default" case and subject raising would be triggered in those languages where it is evidenced in the input, such as in English. If this is the case, then subjects in the very early grammar will occur within VP at S-structure, even where this is not an option for adult speakers of the language. Lebeaux (1988), Pierce (1992), Guilfoyle and Noonan (1990), and Deprez and Pierce (1993) adopt essentially this hypothesis to explain why English-speaking children initially have "sentence external" negation, as in the familiar "No the sun shining" (Klima & Bellugi, 1967; Stage A). On their analyses, children do not have sentence external negation; negation is where it should be (in some I projection). Rather, children have VP-internal subjects, which makes the negation appear to be external. At some point subject raising is triggered and we begin to see subjects appear in the external subject position, evidenced by the onset of sentence internal negation, as in "the sun not shining" (Klima & Belulgi, 1967; Stage B). The two stages are diagrammed in (16).

(16) *Stage A*   *Stage B*

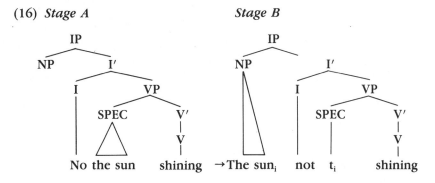

By hypothesis, initial parameter settings are universal and thus we predict that Italian children will also begin with VP-internal subjects. However, because of the differences in the position of the SPEC-VP in Italian and English, Italian subjects will appear in postverbal position. This prediction is confirmed by Bates (1976), who reports that postverbal subjects predominate until about age 2. (See also Schaeffer, 1990, for discussion.)

Interestingly, young Spanish-speaking children show a marked preference for SV(O) word order, in contrast to Italian children (Grinstead, 1992). This is so despite the fact that in the adult language postverbal subjects are quite common. The child's preference for preverbal subjects is also explained under the VP-internal subject hypothesis. Recall that in Spanish the base position for subjects, that is SPEC-VP, is to the left of V'. If Spanish children have neither subject raising nor verb raising at the earliest stage, then their sentences will reflect the basic, nonderived SV(O) order.

Let us turn finally to Irish. Irish presents an interesting case. Despite the fact that the adult language is rigidly VSO, young Irish-speaking children sometimes adopt SVO order. The child's use of SVO word order in the absence of evidence has been argued by some to support the notion that SVO reflects the "natural order" of actions (McNeill, 1975) or concepts (Osgood & Tanz, 1977), or the child's tendency to order the predicate or new information first (MacWhinney & Bates, 1978). Hickey (1990) observed, however, that the children's SVO sentences all occur in the "verbal-noun construction." This is a construction that is similar to the progressive in English in that it is formed with the copula in I. The verbal-noun is marked with a particle *ag*. In the adult language, the presence of the copula in I blocks verb raising and thus *be SVO* word order surfaces, as in (17) (from Hickey, 1990).

(17) Ta an ghaoth ag seideadh.
     (Be the wind blow - Vn)
     'The wind is blowing'

At the relevant stage of development young Irish children (like English-speaking children) omit the copula (indicated by the _____) and thus they appear to have SV(O) word order, as in (18) (from Hickey, 1990).

(18) _____ moncai ag ithe
     (Monkey eat-Vn)
     'Monkey eating'

Hickey showed, however, that Irish children have knowledge of the "positional requirements" of verbs in the language. Outside the verbal-noun construction, Irish children have correct VSO word order, which by hypothesis, is derived through verb raising to I.

To sum up, certain parameters come fixed at an initial, default setting, which may be reset on the basis of language-specific evidence—triggers. These initial settings are presumed to be universal. However, this in no way entails that the "sequence of parameter-testing" is universal, nor that there is a "universal schedule" in the acquisition of particular forms, as suggested by Bates and MacWhinney. We see that children acquiring different languages, children who are at the same developmental level, can have very different grammars. Though parameters arguably have a default value, they can be quickly reset as a function of the input data, for example, the verb raising parameter. Other parameters may remain fixed at the same setting for longer periods of time, for example, the subject raising parameter, but still give rise to different languages—VOS order in Italian, SVO in English and Spanish, and VSO in Irish—through the interaction with other aspects of the grammar, such as the position of specifiers.[17]

There is also evidence that initial parameter settings may be reset (i.e., set to the native language requirement) at different points in different languages. For example, the subject raising parameter seems to be reset in Italian by around age 2;0; at this point Italian children have both postverbal and preverbal subjects. In English, the parameter seems to be reset somewhat later, roughly between ages 2;0 and 3;0, as evidenced by the

---

[17]As an example of the kind of cross-linguistic developmental differences that a parameter model would have difficulty with, Bates and MacWhinney (1987) discussed the well-known observation that children acquiring fixed word order languages learn the correct order early, whereas children learning languages with more flexible word order and rich verbal morphology learn the morphological system at a young age. They correctly noted that there does not seem to be a universal strategy of "word order before morphology" or vice versa. Why Bates and MacWhinney discussed this as a potential counterexample to parameter theory is unclear. There is nothing within the P&P model or the theory of grammar more generally that would lead one to expect that children should have an initial preference for encoding grammatical relations via word order rather than morphology or vice versa.

A second purported universal discussed and rejected by Bates and MacWhinney is the notion that children rely on semantic information such as animacy before using grammatical information such as word order. Bates and MacWhinney noted that whereas English-speaking children rely on word order to uncover grammatical relations, children acquiring languages with freer word order such as Italian, use animacy as a cue to uncovering grammatical functions. Again, they correctly pointed out that there is no universal sequence from semantics to syntax. Although claims have been made that children universally rely on word order (e.g., Sinclair & Bronckart, 1972) or semantic strategies (e.g., Bever, 1970), nothing along these lines has ever been proposed within a P&P framework, and the model in no way predicts such a universal developmental sequence. Hyams (1983, 1986b), one of the earliest acquisition studies within a parameter-setting framework, argued at length against the hypothesis that early grammars are "semantically-based."

appearance of sentence internal negation. Variation of this sort can be explained in one of two ways; either it is due to differences in the children or differences in the input data. It is unlikely, as a general rule, that Italian children mature earlier than English-speaking children, so we must assume that the English "lag" is related to properties of the input. A possible explanation for the lag is that the evidence for subject raising in Italian can be deduced from the order of major lexical categories, whereas in English, it depends on the position of functional elements. Thus, the Italian child hears SVO sentences, and this is sufficient evidence that the subject may raise from its base position. In English, in contrast, subject raising is string vacuous (i.e., the order is SVO whether the subject is internal or external), unless the sentence contains a negative marker or adverbial, for example, 'John does not go' versus '*Not John goes.' If children process functional elements such as negation differently from lexical elements (cf. Garrett, 1980; Lebeaux, 1988; Wu, 1991), then the delay in parameter resetting can be explained as a function of the relative inaccessibility of the English triggering data. A similar kind of explanation would account for the fact that verb raising emerges earlier in German and Irish than in Spanish and Italian.

3.2. Individual Variation

In the previous section, we saw how the interaction of parameter setting with other aspects of grammar and with other components of language (e.g., the processing component) could give rise to different child grammars and different developmental sequences cross-linguistically. But what about the variation that we find among individual children acquiring the same language? According to Bates and MacWhinney (1987), "If parameters are set by 'input data,' then the intermediate stages of acquisition should look the same for all children within a given language—assuming that the linguistic environment is in fact the same on all relevant dimensions" (p. 186).

Individual children raised in the same household receive roughly the same environmental input, yet we are not surprised to find that they develop differently from one another. In the same way, children raised in roughly the same linguistic environment can show individual differences in their language development. Children mature at different rates and within the domain of language there are various components that undergo maturation—the lexicon, the grammar, the language processor, and so on. The rate of maturation in one component may have far-reaching consequences for development in another component. Moreover, there is a difference between "input data" and "intake data" (White, 1981).

Though the input data may be roughly the same for different children in a particular environment, the data that the individual child intakes is dependent on his particular level of maturation. Thus, individual differences may arise out of the different rates of maturation and interactions between the various language-related modules.

To illustrate the point, let us return to our discussion of long-distance reflexivization by English-speaking children (section 2.1.3). We saw that in the early grammar children may allow *himself/herself* to take a nonlocal antecedent contrary to what is possible in the adult language (Chien & Wexler, 1991), and this is arguably due to a morphological misanalysis (Connell & Franks, 1991). The children are analyzing the English anaphors as morphologically simple heads, which may therefore escape the local clause. Recall, however, that not all of the children in the Connell and Franks study had a long distance binding. They found that five of their subjects had long distance binding and allowed only subject antecedents, and five had a strictly local binding and allowed both subject and object antecedents. (Recall that the head movement analysis of long distance binding predicts that these two properties will covary.) The ages of the two groups overlapped and hence there is no reason to assume that these two grammar types represent different developmental stages. Rather, it would appear that some children misanalyze the English anaphors as simple and hence allow long-distance binding, and others have the correct morphological analysis and as a result do not allow long-distance binding. The long distance children will at some point develop the correct morphological analysis of *himself/herself* and the local binding of these elements will follow as a deductive consequence.

There are any number of other examples that illustrate the same point. Even if the data and the sequence of parameters to be set is uniform within a particular language, there are many other aspects of language that fall outside the parameters, but interact with them in crucial ways, for example, morphological analysis, lexical development, pragmatic development, and so on. Individual children may vary in the rate and manner of development in all domains, and depending on the nature of the interaction between the different modules, the effects may be quite widespread and varied. Moreover, Borer and Wexler (1987) and Felix (1986) have argued that parameters themselves may be subject to maturation. To the extent that this is so, individual children may vary in the rate that specific parameters mature.

To sum up, although parameter models predict that certain aspects of development will be universal, this in no way precludes variation at other points. Different languages present different input to the child and individual children (and components) mature at different rates. These factors clearly influence the course of development and provide for a range of cross-linguistic and individual variation. It is important to bear in mind, however, that the variation that we observe in child language exists within well-defined limits. Children do not construct "wild grammars." The challenge for any developmental theory is not simply to account for variation, but to uncover the constraints that narrow the child's hypothesis space.

4. NONDETERMINISTIC MODELS

In this section we return briefly to the issue of discreteness and to the question of how those aspects of language development that appear to be gradual can be explained within a parameter-setting model. I propose that the gradualness is an artefact of the interaction and uneven maturation of different modules of language. There is, however, at least one alternative proposal—gradualness arises because parameters do not come fixed at an initial default value that may be (discretely) reset. Rather, the child's parameters are "open" at the initial state and children analyze the data using *all* values of the parameters. Verrips (in press), for example, proposed that children use a developmental strategy called MAX (maximize input), which states: "For every input string, create as many UG-allowed representations as possible." Representations that are not possible in the adult language are gradually eliminated, eventually leaving the child with the correct parametric setting for his language. So, for example, with respect to the null subject parameter, the particular parameter discussed by Verrips, English-speaking children initially allow both a (Dutch-like) null topic representation (null subject in spec CP), and a (Italian-like) null subject representation (null subject in spec IP) for input sentences such as those in (19).

  (19) a. Want lunch now?
        b. Seems like you're trying to get rid of me.

They have, in Verrips' words, "competing representations," such as those in (20). (Irrelevant details omitted.)

  (20) a.

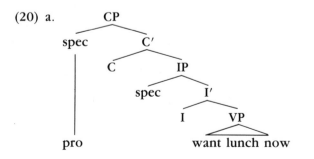

b.

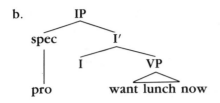

Eventually, the English-speaking child eliminates the null-subject representation in (20b), but this does not completely eliminate null subjects. Rather, the number of null subjects in certain contexts, that is, in spec IP, reduces to zero; whereas those in other contexts, that is, in spec CP (= topic position), with other licensing and identification requirements may still occur. Eventually the child is left with whatever the correct representation is for such sentences in English, and the relevant parameter value.[18] In this way, the loss of null subjects is "gradual," though as Verrips noted, the gradualness is only apparent because what is really involved is a "stepwise" decrease.[19]

Verrips' proposal is similar in many respects to an earlier one by Valian (1990, 1992), who also argued against the idea of an initial setting and the triggering hypothesis, more generally. Valian (1992) proposed a "scale (or hypothesis testing) model" according to which the child "entertains both values (of a parameter) on an equal footing until sufficient evidence accrues to favor one over the other" (p. 2).[20] On Valian's model, development consists of "gathering," "amassing," "tabulating" evidence in favor of one or the other parameter values until "gradually the weight of evidence is clear and weighs down one side very heavily" (1992, p. 12).

Like Verrips, Valian discussed this possibility with respect to the null subject parameter. But the child at the initial state is faced with many parametric options. Pursuing the logic of the competing representations

---

[18]Verrips did not specify what she took to be the representation for sentences such as (19) in English (but see Haegeman, 1990; Hyams, in press-b; Rizzi, in press; for some suggestions), nor how the English-speaking child narrows down the options to precisely these cases, though she did discuss the use of null subjects by German-speaking children in somewhat more detail. This is an important learnability issue, but it is tangential to the central issue discussed in the text, which concerns the plausibility of the nondeterministic, "competing representations" hypothesis.

[19]As Verrips noted, this is an empirical hypothesis. If she is right, we should find null subjects disappearing from specific contexts in a fairly well-defined manner.

[20]Valian's objections to the default setting hypothesis relate to her idea that if children have only one value of a parameter, then they are unable in principle to analyze/parse input data that conflict with that initial setting. As noted in the introduction, however, parameter setting is a "failure-driven" model of development. It is precisely the assumption of a failed parse under some particular parameter value that triggers the resetting to the other value. For discussion of this and other issues raised by Valian (1990, 1992), see Hyams (in press-a) and Kim (1993).

hypothesis, the child would start out with *all* the values of *all* parameters, or in other words, the entire set of possible adult grammars, null subject, non-null subject, verb raising, nonverb raising, subject raising or nonsubject raising, and so forth—a rather implausible assumption on the face of it.

The hypothesis is also implausible from a computational point of view. With respect to Valian's proposal, it is clear that the psychological mechanisms needed to tip the scales in favor of one or the other value would require very large computational resources. At the very least the child must have an accurate memory for previous linguistic data, past failed hypotheses, and parameter settings. The scale model and Verrips' MAX strategy both entail that the child has the ability to represent and compare the multiple, and in principle very large numbers, of representations of a sentence that are generated by the competing grammars. Assuming, for example, that there are five parameters relevant to a particular sentence, the child's grammar would generate 2^5 representations for that sentence. More generally, the grammar would generate 2^n representations for every sentence, where n is the number of relevant parameters, until the child converges on the correct adult value. Thus, the developmental picture that unfolds is one in which the younger you are the more representations/grammars you must cope with.

5. CONCLUSION

In this chapter, we considered the issues of nondiscreteness and variation in child language and the implications of these for P&P models of language development. We have argued that whereas parameter models predict discrete changes in children's system of linguistic knowledge, at least as regards properties of core grammar, they do not necessarily predict discrete changes in their language. The child's language (like the adult's) is epiphenomenal, the result of the interaction of principles and rules in several different components—the grammar, the lexicon, the pragmatic component, language processors, and so forth. Moreover, the child's language is several steps removed from the parameters of core grammar, the level at which parameters are set. We have proposed that interactions between the different modules as well as differences in the rate and manner of maturation of these different modules give rise to the gradual development that we observe in the child's language. Maturational factors in addition to differences in input also account for the cross-linguistic and individual variation that exists across child languages. We considered a number of phenomena (related to binding and word order) in which a particular development (or developments), which are discrete at the level of grammar, show up as "partial" acquisition when viewed from the perspective of the child's E-language. Thus, to understand the developmental process, one must focus on the child's internalized system of knowledge (the I-language). In this respect the study of child language is no different from the study of adult language.

REFERENCES

Baker, M., Johnson, K., & Roberts, I. (1989). Passive arguments raised. *Linguistic Inquiry, 2*, 219–252.

Bates, E. (1976). *Language and context: Studies in the acquisition of pragmatics*. New York: Academic Press.

Bates, E., & MacWhinney, B. (1987). Competition, variation, and language learning. In B. MacWhinney (Ed.), *Mechanisms of language acquisition* (pp. 157–190). Hillsdale, NJ: Lawrence Erlbaum Associates.

Bever, T. G. (1970). The cognitive basis for linguistic structures. In J. R. Hayes (Ed.), *Cognition and the development of language* (pp. 279–362). New York: Wiley.

Borer, H., & Wexler, K. (1987). The maturation of syntax. In T. Roeper & E. Williams (Eds.), *Parameter setting* (pp. 123–172). Dordrecht: Foris.

Chien, Y-C., & Wexler, K. (1991). Children's knowledge of locality conditions in binding as evidence for the modularity of syntax and pragmatics. *Language Acquisition, 1*(3), 225–295.

Chomsky, N. (1965). *Aspects of the theory of syntax*. Cambridge, MA: MIT Press.

Chomsky, N. (1977). Conditions on transformations. In *Essays on form and interpretation* (pp. 81–162). New York: North Holland.

Chomsky, N. (1981). *Lectures on government and binding*. Dordrecht: Foris.

Chomsky, N. (1986). *Barriers*. Cambridge, MA: MIT Press.

Clahsen, H. (1986). Verb inflections in German child language: Acquisition of agreement markings and the functions they encode. *Linguistics, 24*, 79–121.

Clahsen, H. (1991). Constraints on parameter setting: A grammatical analysis of some acquisition stages in German child language. *Language Acquisition, 1*, 361–391.

Connell, P., & Franks, S. (1991, October). *The acquisition of binding theory: A new methodology*. Unpublished manuscript, University of Indiana. Paper presented at the 16th Annual Boston University Conference on Language Development.

Crain, S. (1991). Language acquisition in the absence of experience. *Behavioral and Brain Sciences, 4*, 597–650.

Deprez, V., & Pierce, A. (1993). Negation and functional projections in early child grammar. *Linguistic Inquiry, 24*, 25–68.

Felix, S. (1986). *Cognition and language growth*. Dordrecht: Foris.

Garrett, M. F. (1980). Levels of processing in sentence production. In B. Butterworth (Ed.), *Language production* (Vol. 1, pp. 177–220). London: Academic Press.

Grinstead, J. (1992). *Word order in child Spanish*. Unpublished manuscript, UCLA.

Grodzinsky, Y. (1990). *Theoretical perspectives on language deficits*. Cambridge, MA: MIT Press.

Grodzinsky, Y., & Reinhart, T. (1993). The innateness of binding and coreference: A reply to Grimshaw and Rosen. *Linguistic Inquiry, 24*, 69–102.

Guilfoyle, E., & Noonan, M. (1990). *Functional categories and language acquisition*. Unpublished manuscript, McGill University, Montreal.

Haegeman, L. (1990). Non-overt subjects in diary contexts. In J. Mascaro & M. Nespor (Eds.), *Grammar in progress* (pp. 167–179). Dordrecht: Foris.

Hickey, T. (1990). The acquisition of Irish: A study of word order development. *Journal of Child Language, 17*(1), 17–41.

Hyams, N. (1983). *Acquisition of parameterized grammars.* Unpublished doctoral dissertation, CUNY.

Hyams, N. (1986a, October). *Core and peripheral grammar and the acquisition of inflection.* Paper presented at the 11th Annual Boston University Conference on Language Development, Boston.

Hyams, N. (1986b). *Language acquisition and the theory of parameters.* Dordrecht: Reidel.

Hyams, N. (1988). A principles and parameters approach to the study of child language. *Papers and Reports on Child Language Development, 27*, 153–161.

Hyams, N. (1992a). The genesis of clausal structure. In J. Meisel (Ed.), *The acquisition of verb placement* (pp. 371–400). Dordrecht: Kluwer.

Hyams, N. (1992b). Morphosyntactic development in Italian and its relevance to parameter-setting models: Comments on the paper by E. Pizzuto and C. Caselli. *Journal of Child Language, 19*, 695–709.

Hyams, N. (in press-a). Null subjects in child language and the implications of cross-linguistic variation. In B. Lust (Ed.), *Syntactic theory and first language acquisition: Cross-linguistic perspectives.* Hillsdale, NJ: Lawrence Erlbaum Associates.

Hyams, N. (in press-b). V2, null arguments and C-projections. In T. Hoekstra & B. Schwartz (Eds.), *Language acquisition studies in generative grammar.* Philadelphia: Benjamins.

Hyams, N., & Sigurjónsdóttir, S. (1990). The development of "long-distance anaphora": A cross-linguistic comparison with special reference to Icelandic. *Language Acquisition, 1*(1), 57–93.

Jacubowicz, C. (1984). Markedness and binding principles. *Proceedings of the Northeastern Linguistics Society, 14*, 154–182.

Jacubowicz, C., & Olsen, L. (1988, October). *Reflexive anaphors and pronouns in Danish: Syntax and acquisition.* Paper presented at the 13th Annual Boston University Conference on Language Development, October.

Jaeggli, O. (1986). Passive. *Linguistic Inquiry, 17*, 587–622.

Johnson, K. (1984). *Some notes on binding in Icelandic and subjunctives.* Unpublished manuscript, MIT.

Kim, J. J. (in press). Null subjects: Comments on Valian (1990). *Cognition.*

Kitagawa, Y. (1986). *Subjects in Japanese and English.* Unpublished doctoral dissertation, University of Massachusetts, Amherst.

Klima, E., & Bellugi, U. (1967). Syntactic regularities in the speech of children. In J. Lyons & R. J. Wales (Eds.), *Psycholinguistics papers.* Scotland: Edinburgh University Press.

Koopman, H., & Sportiche, D. (1991). The position of subjects. *Lingua, 85*, 211–258.

Koster, J., & Koster, C. (1986, October). *The acquisition of bound and free anaphora.* Paper presented at the 11th Annual Boston University Conference on Language Development.

Lebeaux, D. (1988). *Language acquisition and the form of the grammar.* Unpublished doctoral dissertation, University of Massachusetts, Amherst.

Lees, R. B., & Klima E. S. (1963). Rules for English pronominalization. In D. A. Reibel & S. A. Schane (Eds.), *Modern studies in English* (pp. 145–159). Englewood Cliffs, NJ: Prentice-Hall.

Maratsos, M., Fox, D., Becher, J., Chalkley, M. A. (1985). Semantic restrictions on children's early passives. *Cognition, 19*, 261–283.

McDaniel, D., Cairns, H. S., & Hsu, J. R. (1990). Binding principles in the grammars of young children. *Language Acquisition, 1*, 121–139.

McNeill, D. (1975). Semiotic extension. In R. L. Solso (Ed.), *Information processing and cognition: The Loyola symposium* (pp. 351–380). Hillsdale, NJ: Lawrence Erlbaum Associates.

MacWhinney, B., & Bates, E. (1978). Sentential devices for conveying givenness and newness: A cross-cultural developmental study. *Journal of Verbal Learning and Verbal Behaviour, 17*, 539–558.

Meisel, J., & Müller N. (1992). Finiteness and verb placement in early child grammars: Evidence from simultaneous acquisition of two first languages: French and German. In J. Meisel (Ed.), *The acquisition of verb placement: Functional categories and V2 phenomena in language development* (pp. 109–138). Dordrecht: Kluwer.

Montalbetti, M., & Wexler, K. (1985). Binding is linking. *Proceedings of the West Coast conference on formal linguistics IV* (pp. 228–245). Stanford, CA: Stanford University Press.

Osgood, C., & Tanz, C. (1977). Will the real direct object in bitransitive sentences please stand up? In A. Juilland (Ed.), *Linguistic studies offered to J. Greenberg on the occasion of his 60th birthday* (pp. 537–590). Saratoga, CA: Anima Libri.

Pica, P. (1987). On the nature of the reflexivization cycle. *Proceedings of Northeastern Linguistics Society, 17*, 483–499. (GLSA) Graduate Linguistics Students Association, University of Massachusetts, Amherst.

Pierce, A. (1992). *On the emergence of syntax: A crosslinguistic study*. Dordrecht: Kluwer.

Pizzuto, E., & Caselli, M. C. (1992). The acquisition of Italian morphology in a crosslinguistic perspective: Implications for models of language development. *Journal of Child Language, 19*, 491–558.

Poeppel, D., & Wexler, K. (1993). Finiteness and V2 effects implicate the existence of functional categories and head movement in early German grammar. *Language, 69*, 1–33.

Reinhart, T. (1983). *Anaphora and semantic interpretation*. Chicago: University of Chicago Press.

Reinhart, T., & Reuland, E. (1991). *Reflexivity*. Unpublished manuscript, University of Tel Aviv and University of Groningen.

Rizzi, L. (in press). Early null subjects and root null subjects. In B. Lust (Ed.), *Syntactic theory and first language acquisition: Cross-linguistic perspectives*. Hillsdale, NJ: Lawrence Erlbaum Associates.

Schaeffer, J. C. (1990). *The syntax of the subject in child language: Italian compared to Dutch*. Unpublished master's thesis, University of Utrecht.

Sinclair, H., & Bronckart, J. (1972). SVO—a linguistic universal?: A study in developmental psycholinguistics. *Journal of Experimental Child Psychology, 14*, 329–348.

Sigurjónsdóttir, S. (1993). *The acquisition of binding in Icelandic*. UCLA Working Papers in Psycholinguistics (Vol. 2). University of California at Los Angeles.

Sigurjónsdóttir, S., & Hyams, N. (1991, October). *The acquisition of binding in Icelandic*. Paper presented at the Boston University Conference on Child Language.

Thornton, R., & Wexler, K. (1991, October). VP ellipsis and the binding principles. Paper presented at the Boston University Conference on Language Development.

Valian, V. (1990). Null subjects: A problem for parameter-setting models of acquisition. *Cognition, 35*, 105–122.

Valian, V. (1992). Children's postulation of null subjects: Parameter setting and language acquisition. In B. Lust (Ed.), *Syntactic theory and first language acquisition: Cross-linguistic perspectives*. Hillsdale, NJ: Lawrence Erlbaum Associates.

Verrips, M. (in press). Learnability meets development: The case of prodrop.

Verrips, M., & Weissenborn, J. (1992). Routes to verb placement in early German and French. In J. Meisel (Ed.), *The acquisition of verb placement* (pp. 283–332). Dordrecht: Kluwer.

Wexler, K. (1991). *Optional infinitives, head movement and the economy of derivations in child grammar*. Unpublished manuscript, MIT.

Wexler, K., & Chien, Y-C. (1985). The development of lexical anaphors and pronouns. *Papers and Reports on Child Language Development, 24*.

Wexler, K., & Culicover, P. (1980). *Formal principles of language acquisition*. Cambridge, MA: MIT Press.

Wexler, K., & Manzini, M-R. (1987). Parameters and learnability in binding theory. In T. Roeper & E. Williams (Eds.), *Parameter setting* (pp. 41–76). Dordrecht: Foris.

White, L. (1981). *Grammatical theory and language acquisition*. Unpublished doctoral dissertation, McGill University, Montreal.

Wu, A. (1991). *A parser-driven model of syntactic development*. Unpublished manuscript, UCLA.

Yang, Q. (1983). The extended binding theory of anaphors. *Language Research*, 19(2).

CHAPTER THREE

Syntax-Semantics Mappings as an Explanation for Some Transitions in Language Development

Paul Bloom
University of Arizona

1. INTRODUCTION

The study of different languages is of obvious relevance to the theory of language development. For one thing, it provides a description of the "target state" of the acquisition process; one could not come to understand the process through which children come to acquire principles of word order in different languages, for instance, without some theory of how word order is understood by adult speakers of those languages. As Macnamara (1982) stressed with regard to cognitive development in general, in order to explain how children come to possess competence within a given domain, we have to have some understanding of just what this knowledge is supposed to be.

Linguistic theory also deals with the unlearned core of linguistic knowledge—what is sometimes called Universal Grammar (UG) (Chomsky, 1981). This is the "initial state" of the acquisition process. To acquire language, children must move from this initial state, which is present in all humans, to possessing properties of adult competence that are not universal and must therefore be learned through attending to adult input (Pinker, 1979, 1984; Wexler & Cullicover, 1980). For instance, languages differ in how they express the thematic roles of arguments; some use word order, others use case markers and order is relatively free. In some languages, wh-movement is overt, in others it is not; some languages draw a grammatical contrast between verbs and adjectives, others do not; and so on. Perhaps the most striking locus of variation is lexical; in English, the word "dog" is used to describe dogs, but French uses the word "chien." The existence of cross-linguistic variation motivates theories of language acquisition, of how children undergo transitions in linguistic knowledge (for a review, see Bloom, in press-b).

One view posits that there exists a Language Acquisition Device (LAD) independent from both linguistic knowledge (either innate or learned) and nonlinguistic cognition, which exists solely for the purpose of facilitating the learning of language. This mechanism is presumed to involve special triggering mechanisms, markedness hierarchies, biases, constraints, and so on. Thus the mechanism of language acquisition is presumed to be distinct from the mechanism of linguistic representation and use.

This chapter explores a "minimalist" alternative, which is that at least some of the transitions in early language development can be explained solely in terms of interaction between linguistic knowledge (UG) and cognitive structures. In particular, it focuses on how children learn the grammatical categories that new words belong to and how they learn the meanings of words. The most developed theories in each of these domains—see Pinker (1984) and Grimshaw (1981) for the grammatical assignment problem and Markman (1990) for the word learning problem—posit that children possess special unlearned mechanisms or biases that exist solely to perform these tasks. But although these proposals largely succeed in describing the transitional process, they fail to capture certain important generalizations. It is argued later that by shifting the focus from special mechanisms of language development to children's knowledge of mappings between syntactic structure and cognitive structure, we can more parsimoniously explain certain transitions in language development.

This chapter is organized as follows. In section 2, the count/mass distinction is introduced, and evidence is presented for the existence of mappings from this syntactic contrast to semantic structure. In section 3, it is argued that children can use these mappings to grammatically encode words as count nouns or mass nouns on the basis of their meaning. In section 4, it is argued that the mappings can work in the other direction, allowing children to use their syntactic categorization of novel words to infer certain core aspects of their meanings. Section 5 focuses on how semantic cues to syntactic structure might interact with syntactic cues to meaning, and a hypothesis about the time-course of language development is defended. Section 6 concludes.

2. A CASE STUDY: THE COUNT/MASS DISTINCTION

No differentiation was made between the standby cars and the ones they often replaced. In the jargon of the precinct they were *all* called "the junk." Cops would pile into the junk when their tour of duty started and would drop off the junk when the tour ended. The junk was both singular and plural. One patrol car was the junk. Six patrol cars were the junk. When a car broke down, it was called "the fuckin' junk." To listen to the motorized cops of Eight-Seven, you'd have thought they were narcotic dealers. (McBain, *Eight Black Horses*, 1985, pp. 99–100)

2.1. Preliminaries

The syntactic count/mass distinction is the contrast between nouns that can follow determiners such as "a" and "another" and can be pluralized ("a dog," "five rocks") versus those that cannot be syntactically individuated and can only follow determiners that pick out an indeterminate quantity of what the noun refers to (e.g., "much water," "a little beer"). Mass nouns can also appear with classifier constructions (e.g., "a piece of furniture," "a grain of sand").

There are reasons for and against using this as a case study for examining the role of syntax-semantics mappings in language development. On the plus side, the count/mass distinction is commonly viewed as a "hard case" for a semantic theory; as discussed later, it is often argued that the semantic basis of the distinction is unreliable at best (and nonexistent at worst). Furthermore, there is a near consensus by developmental psycholinguists, even those sympathetic to semantic approaches (such as Schlesinger, 1988), that syntax-semantics mappings play no role in how young children determine which nouns are count and which are mass. Lastly, the syntactic contrast is assumed to link up with cognitive notions related to quantification that are interesting in their own right. On the negative side, however, the distinction between count nouns and mass nouns is acquired later than other distinctions, such as between nouns and verbs, and is not related to a phrasal contrast, such as between Noun Phrases (NPs) and Verb Phrases (VPs). Given this, and given the general concern that what is true of one domain of language might not be true of all others, the implications of this case study should be treated with caution.

At least for adults, the count/mass distinction certainly has a semantic flavor; objects tend to be described by count nouns and substances tend to be described by mass nouns. This leads to the hypothesis that the only entities described by count nouns are those that have perceptually salient boundaries, and thus those we are able to count, whereas mass nouns describe everything else. Cars and dogs are the sort of things that fall into discrete bounded units—and this explains why one can use "car" and "dog" with count syntax, such as "one car" or "many dogs." In contrast, nonsolid substances and groups of homogeneous particles have no perceptually salient boundaries—what would it be to have "one sand" or "many waters"? One plausible claim, then, is that the count/mass distinction within a language reflects the perceived countability of what the nouns describe.

The claim here is that this is essentially the case: the syntactic count/mass distinction corresponds to a contrast between kinds of entities we perceive as individuals versus those we perceive as nonindividuated entities (or "portions"). But it is equally clear that the count/mass distinction is not defined either in terms of objective properties of entities in the world or in terms of perceptual classes. In particular, the count/mass distinction cannot be defined as a distinction between objects and nonsolid substances. The reasons for this are nicely summed up in the following quote by Ware (1979), but these points are also made by others (including Bloomfield, 1933; Gathercole, 1986; Gleason, 1969; Gordon, 1985; McCawley, 1975; Pelletier, 1979; Quine, 1960; Weinreich, 1966; Whorf, 1956):

> [There is] a tremendous amount of variation that appears unnecessary and inexplicable. . . . There is a count/mass difference between "fruit" and "vegetable" but they apply to things that for all accounts and purposes seem to be alike. Nor can I see anything that would explain the count/mass difference between "footwear" and "shoe," "clothing" and "clothes," "shit" and "turd" or "fuzz" and "cop." These are normally count nouns and mass nouns for basically the same thing. It is also difficult to understand why "knowledge" is a mass noun while "belief" is normally a count noun when our theories tell us they are about such similar material. . . . "furniture" is a difficult case. Although we usually count the pieces in a set, we still talk about how much or how little furniture someone has. Counting is much easier when we are dealing with furniture, but we put up with the mass noun. It would seem more sensible to use a count noun as do the Germans and French. . . . Faced with evidence and examples like these, I become skeptical of finding a general distinction between count and mass occurrences with respect to individuating or anything else. (p. 22)

Several phenomena are introduced above which militate against a semantic account: First, there are cases where the count/mass status of a given word seems unmotivated (e.g., why is "belief" a count noun and "knowledge" a mass noun?). Second, there are pairs of words that have the same extensions but where one is count and the other is mass (e.g., "fuzz"/"cop"). If one could predict the count/mass status of a noun from properties of its extension, these pairs should not exist. Third, there exist cross-linguistic differences and, once again, if the count/mass status of a noun is predictable from the type of entity referred to, languages should not differ. Fourth, there is the existence of words like "furniture," which appear to describe countable entities, but nevertheless get mass syntax. The case of object names that are mass nouns is in apparent violation of the most plausible mapping from count/mass syntax to entities in the world.

Note, however, that all of Ware's objections are against the claim that there is a one-to-one mapping between words and *entities in the world* (see Bloom, 1990a, for discussion). But the sort of mappings relevant to the study of linguistic competence must be between grammatical classes (count/mass, in this case) and *cognitive* classes—not classes of entities in the world. In this sense of the expression, a "semantic theory" is not embarrassed by the fact that the same entity can be described with both a count noun and a mass noun, because this alternation can be viewed as the result of shifting from one construal of that entity to another. Nor is it refuted by the failure to match up linguistic categories one-to-one with classes of entities in the world, because this sort of cognitive theory need not posit that such a relationship exists. Mufwene (1984) put it as follows: "It should be made clear that although communication is about objects and states of affairs in some world, how speakers talk about these is determined more by how they as individual speakers or a community of speakers wish to conceive of/perceive them than by their ontological structures" (p. 204).

Along these lines, one theory of the count/mass distinction is that the contrast between count nouns and mass nouns corresponds to a contrast between those entities that we view as "individuals" versus those we view as "portions" (see, e.g., Bach, 1986; Bloom, 1990a; Jackendoff, 1990; Langacker, 1987; Macnamara, 1986). The notion of individual is related to properties of boundedness and extent and is roughly equivalent to "discrete bounded entity," whereas portion is treated as a default category—any entity not construed as an individual or set of individuals is classified as a portion.

The mapping between the grammatical contrast and the cognitive contrast is most transparent for words that denote material entities—names for bounded objects are count nouns, names for unbounded substances are mass nouns. This brings us back to the observation made earlier: Words such as "dog" and "table" are count nouns and words such as "water" and "sand" are mass nouns. But the explanation is *not* that there are mappings between count/mass and the cognitive notions of object and nonsolid substance, but instead that there are mappings between count/mass syntax and the cognitive contrast between individuals and portions—and, with some rather interesting exceptions (see Bloom, in press-a, for discussion), we are biased to construe physical objects as individuals and nonsolid substances as portions. This semantic basis to count/mass syntax shows up in more abstract domains, as well. For instance, one might argue that "day" is a count noun because it denotes a bounded unit of time, and "race" is a count noun because it denotes a bounded event (see Langacker, 1987, for discussion).

The proposal is summed up here. The syntax-semantics mappings and cognitive biases are presumed to be present for both adults and children.

Syntax-semantics mappings
Count nouns < ----------- > Kinds of individuals
Mass nouns   < ----------- > Kinds of portions

Cognitive biases
There is a strong bias to encode discrete physical objects as individuals.

There is a strong bias to encode substances or collections of particles as portions.

There is some evidence for the first cognitive bias that is independent from linguistic theory and language acquisition. When children are shown a display of objects and asked to count kinds ("How many kinds of animals?") or properties ("How many colors?"), they show a very strong tendency to ignore the question and to only count the discrete objects (Shipley & Shepperson, 1990). Counting involves quantification over individuals, and this result suggests that when children must count entities in the material domain, they are biased to construe objects, and not kinds or properties, as individuals. Note that children are quite capable of counting individuals that are not objects, such as sounds and actions (Wynn, 1990); the suggestion here is that *in the material domain* objects stand out as individuals. And this, combined with the syntax-semantics mapping, explains why they are almost always classified as count nouns.

Wierzbicka (1985) presented a similar account of the cognitive correlates of the count/mass distinction and showed how it can explain some of the cases frequently taken as arbitrary and that vary across languages. She noted, for instance, that the English words "pea" and "noodle" are count nouns, whereas "rice" and "flour" are mass nouns, and she explained this in terms of the physical size of the particles that make up such entities. In general, the bigger the particles are, the more likely a language is to lexicalize the word as a count noun, because people are more likely to construe the word as referring to sets of bounded individuals, and not to an unbounded portion.

She also discussed differences across languages; for instance, in Russian the words for peas and beans and rice and flour are all mass nouns, but the word for broad beans (lima beans) is a count noun. One way to characterize the cross-linguistic phenomena is that languages have different ranges in which they split up a domain into count and mass; very crudely, for English basic-level categories, everything the size of a pea and bigger is construed as an individual and gets described by a count noun, whereas in Russian something has to be as big as a lima bean to be described by a count noun.

Thus although the relationship between objects and count nouns and substances and mass nouns appears to hold across all languages that have the count/mass distinction—names for objects are count nouns, names for substances are mass nouns—there exists variation, which is limited to those cases that can be sensibly viewed as either individuated or non-individuated, such as names for foods like "peas" and "beans," superordinates like "silverware" and "jewelry," and abstract nouns, like "advice" and "information" (see Bloom, 1990a; Markman, 1985; Mufwene, 1984; Wierzbicka, 1985). This suggests that the syntax-semantics correspondence is not something that only exists in the mind of English speakers but instead exists within speakers of all languages. In addition, however, there is some arbitrariness, and children must be sufficiently flexible to semantically categorize nouns solely on the basis of adult input, at least in the more fuzzy cases.

The notion that the count/mass status of more abstract nouns (e.g., "opinion," "advice") is also due to their semantic properties is more contentious, but it is at least plausible that the notion of "individual" can apply outside the material domain. In general, there is nothing implausible about the idea of extending semantic contrasts to abstract thought. We can talk about a single opinion versus many opinions, and the semantic contrast here is the same as if we were talking about one dog versus many dogs. Determiners such as "many" and "few" reflect differences in amount just as clearly when we are talking about prime numbers as when we are asking for cookies. Why should the semantic force of the count/mass distinction be limited to entities we can see and touch? Most likely, this grammatical contrast is not limited to drawing distinctions within the material domain; it can extend to the most abstract aspects of our mental life.

2.2. Psycholinguistic Evidence for an Adult Command of the Cognitive Basis of the Count/Mass Distinction

The strongest test for the semantic basis of a given grammatical distinction is not the existence of correlations within a language (objects tend to be named by count nouns, etc.), but instead emerges from "semantic productivity" on the part of adults and children. The existence of productivity shows that the mappings are present in the minds of naive speakers, rather than the residue of a historical process or the result of a process that only occurs when new words are being coined.

One hardly needs to do an experiment to show that adults possess some semantic productivity, at least with regard to material entities. If adults look at a novel object and hear "look at the blicket," they will encode "blicket" as a count noun; if they see a novel substance and hear exactly the same thing, "look at the blicket," they will take "blicket" as a mass noun. A study (Bloom, 1990a) was conducted to study whether adults are semantically productive outside the material domain. It examined how the *temporal* properties of a noun's referent determine adult intuitions regarding its syntax. According to the theory proposed here, a word describing an entity that is temporally individuated (e.g., "day") is likely to be categorized as a count noun, whereas one describing an entity that is temporally continuous (e.g., "sleep") is likely to be categorized as a mass noun.

Twenty-four MIT undergraduates were tested, and each was presented with four stories. In each story, a new word was used to name either a sensation or a sound, which was described as either occurring as a set of discrete temporal individuals or as a continuous event. Following an idea by Gordon (1985), the words were presented as part of a noun-noun compound (with the key word in boldface) so that it could be taught to the subject without any clue as to whether it was count or mass. The stories are repeated here:

> Sound-individuated: John attached the **moop**-producer to his stereo and switched it on. It started off very loud and then was silent. Then loud, then silent. This went on for many hours.

> Sound-continuous: John attached the **moop**-producer to his stereo and switched it on. It started off very loud and stayed loud, the volume never changed. This went on for many hours.

> Sensation-individuated: The mad scientist attached the **wug**-producer to John's head. John felt the oddest sensation, something that was uncomfortable but not really painful and then it was gone. Then the sensation returned and a second later it was gone. This went on for many hours.

> Sensation-continuous: The mad scientist attached the **wug**-producer to John's head. John felt the oddest sensation, something that was uncomfortable but not really painful. The intensity of the feeling did not change. This went on for many hours.

Following each story were two sentences. In one the word was used as a count noun (e.g., "The machine produced a lot of moops."); in the other, it was used as a mass noun (e.g., "The machine produced a lot of moop."). The subjects were told to circle a number from 1 to 7, according to whether they thought the sentence was "terrible" (1) or "perfect" (7). For each story the subject's preference for the count noun reading was calculated by subtracting the subject's score on the mass noun test sentence from the score on the count noun test sentence. (Thus a negative score indicates a preference for the mass noun sentence). The results are shown in Table 3.1.

For both the sound and sensation stories, there was a statistically significant preference for the count noun reading for the individuated story and the mass noun reading for the continuous story, which suggests that the adult link between count/mass syntax and cognitive structure extends beyond words for material entities.

3. LEARNING THE SYNTACTIC CATEGORIES THAT WORDS AND PHRASES BELONG TO

3.1. Preliminaries

Knowledge of language is expressed in terms of rules and principles mapping over syntactic categories, including "noun" and "adjective," "NP" and "VP," "count noun" and "mass noun." In English, for instance, adult speakers know that adjectives precede nouns within the NP ("the big dog" is appropriate, "the dog big" is not) and this knowledge is not reducible to any generalizations about nonlinguistic categories such as "name for a property" or "name for an object." Syntactic rules and representations appear to be present even in young children; for example, 2-year-old children acquiring English understand that adjectives precede nouns and they obey this generalization even when the noun does not denote a material entity (Bloom, 1990b). This ability requires that they must have somehow learned which words are adjectives and which are nouns. More

TABLE 3.1
Intuitions About the Syntactic Categorization of Novel Words

	Count	Mass	Difference (Count Noun Preference)
Sound (individuated)	4.5	3.3	1.2
Sound (continuous)	2.1	5.5	− 3.4
Sensation (individuated)	5.0	3.0	2.0
Sensation (continuous)	3.0	4.6	− 1.6

generally, the acquisition of syntax requires that children must learn which words and phrases belong to which grammatical categories (Bloom, 1990b; Pinker, 1984; Valian, 1986).

As Fodor (1966) pointed out, this sort of knowledge leaves us with a puzzle. Even assuming that there is a rich store of linguistic knowledge, including a stock of syntactic categories and a set of principles (e.g., "X-bar theory") governing their distribution, the knowledge that the English word "dog" is a count noun and the English word "big" is an adjective cannot be innate. Somehow children must be capable of mapping their linguistic knowledge onto the input that they perceive. This problem is far easier to solve once the child has categorized some words and learned some aspects of grammar; once children know that "big" is an adjective and that English has the rule that NPs are in adjective-noun order, they can infer that "dogs" is a noun by hearing the NP "big dogs" (see Pinker, 1984, 1987, for an explicit model of this process). But this sort of procedure cannot work at the very earliest stage of language development, when children have not yet categorized any words or acquired any rules.

If one does not assume that the linguistic categories themselves are unlearned, then the problem must be expressed differently: It is not that children have to map linguistic categories onto the words and sentences to which they are exposed; instead they must somehow "abstract" these categories from the input. Thus the problem is not mapping the word "dog" onto the preexisting grammatical category of count noun. It is learning that words such as "dog," "cat," and "opinion" share properties that cause them to be grouped into a single category, and then learning rules and principles that apply to this category.

One proposal consistent with this more empiricist view of language is that children perform a distributional analysis on adult speech and classify words as belonging to different parts of speech by virtue of such properties as their position relative to other words and their absolute position within an utterance. As a result of this analysis, it is conceivable that children come to cluster words and phrases into appropriate linguistic classes, such as "noun" and "verb," "count noun" and "mass noun" (see Maratsos & Chalkley, 1981, for discussion, and Levy, 1988a, 1988b, for a defense of this view, in the domain of count/mass and gender contrasts).

This idea has always been popular; distributional learning was called a "discovery procedure" by linguists in the 1940s; Fodor (1966) tentatively adopted it as a solution to the bootstrapping problem, and some computational models for language acquisition have been designed to use this sort of information (see Pinker, 1979). Nevertheless, without constraints (perhaps semantically based) that serve to limit the space of alternatives considered by children, it is doubtful whether such a procedure can work—the search-space is simply too large (Gordon, 1982, 1985; Pinker, 1979, 1984). Gordon (1982), for instance, calculated that a child who searches within the noun phrase for distributional differences between count nouns and mass nouns would have to sift through over 8 billion possible contrasts in order to converge on this distinction. Even assuming that children possess the requisite computational capacities, the search space is so large that it should take a very long period of time for them to acquire the appropriate categories, and this process should be fraught with error. In contrast, the actual process of acquisition appears to be startlingly rapid; children younger than 2½ appear to possess syntactic rules and principles (Bloom, 1990b; Pinker, 1984; Soja, 1992; Valian, 1986), and categorization errors are virtually nonexistent (Brown, 1973; Maratsos, 1982; Pinker, 1984).

A totally unconstrained distributional view is unrealistic for another reason, as it requires there are no unlearned category-specific universals of grammar. The output of such a procedure would be several different classes of words, where each class behaves differently from every other class in the speech of adults. But even assuming that such a procedure exists and could proceed within a realistic time-frame, it does not provide any way for the child to determine which class of words corresponds to "nouns," which to "verbs," and so on. As Pinker (1984) noted, this sort of theory is thus inconsistent with claim that there exists innate syntactic knowledge that is special to these categories. For instance, children could not innately know that all NPs must get case, because there is no way for them to identify which of the different classes of words are NPs. For the same reason, there can be no category-specific semantic knowledge. Under a strong distributional theory, then, one must view it as a historical accident that nouns are names for objects, that prepositions encode spatial relationships, and so on.

All of this appears to be mistaken. There are properties of syntactic categories (both semantic and syntactic) that show up across all or nearly all languages (e.g., Bresnan, 1982; Bybee, 1985; Chomsky, 1986; Greenberg, 1966; Schacter, 1985; Talmy, 1985). Further, when one considers the research showing that 1- and 2-year-olds are capable of drawing inferences from syntactic structure to meaning and vice versa (e.g., Clark & Carpenter, 1990; Hirsh-Pasek et al., 1988; Katz, Baker, & Macnamara, 1974; Naigles, 1990; Slobin, 1985; see also section 4), the notion that they learn language by sorting words into different classes by semantically arbitrary co-occurrence patterns seems very unlikely.

This is not to say that nonsemantic analyses are irrelevant—it is clear, for instance, that children can rapidly acquire morphological distinctions that are not semantically based (Levy, 1988a, 1988b)—but only that they cannot explain how children initially get into the linguistic system and may not even apply prior to the child's determining the syntactic categorization of at least some words. The existence of an immense search space and the fact that very young children possess mappings between grammar and cognition both suggest that more is going on in early language development than an unconstrained distributional analysis.

The existence of syntax-semantics mappings is also problematic for the proposal that children's sensitivity to prosodic cues allows them to syntactically categorize new words, as suggested by L. R. Gleitman, H. G. Gleitman, Landau, and Wanner (1987) and L. R. Gleitman (1990). Children are sensitive to these cues (e.g., Hirsh-Pasek et al., 1987) and it is conceivable that this sensitivity plays some role in solving this problem—but prosody cannot by itself constitute a solution. Suppose 1- and 2-year-olds can use prosody to infer phrase boundaries, and can infer that "the dog chased the cat" has two main phrases: "the dog" and "chased the cat." But which categories do these phrases belong to—which is the NP and which is the VP? Prosody itself tells children nothing, and thus whereas a phrasal parse might play some role in the solution—in combination with a semantic analysis, perhaps—it cannot by itself capture the relevant phenomena: Children do not merely sort words and phrases into different classes, they must categorize them as belonging to specific grammatical categories, categories that have specific syntactic and semantic properties.

3.2. Semantic Competence

A very different sort of solution is as follows: Knowledge of language involves mappings from syntactic structure to cognition (see Enc, 1988, for discussion). Thus "Mary shot John" and "John shot Mary" have the same words but mean different things, presumably because the words occupy different syntactic positions and these syntactic positions have specific cognitive roles associated with them (e.g., Jackendoff, 1983). To take another example, an adult speaker of English will construe "John thinks Fred likes himself" as meaning that John thinks Fred likes Fred, not that John thinks Fred likes John, and this is due to knowledge about the relationships that hold between the NPs "himself," "Fred," and "John," and the mapping between these relationships and intuitions about binding and co-reference (e.g., Chomsky, 1986). In general, there is a systematic relationship between cognitive aspects of sentence understanding—the different roles that participants play in the description of an action, say—and the syntactic structure of the sentence. These mappings are part of what one could call, following Creswell (1978), the child's "semantic competence."

With regard to the problem of determining the syntactic categories that words and phrases belong to, one might suggest that some of these mappings link categories of meaning with syntactic categories, as in the count/mass domain reviewed in section 2. If so, then once children learn (some aspects of) the meaning of a given word, they can (in some cases) use these mappings to infer the grammatical category to which the word belongs.[1]

It is worth comparing this "semantic competence" view to the theory of "semantic bootstrapping," as developed by Grimshaw (1981) and Pinker (1984). Both views posit that children use semantic cues to determine the grammatical category of new words (e.g., If *X* is a name for an object, they can infer that *X* is a count noun). But there is a crucial difference between the two views; the bootstrapping theory posits mappings distinct from linguistic knowledge whereas the "semantic competence" theory does not. Thus Grimshaw (1981, p. 171) posited as a principle of UG (Universal Grammar) that "form and function are independent." The reason why children possess these mappings is because "the LAD . . . gives priority to a grammar with a one-to-one correspondence between form and function." Similarly, Pinker (1984, p. 39) stated, "Although grammatical entities do not have semantic definitions in adult grammars, it is possible that such entities refer to identifiable semantic classes in parent-child discourse." He noted later that these correspondences are only sure to hold in "basic sentences," not in passives, contextually dependent sentences, and so forth (but see Pinker, 1989, for a somewhat different proposal).

To return to the count/mass distinction, the semantic competence theory would state there is a bidirectional mapping between the semantic category "kind of individual" and the syntactic category "count noun," and children can exploit this correspondence when determining the syntactic status of a novel word. Under the semantic bootstrapping account no such relationship would exist, children would instead simply know—as part of their LAD—that names for objects are nouns, and this unidirectional mapping would facilitate their categorization of early words.

---

[1]Note that this is very different from the "semantic assimilation" theory advanced by Schlesinger (1988; chap. 2) where children are assumed to start off only with semantic categories (like "object"), which become more abstract as the result of experience, gradually transforming into syntactic categories (like "noun"). The semantic competence theory assumes that children possess syntactic categories from the very start, which avoids the problem of having to explain how the sort of transformation from semantics to syntax proposed by Schlesinger could ever take place (see also Pinker, 1984). Further, unlike the assimilation proposal, the theory defended here is consistent with children's early acquisition of nouns that are not object names (see section 5), as well as with the fact that even very young children possess a rich understanding of syntactic principles (e.g., Bloom, 1990b).

At first blush, the difference between these accounts might seem like a minor change in emphasis, but some interesting consequences follow from the shift from viewing the child's competence as part of the LAD to explaining in terms of syntax-semantics mappings. First, the semantic bootstrapping theory posits one-way mappings from cognition to syntax and rejects the notion that these mappings can apply in both directions. But there is by now considerable evidence that even young children can draw inferences the other way; they can infer aspects of word meaning from the word's syntactic properties (see section 4). Although it is not impossible that there could exist two separate sets of independent unidirectional mappings—one from semantics to syntax, the other from syntax to semantics—it seems more likely that both sorts of inferences are based on the very same knowledge. Thus the first consequence of a shift from LAD to linguistic knowledge is that, because the mappings would not be limited to the task of determining the syntactic category of words, they could be bidirectional, and thereby also aid in the acquisition of word meanings.

The second consideration has to do with parsimony. It is clear that one needs to posit syntax-semantics mappings that are part of the adult linguistic knowledge (for instance, as part of an explanation for our understanding of thematic roles, binding and coreference, or predicate-argument relations, quantification, and so on). Semantic bootstrapping proposes that in addition to this, there is a set of mappings (actually, as noted earlier, one would have to posit *two* separate sets) that exists solely to facilitate language development. It would be more parsimonious to explain the developmental phenomena in terms of properties of language that we have already posited for independent reasons.

Related to this is the concern that although the generalizations described by the bootstrapping theory are descriptively adequate, there is a large explanatory gap. By simply stipulating the mappings, the bootstrapping theorist cannot explain why these mappings occur and not others. So there is no theory of *why* the mapping is from object names to nouns instead of (say) from object names to verbs or to modals. In general, so long as the form-function mappings exploited in language acquisition are presumed to be distinct from the rest of linguistic theory, systematic relationships between the role of semantics in language acquisition and the role of semantics as part of language itself are left unexplained. Put differently, it would be preferable to have a single theory of linguistic semantics, rather than one for linguistics and one for language development. This is further motivation for capturing the (correct and useful) generalizations discussed by Grimshaw and Pinker in terms of a richer theory of linguistic semantics.

This sets up a further constraint imposed by a shift to UG: The mappings would have to be consistent with linguistic theory. That is, they would have to be couched in the same descriptive terms as statements of semantics. As Grimshaw and Pinker noted, the sort of mappings they proposed, such as "name for object → noun," are not those one would expect to find as part of knowledge of language, which is why they are presumed to be part of a separate LAD. Under a semantic competence account, where there exists no LAD at all, we must posit mappings of quite a different flavor (see Bloom, 1993 for further discussion).

3.3. Previous Research in the Domain of Count and Mass Nouns

If the semantic competence hypothesis is correct, the relevant syntax-semantics mappings must be present in young children. The count/mass distinction is an interesting domain in which to explore this, because it is often argued that the semantic correlates of the syntactic count/mass distinction are not innate but rather come in later, as a result of some sort of linguistic restructuring in the course of language development. Gathercole (1985, 1986) for instance, argued that children start off with distributional categories, with any generalizations regarding the meaning of grammatical categories coming in much later, perhaps by the time they are about 7 or 8 years old. Gordon (1985, 1988) had a rather different view. He concluded that the count/mass distinction is semantic (based on individuation) from the very start, but that young children are insensitive to the perceptual correlates of count/mass syntax; they do not know that names for objects tend to be count nouns and names for substances tend to be mass nouns.

Both Gordon (1985) and Gathercole (1985) presented research suggesting that young children are sensitive to linguistic cues and that they give these cues precedence over perceptual information. This research has been taken as strong evidence against semantic theories of category acquisition. For instance, Levy (1988b) concluded a review of this research by claiming that "Gathercole's conclusions are in complete agreement with the conclusions reached by Gordon (1985); namely that children first learn the linguistic distinction as a morphosyntactic rather than a semantic distinction" (p. 186).

Others have reached similar conclusions. Thus Schlesinger (1988), in his discussion of domains where his semantic assimilation theory does not apply, stated: "Gordon (1985) and Gathercole (1985) have shown that the count/mass distinction is acquired through formal clues rather than via the semantic object-substance distinction. The reason seems to be that, in English, there is not a very consistent correlation between these two distinctions" (p. 147).

These findings have been taken as strong evidence for a nonsemantic view of language development. Levy (1988b) argued, quoting Karmiloff-Smith (1979), that children view language as a formal puzzle, as "a problem space *per se*," which is one version of the distributional theory discussed in section 2.

Some methodological concerns with this research are discussed in detail in Bloom (1990a), but there is a general point worth raising here, also stressed by Gordon (1988). The main result of the count/mass work done by Gordon and Gathercole suggests that when linguistic information and perceptual information are in apparent conflict, children will attend to the linguistic cues. Gordon (1985) found that if children hear something named in a context such as "This is a blicket," they tend to encode "blicket as a count noun; if they hear "This is some blicket," they tend to encode "blicket" as a mass noun. And children will give this linguistic information priority over referential information; so, if they hear "This is a blicket" they are likely to take "blicket" as a count noun regardless of whether "blicket" is describing an object or a substance. Similarly, Gathercole (1985) found that children did not seem to have special difficulties acquiring words where there is an apparent conflict between the perceptual information and the linguistic information as to the word's count/mass status.

These findings are sometimes taken as showing that the child's understanding of count/mass is not semantic; there is an assumption that children have instead memorized some distributional rule such as "Any word following the determiner 'a' is a count noun." This sort of knowledge is distinct from any semantic understanding, which has to be learned at some later point. But although this is logically possible, there is an alternative more consistent with the role of quantifiers in general: When children hear "This is a blicket" and categorize "blicket" as a count noun, they are drawing a *semantic* inference. Specifically, children might represent the determiner "a" as having the semantic role of establishing reference to an individual—because this is in fact what it means—and thus any noun that follows "a" must be able to denote individual entities and therefore must be a count noun. We can express this as follows (see also Bloom, 1990a, chap. 6, for an explicit model of such inferences):

1. "a" is a determiner that has the semantic role of forming an NP that describes a single individual.
2. The head noun within a nonlexical NP that refers to a single individual must have the capacity to refer to a kind of individual—therefore any such noun must be a count noun.

This sort of deduction is just as much an instance of "semantic inference'' as when children categorize ''blicket'' as a count noun through construing the physical object that it describes as an individual. In fact, linguistic cues are a more reliable cue to the semantic status of a novel word than perceptual cues. This is because a given percept can be construed in different ways. If I describe a solid object with the word ''blicket,'' it is *possible* that ''blicket'' is actually a mass noun, because I could be meaning to refer to the stuff that the object is made out of. But linguistic cues are flawless; every noun that can co-occur with a quantifier that has the semantic role of establishing reference to individuals must be a count noun. Given this, the child's early sensitivity to linguistic information might actually support a semantic theory, not refute it. And, as discussed in section 5, there is evidence that even young 2-year-olds possess the requisite semantic understanding of determiners (Soja, 1992).

Besides the research of Gordon and Gathercole, a further motivation for the view that children use distributional information when constructing linguistic categories comes from a set of studies suggesting that children can rapidly acquire semantically arbitrary distinctions, such as the gender contrast in a language like French (see, e.g., Levy, 1988a, 1988b). These results show that children can learn at least some distinctions without the aid of semantics, and they open up the possibility that the categorization of nouns as count or mass is learned the same way.

It is critical, however, to distinguish ''nonsemantic'' from ''distributional.'' Children succeed at acquiring linguistic contrasts such as gender, which shows that they are not limited to categorizing linguistic forms on the basis of meaning. Nevertheless, the fact that children can acquire semantically arbitrary distinctions does not necessarily entail that they must do so through a distributional analysis of the sort assumed by Levy. It seems more likely, given the cross-linguistic similarities in phenomena such as gender marking, that children acquire these semantically arbitrary properties of language through highly constrained analyses of the syntactic tree. For instance, children may attend to agreement markers on determiners because they are disposed to search for morphological regularities between determiners and nouns—not because they are analyzing all possible relations among words within an utterance. Moreover, they might only be able to acquire this sort of semantically arbitrary regularity after they have first used cognition-grammar mappings to determine which words are nouns and which words are determiners in the first place (see also Bloom, in press-b, for discussion).

How can we determine whether children are using semantic knowledge as outlined in the aforementioned inferences, or whether they are merely using memorized distributional rules? Semantic theory predicts that if children do start off with a semantic understanding of count/mass, and if they possess some bias to construe objects as individuals and stuff as portions, then we should expect them to be able to categorize novel words as count nouns or mass nouns via perception. If a word refers to an entity perceived as an individual, they should encode it as a count noun; if something refers to an entity perceived as nonindividuated (as a portion) they should take it as a mass noun. As noted earlier, adults can do this—the studies discussed later concern whether this same capacity exists in young children.[2]

3.4. Evidence for Semantically Based Errors in Children's Speech

One way to explore this issue is by examining how children categorize mass nouns referring to objects, such as superordinates like "furniture" and "money," and food terms like "bread" and "lettuce." These are the sorts of entities that could be construed as either individuals or portions, and are categorized differently across languages. Children often hear these words in grammatically neutral contexts, such as "look at the furniture," where the word can be either count or mass. If children are sensitive to the syntax-semantics mappings, some might mistakenly categorize some of these words as count nouns—because they *do* have to categorize them one way or another and they can readily be construed as referring to individuals. Note that the claim is not that children will use perceptual cues to override linguistic information (we know from Gordon's work that they will not) but rather that in the absence of decisive linguistic cues they will rely on the perceptual information and this might occasionally lead them astray.[3]

---

[2]A study by McPherson (1991, p. 315) is worth mentioning in this regard, as she claimed to show that children younger than 3 "classify words as count nouns or mass nouns on the basis of perceptual information about the extension of words. . . ." Unfortunately, this conclusion is unwarranted. McPherson found that when shown a set of objects and asked to "give me a little vax," children tend to pick out a single small individual. But when shown a collection of particles, and asked "give me a little vax," they tended to scoop out a small portion of these particles. This is an interesting finding, but it does not show that the children are categorizing the noun "vax" as count or mass—in fact, they could succeed at this task without attending to the noun at all. It is quite possible, for instance, that the same result would obtain if the experimenter just pointed to the objects/stuff and told the children "Give me a little." Thus although McPherson's results show that children are sensitive to the object/substance distinction when obeying an instruction, they do not provide any direct evidence that this distinction plays any role in how they determine the count/mass status of novel nouns.

[3]Similarly, we might expect children to occasionally miscategorize certain count nouns as mass nouns. These cases would be very hard to find in spontaneous speech, however. Children frequently omit determiners in their spontaneous speech (e.g., "I want cookie"), and it would be difficult to distinguish cases where children have actually categorized a word as a mass noun and were using a null determiner, from cases where they were merely omitting the appropriate determiner as the result of performance limitations in language production. Because of this, children's miscategorizations of count nouns were not searched for.

This prediction was explored in a study reported in Bloom (1990a), which is summarized here. The spontaneous speech transcripts recorded on the Child Language Data Exchange System (CHILDES) system were studied (MacWhinney & Snow, 1985). The speech of five children was studied: Abe (Kuczaj, 1976); Adam, Eve, and Sarah (Brown, 1973); and Peter (Bloom, 1970). Their ages ranged from 1;6 to 5;2. Two classes of words were searched for: mass nouns that describe entities that can be construed as discrete objects ("bacon," "bread," "cheese," "celery," "clothing," "furniture," "jewelry," "lettuce," "mail," "money," "paper," "spaghetti," and "toast") and mass nouns that describe unbounded substances or substancelike collections of particles ("juice," "milk," "mud," "sand," and "water"). The lists of words were compiled prior to the analysis and are largely based on the transcript search of Gordon (1982).

All utterances with these words were extracted by computer search, and the cases where the words were used in count noun context—with "a," "another," "both," or numerals—were listed. Some examples of the object noun misuses are shown in Table 3.2.

In total, there were 58 cases where the object mass nouns were used as count nouns and 23 cases where the substance mass nouns were used as count nouns. Almost all of the substance errors were instances of one of the following three NPs: "a water," "a juice," and "a milk." These utterances are acceptable under the rule of construal that switches a mass noun to a count noun if the mode of individuating over the substance is contextually available (i.e., "restaurant talk"; Langacker, 1987). In contrast, all of the object mass noun errors are strikingly bad regardless of the context (e.g., "eating a bacon").

Although errors of both sorts were rare, children tend to miscategorize object mass nouns more frequently than substance mass nouns. For three of the five children, this difference is statistically significant (see Table 3.3).

TABLE 3.2
Examples of Object Noun Misuses

I'm gonta have a lettuce (Adam, 3;6)
dat a mail (Adam, 2;7)
here another cheese (Adam, 3;1)
ten money (Adam, 3;4)
I have a new money (Adam, 4;0)
I drop a celery (Eve, 1;7)
eating a bacon (Eve, 2;2)
one spaghetti (Sarah, 2;11)
they have a spooky furniture (Sarah, 4;6)

TABLE 3.3
Relative Proportions of Errors

Child	Object Words (%)	Substance Words (%)
Abe	1.0	1.2
Adam	3.1	0.7*
Eve	5.1	0.5*
Sarah	5.5	2.8
Peter	6.8	2.7*

*$p < .02$, one-tailed

In sum, for at least some children there is a greater proportion of mistakes with object mass nouns such as "money" than for substance mass nouns such as "milk." This suggests that children are sensitive to what a word refers to when determining whether it is a count noun or a mass noun, and provides strong support for the hypothesis that, at least for this linguistic domain, children are capable of using mappings from cognition to grammar when determining the grammatical category that a word belongs to.[4]

4. SEMANTIC COMPETENCE AND THE PROBLEM OF WORD LEARNING

4.1. Constraints versus Mappings

The research discussed earlier concerned how children determine the syntactic category to which new words belong. It was suggested that semantic competence plays some role in how children solve this problem. It is also

---

[4]The precise nature of these errors is open to different explanations. In Bloom (1990a), it was assumed that children who say "a furniture" have actually miscategorized "furniture" as a count noun in their lexicon and have to await positive evidence to attain the correct adult knowledge. But the low rate of errors is consistent with another hypothesis, which is that children have the correct semantic encoding from the very start but sometimes fail to access the relevant memory trace and—as a default—apply the syntax-semantics mappings "on the fly." For a word such as "furniture," this sort of productivity could lead to the child producing the word with count noun syntax, because it can be construed as referring to a kind of individual. This alternative is motivated by the Marcus et al. (1992) theory of children's past-tense overregularization, which suggests that these errors are due to failure to recover the irregular form in memory (such as "went") followed by application of a morphological rule (leading to production of "goed"). The results converge nicely; in an analysis of 25 children, they find an average rate of overregularization of 4.2%; the average rate of count noun errors for mass object names found in the study reported above is 4.3%.

possible that children's knowledge of syntax-semantics mappings might help them in the domain of word learning.

Unfortunately, our understanding of what it is to possess the meaning of a word lags far behind our theory of syntax (Carey, 1982; Premack, 1990) and there is a similar lag in our acquisition theories. Furthermore, whereas syntactic development can be viewed as a deductive process (e.g., parameter-setting), word learning is an inductive process. To take a specific example, consider an adult pointing to Fido and saying to a child "Look at the dog." Assuming that the child can somehow attend to the relevant new word ("dog") and can connect it to the entity that the adult intends to describe (and neither problem is trivial; see Gleitman, 1990), this word could still have an infinity of meanings. Some of these correspond to possible words in a natural language ("dog," "animal," "fido," "large," "brown," "tail"), others do not ("the front half of dogs," "dogs until the year 2000 and then pigs," "dogs and pencils," "dogs and Donald Trump," etc.). The goal of a theory of word learning is to explain both why children never entertain the "crazy" possibilities, and how they so quickly determine which of the "natural" possibilities adults intend to express.

Under the perspective that word learning is an inductive process, it is necessary that the child's hypotheses be somehow ordered or ranked (Fodor, 1975; Goodman, 1983) and there must exist constraints that rule out (or bias against) entire classes of hypotheses. In the domain of language development, Markman and her colleagues presented the following constraints, which are argued to be special to the problem of word learning (e.g., Markman & Hutchinson, 1984; see Markman, 1990, for a review):

1. Whole Object constraint: "A novel label is likely to refer to the whole object and not to its parts, substance, or other properties" (Markman, 1990, p. 59).
2. Taxonomic constraint: "Labels refer to objects of the same kind rather than to objects that are thematically related" (Markman, 1990, p. 59).

There is by now a large body of evidence showing that 2- and 3-year-olds do behave in accordance with these posited constraints. When taught a word for a novel object, children tend to categorize the word as referring to other whole objects of the same kind (e.g., Baldwin, 1989; Clark, 1973; Macnamara, 1982; Markman & Hutchinson, 1984; Markman & Wachtel, 1988; Soja, Carey, & Spelke, 1990; Taylor & Gelman, 1988; Waxman & Gelman, 1986). These constraints appear to be special to language, not the result of more general biases in sorting or categorizing (e.g., Markman & Hutchinson, 1984; Waxman & Gelman, 1986).

It is well-known that such constraints do not apply to adult language—all languages have proper names and pronouns, which do not describe taxonomies, as well as nouns that refer to object parts, solid substances, and so on. The reasonable assumption is that these constraints are independent of adult knowledge of language—they emerge at a very early stage of language development to help children learn words and then they disappear (or, alternatively, they are overridden by other properties of language).

The problem with this, however, is that these same sort of exceptions show up even in the speech of very young children (Bates, Bretherton, & Snyder, 1988; Bloom, in press-a; Gopnik & Choi, 1990; Nelson, 1988, 1990). Even 1- and 2-year-olds use words that do not refer to taxonomies (e.g., pronouns and proper names), words that do not refer to whole objects (e.g., verbs and adjectives), and even count nouns that do not describe whole objects ("nap," "joke," "family," etc.). As Nelson (1990, p. 335) noted, there exist "many abstract social and cultural concepts that are incorporated into the language and presented in passing to children, who pick them up seemingly without effort." She listed some words found in the speech of 20-month-old children (from Bates et al., 1988), including: "bath," "breakfast," "friend," "day," "morning," "week," and "uncle."

Once again, instead of having to posit special innate constraints that exist solely to facilitate language development, it may be possible to get around these descriptive problems by explaining the children's success at word learning in terms of more general properties of linguistic knowledge. In fact, there is an interesting parallel between Markman's constraints on word meaning and the semantic bootstrapping theory discussed earlier. For each, there is a specific mechanism leading that succeeds in explaining the transition for a clear subset of cases. Under semantic bootstrapping, for instance, the child correctly infers that "dog" is a noun because it is the name for a kind of object; for Markman's taxonomic and whole object constraints, the child correctly infers that "dog," because it is a novel label, must refer to a kind of object. But the same question arises for both proposals—does one need to posit special mappings, or could the transition be explained in terms of syntax-semantics mappings that are part of language in general? For word learning, there is a descriptive problem as well; although the whole object and taxonomic constraints succeed in sharply constraining the child's inference, they are overly powerful and thus cannot explain the fact that children appear to have no problem acquiring words that do not refer to taxonomies or do not refer to whole objects.

The idea that syntax-semantics mappings facilitate the acquisition of word meaning is not new. Brown (1957) demonstrated that children are sensitive to the grammatical contrast between count nouns, mass nouns, and verbs when inferring whether a new word refers to an object, a substance, or an action. Katz et al. (1974) showed that even 17-month-olds are sensitive to the noun/NP contrast when determining whether a word refers to an individual versus a kind (see Gelman & Taylor, 1984, for a replication, and Bloom, 1990b, for discussion). More recently, Gleitman and her colleagues argued that these sort of innate mappings play a crucial role in the acquisition of verb meanings (see Gleitman, 1990, for a review). Other relevant theory and research along these lines includes Carey (1982), Landau and Gleitman (1985), Landau, Smith, and Jones (1988), Landau and Stecker (1990), Naigles (1990), and Waxman (1990).

One way to look at this proposal is as follows: A core problem when learning a new word is determining the ontological category that the word meaning belongs to—does the word express a kind or a particular entity, an entity or a spatial relation, an event or a proposition? Languages allow words to appear within only a small number of such categories and, at least in some instances, there may be a one-to-one mapping between ontological class and grammatical category. Thus once a child can distinguish the grammatical categories in the input (e.g., once the child can tell nouns from verbs, or count nouns from mass nouns), this mapping can radically narrow down the search space by directing the child toward the relevant range of meanings. In fact, even if the child does not yet know which words belong to which grammatical categories this sort of one-to-one mapping could still constrain inferences about word learning, because any word has to belong to *some* grammatical category and thus must belong to one of the small number of corresponding conceptual categories.

In sum, once the child can determine the syntactic structure of the words and phrases she is exposed to, mappings from syntax to meaning can play a valuable role in the process of word learning.

4.2. Semantic Competence as an Alternative to Markman's Constraints

One specific proposal (Bloom, in press-a; Macnamara & Reyes, 1990) is that the mappings between count nouns and kinds of individuals can subsume the constraints discussed previously. More generally, there are no constraints on words per se; but only on the possible meanings of members of certain syntactic categories. It's not the fact that "pencil" is a word that constrains children's inferences, it is the fact that it is a count noun. A subset of the mappings that were relevant previously apply here; these are repeated here:

Syntax-semantics mapping
Count nouns < ----------> Kinds of individuals
Property of cognition:
There is a strong bias to encode discrete physical objects as individuals.

This proposal has the immediate advantage that the exceptions suffered by the taxonomic and whole object constraints go away. The mappings supported here are actually true of both child and adult language. Words such as "Fred," "water," and "hit" are exceptions to the constraints discussed by Markman, as they are words that do not describe kinds of objects. But they are not exceptions to the syntax-semantics mappings, as they are not count nouns and the previous mapping does not apply to them. Further, words like "nap" and "forest" *are* consistent with this mapping; although they do not describe whole objects, they do refer to kinds of individuals and as such they are perfectly appropriate as count nouns. As discussed earlier, the notion of individual, although most clear for material entities like dogs and chairs, also extends to bounded units of time, abstract entities, and so on.

This hypothesis makes two predictions about the language and cognition of young children: (a) Children should possess cognitive understanding of the notion "individual" that extends beyond the material domain and (b) they should map this notion onto the grammatical category of "count noun."

4.3. Developmental Evidence for the Role of These Mappings in Word Learning

The notion of infants and children possessing a semantic notion of "individual" that is more abstract than "whole object," one encompassing collections of objects, temporally bounded events, mental states, and so on, would be anathema to someone working within a Piagetian framework of cognitive development. In this framework one of the core assumptions is that the thoughts of very young children are linked to their perceptual experience, and abstract thought only emerges much later, at least past the age of 2 (see Piaget, 1954, for a classic statement of this view).

At least with regard to the concept of "individual," there is good reason to reject this notion. Perhaps the most striking finding is that of Starkey, Spelke, and Gelman (1990). In one experiment, 6- to 8-month-olds were exposed to strings of either two sounds or three sounds. Following this, two pictures were shown simultaneously, one with two objects and one with three objects. Even the youngest infants tested preferred to look at the picture that had the same number of objects as there were sounds. This suggests that infants possess a notion of two individuals or three individuals, where "individual" encompasses both discrete sounds and objects. Along the same lines, Wynn (1990) discovered that almost immediately after children are capable of using the number system to count objects, they can count sounds and actions, further suggesting, quite independently of syntax, that children possess the appropriate abstract semantic notion of "individual."

Given that children have this abstract notion, what is the evidence that they hook it up with count/mass syntax? Probably the strongest support is from Soja (1992), which suggests that as soon as children acquire the surface manifestation of count/mass syntax (i.e., at the point when they learn the semantic properties of the determiners), they can apply the mappings to the acquisition of novel words. She tested children at the point when they start to productively use count/mass syntax (at about age 2½). In one condition, she taught them a new word for a pile of stuff. When the word was presented as a mass noun referring to a pile of stuff, they tended to construe it as a name for that kind of stuff (i.e., as having a similar meaning to "clay"), but when taught it as a count noun, many appeared to construe it as referring not to the stuff itself, but to the bounded pile (i.e., as having a similar meaning to "puddle" or "pile"). This suggests that very young children can use the count/mass syntax of a word to determine the ontological category that it belongs to.

Nevertheless, it is still an open question whether the mapping is from count noun to "individual" (as hypothesized earlier) or whether it is to a less abstract notion such as "bounded material entity." The most direct evidence would be if children at the age studied by Soja could productively extend the semantic implications of count/mass syntax to nonmaterial entities, and there is as yet no support for this claim. There is, however, a study with slightly older children (Bloom, 1990a).

Extending the design of Brown (1957), 3- and 4-year-old children were taught names for perceptually ambiguous stimuli, which could either be construed as a set of individuals or as an unindividuated portion. In one condition, the stimulus was food, either lentils or colored pieces of spaghetti, and it was the sort of entity that could be easily named with either a count noun or a mass noun. In another condition, the stimulus was a string of bell rings from a tape recorder, one after the other at a very fast rate, which could be construed either as a set of discrete bells or as an undifferentiated noise and therefore could be described with either a count noun or a mass noun.

All children were presented with the same stimuli but they were taught the noun in different ways. One group was taught it as a count noun: "These are feps—there really are a lot of feps here"; the other group was

TABLE 3.4
3-Year-Olds

	Object (%)		Sound (%)	
	Count	Mass	Count	Mass
one	75	31.3	56.3	25
more than one	25	68.7	43.7	75

taught it as a mass noun: "This is fep—there really is a lot of fep here." Then the children who were taught the word as a count noun were told to "give the puppet a fep" for the food condition or, in the sound condition, were given a stick and a bell and asked to "make a fep." The children who had been taught the word as a mass noun were told to "give the puppet fep" or to "make fep" with the stick and the bell. If children are sensitive to the semantic properties of count/mass syntax, they should act differently in the count condition than in the mass condition. When asked for "a fep," they should tend to give one object or make one sound; when asked for "fep," they should tend to give a handful of objects or make several sounds.

The results are summarized in Tables 3.4 and 3.5. (The percentages are the proportion of responses that were either to give one object/make one sound, or to give many objects/make many sounds, as a function of whether the word was presented as a count noun or a mass noun.)

For both ages and both conditions (object and sound) there was a statistically significant effect of noun syntax on the children's responses (see Bloom, 1990a, for a more detailed discussion of the stimuli, design, and results). The 3-year-olds tended to give one object/make one sound when exposed to count syntax and to give many objects/make many sounds when exposed to mass syntax. This was also true for the 4-year-olds on the object condition. For the sound condition, they showed a strong tendency to make many sounds regardless of the syntax, though this tendency was significantly diminished when the word was presented as a count noun as opposed to as a mass noun. (This difference should not be taken as showing that there is an actual decrease in the ability to

TABLE 3.5
4-Year-Olds

	Object (%)		Sound (%)	
	Count	Mass	Count	Mass
one	81.3	56.3	37.5	12.5
more than one	18.7	43.7	62.5	87.5

use semantic competence; instead it is most likely due to the fact that the presentation of the stimuli was simplified for the younger children.)

In sum, this study suggests that even children as young as 3 years are sensitive to the semantic implications of count/mass syntax even for entities that are not material.

5. THE TIME COURSE OF TRANSITIONS IN LANGUAGE DEVELOPMENT

The hypothesis so far has been that certain transitions in language development can be explained in terms of mapping relations that are part of linguistic knowledge. In particular, children and adults map count/mass syntax onto aspects of quantificational semantics, and this mapping is used to determine which words are count nouns and which are mass, as well as to narrow down the range of possible meanings that a novel word might have.

Several issues remain. Children somehow have to learn the mapping from quantificational semantics to the surface expression of count/mass syntax; they have to learn that "a" expresses the notion of a single individual, "much" expresses the notion of a sizable quantity of a portion, and so on (see Bloom, 1990a). Further, there are deep parallels between count/mass syntax and aspectual contrasts within the verbal system (e.g., Bach, 1986; Jackendoff, 1990); a more complete theory would explain how the semantic property of quantification applies to events and properties in addition to entities.

These are problems yet to be solved, but what I want to turn to here is an apparent *contradiction* that arises under this theory. The theory advanced in this chapter is not only that children use meaning to learn syntax (as with the semantic bootstrapping theory of Pinker and Grimshaw) but also that they can use syntax to learn meaning (as with the syntactic bootstrapping theory of Gleitman). As it stands, however, this leads to a puzzle: The hypotheses that children use syntax to acquire meaning and that they use meaning to acquire syntax cannot both be true at the beginning of language acquisition—something must break the circle.

There are two possibilities: Children could use some sort of nonsemantic procedure to determine the syntactic structure of sentences, and then use this syntactic information to initially acquire the meanings of some words (as proposed by Gleitman, 1990). Alternatively, they could use some sort of nonsyntactic procedure to determine the meanings of words and then use this semantic information to determine the syntactic categories that the words belong to (as proposed by Pinker, 1984). Each possibility rests on a nontrivial assumption regarding the process of language development. The first assumes that it is possible to learn the syntactic category of a word without knowing what it means. The second assumes that it is possible to learn the meaning of a word without knowing its syntactic category.

There are no knock-down arguments for either theory, but certain factors suggest that the second hypothesis is correct, that is, the course of language development is as follows: Children first use syntax-semantics mappings to learn the syntax of some words from their meanings and later, once they have acquired enough of the syntactic structure, they can use this syntactic knowledge to facilitate the acquisition of word meaning.

The claim that syntactic bootstrapping only operates after some word learning has taken place does not diminish its value as a theory of vocabulary acquisition. It is quite consistent with the previous ordering that 99.99% of the words an adult knows has been acquired with the aid of syntactic structure. However it does entail that the very first words children use can be acquired without syntax. The reasons to adopt this claim are because the syntax-first premise (that children can acquire syntax without the aid of semantics) is problematic, whereas the semantics-first premise (that children can acquire word meaning without the aid of syntax) is quite plausible.

5.1. Why Meaning May Be Necessary for Syntax Learning

The argument against the syntax-first premise was alluded to in the discussion of the problems with distributional theory, but it could be put somewhat differently here: Clearly, the syntactic bootstrapping theory is up to its neck in innate syntactic categories—because it is the purported mapping between such categories and semantic structure that is supposed to aid in the acquisition of word meaning—and thus the problem for the child is to determine which words and phrases in the input correspond to these categories.

But how? Note that children could not very well use syntactic information to solve this problem (e.g., the knowledge that the subjects of verbs are NPs), because they have not yet figured out what verbs are, where their subjects are, and so on. And psychophysical cues are little help either; as far as we know there are no universals of language of the form "Nouns are at the beginning of utterances" or "Verbs are spoken with a higher pitch than adjectives." There is evidence that children are sensitive to prosodic cues and it is possible that they can use them to segment the sentences they hear into discrete phrases—but this will not tell them which phrases belong to which grammatical categories.

There do exist strong and universal generalizations that children are capable of utilizing, but they all have to do with meaning. Names for kinds of individuals belong to the linguistic category "count noun," for instance, and because whole objects are naturally construed by children as individuals, this could enable them to determine that the word "dog" is a count noun. Use of such mappings is the only known procedure that could enable the child to categorize "dog" as a count noun in the absence of any other syntactic knowledge.

This is shaping up as what Fodor (1975) alludes to as a Lyndon Johnson argument ("I'm the only president you've got"): We know that there exist mappings that can solve the problem of syntactically categorizing new words, and because there is no other method that we know of, this serves as a useful working hypothesis. Given our ignorance of language and language development, one should treat this sort of argument cautiously. For instance, it may well be that phrasal information, a constrained distributional analysis, and some set of syntax-phonology mappings could conspire to solve the problem. But as it stands, we know of no such procedure, and this casts doubt on any theory positing a syntactic parse prior to any understanding of word meaning.

5.2. Why Syntax Is Not Needed for Meaning Acquisition

One might object that a semantics-first procedure cannot work, because it is impossible to determine the meaning of a word without already knowing its syntax. Gleitman (1990), for instance, emphasized the serious problems with existing theories of meaning acquisition and suggested that syntactic information plays a crucial role in this process. It is clear that syntax *helps*—as discussed, children younger than 2 are sensitive to syntactic structure in the process of word learning. Furthermore, at least for some words, syntax might be essential. Consider, for instance, the acquisition of words for cognitive states such as "think" or "promise." As Gleitman (1990) suggested, the syntactic properties of these verbs (the fact that they take sentential complements, for instance) might explain how children learn that these are verbs of perception/cognition. Nevertheless, there are three reasons to believe that at least some words can be learned without the aid of syntax (see also Bloom, 1993).

First, children comprehend and produce words long before they show any understanding of syntax, and there appears to be a strict maturational schedule for the emergence of lexical knowledge that precedes the emergence of syntactic knowledge (Meier & Newport, 1990). Whereas there is some evidence that children understand certain aspects of syntax prior to their productive command of these structures (e.g., Hirsh-Pasek et al., 1985), children's first words emerge at about 10 to 12 months and there is no evidence at all that these children at this stage possess any understanding of the syntax of English.

Second, people must be capable of using nonsyntactic means to acquire at least some aspects of word meaning. Even with the aid of cognition-grammar mappings, there is still an infinity of possible meanings that children have to sort out. Knowing that a given word refers to a kind of individual (as a result of hearing it used as a count noun) is only a small part of the word learning puzzle. Children also have to determine which kind of individual the word refers to. From the stand point of syntax, there is no difference at all between "dog" and "cat," "water" and "milk," "whisper" and "shout." The fact that children can learn the semantic differences between these words suggests that they possess the ability to learn at least some properties of meaning in the absence of syntax.

Finally, adults are able to learn the meanings of at least some words without syntactic support. Upon hearing the word "moop" in isolation used to describe a novel animal, an adult could infer that it is a name for that animal, while upon hearing it used to describe a familiar object with a novel color, an adult could infer that it is a name for that color. It should be stressed that it is not clear how far this independence from syntax goes—for instance, could an adult naturally acquire a name for an event ("running") or a name for a spatial relationship ("in") without syntactic support? The answer is not clear. But it does seem that the acquisition of some words—if only names for some entities and some properties—is possible without overt syntactic information. If adults can do this, there is no principled reason to doubt that children can do it as well.

To sum up, the suggestion is that children must initially use meaning to syntactically categorize new words. Further, it was argued children can learn the meanings of some words without syntactic support. This suggests that children first learn the meaning of some words, perhaps only names for objects and substances, and use their semantic competence to categorize these words as belonging to specific grammatical categories. This provides them with enough syntactic knowledge to use the mappings to infer aspects of the meanings of the new words they learn.

6. SUMMARY

One way to explain transitions in language development is through special mappings that exist to facilitate the acquisition process, as argued by Grimshaw (1981), Pinker (1984), and Markman (1990). The alternative explored here is that some transitions in language development are the result of the interaction between (a) mappings that are part of linguistic knowledge (e.g., count nouns refer to kinds of individuals) and (b) cognitive biases (e.g., whole objects are construed as individuals). Studies of children's and adults' understanding of the count/mass distinction show that children are capable of using these mappings to categorize new words as count or mass, which occasionally leads to errors, and that children can determine the ontological status of a novel entity, either material or nonmaterial, by attending to count/mass syntax. This supports the hypothesis that the interaction between linguistic knowledge and cognition is sufficient to explain certain key transitions in language development.

ACKNOWLEDGMENTS

Preparation of the manuscript was supported by a University of Arizona Social and Behavioral Sciences Research Support Grant. I thank Yonata Levy and Karen Wynn for very helpful comments on an earlier draft.

REFERENCES

Bach, E. (1986). The algebra of events. *Linguistics and Philosophy, 9*, 5–16.

Baldwin, D. A. (1989). Priorities in children's expectations about object label reference: Form over color. *Child Development, 60*, 1291–1306.

Bates, E., Bretherton, I., & Snyder, L. (1988). *From first words to grammar: Individual differences and dissociable mechanisms*. Cambridge: Cambridge University Press.

Bloom, L. (1970). *Language development: Form and function in emerging grammars*. Cambridge, MA: MIT Press.

Bloom, P. (1990a). *Semantic structure and language development*. Unpublished doctoral dissertation, MIT. [Available upon request from the author]

Bloom, P. (1990b). Syntactic distinctions in child language. *Journal of Child Language, 17*, 343–355.

Bloom, P. (1993). *Nominal acquisition and the relationship between meaning and form*. Manuscript under review.

Bloom, P. (in press-a). Possible names: The role of syntax in word learning. *Lingua*.

Bloom, P. (in press-b). Recent controversies in the study of language acquisition. In M. A. Gernsbacher (Ed.), *Handbook of psycholinguistics*. San Diego, CA: Academic Press.

Bloomfield, L. (1933). *Language*. New York: Holt.

Bresnan, J. (Ed.). (1982). *The mental representation of grammatical relations*. Cambridge, MA: MIT Press.

Brown, R. (1957). Linguistic determinism and the part of speech. *Journal of Abnormal and Social Psychology, 55*, 1–5.

Brown, R. (1973). *A first language: The early stages*. Cambridge, MA: Harvard University Press.

Bybee, J. (1985). *Morphology: A study of the relation between meaning and form*. Philadelphia: Benjamins.

Carey, S. (1982). Semantic development: The state of the art. In E. Wanner & L. R. Gleitman (Eds.), *Language acquisition: The state of the art* (pp. 347–389). New York: Cambridge University Press.

Chomsky, N. (1981). *Lectures on government and binding.* Dordrecht: Foris.

Chomsky, N. (1986). *Knowledge of language: Its nature, origin, and use.* New York: Praeger.

Clark, E. V. (1973). What's in a word? On the child's acquisition of semantics in his first language. In T. E. Moore (Ed.), *Cognitive development and the acquisition of language* (pp. 65–110). New York: Academic Press.

Clark, E. V., & Carpenter, K. L. (1990). The notion of source in language acquisition. *Language, 65,* 1–30.

Creswell, M. (1978). Semantic competence. In M. Guenther-Reutter & G. Guenther (Eds.), *Meaning and translation* (pp. 9–60). London: Duckworth.

Enc, M. (1988). The syntax-semantics interface. In F. J. Newmeyer (Ed.), *Linguistics: The Cambridge survey: Vol. 1. Linguistic theory: Foundations* (pp. 239–254). New York: Cambridge University Press.

Fodor, J. (1966). How to learn to talk: Some simple ways. In F. Smith & G. Miller (Eds.), *The genesis of language* (pp. 105–122). Cambridge, MA: MIT Press.

Fodor, J. (1975). *The language of thought.* New York: Crowell.

Gathercole, V. (1985). "He has too many hard questions": The acquisition of the linguistic mass-count distinction in *much* and *many. Journal of Child Language, 12,* 395–415.

Gathercole, V. (1986). Evaluating competing linguistic theories with child language data: The case of the mass-count distinction. *Linguistics and Philosophy, 9,* 151–190.

Gelman, S. A., & Taylor, M. (1984). How 2-year-old children interpret proper and common names for unfamiliar objects. *Child Development, 55,* 1535–1540.

Gleason, H. A. (1969). *An introduction to descriptive linguistics.* London: Holt, Rinehart & Winston.

Gleitman, L. R. (1990). The structural sources of word meaning. *Language Acquisition, 1,* 3–55.

Gleitman, L. R., Gleitman, H., Landau, B., & Wanner, E. (1987). Where learning begins: Initial representations for language learning. In F. J. Newmeyer (Ed.), *Linguistics: The Cambridge survey: Vol. 3. Language: Psychological and biological aspects* (pp. 150–193). New York: Cambridge University Press.

Goodman, N. (1983). *Fact, fiction, and forecast.* Cambridge, MA: Harvard University Press.

Gopnik, A., & Choi, S. (1990). Do linguistic differences lead to cognitive differences? A cross-linguistic study of semantic and cognitive development. *First Language, 10,* 199–215.

Gordon, P. (1982). *The acquisition of syntactic categories: The case of the count/mass distinction.* Unpublished doctoral dissertation, MIT.

Gordon, P. (1985). Evaluating the semantic categories hypothesis: The case of the count/mass distinction. *Cognition, 20,* 209–242.

Gordon, P. (1988). Count/mass category acquisition: Distributional distinctions in children's speech. *Journal of Child Language, 15,* 109–128.

Greenberg, J. H. (1966). Some universals of grammar with special reference to the order of meaningful elements. In J. H. Greenberg (Ed.), *Universals of language* (pp. 73–113). Cambridge, MA: MIT Press.

Grimshaw, J. (1981). Form, function, and the language acquisition device. In C. L. Baker & J. McCarthy (Eds.), *The logical problem of language acquisition* (pp. 183–210). Cambridge, MA: MIT Press.

Hirsh-Pasek, K., Gleitman, H., Gleitman, L. R., Golinkoff, R., & Naigles, L. (1988, October). *Syntactic bootstrapping: Evidence from comprehension.* Paper presented at Boston University Conference on Language Development, Boston.

Hirsh-Pasek, K., Golinkoff, R., Fletcher, A., DeGaspe Beaubien, F., & Cauley, K. (1985, October). *In the beginning: One word speakers comprehend word order.* Paper presented at Boston University Conference on Language Development, Boston.

Hirsh-Pasek, K., Kemler-Nelson, D. G., Jusczyk, P. W., Wright, K., Cassidy, K., Druss, B., & Kennedy, B. (1987). Clauses are perceptual units for young infants. *Cognition, 26,* 269–286.

Jackendoff, R. (1983). *Semantics and cognition.* Cambridge, MA: MIT Press.

Jackendoff, R. (1990). *Semantic structures.* Cambridge, MA: MIT Press.

Karmiloff-Smith, A. (1979). *A functional approach to language acquisition.* New York: Cambridge University Press.

Katz, N., Baker, E., & Macnamara, J. (1974). What's in a name? A study of how children learn common and proper names. *Child Development, 45,* 469–473.

Kuczaj, S. (1976). *-ing, -s, and -ed: A study of the acquisition of certain verb inflections.* Unpublished doctoral dissertation, University of Minnesota, Department of Psychology.

Landau, B., & Gleitman, L. R. (1985). *Language and experience.* Cambridge, MA: Harvard University Press.

Landau, B., & Stecker, D. S. (1990). Objects and places: Geometric and syntactic representation in early lexical learning. *Cognitive Development, 5,* 287–312.

Landau, B., Smith, L. B., & Jones, S. (1988). The importance of shape in early lexical learning. *Cognitive Development, 3,* 299–321.

Langacker, R. W. (1987). Nouns and verbs. *Language, 63,* 53–94.

Levy, Y. (1988a). The nature of early language: Evidence from the development of Hebrew morphology. In Y. Levy, I. M. Schlesinger, & M. D. S. Braine (Eds.), *Categories and process in language acquisition* (pp. 3–41). Hillsdale, NJ: Lawrence Erlbaum Associates.

Levy, Y. (1988b). On the early learning of formal grammatical systems: Evidence from studies of the acquisition of gender and countability. *Journal of Child Language, 15,* 179–186.

Macnamara, J. (1982). *Names for things: A study of human learning.* Cambridge, MA: MIT Press.

Macnamara, J. (1986). *A border dispute: The place of logic in psychology.* Cambridge, MA: MIT Press.

Macnamara, J., & Reyes, G. (1990). *The learning of proper names and count nouns: Foundational and empirical issues.* Unpublished manuscript, McGill University and Universite de Montreal.

MacWhinney, B., & Snow, C. (1985). The Child Language Data Exchange System. *Journal of Child Language, 12,* 271–296.

Maratsos, M. (1982). The child's construction of grammatical categories. In L. R. Gleitman & H. Wanner (Eds.), *Language acquisition: The state of the art* (pp. 240–266). New York: Cambridge University Press.

Maratsos, M., & Chalkley, M. A. (1981). The internal language of children's syntax: The ontogenesis and representation of syntactic categories. In K. Nelson (Ed.), *Children's language* (Vol. 2, pp. 127–214). New York: Gardner Press.

Marcus, G. F., Pinker, S., Ullman, M., Hollander, M., Rosen, T. J., & Xu, F. (1992). Overgeneralization in language acquisition. *Monographs of the Society for Research in Child Development, 57*(Serial No. 228).

Markman, E. M. (1985). Why superordinate category names can be mass nouns. *Cognition, 19,* 31–53.

Markman, E. M. (1990). Constraints children place on word meanings. *Cognitive Science, 14,* 57–77.

Markman, E. M., & Hutchinson, J. E. (1984). Children's sensitivity to constraints in word meaning: Taxonomic versus thematic relations. *Cognitive Psychology, 16,* 1–27.

Markman, E. M., & Wachtel, G. F. (1988). Children's use of mutual exclusivity to constrain the meaning of words. *Cognitive Psychology, 20,* 121–157.

McBain, E. (1985). *Eight black horses*. New York: Avon.

McCawley, J. (1975). Lexicography and the count/mass distinction. *Proceedings of the First Annual Conference of the Berkeley Linguistic Society, 1*, 314–321.

McPherson, L. (1991). "A little" goes a long way: Evidence for a perceptual basis of learning for the noun categories COUNT and MASS. *Journal of Child Language, 18*, 315–338.

Meier, R., & Newport, E. (1990). Out of the hands of babes: On a possible sign advantage in language acquisition. *Language, 66*, 1–23.

Mufwene, S. (1984). The count/mass distinction and the English lexicon. In D. Testen, V. Mishra, & J. Drogo (Eds.), *Papers from the parasession on lexical semantics* (pp. 200–221). Chicago: Chicago Linguistics Society.

Naigles, L. (1990). Children use syntax to learn verb meanings. *Journal of Child Language, 17*, 357–374.

Nelson, K. (1988). Constraints on word meaning? *Cognitive Development, 3*, 221–246.

Nelson, K. (1990). Comment on Behrend's "Constraints and Development." *Cognitive Development, 5*, 331–339.

Pelletier, F. (1979). Non-singular reference: Some preliminaries. In F. Pelletier (Ed.), *Mass terms: Some philosophical problems* (pp. 1–14). Dordrecht: Reidel.

Piaget, J. (1954). *The construction of reality in the child*. New York: Basic Books.

Pinker, S. (1979). Formal models of language learning. *Cognition, 1*, 217–283.

Pinker, S. (1984). *Language learnability and language development*. Cambridge, MA: Harvard University Press.

Pinker, S. (1987). The bootstrapping problem in language acquisition. In B. MacWhinney (Ed.), *Mechanisms of language acquisition* (pp. 399–441). Hillsdale, NJ: Lawrence Erlbaum Associates.

Pinker, S. (1989). *Learnability and cognition*. Cambridge, MA: MIT Press.

Premack, D. (1990). Words: What are they, and do animals have them? *Cognition, 37*, 197–212.

Quine, W. V. O. (1960). *Word and object*. Cambridge, MA: MIT Press.

Schacter, P. (1985). Parts-of-speech systems. In T. Shopen (Ed.), *Language typology and syntactic description: Vol. 1. Clause structure* (pp. 3–61). New York: Cambridge University Press.

Schlesinger, I. M. (1988). The origin of relational categories. In Y. Levy, I. M. Schlesinger, & M. D. S. Braine (Eds.), *Categories and processes in language acquisition* (pp. 121–178). Hillsdale, NJ: Lawrence Erlbaum Associates.

Shipley, E. F., & Shepperson, B. (1990). Countable entities: Developmental changes. *Cognition, 34*, 109–136.

Slobin, D. I. (1985). Crosslinguistic evidence for the language-making capacity. In D. I. Slobin (Ed.), *The crosslinguistic study of language acquisition: Vol. 2. Theoretical issues* (pp. 1157–1256). Hillsdale, NJ: Lawrence Erlbaum Associates.

Soja, N. N. (1992). Inferences about the meanings of nouns: The relationship between perception and syntax. *Cognitive Development, 7*, 29–45.

Soja, N., Carey, S., & Spelke, E. S. (1990). Ontological categories guide young children's inductions of word meaning: Object terms and substance terms. *Cognition, 38*, 179–211.

Starkey, P., Spelke, L., & Gelman, R. (1990). Numerical abstraction by human infants. *Cognition, 36*, 97–127.

Talmy, L. (1985). Lexicalization patterns: Semantic structure in lexical forms. In T. Shopen (Ed.), *Language typology and syntactic description: Vol. 3. Grammatical categories and the lexicon* (pp. 57–149). New York: Cambridge University Press.

Taylor, M., & Gelman, S. (1988). Adjectives and nouns: Children's strategies for learning new words. *Child Development, 59*, 411–419.

Valian, V. (1986). Syntactic categories in the speech of young children. *Developmental Psychology, 22*, 562–579.

Ware, R. (1979). Some bits and pieces. In F. Pelletier (Ed.), *Mass terms: Some philosophical problems* (pp. 15–29). Dordrecht: Reidel.

Waxman, S. (1990). Linguistic biases and the establishment of conceptual hierarchies: Evidence from preschool children. *Cognitive Development, 5,* 123–150.

Waxman, S., & Gelman, R. (1986). Preschoolers' use of superordinate relations in classifications and language. *Cognitive Development, 1,* 139–156.

Wexler, K., & Cullicover, P. (1980). *Formal principles of language acquisition.* Cambridge, MA: MIT Press.

Weinreich, U. (1966). Explorations in semantic theory. In T. Sebeok (Ed.), *Current trends in linguistics* (Vol. 3, pp. 395–477). The Hague: Mouton.

Whorf, B. (1956). *Language, thought, and reality.* Cambridge, MA: MIT Press.

Wierzbicka, A. (1985). Oats and wheat: The fallacy of arbitrariness. In J. Haiman (Ed.), *Iconicity in syntax* (pp. 311–342). Amsterdam: Benjamins.

Wynn, K. (1990). Children's understanding of counting. *Cognition, 36,* 155–193.

CHAPTER FOUR

Two Approaches to the Acquisition of Grammar

I. M. Schlesinger
The Hebrew University
Jerusalem

Theorists of language acquisition are divided into two opposing camps. There are those who believe that the adult linguistic system as described by generative grammar must serve as the starting point for explaining language acquisition, and arrive at the conclusion that such an explanation requires the postulation of specifically linguistic innate constraints. The contending view is that semantics provides an entry wedge into the grammatical system and makes it unnecessary to postulate such innate knowledge. The two schools of thought represent two scientific cultures. In each, different kinds of data are looked at for evidence, and the way these data are interpreted and the kinds of arguments deemed relevant differ.

There are actually two separate issues involved in this controversy. One pertains to the role of semantics. According to one view, the child starts out with a grammar defined in terms of formal categories; those taking the semantic approach to language acquisition, by contrast, hold that the child's early system of rules is based on semantic concepts, which are operative in the acquisition process. The second issue is that of the role of specifically linguistic innate knowledge or predispositions. There often is a close relation between the stands taken on these two issues: Most of those working within the framework of generative grammar base their explanations of language learning on formal categories, playing down the role of semantic notions, and embrace a nativist approach. Conversely, the semantic approach was developed as an answer to the challenge issued by work in generative grammar to a learning approach (Schlesinger, 1971b), and at present most "semanticists" opt for a non-nativist theory of language acquisition. It should be clear, however, that the two issues are logically independent. And in fact, there are those who, while holding that innate linguistic knowledge must be postulated, assign to semantic categories a central role in "bootstrapping" the acquisition of grammar (Pinker, 1984, 1987). Similarly, there are those who argue that grammar may be attained by "distributional learning" of purely formal categories, but do not resort to the assumption of such innate knowledge (e.g., Valian, 1986; Wolff, 1988).

On each of the two issues, there are more than two possible positions,[1] but there is no room to discuss these here. This chapter presents one version of the semantic approach and compares it with nativist theories of language acquisition. After presenting the semantic approach in the first two sections, the contending generativist (or nativist) approach is presented (section 3) and the evidence for it examined (sections 4–5). Next I consider the semantic bootstrapping hypothesis and its implications for the nativist-empiricist controversy (section 6). Because the empirical evidence for either side is shown to be inconclusive, the two approaches are evaluated in the light of general methodological criteria, such as parsimony and refutability (section 7). In the final section, I summarize my reasons for preferring the semantic approach.

1. THE SEMANTIC APPROACH

1.1. The Role of Semantics

According to the central tenet of the semantic approach, the early rule system of children learning their native language is based on semantic concepts, which reflect the way children conceive of the world around them. Children interpret the world in terms of such relations as agent, location, and patient, and learn how these are expressed by linguistic means: word order, function words, and inflections. Their early linguistic rule system is a semantic one, and this affords them a way of eventually breaking into the grammar of their native language. The suggestion that the child's earliest "grammar" is semantic in nature has gained widespread acceptance, and it has been shown that early child speech can be accounted for in terms of semantic categories (see, e.g., Bowerman, 1973a, 1973b). Some writers have argued that the language learning child

---

[1]Thus, some theorists would emphasize the role of pragmatic factors in acquisition (Ninio & Snow, 1988). This may be viewed as a variant of the semantic approach.

must be credited with syntactic categories, because there seems to be data showing that the relations expressed by the child cannot be subsumed under the semantic roles usually thought to underlie child language; in section 2.2, I show how these apparent discrepancies can be taken care of.

1.2. The Relation Between Cognitive and Linguistic Development

Some writers who adopt the semantic approach have explicitly or implicitly embraced views that are closely related to the previous claim about the child's early rule system. Among these is the view that semantic notions underlying the children's system are anchored in the way they presumably conceive of the world around them. Cognitive development either leads linguistic development or is a precondition for it; according to others, cognitive development should be expected to correlate with linguistic development. For reviews of these various opinions see, for example, Cromer (1988) and Gopnik and Choi (1990).

Recent findings, however, seem to indicate that the relation between cognitive and linguistic development may be much less close than they were previously thought to be. There are children with severe cognitive retardation—for instance those with William's Syndrome (Karmiloff-Smith, in press)—who are nevertheless very advanced linguistically: They speak fluently and with understanding. Conversely, some children of normal intelligence may have specific language deficits.

It should be clear that these findings do not impugn the central tenet of the semantic approach, pertaining to the way the child breaks into the linguistic system, which is logically independent from any claim regarding the relationship of linguistic and cognitive abilities. The theory that semantics provides an entry wedge to the linguistic system commits one only to the claim that children are able to perceive the world around them in terms of concepts like *actor, action*, and *location*, which figure in semantic roles; no further claim about the relation between cognitive and linguistic development in general is involved.

1.3. Order of Acquisition

Another extrapolation from the central tenet of the semantic approach is that constructions and rules having semantic correlates appear in the child's grammar prior to those that have no such correlates. This does not mean, however, that *all* such purely formal rules appear after the semantically based rules have been mastered. The child may acquire rules about semantic relations, which form the basis of adult phrase structure rules, as the semantic approach has it; and at the same time the child may acquire other, purely formal rules through distributional analysis. Among the factors determining the sequence in which rules are acquired are the complexity of rules and the frequency with which they are instantiated in the input.

It has been shown that certain distinctions that are not semantically based are learned very early, and in learning syntactic constructions that correlate only imperfectly with semantic notions, the child does not seem to capitalize on these correlations. See Gathercole (1985) and Gordon (1985) on the acquisition of the mass/count distinction (but see MacPherson, 1991, and Bloom, chap. 3); Karmilloff-Smith (1978), Levy (1983), and MacWhinney (1978) on the acquisition of gender; and Carpenter (1991) on the acquisition of classifiers by children learning Thai. As stated, these studies are not incompatible with the semantic approach. They are important, however, as a reminder not to construe the central tenet of this approach too restrictively: There are additional ways of learning that do not depend on noting form-meaning correspondences (and proponents of the semantic approach may have erred in not mentioning this rider explicitly). It has been proposed that the earliest relational rules that map meanings into utterances are semantic, whereas syntactic distinctions that have no strong correlations with semantic ones—like gender, and the mass/count distinction—enter the rule system subsequently, as a refinement of the earlier semantic rules (Levy & Schlesinger, 1988).

2. THE TRANSITION TO ADULT GRAMMAR

Early work within the framework of the semantic approach concerned itself with the first stages of acquisition. It was shown that the child's early "grammar" could be accounted for in semantic terms. The objection was then made that this approach does not show how the child progresses from the pristine semantic system to the mature grammar, which, as linguistics has shown, is couched in formal, not semantic, terms. The crucial problem to be tackled by the semantic approach thus is the transition from the early semantically based system to the formal categories of adult grammar.[2]

---

[2]This problem does not arise if one holds (against the opinion of the majority of contemporary linguists) that the adult grammar is organized in terms of semantic concepts. This is the position of Van Valin (1991, in press), who proposed that actor and undergoer are the central adult categories.

2.1. Assimilation Theories

It has been proposed that this transformation comes about by children's gradually extending their semantic categories. For instance, on encountering subjects that are not agents they extend the agent category so as to accommodate this newcomer. Support for this explanation comes from studies by Matthei (1987) and by Braine, Brooks, and Cowan (in press), in which it was found that semantic categories and not syntactic ones are salient for younger children. A theory taking this stance may be called an *assimilation theory*. According to assimilation theory, then, children eventually acquire formal syntactic categories. Findings to the effect that young children deploy formal categories, like subject, and not only semantic ones, like agent (Chien & Lust, 1985; Hyams, 1986), are therefore not incompatible with the semantic approach.

Assimilation theory provides an answer to the charge that the semantic approach involves a discontinuity in the child's linguistic development (e.g., Gleitman & Wanner, 1982). Such a discontinuity would in fact be a serious fault, if it were to entail, say, Gleitman's (1981) "tadpole-and-frog" hypothesis, according to which the acquisition process is saltatory, and some of the child's intellectual attainments have to be discarded in the course of development as being of no further use. Assimilation theory, by contrast, does not assume any saltatory process but a gradual transformation of an early semantic rule system into a formal one.

2.2. Semantic Assimilation

There have been two proposals concerning the way assimilation proceeds. Bowerman (1973b) suggested that the child notes formal similarities between the linguistic realization of early semantic relations and that of other relations. Even in the speech directed at the young child not all subjects are agents; but once children notice that nonagentive subjects are treated in the language likes agents, they assimilate the former into the latter. Another proposal is that semantic as well as formal similarities are the basis of assimilation. This has been called *semantic assimilation* (Schlesinger, 1982, 1988).

Take the agent as an example. Children learning English may have acquired a rule that the agent–action relation is expressed by the word denoting the agent followed by the one denoting the action (as in "daddy runs"). Eventually, however, they will encounter subject–verb constructions that do not express an agent–action relation, in the strict sense of the term, for example, "Johnny fell." This is where semantic assimilation comes in. Children note the formal similarity of this construction to other subject–verb constructions, and their attention is drawn to the similarity of the relation expressed in it to the agent–action relation. "Johnny fell" is construed as a *sort of* action performed by a *sort of* agent, and henceforward they deal with this and similar instances as if they were agents. As a result, the agent category is gradually expanded (and so is the action category).

There exist many such semantic similarities that the child may make use of in applying already acquired rules. Most stative verbs will be uttered in situations where there is some activity going on: "Sleep" is usually heard in the context of activities like lying down, snoring, and turning over; "love" is used in connection with hugging and kissing; and so on. This enables the child to view situations in terms of activities and passive participants (the one who falls, sleeps, loves, etc.)—as agents. The agent category assimilates instances of what, strictly speaking, are not agents at all. Gradually, the child attends more and more to formal cues, and the agent category continues to expand until it eventually coincides with what we call subject in the mature grammar. And the same occurs with other semantic categories.

It has been argued against the semantic assimilation hypothesis (henceforward SA) that many subjects are not construable as agents, even under a very liberal interpretation of the term.[3] This objection rests on a misunderstanding. SA does not claim that subjects *are* agents, objectively speaking. Some subjects are agents, some are similar to agents, and some are regarded by the language as if they were agents. For the child to construe it as an agent it may be sufficient for a given subject to have some agentive feature. The subject category includes several semantic relations between which there is a "family resemblance" (see Schlesinger, 1988 and in press, for a fuller treatment, and Dowty, 1991, for a somewhat similar approach).

What is at issue, then, and what the child attends to, is not what the "objective" world is like, but how it is coded by a linguistic expression and conceived of for the purpose of speaking. This consideration is pertinent also to a related argument against SA: that a given state of affairs

---

[3]Further, it has been argued that child language provides evidence that word classes do not originate in semantic-syntactic correspondences of the most obvious sort: noun = object, verb = action, and so on (Maratsos & Chalkley, 1980). But the semantic approach need not ascribe to such a simplistic view. Schlesinger (1982, section 8.1; 1988) showed how word classes might be formed in the process of acquiring rules mapping semantic relations into surface structures. Braine (1987) proposed a theory of acquisition of word classes on the basis of semantic correspondences in combination with distributional analyses.

may be expressed by alternative linguistic constructions. Thus, a situation that may be described as "A is fleeing from B"—with A as agent—may also be referred to as "B is chasing A"—with B as agent. Here, again, we should appreciate that two identical situations may be conceived of differently, and hence expressed by different linguistic constructions. It has been shown (Schlesinger, 1993) that in "A sells B to C," A, the seller, is conceived of as having the agentive properties Control and Responsibility to a larger extent than in "C buys B from A"; and similar options are provided by other complementary verb pairs, like "lead" and "follow."

Some subjects resist analysis into agentive features (see Schlesinger, in press, for extended discussion). Some of these the child will come to view as realizations of another semantic relation (Schlesinger, in press), and others will be assimilated, along the lines proposed by Bowerman (1973b), on purely formal grounds: The child notices that they behave syntactically like subjects and hence treats them as such. Semantic assimilation should not be expected to furnish an explanation of all phenomena in child speech; it merely lays claim to a central role in acquisition. Many distinctions the child learns to make have no semantic correlate, and their acquisition requires a different explanation.

The Semantic approach is often criticized because its claims are vaguely formulated and it is not made explicit how information is processed. Specifically, it has been commented that semantic categories figuring in the acquisition process are not defined, and hardly any theorists commit themselves to a list of semantic categories operating in child language. When applied to SA, this criticism misses the point: SA envisages a gradual process of forming semantic categories and of expanding these into syntactic ones. Categories are accordingly in continual flux and the nature of the process is such that no single well-defined semantic category is likely to be operative for a protracted period. Contrary to what researchers once thought, the child does not pass through a series of static "child grammars" (Schlesinger, 1982, pp. 11–13).

2.3. Support for the Semantic Assimilation Hypothesis

The fact, alluded to in the foregoing, that semantic categories are continually changing makes it difficult to obtain evidence for semantic assimilation from child language data. Support for the semantic assimilation hypothesis can be obtained, however, from studies of the grammatical system at later ages. The following two predictions may be made:

Prediction 1: For a given syntactic category, those instances will be central that belong to the semantic category out of which the former developed.

Prediction 2: The mature syntactic category—noncentral instances included—will retain the "flavor" of the semantic category out of which it developed.

Take, for instance, the syntactic category subject, which presumably has developed out of the early agent category. According to Prediction 1, the central, or prototypical, subject will be an agent, and the prototypical verb will be an action verb. According to Prediction 2, all subjects will be conceived of as being somehow agentlike, even by adults.

There is some evidence for each of these predictions. A doctoral thesis by Guberman (1992), of Hebrew University is relevant to Prediction 1. Extending the findings of de Villiers (1980), she found that kindergarten children learn a new linguistic construction first for sentences with action verbs rather than with mental or stative verbs. Further, she found that in a lexical decision task, latencies for prototypical verbs are significantly shorter than those for nonprototypical ones, both for 10- and 11-year-olds and for adults. These findings are in line with Prediction 1.

Prediction 2 has been borne out by several studies. Guberman found that verbs are judged to be more active than related nouns (e.g., "to swim" vs. "a swim"). The English language offers the option of referring to the instrument of the action by the subject, as, for instance, in "The dishwasher washed the plates." Now, there are several constraints on subjectivization of the instrument, and these are all accounted for by the fact that the subject is conceived of as having agentlike qualities (Schlesinger, 1989). Further, it has been found that adults consider the subject of mental verbs (for instance, John in "John admires Mary.") to have the agentlike properties control and intention to a greater degree than the direct object (Mary, in this case; Schlesinger, 1992).

It might be argued that these findings do not reflect a semantic assimilation process at all, but are due, instead, to our accumulated linguistic experience with subjects, most of which refer to agents. This alternative explanation seems to me rather implausible. It assumes that whereas adults are aware of a subject-agent correlation, children learning their language are not. This would run counter to the intuition that the language learner is alerted to existing semantic regularities, which the practiced speaker may be quite unaware of. As Brown (1958, p. 253) put it: The semantics of a linguistic construction may "drop from consciousness as language skills become smooth and rapid."

3. THE NATIVIST-EMPIRICIST CONTROVERSY

3.1. The Nativist Challenge

The most serious challenge to the semantic approach has come from nativist theories of language acquisition. When Chomsky's (1965) work came to the fore, it appeared that a learning approach would be faced with what some theorists regarded as an unsolvable problem: How can the child learn deep structure concepts, which by definition are not exhibited in any strings of words that serve as input to the child? This led to the formulation of the nativist thesis. The semantic approach then offered an alternative solution to this problem. But theorists in the tradition of generative grammar argue that the proposals that have been forthcoming are insufficient in principle to account for the acquisition of grammar, particularly in the later stages.

Whereas theorists of the generativist persuasion claim that the assumption of innate constraints is indispensable for an explanation of language acquisition, researchers of a more empiricist bend attempt such an explanation without resorting to assumptions of innate linguistic knowledge. That there are innate propensities that make language learning possible must be conceded by even the most extreme empiricist. The claim made by nativists (as we call them here) is a much stronger one, namely, that language learning is subject to innate constraints that are specifically linguistic, that is, which do not apply to other cognitive functions (Chomsky, 1975).

3.2. The Logic of the Debate

In recent years there has been a spate of empirical work by investigators in the generativist tradition that has been interpreted by them as showing that the child deploys innate knowledge to acquire a given rule of grammar. Nativists regard these phenomena as test cases, presenting a challenge to those who claim that one should explain language learning without assuming innateness.

There is no denying that there has been little in the way of empiricist responses to these challenges. It should be appreciated, however, that it is in the nature of the debate that nativist theorizing will always appear to be on the offensive. This is due to an asymmetry between the claims made. The central claim of the nativist approach to language acquisition—the one that empiricist theorists object to—is that language acquisition can be accounted for only on the assumption of the innateness of linguistic principles and constraints. Like all existential claims, this one cannot be refuted. When it turns out that a phenomenon that has been laid down to innate principles can be explained along empiricist lines, the central claim of nativism is not impugned: No nativist will deny that some things in language have to be learned from the linguistic input (some specific nativist theory may have to be modified, but the nativist position as a whole is not affected). By contrast, the corresponding empiricist claim, namely, that language acquisition can be explained without resorting to specifically linguistic innate principles, can easily be refuted. Once a single phenomenon is shown to be explainable only on the assumption of such innate knowledge, nativism will seem to have won out. Empiricists may in time come forward with an alternative account of the phenomenon in question, but there will always be a backlog of unsolved problems, which may invoke the impression of nativists scoring points all the time.

Phenomena that have *not yet* been accounted for along empiricist lines thus do not constitute a decisive argument for nativism. Theorists of an empiricist persuasion will of course have to deal with these phenomena eventually. But the fact is that at present we have no fully developed empiricist theory; nor is there a fully developed nativist theory. The debate between nativists and empiricists, I propose, should not be viewed as one between theories but rather between research programs. To test a theory empirically it has to be at a reasonably developed stage, and currently theorists of both persuasions are still in the process of formulating testable claims and adjusting these to the incoming data. In other words, there is no fully developed *overall* acquisition theory on the market, but rather a number of hypotheses that are being regarded as tentative and likely to be refined in the light of further evidence. Each of these hypotheses is put up within the framework of one of the two competing research programs. Research programs are not true or false, as theories are, but more or less fruitful. The empiricism I espouse here (please note: empiricism, not behaviorism) is not based on an article of faith, and in fact, there seems at present to be no way to make sure that empiricism is "true." But I do avow that it is the only sound research program, for reasons that will become clear as we proceed.

In the following sections I first discuss some frequently heard arguments to the effect that language acquisition *must* be based on innate linguistic principles. After dealing with this purportedly positive evidence for nativism, I take up the negative evidence adduced by nativists, that is, arguments to the effect that an empiricist theory is unable in principle to explain certain phenomena, which are accounted for on the assumption that certain linguistic principles are innate. This chapter is selective and deals only with the more weighty arguments, and not with those that can easily be seen to be completely inconclusive due to lack of relevant knowledge. To illustrate, take some of the more common arguments against empiricism in language acquisition:

> How could a child ever learn a system as complex as language in such a short time? And how else than by a maturational program can you account for the fact that all children pass through essentially the same stages in their linguistic development?

This presupposes a fully developed theory of language learning that might thus be shown not to fill the bill; but no such theory exists.

> If bird song is innate, human language may be, too.

But the issue is not that of the very possibility of innate linguistic knowledge; rather, what is at issue is the necessity for postulating such knowledge.

Such arguments are best viewed as slogans, useful, perhaps, for making those rally around who have already been convinced from the outset that empiricism (like behaviorism, with which it is often tacitly, and unjustifiably, identified) must be all wrong. The same goes, of course, for similar arguments advanced from the empiricist side.

4. IS THERE EVIDENCE
FOR THE NATIVIST POSITION?

4.1. Universal Grammar

Nativists do not assert that *all* the requisite knowledge is innate, for this would be patently false in view of the many differences between languages. Instead, it is claimed that principles and constraints common to all languages of the world are innate. The bulk of work in generative grammar is concerned with the discovery of this Universal Grammar, and there has been considerable success in revealing abstract linguistic principles that, for all we know, may be universal.

But what might justify the conclusion that these principles are innate? A possible argument would be that, considering the great diversity of physical and cultural conditions, it is implausible that the common features of all languages of the world should be environmentally determined. Instead, they must be due to mankind's biologically determined mental organization. The very existence of universals would thus be evidence for nativism (see also Hoekstra & Kooij, 1988).

However, there are various alternative ways of accounting for linguistic universals. These appeal to semantic factors, processing factors, and various others (Hawkins, 1988). That a rule or principle can be universal and acquired is also argued by Cooper (1975, pp. 170–180) and by Sampson (1978). The existence of Universal Grammar in itself thus does not constitute evidence for nativism.

4.2. Species Specificity of Language

The plausibility of viewing language as part of our innate equipment—as an "organ," as Chomsky put it—appears to be enhanced by the fact that it seems to be species specific: No nonhuman species is known to acquire language spontaneously. Research showing that certain aspects of language can be taught to primates has been viewed by some as scoring a point against the nativist thesis. Nativists, on their part, have made various critical comments on these findings, arguing that sentences of primates have fixed limits (Hoekstra & Kooij, 1988), that no more than simple conditioning is involved, that there is no evidence that complex syntax can be learned by primates, and that they must be taught laboriously and do not evince spontaneous, fast, and easy acquisition.

The question of language learning by primates, however, is only tangential to that of innateness. On the one hand, even if it turns out that primates and other species can learn language, this does not affect the nativist position, because the "language organ" might be innate in not one, but several species. If, on the other hand, the fact of the matter is that no nonhuman species can learn a language comparable in complexity to that of humans, this might be due to the greater general cognitive (as opposed to specifically linguistic) capabilities of humans. Analogously, the fact that all humans, and only humans, wear some kind of clothes does not prove an innate clothes-making faculty; it can be adequately explained as due to certain manipulatory and cognitive skills possessed by all humans, which are made to subserve certain physical needs.

4.3. The Genetic Basis of Linguistic Capacity

According to the nativist thesis, language is in part biologically determined. Evidence has been provided by Gopnik (chap. 11) that linguistic capabilities are inherited. But what does this prove? A given ability may be biologically determined, but the skills for which it is a prerequisite may have to be acquired by those learning mechanisms that are also involved in the acquisition of the knowledge of, say, history and chemistry. The case for nativism would be won, if it could be shown that knowledge of language itself is inherited; but all the reported research has revealed—and all that future research is at all likely to reveal—is innateness of the *ability* to acquire this knowledge, and this implies nothing about the kind of mechanism required to put the ability into effect.

But, it may be argued, if language would be acquired by the same mechanisms as other cognitive skills, one would expect any hereditary impairment of language acquisition to manifest itself in an impairment of other cognitive skills as well; and this is just what Gopnik's research shows not to be the case. This argument is faulted, however, by considering the following alternative. Instead of requiring a different *kind* of ability, the difference between the acquisition of language and that of other cognitive skills may be merely one of the *degree* of abilities involved: Too low a level of a certain ability, or abilities, might impair language acquisition without appreciably affecting other cognitive skills.

An analogy will serve to clarify these points. Suppose that the difference between successful pilots of fighter planes and those that fail in flying tests is shown by research to be accounted for largely by one single variable: Only those candidates who have particularly short choice reaction times become good pilots. However, those who fail, that is, those having somewhat slower reaction times, perform well on all other tasks they are tested on: driving a truck, operating some complicated machinery, tracing aircraft on a radar screen, and so forth. Although an individual's speed of response is probably genetically determined, these findings would of course not be interpreted as showing that there is some innate plane-flying ability that is *qualitatively* different from the abilities underlying those other tasks. And that only plane-flying is affected by this hereditary "impairment" of reaction time does not mean that pilots learn their trade by processes fundamentally different from those other skills are learned by. Innateness of an ability tells us nothing about the processes involved in learning to exercise it.

This analogy is not intended to provide support for the claim that impairment of language is also a matter of degree of ability (for this, like all analogies, may limp a bit). It does show, however, that the same logic of explanation *may* apply to findings of hereditability of linguistic skills, and that these findings therefore cannot be construed as proving the nativist thesis.

5. CAN A GRAMMAR BE INDUCED
FROM LINGUISTIC INPUT ONLY?

We have seen in the preceding section that there is no positive evidence for the nativist thesis. Nativist theorists usually rely on negative evidence for their approach; that is, they purport to show that an empiricist learning theory is incapable in principle of dealing with the complexities of language eventually mastered by the child. If this were so, nativism would win by default. Attempts to prove the impossibility of a learning account, however, are riddled with unwarranted assumptions about the range of possibilities open to a learning theory.

5.1. The Nativist Conception of Learning

Nativist criticisms of empiricist theories of language acquisition are typically based on a very restricted view of available mechanisms of learning. They assume this mechanism to be subject to certain limitations, which in fact characterize only some classical stimulus-response models. The following implicit assumptions underlie nativist arguments:

Assumption A: What can be learned are observable responses, which must be attained by active use through trial-and-error.

Assumption B: What can be learned are only stimulus-response chains.

Putting these fetters on the learning mechanism enables nativist theorists to marshal arguments to the effect that a learning theory is incapable of explaining the acquisition of grammar. But actually, as shown later, there are ways of learning not envisaged by the nativist conception that may make it possible to acquire grammar even without recourse to innate principles.

Here is how Assumption A is deployed in arguing for a nativist theory of language learning. Examples abound in the nativist literature of constructions and principles learned by the child at one go, and any empiricist account, it is argued, would predict the acquisition of these to proceed gradually and gropingly, attended by many errors. Assumption A is unwarranted, however, because it ignores the possibility of passive learning. Presumably, active use by the child is preceded by a long period of registering how a construction is used.

Assumptions A and B, which put a limit to what an empiricist theory might be able to explain, are supplemented by an assumption concerning the product of the acquisition process:

Assumption C: What the child acquires is the system of highly abstract rules specified by generative grammar, which are not exhibited directly in the surface structure of the linguistic input.

Assumption B in conjunction with Assumption C poses a serious problem for the acquisition of deep structures, because these are, by definition, not exhibited in the physical form of speech heard by the child. But Assumption B is unwarranted, because more sophisticated learning models can account for the acquisition of complex hierarchical structures, as shown in Wolff's (1988) computer simulation. As for Assumption C, a possible modification of it is discussed later.

5.2. The Negative Feedback Problem

One of the unsolved problems in learning grammar pertains to the deletion of incorrect rules, once these have been acquired for some reason or other. To get rid of such a rule, the child would have to receive information that it is incorrect, and it has been argued that such negative feedback is not systematically available. This problem has first been discussed by Braine (1971). Some investigators (e.g., Demetras, Post, & Snow, 1986; Moerk, 1991) hold that a more careful analysis of the information available to children shows that they are indeed sufficiently provided with negative feedback to make corrections of rules possible. Because this is a moot point, we assume for the sake of the argument that the problem is a real one. So let us see how it affects the nativist-empiricist controversy.

Explanations that assume innate parameters and initial parameter settings have been argued to solve the negative feedback problem. Without these assumptions, it has been claimed, the child would be bound to overgeneralize from other constructions, and in the absence of negative feedback there would be no way to correct the resulting erroneous rules.

In a trenchant discussion of the problem of overgeneralizations in child language, Bowerman (1988) showed that negative feedback is just as much a problem for nativist as it is for empiricist theories. Here are some observations showing that the nativist solution will not work for every kind of incorrect rule the child may induce from the linguistic input.

1. *Input from bilinguals.* In speaking to the child, caretakers for whom the child's native language is a foreign language are prone to make errors that are influenced by structures and rules carried over from their own native language; in other words, these errors will not contravene any universal of language.[4] Hence innate knowledge of universals will be completely irrelevant to the child's unlearning of such errors. Whether or not such adult errors occur frequently is unimportant in this connection; the fact that they do occur, however rarely, poses a problem for any acquisition theory.

2. *Marked construction.* Adults occasionally use marked constructions

---

[4]In some instances, they may conform to one of the putatively innate settings of a parameter, but often this will not be the case.

that contravene the specific parameter setting of the language in question. For instance, English is a non-pro-drop language, which means that, unlike Spanish and Italian, it does not permit omission of the subject. But the child learning English may hear such utterances as "Forgot to tell you: He won't come tomorrow", "Can't tell what this means", or "Been late again, huh?" As pointed out by Valian (1990b), this might be construed by the child as evidence for English being a pro-drop language. In the absence of negative feedback, one might expect the child to have no means to eliminate this error. But of course such errors do not stay on for ever.

A possible objection might be that the child knows that these utterances are marked, and hence they do not serve as a basis for rule formation. But how does the child find out that they are marked? To argue that the child does so by noting that they are deviant would of course be circular, for the recognition of deviance without negative information is precisely what is at issue here.

3. *Errors*. People often unwittingly commit grammatical errors that do not impair comprehension of the utterance. These are legion, and no one could maintain that they invariably infringe some Universal or other. The innateness hypothesis thus does not solve the problem of how rules educed from such errors are deleted from the child's grammar.

In addition to this evidence from linguistic input to children, there is that from their speech. Children often make incorrect generalizations from grammatically correct input. Many of these—such as generalizations pertaining to the inflectional paradigm of some languages—result in language-specific errors (see, e.g., Levy, 1988). Here, too, the innateness hypothesis is of no help.

The absence of systematic negative feedback thus poses a problem to any theorist of language acquisition, whether or not the empiricist stance is adopted. No completely satisfactory solution is available at present. It seems, however, that frequency of occurrence has a crucial role to play here; erroneous rules may be instantiated too infrequently to take root. Braine (1971, 1988) developed a "sieve" model that sifts out infrequently instantiated rules, and although many unanswered questions do remain, this model seems to be on the right track. Frequency of input also plays a role in the language learning model proposed by Arbib and Hill (1988).

This solution pulls the rug out from under many arguments for the innateness of certain parameters that are based on the unavailability of negative feedback. And, at any rate, whatever the solution will ultimately turn out to be, it will apply also to phenomena for which nativists have proposed explanations that presuppose innate principles.

5.3. The Nature of Rules in an Empiricist Theory

It has been argued that the abstract nature of certain universal linguistic principles precludes explaining their acquisition along empiricist lines. Instead, these principles must be assumed to be innate.

Now, underlying this argument is a certain conception of language learning, which we have formulated earlier on as Assumption C, namely, that the child ends up with a grammar of very general, abstract rules. But there is another possibility. Rather than acquiring rules of very wide application, the child may in some instances acquire what we will call a *compartmental rule*, that is, a rule applying to a much more limited range of cases than provided for by generative grammar. The issue of lack of parsimony that this proposal involves is dealt with in section 7. In the following, the operation of such rules is illustrated by an example from the acquisition of binding principles.

5.4. Binding Principles

Consider the following sentence:

(1) Cinderella's sister pointed to herself.

According to Principle A of binding theory, the reflexive pronoun "herself" is an anaphor that refers to "sister" and not to "Cinderella." The child, it has been claimed, masters this rule without trial-and-error, and this is regarded by nativists as evidence that Principle A (like the other binding principles) is innate.

Innateness need not be resorted to, however. The child will construe (1) correctly without any knowledge of binding principles. Consider all the logical possibilities:

(1) a. Cinderella points at Cinderella.
   b. Cinderella points at the sister.
   c. The sister points at Cinderella.
   d. The sister points at the sister.

In construing (1), the child will not opt for (1a), because this would leave the word "sister" dangling without any purpose. Further, (1b) and (1c) will also be ruled out, because (on the nativist no less than on the empiricist account) the meaning of the reflexive pronoun must be presumed to be known to the child; that is, the child must have learned that the form "____self" signals that the Goal of the action is identical to its

Source, that "point to ___self" means that the one who points is the one pointed at. The child is thus led to construal (1d) as the only possible one, without resorting to any general principles of linguistic theory.

At the time the child can speak and understand sentences like (1) he or she may be presumed to have already acquired the genitive construction, as in "baby's bottle," "daddy's glasses," and the like. Hence the child will understand that it is the sister that is the subject in (1) and does the pointing. This, then, is an additional reason why the child will not opt for (1a) and (1b).

Principle B is involved in sentences with pronominals, like:

(2) Cinderella's sister pointed to her.

Here the pronoun may refer either to Cinderella or to some other person, but not to the sister. Of the five combinations (2 a–e), two are correct construals of (2)—namely, (2c) and (2e):

(2) a. Cinderella points at Cinderella.
    b. Cinderella points at the sister.
    c. The sister points at Cinderella.
    d. The sister points at the sister.
    e. The sister points at some other female person.

The child who hears (2) will rule out (2a) for the same reason as (1a): The word "sister" would be left dangling. Presumably, at the time children can understand (2) correctly, they have already acquired the genitive construction. They will therefore know that an utterance containing "Cinderella's sister" pertains to the sister, and not to Cinderella. This will rule out (2b). They are thus left with the two correct construals (2c) and (2e) and with (2d), which violates Principle B. The availability of more than one construal makes for greater processing difficulty. Sentences like (2) may thus be expected to be relatively difficult for children. There is in fact some evidence that Principle B, exemplified in (2), is acquired later than Principle A, involved in (1) (see McDaniel, Cairns, & Hsu, 1990).

On the empiricist account, then, later acquisition of Principle B is due to processing difficulty, and this difficulty will continue to make itself felt even after the principle has been acquired. A nativist explanation of the later acquisition of Principle B, by contrast, would presumably be based on differential maturation and would predict that, once Principle B has been acquired, the child will not have any more difficulty with it than with Principle A.

In an experiment with Hebrew-speaking adults conducted by a graduate student at Hebrew University, (Hasman, 1991) sentences with pronominals were found to be significantly more difficult to decode than those with reflexive pronouns. Processing these sentences thus involves some cognitive difficulty. This may explain the later acquisition of Principle B by children, thus making the nativist's maturational explanation superfluous.

Eventually, of course, children learn how constructions like (2) are to be understood. Passive learning may play a role here: Children have many occasions to observe adults use sentences with pronouns, as in (2). Presumably they can often make out from the context what the pronoun refers to, and gradually form the relevant rule. They do not get stuck with an incorrect generalization from (1), because only the more frequently instantiated rules are retained, as envisaged by Braine's (1988) "sieve" mechanism.

What is wrong with the nonnativist explanations proposed here? Just about everything, the generative linguist will argue. The strategy proposed for (1) will be of no help in construing other types of sentences involving the same binding principles, for instance:

(3) Cinderella told her sister to point to herself.

This is correct. But what it amounts to is an objection to just the kind of rules that are likely to be predominant in an empiricist theory of language acquisition, namely compartmental rules (i.e., rules of restricted applicability). In tackling sentences like (3), the child may make use of the regularity exemplified in (1), arriving at a rule that includes a wider range of constructions, but not necessarily all those covered by the abstract rules of current linguistic theory. Even if the child at first misconstrues (3), this will do no permanent harm on Braine's assumption of a mechanism that filters out infrequently instantiated rules.

The nativist account here obviously entails greater economy. Due to the innate binding principles, the child acquires the ability to construe (1), (2), and (3)—as well as a host of related constructions—at one fell swoop (so it may seem). This lack of generality of the nonnativist account is discussed further on.

For another proposal of a compartmental rule (refuting a nativist argument against the empiricist approach) see Schlesinger (1982, pp. 31–33). Other empiricist explanations have been advanced by Yamaoka (1988), and—within the framework of Role and Reference Grammar— by Van Valin (1991).

5.5. The Pro-Drop Parameter

The difference between nativist and empiricist explanations of the acquisition of rules can be further illustrated by the case of the pro-drop parameter. Here I compare one particular nativist account, that of Hyams

(1986), of the acquisition of pro-drop and non-pro-drop languages with an empiricist account of the same phenomena. That Hyams no longer adheres to all the views expressed in her 1986 writings[5] need not concern us here, because what is at issue is the nature of empiricist explanations, and these can conveniently be highlighted by this comparison.

Non-pro-drop languages—that is, languages that do not permit subjectless sentences—are more restricted than pro-drop languages because they rule out sentences permitted by the latter. In view of the unavailability of negative feedback, there should be no way for an incorrectly acquired pro-drop rule to be deleted from child language. Some writers in the Government and Binding tradition have therefore argued that the initial innate setting of this parameter has to be non-pro-drop. There are some difficulties with this proposal, however, As pointed out by Hyams (1986), at the very early stages of acquiring English, children frequently make three types of errors: omission of subject (e.g., "see window," "want more apple"), omission of expletives—pleonastic "it" and existential "there" (as in "outside cold," "no more cookies"), and omission of modals and of "be" (as in "see cow," for "I can see a cow," or "you so big"). These three types of utterances are ungrammatical in English, but are grammatical in pro-drop languages, that is, languages that permit null subjects. Hyams therefore claimed that the initial parameter setting is pro-drop. The problem, then, is: How does the child learning a non-pro-drop language reset the parameter, in the absence of negative feedback?

Hyams proposed that resetting the parameter is triggered by the child encountering sentences with expletives, like "it is cold" or "there are no more cookies," which are found only in non-pro-drop languages. As a consequence, errors of all the aforementioned three types disappear from child speech at about the same point in time. The child here capitalizes on the fact that the parameter in question is responsible for a whole range of linguistic regularities, which permits positive information regarding one such regularity to have a pervasive effect (but see Valian, 1990b, pp. 114–115, for a problem with this).

The criticisms that have since been voiced of this proposal need not concern us here; I want to show the ways an empiricist explanation of these phenomena differs from a typical nativist account like that by Hyams. On the empiricist story, each of the various phenomena discussed by Hyams has a different reason.

First, the empiricist may argue, children, as newcomers to language,

---

[5]In response to some criticisms, Hyams since introduced changes into her account (Hyams, 1992). My concern here is only to show how phenomena that have been claimed to pose difficulties for a learning account may be dealt with, and this purpose is best served by contrasting it with Hyams' earlier work.

have difficulty with long utterances. Perhaps there is a production constraint (a possibility first entertained by L. Bloom, 1970, p. 70ff.), perhaps also they are unable to compute more complex structures; at any rate, they tend to drop words from their utterances, which may make them ungrammatical. As they mature, their capability to handle more complex constructions increases, and hence, not too surprisingly, all these errors tend to disappear at approximately the same time.

Hyams objected to this that at the age these observations were made children are in fact capable of more complex utterances. But this is beside the point. That children have the ability to use complex utterances does not mean that they invariably exercise it; rather they may try to save effort. So do adults, who are prone, when the context makes it clear who is meant, to drop the subject, as in: "Forgot to tell you: He won't come tomorrow," or "Going to the movies?"

So far, the foregoing empiricist account is of course only partial; what is missing is a reason for the particular kinds of omissions. Why are subjects deleted rather than objects? Why modals rather than other words? Here are some tentative answers to these questions:

1. Expletive "it" and "there" are semantically empty, and the child at first tends to omit those words that do not carry a message (cf. Slobin, 1985).

2. Like "it" and "there," "be" does little semantic work (note that many languages do not deploy such a link between the subject and the predicative adjective). Hyams countered this argument by citing Brown's (1973) observation that only contractible "be" is deleted. Rather than providing support for her account, this seems to be an obvious result of contractible "be" being perceptually less salient (cf. is—it's; will—you'll), and being less salient, learning is delayed.

3. Modals are conceptually rather complex, which is why they come in later.[6]

4. The subject is typically the least informative part of the sentence and may be taken to be self-evident. Hyams anticipated this explanation by pointing out that the subject is not *always* the least informative and thus not crucial to communication. Perhaps, also, there is a tendency to drop the first element in an utterance, just as adults do (e.g., "Can't tell what this means.").

---

[6]Hyams (1986, pp. 82–85) rejected this explanation on the basis of data from one child who had "hafta" and "gonna" in her speech and no other modals. The former are no less complex than other modals, and Hyams argued that they are not omitted because they have verbal inflections and are therefore analyzed as verbs. However, one cannot rest a case on such an isolated example. A few glitches cannot bolster a theory.

This leaves us with the negative feedback problem. The parameter account avoids this problem: The initial setting of pro-drop is reset on the basis of positive information. But as pointed out in section 5.3, a general solution to the negative feedback problem is needed in any case for empiricist and nativist theories alike.

A different, essentially empiricist, account of the acquisition of pro-drop and non-pro-drop languages has been proposed by Gerken (1991).

These empiricist proposals of course do not affect the linguistic claim concerning the universality of the pro-drop parameter. Linguists of the generative school, however, have made the additional claim that language acquisition can only be explained on the assumption that this parameter and its initial setting are innate. It is this claim that is being argued against here, and the objections made will be pertinent to any nativist proposal of parameter setting, whether that of Hyams or of other theorists.

P. Bloom (1990) analyzed child language data and provided support for the proposal that subjectless sentences are due to production constraints. Contrary to Hyams, he proposed that the initial setting of the parameter is non-pro-drop—favoring the acquisition of languages that permit subjectless sentences, like Spanish and Italian. English-speaking children's omissions of subjects are due, according to Bloom, to performance limitations rather than to parameter setting. A different conclusion is arrived at by Valian (1990a, 1990b), who based her case largely on the occasional omissions of subjects found in informal English speech, and proposed that there is an innate dual-value setting of the pro-drop parameter. This means, in effect, that children innately know that the language they are about to learn is either pro-drop or not, which hardly can be very helpful in mastering the acquisition task. If the processes suggested by Valian for deciding whether the language is pro-drop or not are adequate, they will suffice for the acquisition of the correct rules without any innate parameter.[7]

The assumption of a given parameter as innate is otiose wherever learning processes have to be resorted to in any case to acquire the rules in question. Only a strong commitment to the existence of innate parameters will lead a theorist to hold on to this assumption in such a case. Of course, there is no way at present to disprove the claim that there is after all such innate knowledge even though it is not indispensable for the acquisition process (this is an example of the asymmetry alluded to in section 3.2). But this is hardly a saving grace.

---

[7]It might be argued that the innate parameter with its dual-value setting serves to draw the child's attention to a problem that has to be solved. There is no evidence, however (and it is even hardly plausible a priori), that children need such prompting to find out about just this particular rule, given that they find out about myriads of language-specific rules for which no parameters can be postulated.

6. SEMANTIC BOOTSTRAPPING

We now return to the issue discussed in the first part of this chapter: Are the child's early categories semantic or syntactic? As pointed out in the Introduction, this issue is independent of the nativist-empiricist issue. However, theorists working within the framework of generative grammar have often assumed that the child's categories are syntactic from the outset, and that, being innate, they need not be learned from the input. They thus do not impose on the child any transition from semantic to formal syntactic categories, as the semantic approach does (see in this connection section 2.1 on discontinuity).

But to avoid introducing semantic categories it does not suffice to postulate innate syntactic categories, as Pinker (1984, 1987) showed. The child has to have a way of recognizing an innate syntactic category when it is encountered in the input.[8] Pinker's solution is to postulate innate semantic categories and innate links between these and syntactic categories. The child deploys these links to find out which innate formal categories are instantiated in a given input. Once the latter have thus been bootstrapped, semantic categories cease to function in the acquisition process. It appears, then, that nativist theorists, too, will have to espouse semantic concepts as playing a crucial role in acquisition.

Pinker's proposal depends heavily on nativist assumptions (and Bloom (chap. 3) goes even further in postulating innate meaning-form links). In some aspects, it is very similar to the semantic assimilation hypothesis (see section 2.2), which had been proposed more than a decade earlier (Schlesinger, 1974): According to both theories, syntactic categories are attained by way of semantic ones. Pinker's semantic bootstrapping hypothesis differs from the semantic assimilation hypothesis in that it assumes both semantic and syntactic categories and the links between them to be innate.

According to Pinker, once semantic concepts have bootstrapped innate syntactic categories, they can be dispensed with, because they play no further role in acquisition (and in principle this may occur after a single experience with the semantic-syntactic link). The semantic assimilation hypothesis, by contrast, argues that semantic concepts continue to play a crucial role in the formation of syntactic categories; see Predictions 1 and 2 in section 2.3. Whereas the empirical findings bearing out these predictions are accounted for by the semantic assimilation hypothesis, there seems to be no similar explanation within the framework of the semantic bootstrapping hypothesis, which is not based on gradual

---

[8]A similar problem was faced by Plato, who raised the question of how we gain access to innate ideas. His solution was that particulars, with which we have direct acquaintance, partake of the nature of ideas and remind us of them.

accretion but rather on a short-lived process that serves merely to get syntactic development under way.

The principal difference between Pinker's theory and semantic assimilation is, as stated, that the former resorts to innate categories, whereas the latter does not. Braine (1992) showed that the assumption of innate categories is redundant in the bootstrapping hypothesis: When all claims of innateness of specifically linguistic constructs are deleted from the latter, it converges on an assimilation theory. The latter is thus clearly the more parsimonious theory.

7. PARSIMONY AND REFUTABILITY

The discussion in the previous sections has made it clear that at present there is no empirical evidence for either the nativist or the empiricist approach. Let us see now how these two approaches fare in the light of methodological considerations like parsimony and refutability. Now, these are criteria by which to judge theories, and as stated, in the field of language acquisition we have no fully developed theory, but only research programs. However, there is a point in evaluating the competing research programs in respect to the nature of the inchoate theories they have given rise to.

7.1. Compartmental Rules

The proposal of compartmental rules, made in section 5, might be objected to as involving a less parsimonious grammar at the adult stage than that envisaged by a nativist research program.

This is not necessarily so. Conceivably, the child induces eventually a general principle from several such compartmental rules (just as the linguist induces general principles from apparently unrelated phenomena). On the empiricist account, then, the adult grammar need not be any less parsimonious than it is on the nativist account.

But parsimonious or not, it seems to be a fact of cognitive development that rules of restricted scope are acquired, at least as a first stage. Thus, school children may have compartmentalized knowledge of mathematical rules (Hiebert & Wearne, 1986; Schoenfeld, 1986). While compartmentalization may be disadvantageous in mathematics, it may have its advantages in some other areas. Consider the infant who has learned from observation that unsuspended bodies fall, and then finds out that bodies having certain shapes may roll down an inclined plane. It is highly implausible that she then subsumes both these rules under an infantile version of the law of gravity. It is quite in line with what we know about cognitive functioning that the memory store should carry an extra load of rules so as to achieve greater ease of processing (a point granted by Chomsky, 1982, p. 20). In all these areas, the lack of parsimony in the rule system may be more than offset by parsimony in processing.

7.2. Aspects of Parsimony

Parsimony is a notoriously vague concept. As far as the theory of language acquisition is concerned, the term may refer to the end-state of acquisition (i.e., the adult system), the acquisition process itself, or to the initial state:

1. Parsimony regarding the end state. This is the aspect of parsimony discussed in the foregoing. As stated, a distinction ought to be made between (a) parsimony of the rule system (the grammar), and (b) parsimony in processing (i.e., in deploying the rules of grammar).
2. Parsimony regarding the acquisition process refers to the number of processes required for passing from the initial state of knowledge to the end state, and the complexity of these processes.
3. Parsimony regarding the initial state of the child, that is, the constructs and principles the child is equipped with at the start of language learning.

7.3. Parsimony of Acquisition Processes

It is not clear at all which of the two rival research programs involves the most parsimonious formulations in respect to the process of acquisition. Recent research on constructions exemplifying binding principles has shown that previous explanations in terms of parameter setting have to be modified extensively. Wexler and Manzini (1990) showed on the basis of cross-linguistic data that the acquisition of anaphors and pronouns is based on the correct setting of two parameters. One of these, having no less than five possible values, determines what is the governing category; the other determines the proper antecedent to which the pronoun is bound (two values). Moreover, not only are the values of parameters not generalizable between languages, but they do not even generalize within a single language: The aforementioned parameters must be set for each pronoun and anaphor separately. This is still not enough: The child has to find out for each word whether it is a pronoun or an anaphor; and Hyams and Sigurjónsdóttir (1990) argued that the child must consider also a third possibility, which they called pronominal anaphor. The child learning a "mixed" language (Valian, 1990a) will have to master additional complications in the parameter. In respect to both the acquisition process and the end-state, such an account makes for much less parsimony than earlier ones that envisaged great acquisitional gains from a single parameter setting.

We note parenthetically that through these modifications, nativist theorizing is beginning to move very close to empiricism. With such a complex array of parameter values to be set, so much is left to be learned from the input that one begins to wonder whether innate binding principles really make the child's task any easier.

In comparing empiricist and nativist hypotheses, a distinction ought to be made between two aspects of parsimony. One is the complexity of the theory, as reflected by such properties as the number of processes and constructs involved and their interactions. Another, more crucial, aspect is what may be called the "novelty" of the constructs and processes posited by the theory, where a "novel" construct or process is one that has been introduced for the purpose of that theory only and has no application outside it. It is mainly the novel constructs and processes that affect the parsimony of a theory.

Now, an empiricist theory posits processes that are presumably operative in the acquisition of skills and knowledge in many other domains as well. Processes like storing the input and generalizing from it are not peculiar to language learning, but to almost *any* type of learning. Deploying frequency information—as in Braine's "sieve" model—has also been attested to in various domains (see, e.g., Hasher & Zacks, 1984). These processes, then, are not novel in the sense mentioned, but are needed in a wider theory of learning behaviors and skills. No gain in parsimony is achieved by a language acquisition theory that refrains from including these processes.

7.4. Parsimony of the Initial State

Nativist theories, because they assume a large array of specifically linguistic innate principles, are clearly less parsimonious—in this sense of parsimony—than empiricist theories that assume only general cognitive principles in the initial state.

Here it might be objected that a semantic theory has no edge over nativist accounts, because it merely substitutes innate semantic universals for innate formal ones. Note, however, that the concepts figuring in the semantic approach are not novel in the aforementioned sense, because they will presumably be available for other cognitive tasks. There is no way for children to make sense of the world around them except in terms of who does what to whom, where, and how; in other words, in terms of notions similar to the semantic roles adopted, in one form or another, by theorists of the semantic persuasion. There is thus independent justification for the assumption that these concepts are innate. The nativist, by contrast, postulates constructs that have no function outside of the acquisition of language. There is no other evidence for their being innate.[9]

Furthermore, according the version of the semantic approach advanced in Schlesinger (1982, 1988), one need not assume broad semantic concepts, like *agent* and *patient*, that predate language; they may be formed in the early stages of the process of acquiring the linguistic rule system.

7.5. The Refutability of Nativist Theories

One of the criteria by which a theory may be judged is the degree of its refutability. In the earlier stages of Chomsky's work, specific constructs of deep structure were thought to be universal and innate. This hypothesis was one that could be rather easily refuted. And refuted it eventually was. It was found that central deep structure constructs, like subject and direct object (NP dominated by S and NP dominated by VP) are not universal: the distinction is lacking in the Israeli Sign Language (Schlesinger, 1971a; Namir & Schlesinger, 1978), and some languages have topics rather than subjects (Li & Thompson, 1976). Gradually, universality and the property of innateness have been assigned to more and more abstract principles. It is reasonable to expect that additional principles now believed to be universal will turn out not to be so.[10] With innateness thus receding, nativist proposals become less open to refutation.

The extreme of this development seems to have been reached by Fodor

---

[9]In two nativist theories semantic concepts do exist before language and are a prerequisite for its acquisition: Pinker's semantic bootstrapping theory and Wexler and Culicover's (1980) theory. Braine (1992) showed that Pinker's model may function just as well when it is stripped of its nativist assumption's, and that then it becomes an assimilation theory. Wexler and Culicover's theory is critically discussed in Braine (1988) and in Schlesinger (1982, pp. 79–80).

[10]One of the putatively universal constraints that may be on its way out is Binding Principle A, as suggested by a small study by Hasman (1992). She presented native Hebrew speakers with a small paragraph containing reflexives, for example:

John, Bob, and David were studying for an exam. John told David to force *himself* to go on studying.

Subjects were then asked to indicate to whom the underlined word referred. Twelve out of the 36 subjects violated Principle A in at least one of the eight sentences presented.

& Crain's (1987) proposal that only the mental language in which linguistic rules are formulated is innately constrained. Note that this view is no longer diametrically opposed to that of the empiricist, for there is no reason to rule out the possibility that the resources of this mental language are available to other cognitive tasks as well. Empiricism has no quarrel with innate knowledge that is not specifically linguistic.

In the early days of generative grammar, a putative innate principle or constraint could be refuted by a reported violation of it in child language. In current theories, the possibilities of such refutation are becoming increasingly limited. This development was foreseen in Schlesinger (1982, pp. 21–24), where the status of an innatist theory as an empirical theory was examined. I argued that to deal with a counterexample to the assumption that a given principle P is universal, all the nativist has to do is to state that P and P'—a principle incompatible with P—are both universals; that is, either principle may appear in a language, and it is the disjunction of P and P' that is innate. "Once alternative sets of principles are postulated, [the nativist program] becomes immune to empirical test by cross-linguistic research, and its fruitfulness is bound to be soon exhausted. But sooner or later this option is likely to be taken in order to survive in face of the conflicting evidence" (Schlesinger, 1982, p. 23).

When this was written I did not know how soon this forecast was going to become true. I had not yet heard of Chomsky's (1981) parameter theory, which essentially took the step described in the foregoing: It permitted alternatives the choice between which is presumed to be innate.[11] Obviously, such a theory is far weaker than one involving unique universal principles that do not admit of any alternatives. The theory permitted children to make errors within the limits prescribed by the values of the parameter, and they are then assumed to reset the parameter—that is, to correct these errors—on the basis of subsequent input. Furthermore, as pointed out in section 7.3, in order to deal with counterexamples, generativists have postulated additional parameters, and sometimes additional values for each parameter.

Recent work on the acquisition of anaphora has revealed difficulties in dealing with the facts by a simple assumption of initial parameter settings (see also section 5.5). To account for those errors in early language that would otherwise have counted as evidence against the theory, writers have had to hypothesize that parameters mature (Borer & Wexler, 1987) or that various principles of universal grammar may become available

---

[11]This is not the whole story, of course. Chomsky's parameters (a) pertain to principles that are more abstract than those posited in earlier days, and (b) may entail considerable savings in acquisition, because one setting may prescribe various, possibly superficially disparate phenomena (see, for instance, the discussion of pro-drop in section 5.5).

to the child at different points in time (Nishigauchi & Roeper, 1987). These moves are of course perfectly legitimate; it is the job of the theorist to deal with recalcitrant data. The purpose of the preceding observation is merely to point out that in doing so nativists have been forced into a position where they make much weaker claims than they used to. Gone are the days when children were tightly constrained by universal principles; their task has become much more difficult now.

8. DECIDING BETWEEN APPROACHES

In the foregoing it has been shown that purported evidence against an empiricist theory of language acquisition is seriously flawed. It should be clear, however, that this does not decide the case in favor of empiricism, for there is also no conclusive empirical evidence against nativism. We are left, then, with the question of which of the two research programs holds more promise for a viable language acquisition theory. This question can be decided, if at all, only on the basis of methodological considerations (see the previous section). But in the end, each theorist's decision will be determined by biases, intuitions, and, as proposed in Levy and Schlesinger (1988), the theorist's conception of the child's mind. Although the following remarks may express my own biases, intuitions, and conceptions, I believe they do more than just reflect these subjective factors and have some general validity.

Current nativist explanations of acquisition phenomena have an esthetic appeal exceeding that of similar attempts by empiricists. Nativists display much ingenuity and inventiveness, and they use formalisms in stating their arguments. They are quick to appreciate disconfirming evidence and often have a pat answer ready to deal with it. Empiricist explanations appear much less clever and exciting by comparison. It is therefore easy to understand why the nativist approach should prove seductive to some scholars.

But there is also something profoundly disconcerting in the facility with which nativists are wont to deal with the data. A new innate parameter value or innate triggering rule is often installed as soon as any difficult arises. I propose that in addition to respecting the empirical evidence (which the nativists certainly do), theorists are responsible for the hypotheses they put forward to deal with the evidence. And if these come too easy, they should raise the suspicion that something is wrong. In the end, all the nativist legerdemain is bound to lead to an epicyclical theoretical structure of continually increasing complexity, and section 7.3 shows that we are already well on the way to such excesses.

I believe, therefore, that scientific integrity commits us to the methodological empiricism I have defended in this chapter. One should eschew the postulation of innate knowledge as a panacea for every difficulty that arises, not because one does not believe there is such knowledge (for in the history of science there have been many beliefs that subsequently turned out to be wrong), but because this is an altogether too easy way of doing science. If a linguistic rule under consideration requires knowledge of a certain principle, then we are under an obligation to investigate where this knowledge comes from. Given the impossibility, at present, of obtaining confirming neurological evidence, this obligation cannot be discharged by taking refuge in innateness. A postulated innate principle functions merely as a placeholder for what has not yet been explained. It does no more than give a semblance of having provided an explanation where there really is none. Constructing empiricist explanations is bound to be a slow and painstaking task, but it is one that must not be shirked.

ACKNOWLEDGMENTS

I am indebted to Yonata Levy for valuable comments regarding the presentation of the material; to Iris Levin for helpful bibliographical hints; and to Moshe Anisfeld, Ainat Guberman, Moti Rimor, and Rita Watson for their comments on a previous version. I also thank Paul Bloom for his helpful comments on the penultimate version.

REFERENCES

Arbib, M. A., & Hill, J. C. (1988). Language acquisition: Schemas replace Universal Grammar. In J. A. Hawkins (Ed.), *Explaining language universals* (pp. 31–72). Oxford: Blackwell.

Bloom, L. (1970). *Language development: Form and function in emerging grammars.* Cambridge, MA: MIT Press.

Bloom, P. (1990). Subjectless sentences in child language. *Linguistic Inquiry, 21*, 491–504.

Borer, H., & Wexler, K. (1987). The maturation of syntax. In T. Roeper & E. Williams (Eds.), *Parameter setting* (pp. 123–172). Dordrecht: Reidel.

Bowerman, M. (1973a). *Early syntactic development.* Cambridge: Cambridge University Press.

Bowerman (1973b). Structural relationships in children's utterances: syntactic or semantic? In T. E. Moore (Ed.), *Cognitive development and the acquisition of language* (pp. 197–213). New York: Academic Press.

Bowerman, M. (1988). The "no negative evidence" problem: How do children avoid constructing an overly general grammar? In J. A. Hawkins (Ed.), *Explaining language universals.* Oxford: Blackwell.

Braine, M. D. S. (1971). On two types of models of the internalization of grammars. In D. I. Slobin (Ed.), *The ontogenesis of grammar: A theoretical symposium* (pp. 153–186). New York: Academic Press.

Braine, M. D. S. (1987). What is learned in acquiring word classes—a step toward an acquisition theory. In B. MacWhinney (Ed.), *Mechanisms of language acquisition* (pp. 65–87). Hillsdale, NJ: Lawrence Erlbaum Associates.

Braine, M. D. S. (1988). Modeling the acquisition of linguistic structure. In Y. Levy, I. M. Schlesinger, & M. D. S. Braine (Eds.), *Categories and processes in language acquisition theory* (pp. 217–259). Hillsdale, NJ: Lawrence Erlbaum Associates.

Braine, M. D. S. (1992). What sort of innate structure is needed to "bootstrap" into syntax? *Cognition, 45,* 77–100.

Braine, M. D. S., Brooks, P. J., Cowan, N., & Samuels, M. C., & Tamis-LeMonda, C. (in press) The development of categories at the semantic/syntactic interface. *Cognitive Development.*

Brown, R. (1958). *Words and things.* Glencoe: Free Press.

Brown, R. (1973). *A first language: The early stages.* Cambridge, MA: Harvard University Press.

Carpenter, K. (1991). Later rather than sooner: Extralinguistic categories in the acquisition of Thai classifiers. *Journal of Child Language, 18,* 93–113.

Chien, Y.-C., & Lust, B. (1985). The concepts of topic and subject in first language acquisition of Mandarin Chinese. *Child Development, 56,* 1359–1375.

Chomsky, N. C. (1965). *Aspects of the theory of syntax.* Cambridge, MA: MIT Press.

Chomsky, N. (1975). *Reflections on language.* New York: Pantheon.

Chomsky, N. (1981). *Lectures on government and binding.* Dordrecht: Foris.

Chomsky, N. (1982). *The generative enterprise.* Dordrecht: Foris.

Cooper, D. E. (1975). *Knowledge of language.* London: Prism Press.

Cromer, R. F. (1988). The cognition hypothesis revisited. In F. S. Kessel (Ed.), *The development of language and language researchers* (pp. 223–248). Hillsdale, NJ: Lawrence Erlbaum Associates.

Demetras, M., Post, K., & Snow, C. (1986). Feedback to first language learners: The role of repetitions and clarification questions. *Journal of Child Language, 13,* 275–292.

de Villiers, J. (1980). The process of rule learning in child speech: A new look. In K. E. Nelson (Ed.), *Children's language* (Vol. 2, pp. 1–44). New York: Gardner Press.

Dowty, D. (1991). Thematic proto-roles and argument selection. *Language, 67,* 547–619.

Fodor, J. D., & Crain, S. (1987). Simplicity and generality of rules in language acquisition. In B. MacWhinney (Ed.), *Mechanisms of language acquisition* (pp. 35–63). Hillsdale, NJ: Lawrence Erlbaum Associates.

Gathercole, V. C. (1985). "He has too much hard questions": The acquisition of the linguistic mass-count distinction in *much* and *many*. *Journal of Child Language, 12,* 395–415.

Gerken, L. (1991). The metrical basis for children's subjectless sentences. *Journal of Memory and Language, 30,* 431–451.

Gleitman (1981). Maturational determinants of language growth. *Cognition, 10,* 103–114.

Gleitman, L. R., & Wanner, E. (1982). Language acquisition: The state of the state of the art. In E. Wanner & L. R. Gleitman (Eds.), *Language acquisition: The state of the art* (pp. 3–48). Cambridge: Cambridge University Press.

Gopnik, A., & Choi, S. (1990). Do linguistic differences lead to cognitive differences? A cross-linguistic study of semantic and cognitive development. *First Language, 10,* 199–215.

Gordon, P. (1985). Evaluating the semantic categories hypothesis: The case of count/mass distinction. *Cognition, 20,* 209–242.

Guberman, A. (1992). The development of the verb category in the Hebrew child language. Unpublished doctoral thesis, Hebrew University, Jerusalem.

Hasher, L., & Zacks, R. T. (1984). Automatic processing of fundamental information: The case of frequency of occurrence. *American Psychologist, 39,* 1372–1388.

Hasman, A. (1991). Binding Principles in adults: A comparison between performance of Principle A and Principle B. [in Hebrew] Unpublished manuscript, Hebrew University.

Hasman, A. (1992). Is Binding Principle A universal? An examination of performance by adult Hebrew speakers [in Hebrew]. Unpublished manuscript, Hebrew University.

Hawkins, J. A. (1988). Explaining language universals. In J. A. Hawkins (Ed.), *Explaining language universals* (pp. 3–28). Oxford: Blackwell.

Hiebert, J., & Wearne, D. (1986). Procedures over concepts: The acquisition of decimal number knowledge. In J. Hiebert (Ed.), *Conceptual and procedural knowledge: The case of mathematics* (pp. 199–223). Hillsdale, NJ: Lawrence Erlbaum Associates.

Hoekstra, T., & Kooij, J. G. (1988). The innateness hypothesis. In J. A. Hawkins (Ed.), *Explaining language universals* (pp. 31–55). Oxford: Blackwell.

Hyams, N. M. (1986). *Language acquisition and the theory of parameters*. Dordrecht: Reidel.

Hyams, N. (1992). A reanalysis of null subjects in child language. In J. Weissenborn, H. Goodluck, & T. Roeper (Eds.), *Theoretical issues in language development: Continuity and change in development* (pp. 249–267). Hillsdale, NJ: Lawrence Erlbaum Associates.

Hyams, N., & Sigurjónsdóttir, S. (1990). The development of "long-distance anaphora": A cross-linguistic comparison with special reference to Icelandic. *Language Acquisition, 1,* 57–93.

Karmiloff-Smith, A. (1978). The interplay between syntax, semantics, and phonology in language acquisition processes. In R. Campbell & P. Smith (Ed.), *Recent advances in the psychology of language* (pp. 1–23). New York: Plenum.

Karmiloff-Smith, A. (in press). Piaget and Chomsky on language acquisition: Divorce or marriage? *First Language.*

Levy, Y. (1983). It's frogs all the way down. *Cognition, 15,* 75–93.

Levy, Y. (1988). The nature of early language: Evidence from the development of Hebrew morphology. In Y. Levy, I. M. Schlesinger, & M. D. S. Braine (Eds.), *Categories and processes in language acquisition theory* (pp. 73–98). Hillsdale, NJ: Lawrence Erlbaum Associates.

Levy, Y., & Schlesinger, I. M. (1988). The child's early categories: Approaches to language acquisition theory. In Y. Levy, I. M. Schlesinger, & M. D. S. Braine (Eds.), *Categories and processes in language acquisition theory* (pp. 261–276). Hillsdale, NJ: Lawrence Erlbaum Associates.

Li, C. N., & Thompson, S. A. (1976). Subject and topic: A new typology of language. In C. N. Li (Ed.), *Subject and topic* (pp. 457–489). New York: Academic Press.

Maratsos, M. P., & Chalkley, M. A. (1980). The internal language of children's syntax. In K. Nelson (Ed.), *Children's language* (Vol. 2, pp. 127–214). New York: Gardner Press.

McDaniel, D., Cairns, H. S., & Hsu, J. R. (1990). Binding principles in the grammar of young children. *Language Acquisition, 1,* 121–139.

MacPherson, L. M. P. (1991). A *little* goes a long way: Evidence for the perceptual basis of learning for the noun categories COUNT and MASS. *Journal of Child Language, 18,* 315–338.

MacWhinney, B. (1978). The acquisition of morphophonology. *Monographs of the Society for Research in Child Development, 43* (1–2, Serial No. 174).

Matthei, E. H. (1987). Subjects and agents in emerging grammars: Evidence for change in children's biases. *Journal of Child Language, 14,* 295–308.

Moerk, E. L. (1991). Positive evidence for negative evidence. *First Language, 11,* 219–251.

Namir, L., & Schlesinger, I. M. (1978). The grammar of sign language. In I. M. Schlesinger & L. Namir (Eds.), *Sign language of the deaf: Psychological, linguistic, and sociological perspectives* (pp. 97–140). New York: Academic Press.

Nishigauchi, T., & Roeper, T. (1987). Deductive parameters and learnability in binding theory. In T. Roeper & E. Williams (Eds.), *Parameter setting* (pp. 91–121). Dordrecht: Reidel.

Ninio, A., & Snow, C. E. (1988). Language acquisition through language use: The functional sources of children's early utterances. In Y. Levy, I. M. Schlesinger, & M. D. S. Braine (Eds.), *Categories and processes in language acquisition theory* (pp. 11–30). Hillsdale, NJ: Lawrence Erlbaum Associates.

Pinker, S. (1984). *Language learnability and language development*. Cambridge, MA: Harvard University Press.

Pinker, S. (1987). The bootstrapping problem in language acquisition. In B. MacWhinney (Ed.), *Mechanisms of language acquisition* (pp. 399–441). Hillsdale, NJ: Lawrence Erlbaum Associates.

Sampson, E. (1978). Linguistic universals as evidence for empiricism. *Journal of Linguistics, 14*, 183–206.

Schlesinger, I. M. (1971a). The grammar of sign language and the problem of language universals. In J. Morton (Ed.), *Biological and social factors in psycholinguistics* (pp. 98–121). London: Logos Press.

Schlesinger, I. M. (1971b). Learning grammar: From pivot to realization rule. In R. Huxley & E. Ingram (Eds.), *Language acquisition: Models and methods* (pp. 79–93). London: Academic Press.

Schlesinger, I. M. (1974). Relational concepts underlying language. In R. L. Schiefelbusch & L. L. Lloyd (Eds.), *Language perspectives—Acquisition, retardation and intervention* (pp. 129–151). Baltimore: University Park Press.

Schlesinger, I. M. (1982). *Steps to language: Toward a theory of language acquisition*. New York: Lawrence Erlbaum Associates.

Schlesinger, I. M. (1988). The origin of relational categories. In Y. Levy, I. M. Schlesinger, & M. D. S. Braine (Eds.), *Categories and processes in language acquisition theory* (pp. 121–178). Hillsdale, NJ: Lawrence Erlbaum Associates.

Schlesinger I. M. (1989). Instruments as agents. *Journal of Linguistics, 25*, 189–210.

Schlesinger, I. M. (1992). The experiencer as an agent. *Journal of Memory and Language, 31*, 315–332.

Schlesinger, I. M. (1993). If Saussure was right, could Whorf have been wrong? In E. Dromi (Ed.), *Language and cognition: A developmental perspective* (pp. 202–218). Norwood, NJ: Ablex.

Schlesinger, I. M. (in press). *Cognitive space and linguistic case*. Cambridge: Cambridge University Press.

Schoenfeld, A. H. (1986). On having and using geometric knowledge. In J. Hiebert (Ed.), *Conceptual and procedural knowledge: The case of mathematics* (pp. 225–264). Hillsdale, NJ: Lawrence Erlbaum Associates.

Slobin, D. I. (1985). Cross-linguistic evidence for the language-making capacity. In D. I. Slobin (Ed.), *The crosslinguistic study of language acquisition* (Vol. 2, pp. 1157–1249). Hillsdale, NJ: Lawrence Erlbaum Associates.

Valian, V. (1986). Syntactic categories in the speech of young children. *Developmental Psychology, 22*, 562–579.

Valian, V. (1990a). Logical and psychological constraints on the acquisition of syntax. In L. Frazier & J. de Villiers (Eds.), *Language processing and language acquisition* (pp. 119–145). Dordrecht: Kluwer.

Valian, V. (1990b). Null subjects: A problem for parameter setting models of language acquisition. *Cognition, 35*, 105–122.

Van Valin, R. (1991). Functionalist learning theory and language acquisition. *First Language, 11*, 7–40.

Van Valin, R. (in press). Semantic roles and grammatical relations. *Papers and Reports on Child Language Development*.

Wexler, K. & Culicover, P. W. (1980). *Formal principles of language acquisition*. Cambridge, MA: MIT Press.

Wexler, K., & Manzini, R. (1987). Parameters and learnability in binding theory. In T. Roeper & E. Williams (Eds.), *Parameter setting* (pp. 41–76). Dordrecht: Reidel.

Wolff, J. G. (1988). Learning syntax and meanings through optimization and distributional analysis. In Y. Levy, I. M. Schlesinger, & M. D. S. Braine (Eds.), *Categories and processes in language acquisition theory* (pp. 179–215). Hillsdale, NJ: Lawrence Erlbaum Associates.

Yamaoka, T. (1988). A semantic and prototype discussion of the "be easy to V" structure: A possible explanation of its acquisition process. *Applied Linguistics, 9,* 385–401.

PART TWO

CROSS-LINGUISTIC PERSPECTIVES

CHAPTER FIVE

The Acquisition of Functional Structure

Teun Hoekstra
Leiden University
Netherlands Institute for Advanced Studies

1. INTRODUCTION

Early stages of acquisition are characterized by the absence of various elements that are required in adult speech, specifically functional elements such as determiners, complementizers, grammatical prepositions, auxiliaries, and the like. Various theoretical positions have been taken in the recent literature with respect to this lack of grammatical elements.

1.1. Parametric Variation

One line of thinking holds that stages of acquisition may differ from adult systems in ways in which adult grammars may vary (cf. Hyams' view on the absence of pronouns in English, which she characterized in terms of properties of the grammar as equaling the grammar of a pro-drop language). According to this view, then, the child's grammar is a complete grammar, consistent with Universal Grammar (UG) in all respects. This requires, then, that there are languages in which such functional elements are also lacking. Such languages thus represent a particular parametric value of UG. Clearly, such languages appear to exist, Chinese being a famous example of a language that is extremely poor in this respect. On this view, then, English children go through a stage in which they are speaking according to a Chineselike grammar.

1.2. The Subgrammar Approach

A second approach is that the grammar underlying these early stages constitutes a proper subgrammar. There are various executions of this idea (e.g., Lebeaux, 1988; Radford, 1990). According to one idea, certain modules of the full grammar are absent (e.g., case theory). Another idea, specifically defended by Radford, purports that the class of functional categories is subject to maturation. The details of this hypothesis are discussed later.

1.3. External to UG

There is also a third approach, according to which child grammars are neither subgrammars, nor necessarily consistent with UG. Obviously, this broad idea can be implemented in various different forms. Consider, for example, the category INFL (inflection). In recent work, it is suggested that INFL be split up in at least the categories Tense and AGR[eement] (cf. Belletti, 1990; Chomsky, 1989; Pollock, 1989). This so-called split-INFL hypothesis has generated a host of proposals on the characterization of early stages. Among these, we find a proposal that children may have a functional category F (cf. Clahsen, 1990), something in between Tense and AGR (more like Finite), which itself would not occur in any adult grammar. F would, technically speaking, be outside of UG, or, put differently, would be restricted to child grammars. This view is the weakest position to take, in that it does not restrict early grammars in any specific way.

1.4. Structure of this Chapter

After a brief introduction of the relevant notions, I discuss four sets of developmental data from Dutch involving the acquisition of functional structure. I demonstrate that in all four cases the child misrepresents certain expressions from the point of view of the target grammar in a particular way. More precisely, expressions that have the status of a functional category in the adult system are represented as adjuncts. Even though at odds with the target grammar, the relevant representations are within the confines of UG. I then discuss the implications of these findings for the theories of acquisition mentioned earlier.

2. FUNCTIONAL CATEGORIES, LEXICAL CATEGORIES, AND ADJUNCTS

The total inventory of expressions is split into two classes: the major lexical categories—noun, verb, and adjectives (possibly prepositions)—and nonmajor categories. More recently, it has been suggested that this latter category also can be subdivided into two classes: those that behave as adjuncts to some projection of another category, and those that behave as a head, referred to as functional heads, selecting a specific complement and projecting a phrasal structure.

To illustrate this consider the contrast in (1):

(1) a. *John not sees a donkey.
     b. John does not see a donkey.
     c. John never sees a donkey.

Assuming a clause structure for English as in (2), with I(nfl) the base position of the inflection, we see that *not* behaves differently from *never*, in that it blocks the connection between I and V, triggering the auxiliary device *do*, which bears the inflectional morphology. *Never* does not have such a blocking effect, in that it allows the inflectional morphology to be associated with the verb. I and V being heads, the difference between *not* and *never* is explained if it is assumed that *not* constitutes the head of a NEG-projection, and therefore functions as an intervening head, given the structure in (3a). *Never*, on the other hand, is a VP-adjunct, as in (3b), and therefore does not function as an intervening head. Only intervening heads induce blocking effects, something that is formulated in the head movement constraint (see Chomsky, 1989; Pollock, 1989; Travis, 1984).

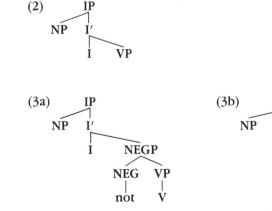

This then leads to a bipartitioning in the class of nonmajor categories: those that have the status of functional category, like English *not*, and those that have adjunct status, like English *never*. Among these functional categories we find I elements (Tense, Agr), NEG, Aspect, Number, Determiner, Quantifier, Person, to mention just a number of recently proposed ones. Let me give one further illustration, which plays a role in the discussion later (viz. Determiners). The category of nominal phrases was traditionally regarded as a projection NP, headed by the noun, and taking the determiner as its specifier. More recently, however, it has been proposed that determiners are heads, taking projections of nouns (NPs) as their complement (cf. Abney, 1986). The structure of a nominal phrase such as "the book" or "John's book" under this proposal looks like (4).

(4)

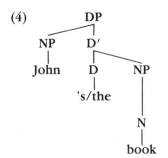

We see a parallelism with the structure of clauses in (2): Inflectional or functional information is separated from the lexical element, and given an independent status in the representation, as a head, projecting a full phrase, and taking the projection of the lexical category as its complement.

The fact that the D-element *the* does not allow a specifier, as in '*John the book', whereas the D-element -*s* does, requires independent explanation, for example, in terms of case theory, an issue with which I am not concerned.

3. THE ACQUISITION DEBATE

Expressions belonging to these functional categories are typically absent or sporadic in early stages of acquisition. Determiners, complementizers, wh-expressions, auxiliaries, and pronouns are left out. Some people (Guilfoyle & Noonan, 1990; Radford, 1990; Tsimpli, 1992) attempt to explain this by suggesting that functional categories "mature." The maturational theory of acquisition, proposed by Wexler and others (cf. Borer & Wexler, 1987), holds that each stage must be compatible with UG, but that certain portions of UG are subject to maturation. This theory is opposed to the continuity hypothesis, which maintains that all of UG is available as of the beginning. Those who insist that these functional categories are available in the grammar of children in the earliest stages therefore have to explain the absence of elements instantiating these categories along different lines. Typically, one would say that even though the categories are present, the items to instantiate these categories still have to be learned (the so-called lexical learning hypothesis). An underlying assumption behind the maturational account would seem to be that if a particular functional category X were available in the grammar of a child, there would not be an acquisition problem, that is, the child would be able to directly map expressions belonging to X in the adult grammar onto the category X in his own grammar. This logic sounds quite reasonable, specifically in view of the high frequency with which functional expressions occur in the language. This type of problem is known as the triggering problem, and the theory of maturation is proposed as a solution to this problem: The abundance of X in the input is irrelevant for the acquisition of the category X in the grammar, as X still has to mature.

However, the basic assumption that there would not be an acquisition problem if the category X were present in the grammar rests itself on a faulty premise, namely, the premise that in all cases the determination that a particular expression instantiates category X can be uniquely established. However, this is certainly not true in all cases. This then is the starting point of my argument, formulated in I:

I. There is in general no unique relationship between the meaning of a particular expression and the status of functional head.

Consider possessives. In some languages (e.g., English) possessive pronouns are in complementary distribution with determiners, and may hence be taken as instances of the functional category Determiner. In other languages, however (e.g., Italian), possessives have the status of adjectives rather than determiners. Hence, UG cannot map possessive pronouns uniquely onto a functional node Determiner or represent it as an adjunct, given that languages vary in this respect. Other evidence than just its meaning are relevant in determining the status of a particular expression, that is, evidence such as complementarity, agreement, and so forth, in short distributional and morphological evidence. Negation constitutes another example of the same point. As Zanuttini (1990) argued, the expression of negation is a functional head in some languages, as illustrated for English *not* above, whereas it has the status of a VP-adverb in other languages (e.g., French *pas*).

Given this state of affairs, the child is confronted with a choice as to the representation of such elements of which UG cannot uniquely determine the status. This choice exists even if the concept of functional categories is available throughout. Concretely, the English child may have a UG determined choice with respect to *not* between the representation in (3) and (4). The issue, then, is which of these choices will initially be taken.

Consider the relationship between some expression X and some projection YP in abstract terms. If X relates to YP as a functional head, this has a number of consequences: X is restricted to single elements (i.e., a head, not a phrase), X is in complementary distribution with other members of its category, and X selects YP. Finally, as I illustrated with English *not*, a functional head may evoke intervener effects on head movement. If X relates to YP as an adjunct, on the other hand, none of these restrictions hold. These differences between adjunction and complementation are summarized in II.

II.

	Y(head) + XP	Y(adjunct) + XP
Y only a single word	yes	no
XP of fixed category	yes	no
complementary distribution	yes	no
intervener effects	yes	no

The assumption of an adjunct status for X therefore requires less information than the assumption of a functional head status. There are two theories that lead us to a particular expectation as to which UG-determined option the child will select. On the one hand, the learning theoretic perspective of the set theoretic approach advocated in Wexler and Manzini (1987), that is, the no-negative-evidence point of view, the most restricted option, in this case of a functional head, would be expected, as this option might be inconsistent with positive evidence, forcing the learner to replace the more restricted option by a more liberal one. On the other hand, if we maintain that the learner does make decisions for which sufficient evidence is not available, we are to expect that the option that presupposes the least is selected, that is, the status of an adjunct. Clearly, just as selection of the adjunct option does not require much information, it is also less restrictive, hence bringing the child in an overly permissive grammar at that point. This raises the question as to how the learner ever recovers from this choice, under the assumption that negative evidence is not available.

I discuss four examples from Dutch that suggest the adjunct structure is taken first, and restructuring takes place later. This empirical evidence therefore supports a cautious learner model over a bold learner, which is driven by set theoretic considerations. I return to the learning problem which the child runs into by this strategy in section 7.

4. THE ACQUISITION OF NEGATION AND MODALITY

Our first example concentrates on the acquisition of negation and modality in Dutch in the very early stages (from 1;7 to 1;11). The discussion is based on an investigation of longitudinal diary data, ranging from age 1;3 until 6;0, collected by Jordens from his child, Jasmijn. Two negative elements are used in this period: *nee* 'no' and *niet* 'not', with *nee* dying out at 1;11. Before 1;11, however, both are used, and it would be misleading to suggest that the use of the *nee* constitutes a stage prior to the use of *niet*.[1]

Before analyzing the system of negation and modality as it is used in this stage of acquisition, it is perhaps useful to give a brief description of the corresponding elements in the target language. Dutch is a so-called SOV language with verb second order in main clauses. This means that the finite verb occurs basically in final position in embedded clauses (certain PPs and embedded clauses follow the finite verb). We take this to result from the headedness of IP,[2] that is, we assume that the basic structure of CP is as in (5):

(5)

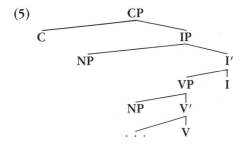

Given this structure, it is in fact hard to decide whether the association of I and V comes about by V movement to I or by lowering of I to V, but as the choice is irrelevant in the present context, we do not discuss this issue. The C-position is occupied by complementizers in embedded clauses, but serves as the landing site of the finite verb in main clauses, yielding the V second effect when the [SPEC, CP] is filled by some phrasal constituent from the IP domain.

Modal verbs in Dutch differ from modal verbs in English in that they are not restricted to finite forms. In fact, there is no reason to assume any special status for modal verbs in Dutch with respect to INFL. It is

---

[1]For further details concerning the quantificational aspects, I refer the reader to Hoekstra and Jordens (1993).

[2]Although the notion of INFL should probably be split up into more elementary components, along the lines of Pollock (1989), I use the label INFL here, as further refinements are irrelevant for present purposes.

possible to combine modal verbs with aspectual verbs as well as with other modal verbs, as in *hij moet het gedaan kunnen hebben* ('he must it done can have' = 'he must have been able to do it').

As for negation, the typical element expressing negation in adult Dutch is *niet*. It may combine with expressions of various types, as may English *not*, for example, with quantifiers (*niet veel pijlen* = 'not many arrows') and with adjectives (*een niet zo groot huis* 'a not so big house'). It is also used to express sentential negation. As for its position, we may assume that it occurs in pre-VP position, but due to various movement processes, elements belonging to the VP-domain may end up to the left of the negation. One such movement concerns the subject, which we take to be base-generated internal to VP, and subsequently moved to the [SPEC, IP]-position. Other movement operations can be subsumed under the heading of scrambling, to which we direct our attention in section 5. A number of negative sentences is provided in (6):

(6) a. *dat Jan niet lacht*
       that John not laughs
    b. *dat Jan niet over het weer spreekt*
       that John not about the weather talks
    c. *dat Jan gisteren niet met z'n broer naar Amsterdam ging*
       that John yesterday not with his brother to Amsterdam went

The element *nee* occurs in adult Dutch, functioning, like its German congener *nein* and its English counterpart *no* as an anaphoric negation, giving a denial answer to a previous question.[3]

In the stage under investigation, both *niet* and *nee* are used by the child to express sentential negation. Given the existence of two elements, we face the question of their relative distribution. The following is a fair summary:

(7) relative distribution of *niet* and *nee*
    a. *nee* never occurs with modal verbs such as *kan* and *mag*: here
       we find *niet*, or rather *nie* exclusively.
    b. *nee* never occurs with finite verbs.
    c. *niet* never occurs with non-finite verbs.
    d. in nonverbal sentences, both *niet* and *nee* are used.

Clearly, then, their relative distribution is not random, but results from

---

[3]English *no* has two uses: Apart from its anaphoric use, *no* is also used as a fused negator in cases like "no person entered the room," where it may be considered a fusion of NEG and an indefinite determiner (cf. "not a person entered the room"). The Dutch equivalent of this *no* is *geen*, which is discussed in section 5.

some system. What is this system? We claim that the distribution follows from the following:

(8) a. *niet* is a pure negation: It negates a description pertaining to the here-and-now.
   b. *nee* is a modal negation, meaning "I do not want."

The claim that *nee*, the anaphoric negation in the adult language, is a modal negation makes it understandable why the anaphoric negation is used as a sentential negation, while it is used anaphorically as well. From an anaphoric negative response (Do you want to sit here? No, I don't want to sit here.) it is generalized to other negative wishes: *nee poes hier zitten* 'I don't want the pussy cat to sit here').

Consider how (7) follows from (8). (7a) follows from (8b): If *kan/mag* expresses modality, and *nee* also expresses modality, then *nee* is incompatible with these contexts. Although there is no restriction per se on combining modal elements, not all combinations are possible. In particular, embedding of a boulemaic negation under epistemic modality (I cannot want this) appears very unlikely.

The statements in (7b) and (7c) express a complementarity of *niet* and *nee* in the domain of finiteness. As is well known, at the relevant stage we find both infinitival and finite constructions, be it that the latter are rather limited. These two show different patterns of negation: In finite contexts, we have postverbal negation, whereas nonfinite constructions feature preverbal negation. This is not only true for Dutch, but appears to be a rather general phenomenon, reported for Swedish (Lundin & Platzack, 1989; Plunkett & Strömqvist, 1990), French (Pierce, 1989; Weissenborn, Verrips, & Berman, 1989) and German (Clahsen, 1988). The difference in position can be explained by assuming that the negation occupies a pre-VP position, with finite verbs moving to its left to some functional position, a difference that is then captured in the same way as in adult grammars. So, in French, finite verbs move to the left of *pas*, whereas nonfinite verbs (with the exception of *être* and *avoir*) remain to the right of *pas*, as shown in (9):

(9) a. *Jean ne lit pas un livre*
       John NEG reads NEG a book   'John doesn't read a book'
   b. *ne pas lire un livre*
       NEG NEG read a book   'to not read a book'

Similarly, in adult Dutch, the finite verb in main clauses occurs to the left of *niet*, as a result of movement to C of the finite verb, and it occurs to the right of *niet* in embedded clauses, as shown in the examples in (6).

The difference between adult systems and the grammar of children displaying both preverbal and postverbal negation is first and foremost due to the possibility of nonfinite main clauses in the latter. Poeppel and Wexler (in press) referred to this stage as the "optional infinitive stage." Despite the notion of optionality here, I want to maintain that, just as the use of *nee* versus *niet* is not an arbitrary matter, the choice between a finite and a nonfinite construction is likewise not just an arbitrary choice between two equivalents. We maintain the following:

(10) Finite constructions describe the here-and-now.
Nonfinite constructions do not describe the here-and-now.

Note that lack of here-and-now implies modality: Whatever is being said relates to some other world/time coordinate, to which the speaker relates the proposition in some modality or other. This concurs with the intuition that many researchers have had concerning nonfinite sentences as if some modal verb were lacking.

It is not easy to provide clear evidence in favor of (10), as it often depends on the interpretation of the context. However, indirect evidence may be put forth. We feel that the system of negation constitutes such indirect evidence. *Niet*, being an pure negator, may combine with finite constructions, which lack modality (or in the case of an overt modal express this modality separately), but *nee* is not suitable in finite constructions because of its inherent modality. Vice versa, *niet* is incompatible with the inherent modality of nonfinite constructions, but *nee* is well suited in this context. Put differently, in infinitival contexts, *kan/mag* + *niet* are in complementary distribution with *nee*, while this entire context itself is in complementary distribution with finite-verb + *niet*, as in (11):

(11) distribution of negation in verbal contexts
finite   nonfinite
niet   kan/mag + nie vs. nee

If these claims are correct, the fact that *niet* and *nee* have an overlapping distribution in nonverbal contexts hardly comes as a surprise. Our analysis entails, however, that nonverbal utterances with *niet* differ in interpretation from such utterances with *nee*. Some examples are given in (12) and (13):

(12) a. *die niet*   1;10
       that not
     b. *die niet goed*   1;10
       that not good

    c. *Peter niet oppe hand*   1;11
       Peter not on his hand
    d. *niet voor poes*   1;11
       not for pussy cat

(13) a. *nee poes vlees*   1;10
       no pussycat meat
    b. *nee thee*   1;10
       no tea
    c. *nee Tom Poes buiten. Cynthia ook niet*   1;10
       no Tom Poes outside. Cynthia also not

Again, it is hard to go beyond the impressionistic level, but our interpretation is that the utterances in (13) do not describe the current situation, for example, in (13a) the situation that the pussy cat has no meat, but rather the negative desire with respect to that situation: "I don't want the pussy cat to have meat." The utterances in (12), on the other hand, give just an assessment of the situation.

We see, then, that the semantic difference we postulate in (8) captures the distribution described in (7).

This system changes in a period of 2 months. In this period, *nee* disappears. At the same time, the use of modal verbs expands. How can we interpret this acquisitional process? So far, we have not been very specific about the syntactic analysis of the modal system, but one may have wondered why we put the negative modal *kan/mag* + *niet* in a separate category from the finite verbs. The claim we want to make is that until age 1;10 there is no syntactic difference between these negative modals and *nee*. In adult grammar, *nee* is an adverb, and *kan/mag* is a finite verb, but we propose that at the relevant stage, there is no syntactic distinction.[4] Instead, we propose that both *nee* and *kan/mag* + *niet* are adjoined to the projection of which the nonfinite verb is the lexical head. We use the label VP for this projection. So, the structure we propose is as in (14):

(14) syntactic structure of modal system at age 1;10

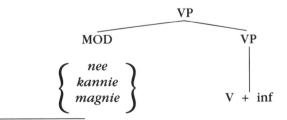

----

[4]Klima and Bellugi (1967) made the same claim for English *can't* and *don't* in the same period.

(the internal structure of *kan/mag* + *niet* is irrelevant for our purposes). A developmental change that takes place around 1;11:

1. The intonational pattern changes from the typical doubly stressed adjunction pattern to a integrative pattern with a single stress on the infinitive: *kánnie zítten* becomes *kannie zítten*. This integrative accentuation is typical of a head-complement structure, where stress is placed on the lexical head of the complement.

2. The nonverbal modal *nee* disappears.

3. Whereas earlier *kan/mag* + *nie* can either precede or follow the nonfinite construction, it now precedes it. This change can be represented in the grammar if we assume that instead of the adjunctional structure in (14), the grammar has a head-complement structure, with a requirement on the head that it be verbal, that is, the structure is as in (15). Although the hierarchical relation remains the same, the functional relation as well as the categorical labeling has changed.

(15) sentence structure at age 1;11

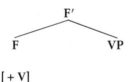

[+ V]

The final question concerns what triggers this restructuring. This question is related to the question as to what allows the child to use nonfinite main clauses. Here I would like to follow Rizzi (1993), who argued that presence of a functional category may be optional. In the case at hand, I assume that the optional infinitive stage is a consequence of the optionality of the F-position: In finite-constructions this position is available as a landing site for the finite verb, but in infinitival constructions, the F-position is lacking. Infinitival clauses become impossible once the presence of the F-position becomes obligatory. With respect to the category of (negative) modal, the child then has to either discard the use of these elements, or reanalyze them as finite verbs, occupying the F-position. This is indeed what happens, in a way that is consistent with the input: *Nee* is discarded, as it is nonverbal, whereas the modals are reanalyzed as verbs, occupying the F-position, and taking the infinitival projection as its complement. The stress shift and positional fixation are consequences of this reanalysis.

The shift from (14) to (15) thus constitutes our first example of the development from modifying adjunct to governing functional head. We now turn to our second example.

5. SCRAMBLING AND SUBSCRAMBLING

We now move on to a later stage of development, starting at age 2;1. At this age, the only negator is *niet*: *nee* has disappeared. *Niet* itself functions in the same way as in adult Dutch. An analysis of *niet* as part of (some of the) verbs is excluded, as *niet* is separated from the finite verb in second position by intervening subjects, both pronouns and lexical NPs. The system of negation only differs from the adult system in two respects:

1. The fused negator *geen* is not available and it remains absent until 2;9. I do not discuss the acquisition of *geen* here, but restrict myself to noting that *geen* in the adult system stands in opposition to *niet* in function of the determiner system and its semantic properties. Basically, *geen* occurs in combination with count nouns, both plural and singular if there is no specific reference, and with mass terms. The use of *geen* in adult Dutch is illustrated by the examples in (16c).

2. The position of *niet* vis à vis the object NP is incorrect in many instances, at least at 2;1. Basically, NPs denoting strong quantifiers (i.e., proper names, pronouns, definite noun phrases, indefinite specific noun phrases) scramble to the left of the negation, unless there is constituent negation. In other circumstances, *geen* is used.

(16) a. *dat Jan **het boek** niet leest*   definite NP
    that John the book not reads
  b. *dat Jan **een boek** niet leest*   specific indefinite NP
    that John a book not reads
  c. *dat Jan **geen boek** leest*   unspecific indefinite NP
    that John no book reads

In conclusion, then, at 2;1 the interaction of semantic/syntactic properties of the object NP and negation is not yet acquired.

Gradually, scrambling of strong NPs is acquired. Pronouns are the first to scramble, followed by proper names. These NPs are strong NPs inherently, that is, their strength is not a function of a determiner element. Typically, determiners are absent at this stage. To the extent that they do occur, their occurrence is mainly restricted to NPs in the complement of prepositions. As soon as determiners are acquired, the NPs they are part of behave as expected. Some illustrative examples of transitive constructions at 2;1 are given in (17) and (18) illustrates the system at 2;8:

(17) a. *ik mag niet **modewijzer***   2;1
    I may not fashion designer
    'I may not have the/a fashion designer'   (name of a toy)

    b. *ik kan niet **Maria** zoeken*   2;1
      I can not Mary search
      'I can't search Mary'
    c. *ik wil niet **dit***   2;1
      I want not this
      'I don't want this'

(18) a. . . . *dat jij niet **lolly** heb*   2;8
      . . . that you not lollipop have
      'that you don't have a lollipop'
    b. *ik vin **dat jongetje** niet lief*   2;8
      I find that boy not sweet
      'I don't find that boy sweet'
    c. *ik kan **dat** niet*   2;8
      I can that not
      'I can't do that'

As we see in (17), a definite NP, a proper name and a pronoun occur to the right of *niet*, which we may interpret as resulting from the lack of scrambling. In (18b) the full NP object is correctly scrambled to the left of *niet*, as is the pronominal object in (18c). There are no mistakes in the positioning of pronominal objects, or proper name objects, and there are no mistakes in the position of NPs with a definite determiner. There still is one type of mistake, from an adult perspective, which is displayed by (18a). Instead of *niet* we should have the fused negator *geen* (cf. 16c), but this element does not occur.

The acquisition of scrambling is not what interests us here. Rather, in the investigation of scrambling I noted that during the development of scrambling, there are quite a few cases of the type in (19), in which part of the NP is scrambled, in apparent violation of the so-called left branch condition.

(19)a. *die heb ik niet **sok** aan*   2;3
      that have I not sock on
      'I am not wearing that sock'
    b. ***jou** niet **pyama***   2;5
      you not pyjamas
      'that is not your pyjamas'
    c. ***Cynthia** is dat niet **pyama***   2;5
      Cynthia is that not pyjamas
      'that is not Cynthia's pyjamas'
    d. ***Cynthia** mag **mij** niet **navel** zien*   2;7
      Cynthia may me not bellybutton see
      'Cynthia may not see my bellybutton'

    e. *jij ziet **mij** niet **ogen***   2;7
       you see me not eyes
       'you don't see my eyes'

    f. *ik vin **Cynthia** niet **tekening** leuk*   2;8
       I find Cynthia not drawing nice
       'I don't like Cynthia's picture'

    g. *ik kan **die** niet **vis** vange*   2;8
       I can that not fish catch
       'I cannot catch that fish'

    h. *Cynthia mag **mij** niet **pyama** zien*   2;8
       Cynthia may me not pyjamas see
       'Cynthia may not see my pyjamas'

In all these examples, the bold faced parts would form a single constituent in the adult grammar. The splitting results from topicalization in (19a–c), and from scrambling in the other examples.

Under a DP hypothesis (cf. section 3; Abney, 1986; Szabolcsi, 1986), some of the examples involve extraction of the specifier (19c and 19f), others involve extraction of the head of DP (19a and 19g), and other cases are not clear, as they depend on the analysis of these pronouns, either as personal pronouns in [SPEC, D] or as possessive pronouns in head position. The relevant generalization to make, here, is that all the leftward scrambled parts can be independent NPs, that is, they can function as object NPs by themselves. Moreover, they are NPs of the type that are scrambled at this stage (i.e., pronouns and proper names). There are no instances of any such split involving a determiner that cannot occur by itself, such as *de* 'the' or *een* 'a'. So, in terms of surface syntactic distribution, the object may be split up in two parts if each of the two parts can be used as an independent NP, and each part also occupies the position expected for its type. So, the pattern is as in (20):

(20) . . . NP1 *niet* NP2 V

where NP2 is a bare common noun, and NP1 either is a pronoun or a proper name. By virtue of the theta criterion and the projection principle, we are forced to assume that these two parts together constitute a single argument, that is, together they function as the object of the verb. One might attempt to provide alternative analyses, according to which we are not dealing with a single, split-up constituent. One such alternative might be to draw an analogy with possessive dative constructions, as in *Je lui ai coupé les cheveux* 'I to-him have cut the hair', as discussed by Guéron (1985). However, this might be a possible analysis for cases where NP1 is a proper name or a personal pronoun, but not for those cases where NP1 is a demonstrative. The second possibility might be to assume that the common noun NP2 is not an NP, but rather part of a compound verb. So, (19g) might be analyzed as involving the compound verb *vis vangen* taking *die* as its object. Yet, this also does not provide an unified analysis, as it is inapplicable in most other cases.

The conclusion has to be that NP1 and NP2 do form a single constituent that is split up by movement of NP1 away from NP2 (i.e., by subextraction). As stated earlier, from a DP structure point of view, these subextractions either involve extraction of the specifier or of the head. Let us look at the specifier cases first. In adult grammar, such extractions used to be excluded by an appeal to the left branch condition, which stipulates that material from a left branch may not be extracted. From a more recent perspective, however, in particular from the DP analysis perspective, it is not immediately clear how the left branch condition can be operative with respect to the specifier of DP, without being operative with respect to the specifier of IP, these two being completely parallel (cf. Corver, 1990, for discussion). We therefore need to find another reason why extraction of the specifier of DP is excluded in the adult grammar. It is important in this context to observe that the genitive marker is generally lacking at the relevant stage. The same has been widely reported for English genitival -*s* (cf. Bloom, 1970; Brown, 1973; and many others). So, instead of *papa's horloge* 'daddy's watch', the child says *papa loozje*. Similarly, the child uses personal pronouns instead of possessive pronouns. So, if we adopt the structure in (21), we may suggest that the fact that "possessor" extraction is impossible in adult grammar is not due to the left branch condition, but is a consequence of the relationship with the genitive marker:

(21)

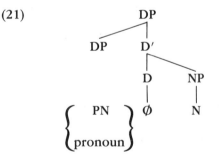

Consider the subscrambling of demonstratives next. Starting out with a structure such as (21) again, with the demonstrative in head position, this subscrambling would be an instance of head movement, and as such in principle is not allowed by structure preservation, unless the position of NP1 in (20) is some kind of head position, for which there is no indication, nor would it allow for a unified analysis. In conclusion, then, if the structure of nominal phrases in this stage were identical to the adult model, the subextractions illustrated in (19) would be excluded by UG principles, basically the same principles that would supposedly lead the child to analyze the demonstrative as the head of a DP.

We therefore would like to propose an alternative to the structure in (21), namely the structure in (22), with the proper names and demonstratives in adjoined, rather than in head position.

(22)

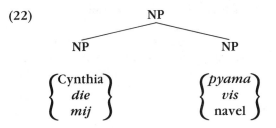

Again we face the question as to what induces the change from (22) to (21). As in the case of modals, this question relates to the more general question as to what allows the absence of determiners in children's grammar. The answer may likewise be that the presence of a D is optional at first, but obligatory later on, analogous to the CP-requirement with respect to the optional infinitive stage. Once the DP-structure becomes obligatory, the elements that were adjoined have to be reanalyzed in conformity with the DP-structure.

6. TWO SPECULATIVE OTHER EXAMPLES

We now turn to a different case that might also provide an example of the same developmental schema. It is exemplified in (23):

(23) *kijk eens hoe ik groot ben*
look how I big am

This type is not evidenced in the recorded data, but such constructions can be heard in spontaneous data. If the structure of the construction *hoe groot* is as in (24), this case also involves an apparent violation of the left branch condition.

(24)

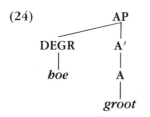

Yet, as we said, the status of the left branch condition is rather problematic in current theory. It is interesting that Corver (1990) argued that *hoe* and elements like it should not be considered specifiers of the AP, but rather as heads of a DEGR phrase, a functional category in his view, taking AP as its complement. The structure of the construction under this proposal would be as in (25), rather than as in (24), and the lack of movement in the adult grammar can then be seen as a consequence of the absence of a suitable landing site for movement of the head of the DEGR-phrase.

(25)

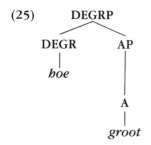

However, if in the child's grammar the structure is as in (26), with *hoe* adjoined to the AP rather than in the specifier position, the extraction as found in (23) is no longer problematic. We would then have yet a further instance of the acquisition schema proposed in this chapter.

(26)

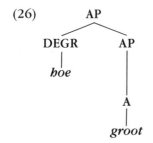

As a final example, consider the acquisition of embedded clauses. The earliest embeddings are found at 2;1, but lexical complementizers as well as wh-phrases are lacking at this point (cf. Rothweiler, 1989, who reported the same for German):

(27) a. *ik weet niet cookmonster is*
         I know not Cookie Monster is
         'I don't know *where* CM is'
     b. *vin je niet leuk is*
         find you not funny is
         'don't you think *that* that is funny'

Wh-expressions in embedded questions are found before overt complementizers show up. We might interpret this as evidence that these embeddings are initially IPs, to which the wh-expressions are initially adjoined. After the acquisition of complementizers, this situation is reanalyzed, and wh-expressions occur in SPEC of CP. This development would then also instantiate the proposed schema. The claim that children initially adjoin wh-phrases to IP is also made in de Villiers (1991), who made this claim to explain the absence of inversion in English wh-questions. She furthermore argued that inversion in main clauses develops after embedded wh-questions turn up. Clearly, the relationship between the issue of the status of embedded clauses and that of main clauses requires much further investigation, but I think that these phenomena allow the interpretation that wh-phrases may first adjoin, to only later be reanalyzed as occupying a specifier position of CP.

There is one piece of additional evidence in favor of this tentative proposal. Even though the nominative forms of subject pronouns are already available, the earliest examples of embeddings with pronominal subjects feature accusative rather than nominative pronouns, as in the examples in (28):

(28) a. weet ik niet *jou* is
         know I not you-ACC is
         'I didn't know where you were'
     b. Dan weet Papa niet waar *mij* is
         then knows daddy not where me is

Under an analysis of the embedding as IPs instead of CPs, there would be no barrier to protect the embedded subject from government by the matrix verb, which may hence assign accusative case.[5]

----

[5]The accusative pronouns in subject position may only be taken as evidence if there are no accusative pronouns in matrix subject position. This is not the case in early English, where both nominative and nonnominative pronominal subjects occur. I have not found any clear cases of accusative pronominal subjects in the data in clearly verbal sentences.

7. THE TRIGGERING PROBLEM

Having provided the evidence for the proposed schema of acquisition, the question arises as to what will trigger the child to reanalyze the adjunct structure to a functional head-complement structure. The maturational hypothesis intends to provide an account of this triggering problem, by stipulating that the question whether X is a functional head arises only at the point in which functional categories mature. However, this hypothesis explains this situation only in part. Whereas the hypothesis explains the absence of certain expressions qua functional heads, it does not explain their absence itself. The child can always misrepresent a certain expression.

A further problem with the maturational account is that it is just not true that all of the members of a particular functional category in the adult language are always absent. This was shown earlier with determiner elements, like the demonstratives, which are present at a very early age, while other determiners are still lacking. Similarly, although adult grammars are generally restricted by a finiteness requirement (i.e., the requirement that a sentence be finite), children allow nonfinite sentences while at the same time using finite verbs. As in the case of determiners like *de* in Dutch, the syntax of these finite verbs is correct at a very early stage, basically from the beginning of their usage. So, the earliest finite verbs in Dutch occur in second position, in conformity with the adult grammar. Yet, at the same time, children also use nonfinite verbs, in a syntax that equally matches that of the adult language (i.e., in final position in Dutch). This suggests that it is not so much maturation of a category, but rather maturation or development of a certain requirement, which has the obligatory presence of a category as a consequence. This is essentially what Rizzi (1992) proposed. I do not speculate on the nature of these requirements here.

If my analysis of the acquisitional schema is correct, the question that has to be answered is why a "misrepresentation" (i.e., as adjuncts) is not open to all members of a particular functional category in the adult language. What we need, therefore, is a condition on adjunction that allows certain members of, for example, the adult category Determiner to be treated as an adjunct, but not others.

I propose a condition on adjuncts that has the desired effect, namely, the condition that X can only be treated as an adjunct if X can occur independently in the input. Note that this is precisely the difference between a determiner like *de* 'the' and *die/dat* 'those/that': Whereas the latter may constitute an independent phrase, *de* can only occur in combination with an NP. Recall that all subscrambled parts of objects (i.e., all elements capable of occupying the NP_1 position in (20)) could occur as independent objects. Typically, subscrambling stops when determiners like *de* come in. Assuming the condition on adjunction just proposed, such weak determiner elements have to get the status of a functional head, thereby generating a structural position open for other determiners as well.

Although this condition on adjunction explains why only certain members of a functional category in the adult language occur in early stages, we are still left with the question why other members are not available. For this, there are still two options: Either the elements concerned take more time to be acquired, or the categorical structure to host these elements is unavailable, due to lack of maturation. The evidence reviewed here is compatible with both options, it seems to me. The only point worth mentioning in this connection is that the developmental shifts we argued for spread out over a rather large period of time, suggesting that if maturation is involved, it would be a rather complex matter—that is, it is not the case that the notion of functional structure per se can be said to mature at a certain point, but rather certain functional categories would have to mature earlier than others, a scenario that is not so much impossible, but certainly not very appealing either. Rather, it seems more likely that the concept of functional structure is available throughout, but that it is exploited as a last resort (i.e., if the more elementary adjunction strategy no longer suffices).

ACKNOWLEDGMENTS

This chapter was written while I was at the Netherlands Institute for Advanced Studies (NIAS). The research was done in close collaboration with Peter Jordens, whose contribution is gratefully acknowledged. I am also grateful to him for giving me access to the wealth of material that he so carefully collected from his daughter's speech. I also want to thank Tom Roeper for many helpful discussions, and Nina Hyams for a number of useful comments.

REFERENCES

Abney, S. (1986). *The English noun phrase in its sentential aspect.* Unpublished doctoral dissertation, MIT, Cambridge, MA.

Belletti, A. (1990). *Generalized verb movement.* Turin: Rosenberg & Sellier.

Bloom, L. (1970). *Language development: Form and function in emerging grammars.* Cambridge, MA: MIT Press.

Borer, H., & Wexler, K. (1987). The maturation of syntax. In T. Roeper & E. Williams (Eds.), *Parameter setting* (pp. 123–172). Dordrecht: Reidel.

Brown, R. (1973). *A first language: The early stages.* Cambridge, MA: Harvard University Press.

Chomsky, N. (1989). Some notes on economy of derivation and representation. In I. Laka & A. Mahajan (Eds.), *MIT working papers in linguistics 10* (pp. 43–74). Cambridge, MA: MIT, Department of Linguistics and Philosophy.

Clahsen, H. (1988). Critical phases of grammar development: A study of the acquisition of negation in children and adults. In P. Jordens & J. Lalleman (Eds.), *Language development* (pp. 123–148). Dordrecht: Foris.

Clahsen, H. (1990). *Constraints on parameter setting: A grammatical analysis of some acquisitional stages in German child language.* Paper presented at the Boston University Conference on Language development, Boston.

Corver, N. (1990). *The grammar of left-branch extractions.* Unpublished doctoral dissertation, Tilburg University, The Netherlands.

de Villiers, J. (1991). Why questions. In T. L. Maxfield & B. Plunkett (Eds.), *Papers in the acquisition of WH.* UMASS Occasional Papers, distributed by the GLSA, University of Massachusetts, Amherst.

Guéron, J. (1985). Inalienable possession, PRO-inclusion and lexical chains. In J. Gueron, H.-G. Obenhauer, & J.-Y. Pollock (Eds.), *Grammatical representation* (pp. 43–86). Dordrecht: Foris.

Guilfoyle, E., & Noonan, M. (1990). *Functional categories and language acquisition.* Unpublished manuscript, McGill University, Montreal.

Hoekstra, T. A., & Jordens, P. (1991, March). *From adjunct to head.* Paper presented at the GLOW-workshop on the acquisition of heads, Leiden, The Netherlands.

Lebeaux, D. (1988). *Language acquisition and the form of grammar.* Unpublished doctoral dissertation, University of Massachusetts, Amherst.

Lundin, B., & Platzack, C. (1989). The acquisition of verb inflection, verb second and subordinate clauses in Swedish. In Working Papers in Scandinavian Syntax (*WPSS*), *42*, 43–55. Dept. of Linguistics, Lund, Sweden.

Pierce, A. (1989). *On the emergence of syntax: A crosslinguistic study.* Unpublished doctoral dissertation, MIT, Cambridge, MA.

Plunkett, K., & Strömqvist, S. (1990). *The acquisition of Scandinavian languages.* Gothenburg papers in theoretical linguistics. Gothenburg, Sweden: University of Gothenburg.

Poeppel, D. & Wexler, K. (in press). The full competence hypothesis of clause structure in early German. *Language.*

Pollock, J-Y. (1989). Verb movement, Universal Grammar and the structure of IP. *Linguistic Inquiry, 20,* 365–423.

Radford, A. (1990). *Syntactic theory and the acquisition of English syntax.* London: Blackwell.

Rizzi, L. (in press). Early null subjects and root null subjects. In T. Hoekstra and B. D. Schwartz (Eds.), *Language acquisition studies in generative grammar.* Amsterdam, Benjamins Publishing Company.

Rothweiler, M. (1989). *Nebensatzerwerb in Deutschen.* Unpublished doctoral dissertation, University of Tubingen.

Szabolcsi, A. (1986). The possessor that ran away from home. *The Linguistic Review, 3,* 89–102.

Travis, L. (1984). *Parameters and effects of word order variation.* Unpublished doctoral dissertation, MIT, Cambridge, MA.

Tsimpli, Y. (1992). *Functional categories and maturation: The prefunctional stage of language acquisition.* Unpublished doctoral dissertation, University College, London.

Weissenborn, J., Verrips, M., & Berman, R. (1989). *Negation as a window to the structure of early child language.* Unpublished manuscript, Max Planck Institute, Nijmegen.

Wexler, K., & Manzini, R. (1987). Parameters and learnability in binding theory. In T. Roeper & E. Williams (Eds.), *Parameter setting* (pp. 41–76). Dordrecht: Reidel.

Zanuttini, R. (1990). Two types of negative markers. In *Proceedings of NELS 20*. University of Massachusetts, Amherst: Graduate Linguistics Students Association.

CHAPTER SIX

The Acquisition of
Italian Verb Morphology in a
Cross-Linguistic Perspective

Elena Pizzuto
Maria Cristina Caselli
Institute of Psychology
National Research Council
Rome, Italy

1. INTRODUCTION

Children acquiring Italian must learn a very rich system of verb inflections. Verbs never appear as unmarked forms but always bear inflectional affixes. It has been proposed (Jaeggli & Safir, 1989a, pp. 29–31) that inflectional paradigms in which all forms are always complex (that is, divisible into stem and affixes, as in Italian), or none of them are (as in Chinese), can be characterized as morphologically uniform. In contrast, mixed morphological paradigms in which some forms are inflected, and others correspond to the verb stem are not morphologically uniform. This is the case of English in which, for example, the third-person regular present-tense form is divisible into stem plus affix (*speak-s*), and the remaining present-tense forms correspond to the verb stem (*speak*). From a cross-linguistic perspective, the question arises whether, or to what extent, the developmental patterns observable in the acquisition of a morphologically rich and uniform language like Italian are comparable to those noted in the acquisition of other, morphologically impoverished and not uniform languages such as English.

In an earlier, more extensive study, we described the development of the morphological paradigms of Italian pronouns, definite articles, simple and compound (or periphrastic) forms of main verbs, auxiliaries and copulas in three children's spontaneous production (Pizzuto & Caselli, 1991, 1992). In the present chapter, we use the same set of spontaneous

137

production data to focus on a more restricted aspect of the developmental process: the acquisition of main verbs' simple, finite forms. We pursue three major objectives: (a) provide new information on the acquisition of verb inflectional morphology in Italian; (b) compare this information with data on the spontaneous acquisition of English verb inflections; (c) explore whether, and/or to what extent, the patterns identified can be explained within current approaches to language development. In particular, we evaluate the plausibility of a nativist, parameter-setting account of the development of verb inflectional morphology as proposed for Italian and English by Hyams (1986a, 1986b, 1991, 1992). The data we provide hopefully clarifies some theoretical and methodological issues concerning cross-linguistic variation in language acquisition. A brief description of the Italian verb system is necessary.

1.1. The Italian Verb System

As noted, in Italian, unlike in English, verbs never occur as unmarked, bare stem forms (e.g., *speak*) to which inflectional suffixes can then be added (e.g., as in *speaks, speaking*). However, as pointed out by Scalise (1990, pp. 117ff.), the notion of stem used in the description of English verbs cannot be directly applied to Italian. Whereas an English verbal stem is monomorphemic, its Italian counterpart is bimorphemic: It consists of a verbal root followed by a characteristic thematic vowel, distinctive for each of the three major conjugations. This segmentation of Italian verbs, the same described in standard Italian grammars (Dardano & Trifone, 1985; cf. Vincent, 1987), is illustrated in Table 6.1: the citation, infinitival forms of the regular verbs *chiamare* 'to call', *battere* 'to bang' and *dormire* 'to sleep' are decomposable into: the roots *chiam-, batt-,* and *dorm-*; the stems *chiam-a, batt-e,* and *dorm-i*, where the vowels *a-, e,* and *-i-* define, respectively, the first, second, and third conjugation class; the ending suffix *-re* marking the infinitive. Because verbal roots and stems can only appear as part of a larger form or larger sequences of morphemes, they can be considered as *bound forms* (Matthews, 1974, pp. 160ff.). Stems, however, are also homophonous with some inflected forms.

The first conjugation is the largest verb class, and newly coined verbs tend to follow its pattern. All conjugations comprise both regular and irregular verbs. Most irregular verbs belong to the second conjugation, a much smaller number to the third conjugation, and there are only four, but highly frequent irregular verbs in the first conjugation (*andare* 'to go'; *dare* 'to give'; *fare* 'to make'; *stare* 'to stay'). As shown in Table 6.1 by the irregular patterns of *andare*, and *tenere* 'to hold', most ir-

TABLE 6.1
Examples of Regular and Irregular Patterns in Italian Verbs of the
First, Second, and Third Conjugation: Root, Stem, Citation Form (Infinitive),
Indicative Present, Imperfect, Future, and Imperative Present Inflections

	Conjugation				
	1st Reg.	*2nd Reg.*	*3rd Reg.*	*1st Irreg.*	*2nd Irreg.*
Root	chiam	batt	dorm	and	ten
Stem	chiam-a	batt-e	dorm-i	and-a	ten-e
Infinitive	chiam-a-re	batt-e-re	dorm-i-re	and-a-re	ten-e-re
	'to call'	*'to bang'*	*'to sleep'*	*'to go'*	*'to hold'*
	Roots:				
	chiam	*batt*	*dorm*	*and*	*ten*
-Inflections:					
-Indic. Pres.					
1SG	-o	-o	-o	vado	tengo
2SG	-i	-i	-i	vai	tieni
3SG	-a	-e	-e	va	tiene
1PL	-iamo	-iamo	-iamo	andiamo	teniamo
2PL	-ate	-ete	-ite	andate	tenete
3PL	-ano	-ono	-ono	vanno	tengono
	'call/s'	*'bang/s'*	*'sleep/s'*	*'go/goes'*	*'hold/s'*
-Indic. Imperf.					
1SG	-avo	-evo	-ivo	and-avo	ten-evo
2SG	-avi	-evi	-ivi	-avi	-evi
3SG	-ava	-eva	-iva	-ava	-eva
1PL	-avamo	-evamo	-ivamo	-avamo	-evamo
2PL	-avate	-evate	-ivate	-avate	-evate
3PL	-avano	-evano	-ivano	-avano	-evano
	'was/were calling'	*'was/were banging'*	*'was/were sleeping'*	*'was/were going'*	*'was/were holding'*
-Indic. Fut.					
1SG	-erò	-erò	-irò	andrò	terrò
2SG	-erai	-erai	-irai	andrai	terrai
3SG	-erà	-erà	-irà	andrà	terrà
1PL	-eremo	-eremo	-iremo	andremo	terremo
2PL	-erete	-erete	-irete	andrete	terrete
3PL	-eranno	-eranno	-iranno	andranno	terranno
	'will call'	*'will bang'*	*'will sleep'*	*'will go'*	*'will hold'*
-Imper. Pres.					
2SG	-a	-i	-i	vai ~ va'	tieni
1PL	-iamo	-iamo	-iamo	andiamo	teniamo
2PL	-ate	-ete	-ite	andate	tenete
	'call'	*'bang'*	*'sleep'*	*'go'*	*'hold'*

regularities concern alterations of the verb *root* rather than its inflectional endings. Irregularities are spread across several morphological sub-paradigms, except the indicative imperfect, which is always regular. Inflections convey information about one or more of the following: mood (e.g., indicative, imperative, subjunctive); time (present, past, future); aspect (e.g., imperfect vs. perfect/historic past); person and number (first-, second-, and third-person singular and plural). Table 6.1 schematically illustrates some of the most commonly used inflections (indicative present, imperfect, future and imperative present) in regular and irregular verbs.

Some inflected forms, shown in bold in Table 6.1, are homophonous with, albeit formally distinct from verb stems (Scalise, 1990). These include: (a) the indicative present third person singular forms of first and second conjugation verbs (*chiama, batte*), usually described as the most unmarked or basic verbal forms across languages (Bybee, 1985; Bybee Hooper, 1979; Greenberg, 1966; Matthews, 1974); (b) the imperative second-person singular of first conjugation verbs (*chiama*), and the indicative and imperative second-person singular of third conjugation verbs (*dormi*)—all forms that are "more marked" than the third singular, but less marked than other inflected forms (cf. Bybee, 1985). The full inflectional system includes 21 simple and compound, finite and nonfinite forms, 16 of which are commonly used. Compound or peryphrastic forms (Matthews, 1974, p. 172) require the auxiliaries *essere* 'to be' or *avere* 'to have' plus the verb past participle, and are used in several sub-paradigms (e.g., indicative perfect, future perfect, pluperfect, past anterior). The present work focuses only on simple, finite forms. Data on the acquisition of compound and nonfinite forms (e.g., gerunds, infinitives, participles) are reported elsewhere (Pizzuto & Caselli, 1992), and are only mentioned as needed at relevant points throughout this chapter.

The inflectional patterns illustrated in Table 6.1 attempt to highlight the synthetic-fusional characteristics of Italian verbal morphology. The morphemes for mood, time, and aspect as well as those for person and number are not easily segmentable one from the other: In the form *chiamavo* 'I was calling', for example, the infix -*v*- marks both indicative mood and imperfective aspect, whereas the categories of first person and singular number are conflated into the single ending suffix -*o*. Due to these typological features, Italian can be likened more to other synthetic-fusional languages such as Hebrew (Berman, 1985; Dromi & Berman, 1982; Levy, 1983a, 1983b), than to richly inflected but analytic-agglutinative languages such as Turkish, or Hungarian, in which linearly arranged morphemes provide more transparent, one-to-one mappings between morphological forms and their meanings (Aksu-Koç & Slobin, 1985; MacWhinney, 1985; Slobin, 1982).

Two important features differentiate some inflections from others. The first is whether the inflection involves a single vowel (as for example in the singular indicative and imperative inflections -*a/-e/-i*), or two or more syllable morphemes (as for example in all plural inflections -*iamo/-ate/ -ano*, and in most other singular inflections). The second is stress. Primary stress can fall on the verb root, as in the indicative and imperative forms for first, second, third person singular and third person plural (e.g., *chiàmo/chiàmi/chiàma/chiàmano*), or on the inflectional morpheme itself, as in the indicative and imperative first- and second-person plural (e.g., *chiamiàmo/chiamàte*). When primary stress falls on the root, there is no way of predicting on which syllable it will fall, because Italian is a "free stress" language. However, the vast majority of words are paroxitonic, or stressed on the penultimate syllable, as in *chiàma* (Dardano & Trifone, 1985; A. L. Lepschy & G. Lepschy, 1988; Vincent, 1987). Inflections that receive primary stress such as -*iàmo* have greater perceptual salience than unstressed ones. Within forms bearing unstressed inflections, the syllable next to the stressed one (e.g., *chià*ma) has greater perceptual salience than more distant syllable(s) (e.g., *chià*mano) (Bortolini, personal communication, December 1992). Unstressed syllables are also subject to the phonological process of weak syllable deletion (L. B. Leonard, Sabbadini, J. Leonard, & Volterra, 1987).

The rules governing the choice of mood/time/aspect inflections are complex and cannot be discussed here, except for noting that the indicative and, in part, the imperative present-tense inflections can be considered the least marked forms (Matthews, 1974, p. 152); the imperfect has been characterized as the unmarked past tense (Vincent, 1987, p. 296). The main rule governing agreement inflections is that verbs agree with their subject in person and number. Subject pronouns are optional in Italian. At the level of semantic and pragmatic relations, this entails that in Italian, unlike in English or in other languages in which subject pronouns are obligatory, the deictic category of person is to a large extent grammaticalized via verb inflections, rather than lexical subject pronouns. At the syntactic level, the presence of overt verb agreement and the possibility of deleting subject pronouns with tensed verbs have led to the characterization of Italian as a pro-drop or null-subject language (Chomsky, 1981; Rizzi, 1982, 1986).

1.2. Hypotheses Concerning Acquisition

On theoretical grounds, different hypotheses can be made concerning the acquisition of Italian verb inflections. We consider here two different sets of hypotheses stemming from two, likewise distinct broad, general views. Simplifying greatly, and recognizing the existence of a remarkable variety of subschools and differences of focus and orientations, we distinguish between: (a) a psychological, developmentally oriented approach and (b) a linguistically oriented approach articulated within parameter-setting theory.

As noted by Slobin (1988, p. 131) within the first approach one starts "from individual children and individual languages, rather than a preconceived view of universal grammar, trying to characterize the strategies or 'operating principles' that children use in building up grammars within the context of developing cognition and communication." In our view, perhaps the most common, defining feature of this approach, expressed in different ways in the work of different investigators (cf. Bates, Bretherton, & Snyder, 1988; Bates & MacWhinney, 1982, 1989; Berman, 1991; Karmiloff-Smith, 1979; MacWhinney, 1978, 1985; Maratsos, 1983; Maratsos & Chalkley, 1980; Slobin, 1973, 1982, 1985a, 1985b), is the effort to explain language development in terms of underlying psychological processes and mechanisms that are, or in principle may be, at least in part, shared with other perceptual and cognitive domains. As stressed by Berman (1991, p. 613) "in acquiring language the child is not only attentive to structural constraints and principles, but has recourse to a 'confluence of cues,' which are perceptual and semantic as well as structure-dependent, and are sensitive to the relative productivity of devices within a given target language." The cues or distributional regularities that are present in the child's linguistic input play a major role in the developmental process (Bates & MacWhinney, 1989; Maratsos & Chalkley, 1980). This latter point has recently received considerable support from connectionist simulations of morphological learning in which the statistical structure of the input is varied systematically (MacWhinney, 1991b; MacWhinney & Leinbach, 1991; MacWhinney, Leinbach, Taraban, & McDonald, 1989; Pizzuto, Caselli, & Tangorra, 1991; Plunkett & Marchman, 1990; Rumelhart & McClelland, 1986). One other important trait is the attention paid not only to the adult, end-state model, but to the developmental process of language learning per se, in an attempt to provide psychologically valid, motivated explanations for the changes observed over time in children's performance and knowledge systems (Bates & Carnevale, 1992; Berman, 1991; Grant & Karmiloff-Smith, 1991; Karmiloff-Smith, 1979; Slobin, 1982, 1985a, 1991).

From this perspective, we expect that a number of interrelated formal, distributional as well as pragmatic, semantic and cognitive factors may influence the acquisition of Italian main verb inflections along patterns that may in part resemble, and in part differ from both those found in poorly inflected, analytic languages such as English, and other richly inflected, typologically similar or dissimilar languages.

There are no bare verbal roots/stems, and roots/stems must be characterized as bound forms, so the Italian child faces the task of acquiring word-alternation patterns. As noted by Smoczinska (1985, pp. 596–597) with respect to similar features of Polish, this requires the ability to *replace* grammatical morphemes according to the rules of the language, rather than the ability to *add* them to basic forms when required (as in English).

The various pragmatic, semantic, and grammatical distinctions carried by verb inflections can be characterized as different subdomains that presumably require the development of likewise different skills in the course of acquisition—hence we can expect different phases in the acquisition process, with different forms being acquired earlier (or later) than others. For example, one aspect of the agreement inflections is that they grammaticalize the pragmatic and semantic category of person deixis. Because person is obligatorily marked on the verb, the Italian verb inflections can be described, following Slobin (1982, p. 138) as *local cues* to such grammatical distinctions, and local, obligatory cues are known to facilitate the acquisition process (Slobin, 1982, 1985a). Using the terminology proposed by Bates and MacWhinney (1989, pp. 41ff.) within their "competition model," we can say that some of the available cues are also particularly reliable, and have thus particular strength. For example, the present indicative first- and second-person inflections are the same across the three conjugations, in regular and irregular verbs alike (see Table 6.1), hence the child can form some strong generalizations about the inflectional ending—though errors can be expected on the root alternations that distinguish regular and irregular forms. On these grounds, and taking into account the relatively early appearance of person pronouns in children acquiring English and other languages (Brown, 1973; Chiat, 1986), we can expect that Italian children will use verb inflections to mark the major distinctions of person deixis at a comparable, or even earlier age than their English counterparts acquiring subject pronouns. Possible differences will be revealing of the role played by language-specific features, such as the availability of lexical versus morphological-inflectional devices.

The relative unmarkedness of some inflected forms as compared with others may also be expected to play a role. For example, it is plausible to hypothesize that the indicative present third-person singular of first and second conjugation verbs, homophonous with the verb stem—hence less marked than other forms—may be acquired earlier and with less difficulty than other inflected forms. On similar grounds, we can expect that present-tense inflections will emerge earlier than more marked inflections such as those for future or past tense, or imperfective aspect. In addition, compared with simple present-tense inflections, those for past and future time, or for aspect, presumably require more complex cognitive skills—hence can be expected to develop at a later age. Differences in the frequencies of each conjugational pattern (or of the more regular as compared with the more irregular patterns) may facilitate and/ or hinder the acquisition of some inflected forms, leading for example to an earlier development of the overall more regular and productive first conjugation verb pattern, and to a delay over the second and third conjugation patterns, where more irregular verbs are found.

Finally, surface features of the syllabic and stress patterns of Italian verb roots and inflections are likely to exert a role in the developmental process, and may for example facilitate the acquisition of bisyllabic, stressed inflections, or render more problematic the acquisition of unstressed inflections. This hypothesis is particularly plausible in the light of: (a) data reported by Leonard et al. (1987), and Leonard, Bortolini, Caselli, McGregor, and Sabbadini (1992), showing that the presence or absence of stressed, vowel-final syllabic inflections significantly influences the performance of Italian children with specific language impairment; (b) Pye's (1983) findings showing that in the Mayan language K'ich'e, syllable structure and stress rules enhance the perceptual salience of specific verb terminations, and promote a very early, almost errorless acquisition of these particular morphemes, despite the fact that they do not encode any simple semantic or syntactic meaning.

There are at least two features of Italian verb morphology that may generate particular difficulties in the acquisition process. The synthetic-fusional characteristics of verb inflections, whereby different morphological distinctions are conflated into a single segment, presumably render more difficult for the child the segmentation of the appropriate morpheme-meaning mappings (Slobin, 1982, p. 151). Thus, we could expect that in Italian the acquisition of mood/time/aspect inflections be less precocious than it could be, for example, in a language of agglutinative type such as Turkish, where the linear arrangement of morphemes, and the more transparent form-meaning mappings they provide, is reported to promote a very early mastery of tense/aspect distinctions (Aksu-Koç & Slobin, 1985).

A second problematic feature of Italian verb morphology is the homonymy of some inflections (in regular and irregular verbs) across different conjugations, moods, or subparadigms. For example, the imperative and indicative second-person forms (singular and plural) are homonymous in all three conjugations, with one exception: Verbs of the first conjugation like *chiamare* distinguish between the second-person singular of the indicative *chiami* and the imperative *chiama*; in first conjugation verbs, the inflection -*a* is used for both the indicative present third-person singular and the imperative second-person singular. Homonymy is held to be a source of ambiguity and confusion for small children (Slobin, 1973, p. 203; 1982; 1985a)—hence we should expect that children encounter some difficulty in acquiring these forms.

The hypotheses generated within a parameter-setting approach to language development are based primarily on linguistic models of the adult language, privileging for the most the domain of syntax as the major focus of investigation. Inspired by the generative tradition of linguistic research as it has evolved over the last 10 years (Chomsky, 1981), parameter-setting theory appears to offer a way of reconciling nativism with wide variations across languages in the pace and nature of grammatical development. Cross-linguistic variation is used within parameter-setting theory to argue in favor of the idea that children are equipped with an innate set of options for acquiring distinct language types (Roeper & Williams, 1987).

It is beyond the scope of this chapter to survey the different positions that characterize parameter-setting approaches to language acquisition. We mention here only some of the major assumptions that, in our view, are shared by most researchers working in this field. A limited set of strictly linguistic universal (hence putatively innate) principles of grammar formation are postulated as determinants of language acquisition. The theory of Universal Grammar (UG) adopted within this approach is intended not just as a linguistic theory that aims to identify and describe the defining features of human language beyond interlanguage differences, but as a "theory of the internal organization of the mind/brain of the language learner" (Crain, 1991, p. 598). As put by Roeper (1988, p. 35), it is hypothesized that UG "will eventually explain all the significant structural and semantic aspects of child grammar, while the role of pragmatics and cognition, though intimately connected with language, will be seen as external to the grammatical heart of language." Language is viewed as an autonomous human faculty or module (Newmayer, 1988), and grammar itself is represented as a set of modules, each governed by a set of general principles that are assumed to be part of the child's innate knowledge. The extensive variation exhibited by different languages is explained by positing language-particular parameters of variation in the modules. Any given parameter controls a cluster of properties that languages may or may not exhibit, and the child's task is to set the appropriate values for each particular parameter. Because each parameter governs a cluster of features, the setting (or resetting) of even a single parameter has far-reaching consequences into a child's grammar, determining the appearance (or disappearance) of a variety of seemingly unrelated features (Roeper, 1988).

A parameter that has received considerable attention is the "pro-drop" or "null subject" parameter. This has been proposed to characterize the differences between languages with rich verb agreement systems—like Italian, Portuguese, or Spanish—that allow subjects of tensed sentences to be "dropped," or to be realized as phonetically null, empty categories that are nonetheless interpreted as having definite pronominal reference, and languages that do not possess such rich agreement systems, in which subjects are generally obligatory in sentences with tensed verbs—like English or French (Chomsky, 1981; Rizzi, 1982, 1986). In addition to the optionality of subject pronouns, the null subject parameter carries with it a cluster of related properties. A precise characterization of all the properties that uniquely distinguish pro-drop from non-pro-drop languages, or even the standardization of the formalism that captures such properties, is still the topic of much current investigation that cannot be summarized here (e.g., compare Chomsky, 1981, pp. 240–284; Hyams, 1986b, pp. 26–62; 1987, pp. 3–8; Jaeggli & Safir, 1989b; Rizzi, 1982, pp. 117–184). Some of the distinctive properties that have been reported include: (a) the use of lexical expletives: Non-null-subject languages possess referentially empty pronouns like *it* in *It is raining*. This kind of pronouns are typically absent in null-subject languages; (b) properties of the auxiliary and modal system: In non-null subjects languages like English, modals (e.g., *must, can*), auxiliary verbs *have* and *be*, and also the copula *be*, are syntactically and morphologically distinguished from main verbs, whereas in null-subject languages they exhibit most of the syntactic and morphological properties of main verbs (Hyams, 1986b, pp. 26–62); (c) morphological uniformity: Null subjects would be permitted in all and only languages with morphologically uniform inflectional paradigms as previously characterized (Jaeggli & Safir, 1989a; cf. Radford, 1990).

Applying this analysis of adult languages to data on the acquisition of English and Italian, Hyams (1986a, 1986b, 1987, 1988, 1991, 1992) proposed that in the acquisition of both languages the parameter in question is initially set at the "pro-drop" value, which is incorrect for English but appropriate for Italian. This would explain several, previously unrelated salient properties of children's English (in the age range from, approximately, 1;6 to 3;0), including not only the absence of lexical subjects in sentences with tensed verbs, but also the lack of expletives, and the delayed emergence of modals. At some point during the third year, a resetting of the parameter occurs, apparently triggered by the use of the lexical expletives *it* and *there*, and the properties connected with the appropriate, non-pro-drop setting of the parameter—use of lexical subjects, modals—also appear in the language of English children. For the purpose of this chapter, we do not consider in further details the pro-drop parameter,[1] but rather focus on another parameter that has been

---

[1]An appropriate discussion of this topic would require a detailed examination not only of all the cross-linguistic developmental data considered by Hyams and other authors (i.e., on German besides English and Italian), but also of a number of subtle yet, in our opinion at least, rather significant modifications that can be noted in Hyams' different presentations of her own work and, finally, of some of the more general theoretical principles of

proposed to account for the development of verb inflectional morphology in Italian and English.

In order to explain why an impoverished morphological system like that of English is so difficult to acquire, whereas "children acquiring more richly inflected languages learn the inflectional system of these languages at a strikingly early age and with relatively few errors," Hyams (1986a, pp. 4–5, but see also 1986b, 1988, 1991, 1992) hypothesized the existence of a stem parameter of the following form: "A verbal stem does/does not constitute a well-formed word." English takes a positive value (+ uninflected stem) along this particular parameter, because verbs can surface as bare stems. In Italian, the parameter takes the opposite value (– uninflected stem), because verbs cannot surface as bare stems. Hyams (1986a, p. 3) observed that the numerosity of inflectional elements renders the Italian system intuitively "more complex" than the English one: "Common sense (and any learning theory) tells us that it should be more difficult to learn the six Italian affixes than the single English one."

In discussing the role of the stem parameter in language acquisition, Hyams utilized the notions of *core versus peripheral* grammars (Chomsky, 1981), and proposed that verb inflections are linguistically specified as a *core property* of a language like Italian, where verbs never surface in uninflected forms, and as a *peripheral property* of a language like English, in which verbs also appear in unmarked, uninflected forms. In both English and Italian children the setting or fixing of the appropriate parameter is said to be triggered by the language-specific input to which they are exposed, but "the difference in linguistic behavior exhibited by the two populations is strictly an effect of different setting along a particular parameter" (Hyams, 1986a, p. 6), and it is also contingent on whether inflections are, or are not, part of the language core grammar. Accordingly, because English children hear verbs that are largely invariant in form, they set the verb stem parameter at its positive value (i.e., + uninflected stems). Furthermore, because inflections are a peripheral, marked property in English, and the acquisition of such properties presumably requires "more exposure to data or more computation" (Hyams, 1986a, p. 8), the learning of inflections by the English child also requires a "relaxation" of the initial parameter setting. This initial

---

government and binding theory (e.g., as presented in Chomsky, 1981; Rizzi, 1982, 1986) from which this line of work stems. For limits of space and focus, we limit our attention to those aspects of Hyams' work that are most directly relevant to the topics explored in the present work, and that we believe need to be clarified. For important issues (e.g., the "R-Rule" Parameter), as well as minor topics we disregard, the reader is referred to Hyams' original work, cited in the text, and to recent reviews and criticism (e.g., Drozd, 1989; Lebeaux, 1987; Loeb & Leonard, 1988; O'Grady, Peters, & Masterson, 1989; Pizzuto & Caselli, 1992; Radford, 1990; Smith, 1988; Valian, 1990, 1991.)

parameter setting, and the subsequent relaxation it requires, would explain, according to Hyams, the systematic omissions of verb inflections by English children in the early stages of development and, more generally, the "delayed" acquisition of English verbal morphology.

For languages of the Italian type, two specific predictions are made, stated by Hyams (1992, p. 696) as follows: "The first is that Italian children will never produce verbs in their bare stem form (while English speaking children, who learn inflection as a 'marked' property of the language, will use bare stem forms). The second prediction, which is not a direct deductive consequence of the stem parameter but related to it, is that children acquiring Italian will learn the inflectional affixes earlier than English speaking children because, given the Italian setting of the parameter, they do not have the option of omitting these inflectional elements" (cf. also Hyams, 1986a, p. 4; 1991). In a number of different contexts Hyams (1986a, p. 3; 1986b, fn. 18; 1991; 1992) claimed that data on the spontaneous acquisition of Italian, including new data recently reported by Pizzuto and Caselli (1991, 1992), fully supports these two predictions, and corroborate a parameter-setting account of the development of Italian and English verb morphology.

The evidence we review and discuss in the present chapter allows us to assess the plausibility of Hyams' predictions and claims. Before proceeding any further, however, it is useful to point out some problems inherent in Hyams' proposals.

One rather substantial problem regards Hyams' general prediction that Italian children should not produce bare-stem, uninflected verbs. A serious shortcoming of this prediction is the difficulty in seeing not only how it could ever be falsified, but also how it can be appropriately defined as a prediction (or, if supported by empirical evidence, even a claim about Italian). This is due to the following.

In her sketch of the Italian verbal structure, Hyams (1986a, p. 3) appears to apply to Italian stems the same description that is used for English stems (e.g., the form *parl-* is described as the stem of the verb *parlare* 'to speak'). As noted, Scalise (1990) explicitly questioned this English-based representations of Italian verb stems, and in Italian grammars forms like *parl-* are clearly classified as verbal roots. From this standpoint, Hyams' prediction should thus be rephrased as follows: "Italian children will never produce verbs in their bare root form." With this clarification, and provided that our interpretation of Hyams' views is appropriate, the following must be noted.

In factual terms, all Italian content words—nouns and adjectives as well as verbs—never surface as bare roots. Verbal, nominal, or adjectival forms such as *chiam-* (for *chiama* 'calls'), or *bimb-* (for *bimbo* 'child-masculine & singular'), or *buon-* (for *buono* 'good-masculine & singular'), simply are never uttered or heard by an Italian speaker. Insofar as we can assume that children will not learn constructions they never hear in their language (Brown, 1973, p. 409), it is thus unlikely that Italian children will produce bare roots to which they are never exposed. In the early stages of development children do produce word fragments in which the intended adult targets can often be recognized. Examples from our own records include <*pello*> for *cappello* 'hat', <*picco*> for *piccola* 'little-feminine & singular', <*amo*> for *andiamo* 'go-first person plural'. No one has ever reported bare roots among these word fragments. However, it seems to us implausible to attribute the absence of bare roots in the speech of Italian children to the working of a stem (or root) parameter of the kind hypothesized by Hyams. Bare roots end in consonant, whereas Italian words typically end in vowel. Although many commonly used foreign loans (e.g., *sport*), few grammatical morphemes (e.g., the article *il*), and acronyms (e.g., *FIAT*) end in consonant, the final-consonant pattern cannot be considered a productive phonological pattern of Italian (Bortolini & Zampolli, 1979; Vincent, 1987). The production of bare roots would be a violation of the basic phonological pattern of Italian. Thus, even if we observe that Italian children only produce inflected verbs (or nominals, or adjectives), on which basis can we say that they are doing so because they are avoiding bare roots, and not simply because they are striving to approximate the sound patterns of their language? Given the structure of Italian words, there seems to be no way for discriminating whether the children's behavior is determined by the single, very specific linguistic principle postulated by Hyams, or by the children's developing articulatory-phonological abilities (Bortolini, 1987; in 1993; in press). In sum, by predicting that the production of inflected verbs by Italian children is determined by their knowledge that only inflected words are well formed, the parameter provides under the surface form of a prediction (and subsequently, of an explanation) nothing more than a description of the very same regularity of the Italian language it is supposed to explain (and/or to determine in development). In our opinion, this is a tautological statement, rather than an appropriate, empirically testable prediction.

The second, and most important question raised by a parametric account of language learning, and particularly by the one proposed by Hyams, is what specifically and unambiguously distinguishes such an account from other models of language development, that is, what developmental patterns can be considered distinctive of the phenomena determined by the parameters. Crain (1991, p. 600) recently noted that "it is important to appreciate . . . that parameter-setting models do *not* entail slow, piecemeal acquisition of linguistic knowledge." When referring to real time acquisition, several authors described the setting or resetting of any given parameter as an abrupt transition from a stage in which the parameter is not operating to one in which it is operating, and the cluster of properties that are governed by the parameter in question, previously absent from the child's language, suddenly appear. For example, Roeper (1986, pp. x–xi), commenting on Hyams' work on English and Italian, and on Clahsen's work on German, stressed how the appearance of expletives in English *immediately triggers* the subject requirement in English, or how the appearance of obligatory subjects in German is found at *exactly the moment* when tense marking appears on the auxiliary, and this is held to be a predictable variant on the trigger for obligatory subject in German. Similar views are expressed in Hyams (1986b, p. 92; 1987, pp. 1,1–12), Jaeggli and Safir (1989), and Roeper (1988, p. 42).

If our interpretation of this general view is correct, there seem to be two major predictions that distinguish a parameter model from other kinds of models. First, because the parameters operate in a discrete, categorical manner, the acquisition of particular morphological or morphosyntactic regularities that are assumed to be dependent on a specific parameter should be triggered in an all-or-none fashion. No gradual learning processes should be noted. Second, and concurrently, elements and structures that are described as interdependent manifestations of one and the same parameter (or parameter setting) should appear, and/or be mastered at one and the same point in development.

Thus, for example, if we assume, following Hyams, that the stem parameter is set correctly from the start for Italian children, and that inflection is specified as a core property of Italian, we should expect that Italian children master all verb inflections (because the parametric principles in question are assumed to operate on the entire verb paradigm, and not on a fraction of it), and that they do so more or less instantaneously, at the same time as, or shortly after they begin to produce verbs (because the same principles operate in a discrete, categorical manner).

This interpretation of the predictions that can be considered distinctive of a parameter account, has been strongly criticized by Hyams (1992, pp. 697ff.), who stated that "the stem parameter does not require or predict instantaneous and simultaneous acquisition across several inflectional paradigms. . . . [Rather] the setting of the stem parameter entails only that the child knows a specific condition on word formation, not that he or she knows all the individual inflectional forms." Hyams pointed out that "within parameter theory there is an important distinction made between those properties of the grammar that are triggered by virtue of the parameter setting, which are predicted to develop in a discrete manner, all else being equal, and those aspects of language which reside in the lexicon (i.e. the learning of particular morphemes and their associated syntactic, semantic and phonological properties), which is likely to be piecemeal and gradual.'' Hyams stressed that there is an important difference between ''setting the parameter to determine the well-formedness of bare stems in a language, and the learning of particular affixes, which is dependent on a number of factors.''

We acknowledge Hyams' clarifications. However, we must note the following: (a) If the stem parameter only ''controls'' the well formedness of bare stems in a language, then it is subject to the criticism we made earlier: It is difficult to see how it can be considered anything more than a description, or a restatement, of the surface (primarily phonological) regularities of Italian (or English) and of Italian (or English) child language, and/or how it can contribute to our understanding of the developmental process. (b) If the learning of individual verbal inflections is likened to lexical learning, the stem parameter becomes largely irrelevant for addressing the question originally formulated by Hyams: why the inflectional *systems* of richly inflected languages are (supposedly) acquired at a strikingly early age, and earlier than in English. Furthermore, if the stem parameter does not allow any specific prediction concerning the learning of particular inflections or morphological paradigms, then it is not clear how the postulated parameter can be distinguished (other than terminologically) from any of the other ''semantic, syntactic and phonological factors'' that Hyams (1992, p. 697) noted, certainly play a role in children's acquisition of grammatical morphemes and morphological paradigms. In other words, it is not clear how, with reference to the stem parameter, one can identify those ''properties of the grammar that are triggered by virtue of the parameter setting, and which are predicted to develop in a discrete manner.'' (c) Hyams' (1991, 1992) recent statements on the possibility that, in richly inflected languages like Italian, the learning of particular affixes may proceed in a piecemeal fashion contradict the description of morphological development in Italian sketched by the same author in the same context, and in several other published and unpublished works cited previously. This description stresses Italian children's striking precocity in learning inflections and/or large portions of the inflectional paradigms of their language (e.g., Hyams [1986a, p. 3] stated that the Italian children she studied had ''*mastered the present tense verbal paradigm by roughly age 2;0*''; elsewhere, Hyams [1986b, p. 104, fn. 18] noted that ''Weist and Witkowska (1985) report that Polish speaking children have *complete productivity in the tense and aspect system of Polish prior to age 2;6. Similar facts hold for Italian speaking children*'' [emphasis added]). These observations suggest the need for more detailed characterizations of the differences (and/or similarities) between parametric models and other models, and of more explicit statements on the amount and type of evidence that would unequivocally support a parameter account of the learning of verbal inflections in typologically different languages.

In the absence of more satisfactory accounts, we maintain that the two major predictions specified earlier—absence of gradual learning processes, and simultaneous appearance and/or mastery of a large variety of verbal inflections in richly inflected languages like Italian—distinguish parameter theory from psychological, developmentally oriented models of language development. In our view, the parameter-setting account is interesting precisely because it makes these strong predictions. If the data do not conform to these predictions, and/or if the parameter theory itself is modified to permit gradual and piecemeal learning, then the parameter-setting approach to language acquisition becomes empirically indistinguishable from other theories or models that attempt to explain language development in terms of a variety of underlying processes and mechanisms. Some such mechanisms and processes may be common to other, nonlinguistic domains, and/or may *become* specific of the linguistic domain, or "modularized," as a *result*, rather than the starting point, of the developmental process itself, as suggested by Karmiloff-Smith (1991).

There is a final point we would like to make. Under careful scrutiny, the data on the acquisition of Italian that has been adduced thus far in favor of a parameter-setting account is surprisingly limited, and clearly insufficient to assess the cross-linguistic relevance of such an account. Hyams' description of the acquisition of verb inflections by Italian children hardly—if ever—includes quantitative information to assess the productivity of a given process (e.g., number of obligatory or nonobligatory contexts for production of the relevant forms; proportion of correct vs. erroneous or inappropriate usage, variety of instantiation of the inflections observed), or the stage or level of linguistic development at which it is observed (e.g., mean length of utterance, MLU, or one-word as compared with two-word stage of linguistic development), or clear indications on the time slots that can be considered critical in assessing relative precocity and/or delay with which a given parameter governed (or otherwise innately driven) behavior appears.

This is all the more surprising if one considers that most of the critical information on English children Hyams used for comparative purpose is drawn from the very detailed studies of Brown (1973) and Cazden (1968)—who proposed such explicit criteria to evaluate the development of English morphology. In this chapter we wish to pursue the same line of investigation described in Pizzuto and Caselli (1992). By providing relevant new information, and using the same methodology that has been successfully employed by Cazden and Brown in the exploration of the spontaneous acquisition of English, we aim to clarify empirical and theoretical issues concerning both the actual course of development, and the models that can account for it.

2. METHOD

The data analyzed for the present study are in the form of transcripts, and were taken from a larger corpus of longitudinal records on the acquisition of Italian.

2.1. Subjects

The subjects were three middle-class, first-born Italian children: one girl (Claudia) and two boys (Francesco and Marco). The children's spontaneous production was audiorecorded and studied longitudinally from the ages of 1;3 to 2;9 (Claudia), 1;4 to 3;9 (Francesco), and 1;5 to 3;0 (Marco). The data on Claudia and Francesco were collected and transcribed by Antinucci, Tieri, and Volterra at the Institute of Psychology of the CNR in Rome, Italy, and have been analyzed and described from a variety of perspectives in several published and unpublished papers (see Antinucci & Parisi, 1973; Antinucci & Miller, 1976; Bates, 1976; Leonard et al., 1987; Pizzuto & Caselli, 1992; Volterra, 1976). The data on the third child, Marco, were collected by the second author of this chapter (who is also the child's mother) and were transcribed with the assistance of Calabrese.

2.2. Procedure

Data collection procedures for Claudia and Francesco were as follows: The children were visited in their homes, at 2-week intervals, by one or two external observer(s) who were well acquainted with the family and the child. Approximately 2-hour audiorecordings were made at each visit. The records include both child–mother interaction and a considerable proportion of child–observer interaction. For Marco, 1-hour audiorecordings were made at home, at approximately 1-month intervals, and include mostly child–mother interaction. No records were made at the age of 1;6, in the period between ages 2;6 and 2;9, and at age 2;11. Compared with the corpora of the other two children, Marco's corpus is thus smaller, though it perhaps reflects more closely the child's actual linguistic environment.

All transcriptions were made by hand in standard Italian orthography. Italian spelling bears an almost one-to-one correspondence between sounds and graphemes (A. L. Lepschy & G. Lepschy, 1988; Vincent, 1987), thus it is possible to describe rather closely a speaker's pronunciation. Typical errors or mispronunciations were clearly indicated. For example, the word /apro/ 'open-1stSG', mispronounced by one of the chil-

dren as /apo/, was transcribed as < *apo* >. The transcripts thus provide
a reasonably accurate picture of the children's morphophonemic development. The transcripts include all the child's and the adults' utterances,
and relevant information on the nonlinguistic context of interaction.

For the present study we used only part of the data available for the
three children, analyzing only the samples that were recorded at 1-month
intervals. Table 6.2 shows the transcripts we analyzed for each child (transcript numbers are as indicated in the original corpora), the age (round-
ed) of the child at the time of each sample we analyzed, the number of
distinct verbs used categorized by verb roots (types), and the cumulative
number of all inflected verb forms (tokens) produced by each child in
the individual samples and across samples (e.g., 4 occurrences of the form
chiami 'call-2SG' and 2 occurrences of *dormi* 'sleep-2SG' were counted
as 2 distinct root types, and 6 tokens of second-person singular inflections). The Mean Length of Utterance in words (MLUw) in each sample,
and the age at which each child was defined as having reached the "two-
word stage" (indicated by a starred line) are also shown. Two 30-min
samples of Marco's corpus (sessions 19 and 20) were taken at the ages
of 2;4;13 and 2;4;29, but were grouped in Table 6.2 into one single sample for age 2;5, in order to facilitate the comparison between the data
on this child and those on Claudia and Francesco (see Brown, 1973, p.
257, on the feasibility of such a procedure).

2.3. Coding and Analysis

The data were coded and analyzed following as closely as possible the
procedures originally proposed by Cazden (1968) and Brown (1973) for
the study of grammatical development in the spontaneous acquisition of
English. In particular, we used Cazden's criteria for: (a) identifying in the
children's production obligatory contexts of use for each of verb forms
studied; (b) scoring the children's performance on each verb inflection;
(c) identifying morpheme acquisition points.

We thus extracted from the transcripts all the children's utterances that
contained what, from the standpoint of the adult observer, could be classified as verbs. Correct and erroneous productions, and any other atypical phenomena were then coded, and the proportion of correct versus
all other kinds of productions was computed. The point of acquisition
of each verb inflection was defined, following Cazden (1968, p. 435),
as "the first out of three consecutive speech samples such that in all three
a given morpheme is supplied correctly in at least 90% of the contexts
in which it is clearly required." However, there were samples in which
only one or two required contexts could be identified; knowing that in
these cases children's performance cannot be appropriately assessed, we

TABLE 6.2
Longitudinal Data Used for the Study and Number of Distinct Verb Roots and Simple Tense, Finite Main Verb Forms in the Three Children's Production

Claudia

TN	Age	Verb Forms		
		Typ	Tok	MLUw
2	1;4	4	11	1.91
*****	*****	*****	*****	*****
4	1;5	2	4	2.0
6	1;6	6	8	1.76
7	1;7	9	18	2.02
9	1;8	19	58	2.67
11	1;9	22	77	2.46
13	1;10	20	62	2.76
14	1;11	30	145	2.65
15	2;0	31	139	3.19
17	2;1	38	148	2.86
19	2;2	24	71	3.16
20	2;3	47	140	3.23
21	2;4	41	130	3.70
Tot:		**94**	**1011**	

Francesco

TN	Age	Verb Forms		
		Typ	Tok	MLUw
—				
3	1;5	3	14	1.49
5	1;6	3	22	1.25
7	1;7	3	4	1.12
9	1;8	2	6	1.46
11	1;9	5	13	1.46
*****	*****	*****	*****	*****
13	1;10	9	20	1.75
15	1;11	9	18	1.73
17	2;0	14	25	1.97
19	2;1	24	47	2.54
21	2;2	28	78	2.52
23	2;3	33	98	2.52
25	2;4	23	45	2.88
27	2;5	31	74	3.09
29	2;6	26	81	2.70
30	2;7	27	84	3.57
32	2;8	27	62	3.57
34	2;9	32	111	3.55
36	2;10	26	79	4.53
Tot:		**97**	**881**	

Marco

TN	Age	Verb Forms		
		Typ	Tok	MLUw
—	1;5	3	3	1.31
4	1;6	—	—	—
—	1;7	1	2	1.35
6	1;8	3	3	1.30
7	1;9	5	9	1.48
8	1;10	8	10	1.33
9	1;11	9	15	1.40
*****	*****	*****	*****	*****
10	2;0	8	24	1.37
11	2;1	24	38	1.97
12	2;2	11	23	1.65
13	2;3	22	45	2.30
15	2;4	22	41	2.31
18	2;5	27	81	
19/20	2;6	—	—	—
—	2;7	—	—	—
—	2;8	—	—	—
—	2;9	—	—	—
21	2;10	6	12	1.97
22	3;0	24	45	2.65
Tot:		**72**	**351**	

Note: TN: number of the transcripts in the corpora from which the data were extracted. Under Verb Forms, the number of distinct verb roots used by each child is shown under Typ(es), while the cumulative number of inflected forms produced for all stems is shown under Tok(ens). The Total number of types and tokens across all samples is shown in bold. A "*****" line is placed under the age points at which each child reached the two-word stage. MLUw = Mean Length of Utterance in words as defined in the text.

adopted the procedure followed by J. G. de Villiers and P. A. de Villiers (1973; cf. also Brown, 1973, p. 273) in analogous cases: They required that each of the samples crucial for scoring the acquisition point of a given verb inflection contain at least five obligatory contexts of use.

In the early samples there were cases in which, regardless of the number of verb tokens produced by the child, and of the number of required contexts we could identify, one type of person inflection occurred only with a specific verb. For example, the *-i* ending of the second-person singular, present-tense inflection occurred only with the form *api* for *apri* 'open-2SG'. As noted by MacWhinney (1978, p. 1084), with respect to Hungarian, it is difficult to demonstrate the productivity of these early inflections, which can be considered more as 'amalgams', or unanalyzed units than truly productive morphological combinations of roots/stems and inflectional endings. Early inflections may be item based rather than class based (Gordon & Chafetz, 1990; cf. also Bloom, Lifter, & Hafitz, 1980). Taking into account different procedures that have been proposed (cf. Bates et al., 1988; Bloom et al., 1980; Clark & Berman, 1984; Mac-Whinney, 1978), we attempted to assess the productivity of the various inflected forms in the children's language by examining (a) the number of inflected forms used for each verb root (i.e., whether in addition to the form for *apri* the child also used those for *apro* 'open-1SG' or *apre* 'open-3SG'); (b) the number of distinct verb roots used with each inflection (i.e., whether the child produced the second-person inflection not only with the form for *apri* but also with that for *vedi* 'see-2SG'). We estimated that any given inflection was beginning to be used productively by each child when (a) the same verb root appeared in at least two distinct inflected forms, and (b) the same inflection was used with at least two different verbs. We also examined the frequencies of different conjugational patterns, and of regular versus irregular verbs.[2]

---

[2]We are in the process of transferring these data in a computerized form, using the CHAT format of the CHILDES system (MacWhinney, 1991a; MacWhinney & Snow, 1985, 1990). The corpora of Francesco and Marco have been put in CHAT format, and will be available for use within the CHILDES system as soon as we complete checking the accuracy of the computerized transcriptions as compared with the original records. As the CHAT formatting of the data is still in progress, most of the coding and analyses described in the present work, as well as those reported in Pizzuto and Caselli (1991, 1992, 1993), were done on the handwritten transcripts. Many of the type/token analyses we performed for the present work, however, were done transferring in a simplified CHAT format all the verb tokens we had previously manually extracted, and coded, from the children's corpora. We then used the CLAN program 'freq' to ascertain the frequency of various patterns of interest. The greater precision permitted by these computerized tools of coding and analysis is in part responsible for some discrepancies between the results described in the present work, and those reported in Pizzuto and Caselli (1991, 1992). In particular, the CLAN analyses uncovered one error we committed, and for which we apologize to our readers, in scoring one child's performance over first-person plural verb inflections. In Pizzuto and Caselli (1991, 1992) we incorrectly reported that no plural inflections attained our

Other methodological problems were similar to those encountered in any study of spontaneous production (see Kuczaj, 1977; Maratsos, 1983). These revolved primarily around ambiguous cases of two types: (a) unclear verb forms with various endings, mostly produced as one-word utterances where neither the linguistic nor the extralinguistic context was sufficient to determine the appropriateness of the form produced. For example, at 1;6 Francesco produced as one-word utterances several tokens of the form /api/, which superficially could have been interpreted as the second-person indicative/imperative form for 'apri' 'open-2SG'. However, this interpretation was questionable because the child used the form both to refer to himself while he was opening or also closing a drawer, and to adults when asking them to open or close a box or a drawer for him. (b) A second type of unclear forms included *-a* ending verbs, which in some cases, especially when produced as one-word utterances, could be interpreted either as a third-person indicative or as a second-person imperative form (see Table 6.1). All of these ambiguous or entirely dubious productions were coded as "unclassifiable."

Finally, there was the problem of distinguishing indicative from imperative forms in all those cases in which the forms are homonymous, that is, in the first- and second-person plural of all regular verbs, and in the second-person singular of second and third conjugation verbs (see Table 6.1). In some such cases, the presence of a direct or indirect object clitic following or preceding the verb permitted to discriminate very clearly an imperative form (e.g., *prendi* + *lo* 'take-2SG + it'), from an indicative one (e.g., *lo* + *prendi* 'it + take-2SG'). In other cases, contextual information was sufficient to disambiguate the child's utterance. In many other cases, however, the distinction could not be drawn consistently, and an imperative or a declarative interpretation were equally plausible for forms like *prendi*, especially when the verb was used as a one-word utterance. Because we could not find consistent criteria for distinguishing indicative and imperative forms (cf. also Bates, 1976), we decided to include these forms into a single class indicative/imperative.

In order to provide a measure of reliability of our analyses, each of the two authors independently extracted and coded all the utterances, including verbs from the children's corpora. Interjudge reliability was then computed by comparing the two authors' coding and analyses of all samples examined. Agreement ranged from 96% to 100%.

Two quantitative measures of the children's overall linguistic maturity were computed. The first was the MLUw, shown in Table 6.2. As other investigators have noted, a computation of MLU in morphemes is problematic in richly inflected languages like Italian (Bates, 1976, pp. 117–119; Leonard et al., 1987, p. 238; Slobin & Bever, 1982). In accord

---

acquisition criteria in any of our subjects. In the present work this result is replicated for two of our subjects, but not for one of them (Claudia), who acquired one plural inflection.

with Leonard et al. (1987), we found that an MLU computation in words was the most reasonable solution for Italian data (cf. also Dromi & Berman, 1982, on Hebrew; Hickey, 1991, on Hirish). Knowing that in Italian, as in other languages, important changes take place when the child's utterances no longer consist of single units only, but combinations of two and more major lexical items begin to be consistently produced (Caselli & Casadio, in press; Chilosi & Cipriani, 1991), we attempted to have an index of this transition from the one-word to what is commonly called the *two-word stage*. We examined combinations of items from major lexical categories: verbs, nouns, adjectives, adverbs (vs. pronouns, articles, prepositions); we then identified in each child's corpus the first out of three consecutive age samples such that in all three at least 20% of the child's total utterances were composed of two or more such content words. We assumed that a 20% proportion of two (or more) content word utterances was a reliable index that the child was no longer at the one-word stage, but had entered the two-word stage.

3. RESULTS

3.1. Major Regularities in the Three Children's Overall Production of Verbs

Table 6.2 shows the total number of simple tense, finite main verb forms identified in each child's corpus. We reported elsewhere that this type of verb productions were the first to appear in the children production and accounted for the largest part of the children's total verb repertoires. The remaining part of the children's production of verbs included copulas, compound forms, infinitive, gerund, and participial forms. However, no compound forms attained our acquisition criteria; the third-person singular indicative present copula reached criterion in two of the three children, and other forms were so sparsely represented that they could be considered virtually absent from the children's repertoire (Pizzuto & Caselli, 1992).

Later we focus on simple tense, finite verb inflections. Although the large majority of productions were clearly classifiable by the criteria described earlier (96%, 95%, and 93% for Claudia, Francesco, and Marco, respectively), a small proportion of unclassifiable verbs (N from 25 to 53 tokens or 4% to 7%) were found in each child's corpus. These figures are comparable to reports in the English literature, when the proportion of unclassifiable utterances is reported at all (e.g., see Bloom et al., 1980; Cazden, 1968, p. 439; J. G. de Villiers & P. A. de Villiers, 1973, p. 269). Unclassifiable forms comprised verbs with various endings, mostly produced as one-word utterances, where neither the linguistic nor the extralinguistic context was sufficient to determine the appropriateness of the form produced. In most cases, these forms were entirely ambiguous, or uninterpretable even for the adults who were interacting with the child. In a previous study (Pizzuto & Caselli, 1992), we had simply noted the existence of these unclassifiable verb utterances, but considered them uninformative with respect to the pattern of acquisition of *individual* inflected forms (e.g., of the inflections marking first, second, third person). Additional analysis indicates that consideration of these unclassifiable forms provides relevant information on the developmental pattern followed by Italian children in the acquisition of the *system* of verb inflection.

3.2. Appearance and Acquisition of Simple Tense, Finite Main Verbs Inflections

Table 6.3 shows all the different forms we identified in each child's production along with two kinds of information: On the left, in normal characters, we show the age at which a given form was first noted, that is, its *first appearance*; on the right, in bold, italics, and only for the forms that attained our acquisition criteria as previously defined, we show the *age of acquisition* of a given verb inflection.

The data in Table 6.3 clearly indicate that a rich variety of distinct inflections (from 8 to 10) were found, beginning at the earliest ages: At ages 1;4 to 1;9 all three children used present-tense first-, second-, and third-person singular. The patterns of appearance of the different verb forms were relatively similar across children: Singular forms appeared earlier than plural ones; present-tense forms appeared earlier than past and future forms; with few exceptions, the various inflections for first, second, and third person did not appear all at the same time, but rather at time intervals lasting from one to several months.

Compared with the data on first appearance, the data on those forms that reached our acquisition criteria provide a strikingly different picture. Looking at Table 6.3, it can be seen that in all three children only a small set of present-tense inflections attained criterion: the third-person singular indicative in all three children, the singular first-person indicative and second-person indicative/imperative in both Claudia and Francesco, and the first-person plural indicative/imperative in Claudia only (see fn. 2). The time interval that elapsed between the first appearance and the acquisition of these few verb forms ranges from a minimum of 1 (in one case only) to a maximum of 8 months, with an average from 4 to 6 months.

In all three children, plural forms constituted a very small proportion in comparison with singular forms (total N: from 63 to 131 tokens, or 9% to 19%). This in part explains why only a single plural form (the first-

TABLE 6.3
Simple Tense Finite Main Verb Forms Inflected for Person and Number
in the Three Children's Production: Age of First Appearance
as Compared with Age of Acquisition

Subjects		Claudia		Francesco		Marco	
		1st App.	*Acq.*	*1st App.*	*Acq.*	*1st App.*	*Acq.*
Present							
Ind.	1SG	1;6	*1;8*	1;5	*2;1*	1;8	—
Ind. & Imp.	2SG	1;4	*1;8*	1;5	*2;0*	1;5	—
Ind.	3SG	1;4	*1;9*	1;9	*1;10*	1;9	*2;1*
Ind. & Imp.	1PL	1;7	*1;10*	1;7	—	2;0	—
Ind. & Imp.	2PL	—		2;9	—	—	
Ind.	3PL	1;11		1;11	—	2;0	—
Conditional	1SG	1;10	—	—		—	
Past							
Imperfect	1SG	2;1		2;7	—	—	
	2SG	—		—		1;10	—
	3SG	2;1	—	2;3	—	2;2	—
	3PL	1;10	—	2;10	—	—	
Hist. Past	3SG	2;3		—		—	
Simple Future	3SG	—		—		2;4	—

Note: Verbs forms are described on the left. Ind.: Indicative; Imp.: Imperative; Hist. Past: Historic Past (see the text). For each subject the age (in years; months) of first appearance is shown on the left, in normal characters, the *age of acquisition* on the right, in *italic, bold characters*. Acquisition criteria are defined in the text. Additional details are given in the text.

person plural indicative/imperative), in only one child, met our acquisition criteria: All the other forms were not sufficiently represented in each corpus (nor in individual samples) to allow appropriate assessment of the children's performance.

Errors occurred in small proportions (total *N*: from 20 to 21 tokens, or 3% to 4%), were noted in all three children's corpora, but were not homogeneously distributed across inflections: In all three children they occurred with the singular inflections, and in Francesco and Marco they also occurred with the third-person plural inflection. The production of the indicative/imperative first-person plural (by all three children), and second-person plural (by Francesco only) was instead errorless. The most frequent types of errors, produced by all three children, included:

(a) Errors of agreement in person and number, for example:
   (1) F: 1;10 *aggiusta* (= *aggiusto*) io '*fix-3SG (= fix-1SG) I'
   (2) C: 1;7 pallone l'*ape* (= *apri*) 'ball it *open-3G (= open-2SG)'
   (3) M: 2;1 *piango* (= *piange*) Marco '*cry-1SG (= cry-3SG) Marco'

(b) Errors with the imperative inflections. In the second and third con-jugations the indicative and imperative second-person singular forms bear the same -*i* ending (e.g., *batti*), whereas in the first con-jugation the indicative ends in -*i* (*chiami*), the imperative in -*a* (*chiama*). The children erroneously used the -*i* ending, instead of the required -*a*, with imperative forms of 1st conjugation verbs, as in (4) to (6):

(4) F: 2;6 **raccontila!* (= *raccontala*) 'tell-2SG-it!'
(5) C: 1;9 **palli!* (= *parla*) 'speak-2SG!'
(6) M: 2;3 **levi!* (= *leva*) 'take-away-2SG!'

Errors of this kind, which we expected from the regularities and the homonymy proper of the inflectional patterns, suggest a tendency to: (a) mark second-person inflections, irrespective of mood distinctions, with the -*i* ending proper of the three conjugations; (b) avoid the homony-mous -*a* marking of second-person imperative and third-person singu-lar, first conjugation verbs. In all three children, the indicative/imperative -*i* inflection appeared earlier than more marked -*a* inflection.

Another type of error, root regularization, was very infrequent, and was produced only by Claudia and Francesco, for example:

(7) F: 2;7 **vieno* (= *vengo*) 'come-1SG irreg'.
(8) C: 1;10 **dicio* (= *dico*) 'say-1SG irreg'.

In most cases, and in all three children, these erroneous productions occurred along with correct ones: Often within the same sample, or even within the same utterance or set of related utterances, the same verb was produced once in a correct and once in an erroneous form. For example Claudia, immediately after having produced the erroneous imperative form **palli!* (for *parla!*), produced the correct utterance *palla tu!* ('speak-2SG you!'), where she used the -*a* inflection required for this first conjugation verb, and clarified her intent with the emphatic use of a second-person pronoun.

Another interesting feature of verb production were utterances in which the children referred to themselves using a third-person instead of a first-person verb, in most cases along with their own names instead of a first-person pronoun, as identifying expressions. Consider examples (9) to (11):

(9) C: 1;9 *maggia Cadia?* for *mangio io?* 'eat-3SG Claudia?' for 'eat-1SG I?'
(10) F: 1;10 *Checco batte* for *io batto* 'Francesco bang-3SG' for 'I bang-1SG'.
(11) M: 2;3 *Marco vuole* for *io voglio* 'Marco want-3SG' for 'I want-1SG'.

Unless they were clear instances of agreement errors (cf. example 1), we included these third-person verbs among the morphologically correct occurrences of third-person verb inflection, but we considered them atypical or inappropriate with respect to the requirements of discourse pragmatics in adult Italian. In normal dialogue, a first-person verb inflection and, optionally, a first-person pronoun, are the only appropriate means for self-reference: Third-person verbs, and nominal expressions, must be restricted to nonspeaker/nonaddressee participants, or inanimate objects.

These data, albeit informative, do not clarify two major questions: (a) How productive was the use of inflections by the children? (b) In the time lapse between first appearance and acquisition, does development proceed abruptly, going in one single step from incomplete to full mastery of a given morpheme (or set of morphemes), or is it rather a gradual (albeit not necessarily linear) process, in which correct performance rises slowly over time? In order to answer these questions, we examined (a) verb types and tokens in the children's total production, attempting to ascertain the productivity of individual verb roots and/or inflectional paradigms; and (b) the children's performance across all age samples on all tokens of verb inflections considered as an undifferentiated set, and individual inflected forms that were productively used by all three children.

3.3. Productivity of Different Patterns in the Children's Total Production

The analysis of the distinct verb roots, or root types, used by the children (Table 6.2) revealed several regularities. As expected on the basis of the patterns of adult Italian, a large majority of the verbs used by the children belonged to the first conjugation (from 42 to 57 roots across children), whereas second (N: 20 to 27), and third (N: 9 to 12) conjugation verbs were represented in much smaller numbers. Irregular verbs of all three conjugations were found (N: from 4 to 15 depending on the child), and included in all three children the same four highly frequent first conjugation verbs *andare, dare, fare, stare*.

The total number of root types used by the children was much smaller than the cumulative number of all inflected verb tokens (N type/tokens: 94/1011; 97/881; 72/351 in Claudia, Francesco and Marco, respectively—see Table 6.2). This low type/token ratio could suggest that on the whole the children's use of verbal inflections was highly productive. However, closer inspection of the data provided different indications. First, we examined in each child's total production the number of root types that appeared in only one inflected form (e.g., *tiro* 'pull-1SG'), as compared with those that appeared with two or more in-flections (e.g., *mangio/mangi/mangia* 'eat-1SG/eat-2SG/eat-3SG'). We found that in all three children approximately one half of the different verb roots appeared in only one inflected form (*N:* 42, 51 and 36 in Claudia, Francesco and Marco). A considerably smaller number appeared in two inflected forms (*N:* 27, 20, and 22), an even smaller number in three (*N:* 13, 16, and 11), and in four or more inflected forms (*N:* 12, 10, and 13 for Claudia, Francesco and Marco, respectively). In each child, approximately one half of the few roots appearing with more than three inflected forms were irregular, highly frequent verbs (e.g., *andare, fare, stare*), which presumably are learned by rote.

Second, we analyzed the distribution of the different *inflection types* over distinct verb roots, excluding all repetitions of the same form (e.g., if each of the forms *apro* 'open-1SG', *mangio* 'eat-1SG', *gioco* 'play-1SG' and *chiamava* 'was-calling-3SG', was produced two times by one child, we classified these productions as 3—not 6—tokens of the first-person singular inflection type, distributed over three different verb roots, and as 1 token—not 2—of the imperfect 3SG inflection type). We found that the distribution of inflection types over distinct verb roots was uneven for both mood/tense/aspect and person/number inflections. Inflection types, like their corresponding tokens, were essentially limited to indicative and, to a much smaller extent, imperative present-tense forms. Within the more productive category of person/number distinctions, Claudia, Francesco, and Marco produced, respectively, a total of 181, 186, and 111 inflection types. In all three children, singular inflections were produced with a significantly larger number of verb roots than plural inflections (SG/PL *N:* 142/39; 161/25; 91/20). Within *singular* inflection types, the third person was used with a larger number of verb roots by both Claudia (*N:* 56 vs. 44 and 42 roots used with first and second person), and Marco (*N:* 44 as compared with 23 for first and 24 for second person); in Francesco, a greater number of roots appeared with first person (*N:* 60 vs. 51 and 50 for second and third person). With *plural* inflection types, in Claudia the first-person plural indicative/imperative inflection occurred with a fairly large number of roots (*N:* 32 vs. 11 and 10 roots in Francesco and Marco); second- (in Francesco's corpus only) and third-person inflections were used with a much smaller number of distinct verb roots (*N:* 4 to 11 across children). Taken together, all of these data indicate that across samples only the three singular present-tense inflections were used productively by all three children, whereas the first-person plural (indicative/imperative) was used productively only by Claudia.

Examining developmental changes in these patterns, we found that there was no productive use of inflections in the early samples: with some negligible exception, from the ages of 1;4 to 1;7 for Claudia, 1;5 to 1;8 for Francesco, and 1;5 to 1;11 for Marco, each root (*N*: 5 to 10 across children) was used with only one inflection. Roots bearing two (or more) inflections began to appear after these ages. Although, as noted, a large proportion of individual roots continued to be produced in a single form, the number of regular and irregular roots with more than one inflection gradually increased, especially within the subparadigm of singular inflections. In partial accord with these observations, the two a priori criteria we had formulated for assessing the *beginning* of productivity for each inflection type—use of the same inflection with two roots, and of the same root with two inflections—indicated similar discrepancies between singular as compared with plural inflections (the age ranges for initial productivity of SG vs. PL were, in Claudia: 1;7–1;8 vs. 1;8–2;1; in Francesco: 1,8–1;9 vs. 2;3–2;9; in Marco: 1;11–2;0 vs. 2;4).

3.4. Developmental Patterns in the Acquisition of Inflected Forms

Figure 6.1 shows the proportions of classifiable as compared to unclassifiable inflected verbs (top section), and the proportion of overall correct verbs (bottom section), in all three children's production, as a function of age. All tokens of finite, simple tense main verb inflections are collapsed together into a single category. The proportion of overall correct verbs is computed as the ratio between morphologically correct productions (numerator) and incorrect plus unclassifiable productions (denominator). A ' < ' mark indicates samples with less than five tokens of verb forms (e.g., Claudia's sample at age 1;5 included only 4 verbs).

Previous studies on the development of verb morphology in both English and Italian have usually excluded from analysis ambiguous or, in our coding, unclassifiable verbs (e.g., Bloom et al., 1980; Cazden, 1968; Pizzuto & Caselli, 1992). The reason for this is straightforward: "*Often* the children used unmarked verbs *where some inflection was clearly required.* But unless there was a clear indication of *which inflection should have been supplied*, these cases were excluded from analysis" (Cazden, 1968, p. 231, emphasis added). Unclassifiable verb utterances clearly cannot be used to chart the development of *individual, specific* inflected forms—precisely because the investigator is unable to ascertain with some degree of confidence which specific inflection the child should have supplied in the ambiguous context. In the analysis of individual inflections this methodological constraint applies equally to English and Italian. Thus in Italian, as in English, the development of individual inflections must be charted considering only the set of clearly classifiable verb utterances. However in Italian, unlike in English, verbs never appear "unmarked,"

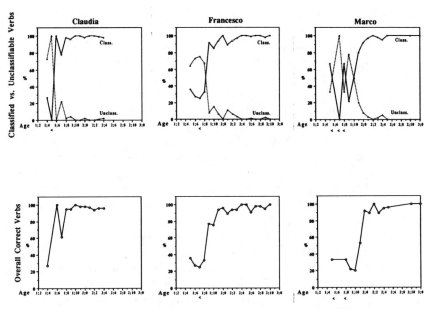

FIG. 6.1.   Proportion of classifiable as compared with unclassifiable verbs
(top section), and proportion of overall correct inflected verbs in the three
children's production as a function of age (bottom section). <, Samples
with fewer than five verb tokens.

but always bear some inflection. The status (and/or import) of the Italian
unclassifiable inflected verbs is thus clearly different from their English
equivalents.

Our analysis suggests that ambiguous, unclassifiable verbs provide important information on the developmental process in a language like
Italian. The production of unclassifiable verbs reflects not just the child's
(and the investigator's) limitations, but also the learning pattern followed
by Italian children on their road to master the various inflections in their
language—most notably the "degree of uncertainty" the children seem
to manifest, at certain points in development, in choosing the "right"
inflected form for the meaning they are trying to convey. We thus felt
it appropriate to include unclassifiable verbs, albeit at a global level, with
all the inflected verbs grouped into a single, undifferentiated category.

Figure 6.1 reveals that early in development, and for periods lasting
from 4 to 6 months, unclassifiable verbs constitute a considerable proportion of all three children's repertoire (from 25% to 100%, depending
on the sample). Classifiable verbs begin to be consistently represented
in the three children's repertoires (at levels of 90% or more), only 5 to
6 months after their first appearance (at the ages of 1;8 for Claudia, 1;9
for Francesco, and 2;0 for Marco). This is of particular interest if we recall

that the overall proportion of unclassifiable verbs in the three children's corpora was very small (from 4% to 7%). The information in Fig. 6.1 shows that unclassifiable verbs were *not* evenly distributed across all age samples, but were a characterizing feature of the earliest developmental stages.

Across verb forms and across children, correct performance rises rather slowly over time, with the growth curves exhibiting more or less marked up and down drops in performance in the course of development. The developmental curves of overall correct productions and of classifiable verbs are very similar (with the exception of Marco's performance in samples 1;5 to 1;8), and often coincide. This indicates that the classifiable verbs produced by the children were also, in most cases, correct occurrences. And, as noted, the overall proportion of errors was very low in all three children (3% to 4%).

Figure 6.1 shows that *all* inflections attained, or were very close to attain, our acquisition criterion (90% correct) at age 1;8 for Claudia, 1;11 for Francesco, and 2;0 for Marco. However, the inflections that attained criterion were only a small subset of present-tense, indicative/imperative forms: four in Claudia, three in Francesco, only one in Marco. The ages at which each inflection from this subset attained criterion were also different (Table 6.3). None of the other forms that occurred in the children's production attained criterion. This clearly reveals how collapsing different inflections into one undifferentiated category may lead to improper assessment of the children's actual performance, hence also to an over or underestimation of the children's actual control of a given morphological paradigm.

Figure 6.2 illustrates, in relation to classifiable verbs only, the development of the specific inflections that were used productively by all three children, and that attained criterion in one or more children: first-, second-, and third-person SG present indicative and imperative.

Figure 6.2 shows that, with two exceptions to be noted separately, the children's performance curves describe two major developmental phases: In the first phase, as indicated by the '<' marks in several samples, there are often few required contexts, and thus also few actual productions of each type of inflection. In this period—of varying length depending on the child or the inflection—there is variation even between extremely high or low levels, and this yields up and down swoops in the acquisition curves. This pattern is very similar to that noted by Brown (1973) in the early development of English morphemes. Brown observed that in this phase production-where-required is probabilistic, and that "the number of clearly obligatory contexts is smaller in the early samples than in the later ones because, in general, the constraints that define obligation are themselves acquired over time. Therefore the number of instances

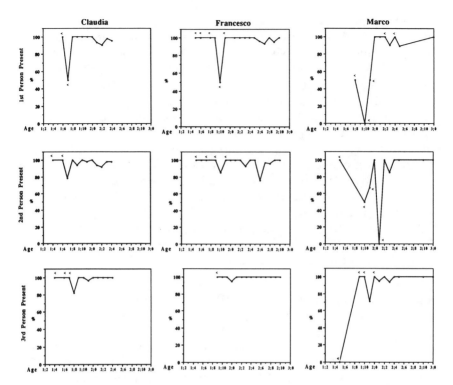

FIG. 6.2. Proportion of correct indicative present-tense first-, second-, and third-person singular inflected verbs in the three children's production as a function of age. <, Samples with fewer than five contexts of obligatory use.

determining each data point is smaller in the earlier samples than in the later" (Brown, 1973, p. 257). This developmental period coincides approximately with the first three to six samples (depending on the child) in which, as noted, most verb roots appear in one form only.

In the second phase, the number of obligatory contexts and actual productions increases (see the disappearance of the ' < ' marks in Fig. 6.2), whereas the performance patterns stabilize in the acquisition range. With some negligible exceptions (e.g., Francesco's performance on second-person verbs at age 2;6), once performance reaches or exceeds the 90% correct level, in samples containing a sufficient number of contexts, the curves stabilize over several consecutive samples within the 90% to 100% correct range. Like the previous unstable pattern, this one was also noted by Brown in the development of English morphemes, and described as "a fairly general property of the curves for inflections and other morphemes" (Brown, 1973, p. 258). It was indeed the observation of this pattern that led Brown and Cazden to adopt their "90% correct use over three consecutive samples'' as the morpheme acquisition criterion. During this phase, the variety of instantiation of each inflection increases significantly. Insofar as the observed changes in development can be taken as an indication of learning, that is, as systematic changes in the children's performance as a result of experience, we can characterize the first phase as a learning stage prior to the second acquisition stage.

There are two exceptions to the pattern described. One is Francesco's performance on third-person verbs, which appears 100% correct from the start, at age 1;9 (see Fig. 6.2). Regardless of individual differences, a comparison of the performance curves over third-person inflections and those over first- and second-person inflections indicates that in all three children morphologically correct third-person verb inflections developed with a more regular pattern than first- and second-person inflections. The second exception, not illustrated in Fig. 6.2, was the first-person plural indicative/imperative inflection, which, as noted, all three children used always correctly.

3.5. The Acquisition of Verb Inflections, MLU and the Two-Word Stage

Consider, next, the relationship between verb inflections and overall linguistic maturity, on the one hand, and how these patterns compare with those found in English. Table 6.4 summarizes the relevant data on our three subjects, and presents a rough comparison between these data and those reported by Brown (1973, p. 271) in his longitudinal study of Adam, Eve, and Sarah, and by J. G. de Villiers and P. A. de Villiers (1973, p. 270) in their cross-sectional study of the acquisition of English grammatical morphemes. For this comparison we applied to the Italian MLUw scores the same *quantitative* distinctions in MLU stages originally proposed by Brown (1973, pp. 53ff., 270ff.) for English. Thus, for example, MLUw Stage I for the Italian children is defined as the phase in which MLUw scores are comprised between 1.00 and 2.24, and is compared to the phase in which MLU scores for the English children are in the same range. We do not attribute to the Italian MLUw stages the same *qualitative* differences that, following Brown, are commonly made for English (e.g., characterizing Stage I as the phase of basic semantic roles and grammatical relations; Stage II as the phase of grammatical morphemes and the modulation of meaning). Further research is needed before characterizations of this (or, more likely, different) kind can be proposed for Italian. The comparison is limited to the Italian and English verb inflections that were mastered during MLUw/MLU Stages I to III.

It should be clear that a precise comparison between the Italian and the English data cannot be made: The measure of developmental level

TABLE 6.4

The Acquisition of Verb Inflections in Italian and English in
Relation with MLUw/MLU Stages I–III and Age: A Comparison
Between the Three Italian Children, Brown's Subjects Eve, Adam, and
Sarah, and 12 Subjects of de Villiers and de Villiers' Cross-Sectional Study

| | MLUw/MLU Stages | | | | | |
| | I—1.00–2.24 | | II—2.25–2.74 | | III—2.75–3.49 | |
Subjects	Age	V.Infl.	Age	V.Infl.	Age	V.Infl.
Claudia	1;4–1;7 2-wS	—	1;8–1;9	V-1/V-2 V-3	1;10–2;3	V-1PL
Francesco	1;5–2;0 2-wS	V-3 V-2	2;1–2;2	V-1	2;3–2;5	
Marco	1;5–2;2 2-wS	V-3	2;3–3;0			
Eve	1;6–1;8	—	1;9–1;10	V-ing	1;11–2;1	
Adam	2;3–2;5	—	2;6–2;10	V-ing	2;11–3;1	V-p.irreg.
Sarah	2;3–2;9	—	2;10–3;0	V-ing V-p.irreg.	3;1–3;7	
Zoe	1;4	V-ing				
Rachel	2;2	V-ing				
Hilary	2;2	V-p.irreg.				
Caleb	2;6	V-ing				
Chris			2;4	V-ing		
John			2;7	V-p.irreg.		
Karen					2;6	V-ing
Mary					2;8	V-ing
Andrew					2;4	V-ing
Hannah					1;9	V-ing
Eric					2;9	V-ing
Amy					2;4	V-ing/V-3 irreg.

Note: MLUw is used for the Italian children and is defined in the methodology section
of the present paper. MLU is used for the English-speaking children. The data on Eve, Adam,
and Sarah are adapted from Brown (1973, p. 271), and the data on the remaining English
subjects are taken from J. G. de Villiers and P. A. de Villiers (1973). MLU/MLUw stages
are distinguished after Brown (1973, pp. 53ff., 270ff.). Age: age ranges of the children at
each MLUw/MLU stage. 2-wS: age range at which the two-word stage had stabilized in the
Italian children (see the text). V.Infl.: verb inflections acquired at each MLUw/MLU stage
and age range. Comparable acquisition criteria are used for the Italian and English children
(see the methodology section). For Italian children and the 12 J. G. de Villiers and P. A.
de Villiers' subjects inflections that attained criterion simultaneously are shown on the same
line, separated by a '/'; inflections placed on different lines represent sequential order of
acquisition. For comparable information on Eve, Adam, and Sarah see Brown (1973, pp.
270–271). In the Italian data the glosses V-1, V-2, V-3, V-1PL stand for, respectively, main
verbs indicative present-tense singular first, second, and third person, and first-person plural
forms. In the English data V-ing, V-p.irreg. and V-3 irreg. indicate, respectively, the present
progressive and the irregular past and third-person singular inflections. For additional details refer to the text.

that we used for the Italian children (MLUw) is not strictly comparable to the measure of MLU for English. There are also clear differences between English and Italian in the number of contrasts that must be acquired, as well as at a local, morpheme-by-morpheme level. Nonetheless, several observations can be made.

In Italian, as summarized in Table 6.4, mastery of a single (in Marco), three (in Francesco), and four (in Claudia) inflections was achieved only after the two-word stage had stabilized. Thus no productive use of verb inflections is found at the one-word stage. There are clear individual differences in overall linguistic development: Although MLUw increases systematically with age for all three children, Claudia is the most advanced (e.g., she reached Stage III by age 1;10), followed by Francesco and, at some distance, Marco (both were still at MLUw Stage I until age 2;0 to 2;2). These same differences are reflected in the ages at which each child reached the two-word stage: Claudia at 1;4, Francesco at 1;9, and Marco at 1;11.

Regardless of age, each child achieves productive control of at least one verb inflection when MLUw nears, or goes beyond, point 2.00 (range: 1.75–2.46). The most advanced child, Claudia, was also the one who controlled the largest number of inflections at the youngest age (by 1;10). These patterns suggest that MLUw may predict morphological development more accurately than age. This is similar to what was found in English with respect to age and MLU stages, and is consistent with what was found in other languages (cf. Dromi & Berman, 1982; Hickey, 1991, among others).

Looking now at the English data in Table 6.4 first note the individual differences. There is also considerable variation in the ages at which the subjects reached (or were already, as in J. G. de Villiers & P. A. de Villiers' study) MLU Stages I to III: In Brown's sample, Eve was already at Stage II at age 2;1, whereas Adam and Sarah were still at Stage I through ages 2;5 to 2;9; in J. G. de Villiers and P. A. de Villiers' sample, MLU Stage I comprises one subject as young as 1;4, and three subjects in the age range 2;2 to 2;6. At MLU Stage III we find one subject of age 1;9, and three subjects in the age range 2;4 to 2;6.

Variation is also noted in the ages/MLU stages at which the children mastered the English verb inflections indicated in Table 6.4. Thus, for example, whereas Brown's three subjects acquired the present progressive '-ing' inflection at MLU Stage II (age range: 1;9–3;0), in J. G. de Villiers and P. A. de Villiers' sample three of the four subjects who were at MLU Stage I (age range: 1;4–2;6) already exhibited productive control over this inflection. Similarly, the English past irregular inflection is mastered by Sarah and Adam at, respectively, MLU Stages II and III whereas, among J. G. de Villiers and P. A. de Villiers' subjects, one (Hilary) mastered it earlier, at MLU Stage I, another one (John) later, at MLU Stage II, and the remaining ones did not productively use this inflection (see Table 6.4).

Finally, comparing the Italian and the English data, we can observe the following. Regardless of individual differences in Italian, as in English, the acquisition of verb inflections appears to be more closely related with overall linguistic development as reflected into MLUw/MLU stages than with simple chronological age. In both languages, the acquisition of verb inflections is far from having been completed by MLUw/MLU Stage III: Only some specific inflections have been acquired, and these range in number from one to four in the Italian children, and from one to two in the English-speaking ones. In both languages, some inflections are clearly acquired earlier than others. However, there are obvious differences in the specific inflections that are acquired.

Two inflections are present in both English and Italian: One is the third-person present; the other is the English present progressive, which is comparable, under several aspects, to the Italian present gerund inflection (e.g., *speak-ing* = *parl-ando*). Yet the patterns of acquisition of these two inflections are very different in the two languages: The Italian third-person inflection is acquired very early, by MLUw Stages I or II, whereas its English equivalent is among the latest inflections to be acquired (by MLU Stages IV and V). The English present progressive is the earliest verb inflection mastered (by MLU Stages I or II), whereas its Italian counterpart is virtually absent from the Italian children's repertoires (Pizzuto & Caselli, 1992).

4. DISCUSSION

The first objective of the present study was to explore the acquisition of verb inflections in Italian as compared to English. We did so by analyzing longitudinal data from three children, using methods comparable to those that are widely employed in the study of spontaneous morphological development in English.

In the age range from 1;4–1;5 to 2;10–3;0, we found a rich variety of simple tense, finite main verb inflections. It we had limited our observations to these examples of the children's production, without imposing acquisition criteria (cf. Hyams, 1986a, 1986b, 1987), or to only one fairly advanced child such as Claudia, we might have been tempted to conclude that the Italian system of verb inflectional morphology is mastered very early. However, and quite significantly, very few of these inflected forms attained our acquisition criterion. Despite differences in the children's age, and in the sizes of the corpora analyzed, the developmental patterns identified in the three children exhibited some major similarities. These include the following:

1. All verb inflections that reached criterion were present-tense, indicative/imperative forms, and all but one were singular.

2. In all but one case, there was a consistent time lag, lasting on the average from 4 to 6 months, between first appearance and point of acquisition for those inflections that did reach criterion. In all cases, a period of varying length elapsed between initial nonproductive and subsequent productive use of each inflection.

3. Summing correct performance across all verb inflections, similar, rather gradual growth curves were noted. Correct performance was initially unstable for almost every inflection we considered; patterns stabilized weeks or months after this point.

4. We found evidence for morphological errors (albeit at low levels), which co-occurred with correct production during this protracted period of development.

In addition to these similarities we also found remarkable individual *differences* among the children and among the inflections. These concerned (a) the age at which the verb inflections were acquired; (b) the order of acquisition for these inflections, above and beyond the similarities noted earlier (e.g., Claudia acquired first- and second-person verbs at the same time, whereas Francesco acquired the second person 1 month earlier than the first; and (c) the first-person present indicative/imperative plural inflection, which, unlike other inflections, was always used correctly by the children.

These results corroborate and extend recent findings on the acquisition of Italian reported by Caselli, Leonard, Volterra, and Campagnoli (1993), and by Pizzuto and Caselli (1991, 1992, 1993). One of the results reported by Pizzuto and Caselli (1991, 1992)—that no plural inflections attained criterion—must be amended on the basis of the present work. As noted, the first-person plural inflection attained criterion in one of our three subjects, Claudia (see fn. 2). Caselli et al. (1993) conducted a cross-sectional study exploring children's elicited production and comprehension abilities in specific experimental tasks. One finding from this study confirms the disparity between singular and plural present-tense indicative inflections: The third-person singular inflection is mastered earlier, by age 2;6 to 3;0; the corresponding plural inflection is mastered later, by age 3;6 to 4;0. The findings of earlier studies on the acquisition of Italian, which employed part of the same data as the present work, are also partially confirmed (e.g., Bates, 1976; Leonard et al., 1987), although precise comparisons with our results cannot be made, due to differences in focus and methodologies.

The comparison between our data and those on English-speaking children reveals that, in the early stages of development at least, the general developmental patterns are similar in the two languages, from both a quantitative and a qualitative standpoint. Neither the English nor the Italian children have achieved complete productivity in the verb inflection *system* of their language: They control, at most, a limited number of individual inflections, and this number is not very different in the two languages (one to four for the Italian children; one or two for the English children). From a qualitative standpoint, the major regularities noted under the previously listed points 2 to 4 have all been extensively documented in English (cf. among others, the classical works of Brown, 1973; Cazden, 1968; J. G. de Villiers & P. A. de Villiers, 1973, 1985; Maratsos, 1983).

Concerning the developmental curves of individual verb inflections, J. G. de Villiers and P. A. de Villiers (1973, p. 271) found that some morphemes of English, including for example the third-person regular inflection show gradual growth curves. Other morphemes have either very sparse data, or reach criterion very early. Their cross-sectional data show that the present progressive inflection reached criterion very early: Three subjects of J. G. de Villiers and P. A. de Villiers' study had already mastered this inflection at MLU Stage I, and produced it correctly in 93% to 100% of the cases in which it was obligatorily required; the 100% correct performance level was also noted in all the other subjects who produced this inflection, and who were at MLU Stages II and III. These patterns differ in part from those described by Brown (1973), and resemble in part those we noted in the development of the Italian third-person singular and first-person plural inflections.

Several general aspects of morphological development in Italian and English appear similar, but some interlanguage differences are evident. Perhaps the most conspicuous concern is the development of (a) the third-person singular inflection, which can be considered semantically and structurally equivalent in Italian and English, and (b) the English present progressive inflection, which corresponds to a large extent to the gerund inflection of Italian. The acquisition of the third-person inflection appears strikingly precocious in Italian as compared with English, whether by chronological age or linguistic stage. Conversely, the acquisition of the present progressive inflection appears strikingly precocious in English. We consider some of the reasons that may lead to this disparity shortly.

Another objective of this study was to evaluate the plausibility of Hyams' predictions and claims based on the stem parameter account of verb inflections in English and Italian. Our data do not disconfirm Hyams' major prediction, and its related claim, concerning the absence of verb roots in the acquisition of Italian. However, we argued earlier in this chapter and in Pizzuto and Caselli (1992) that this prediction and claim are not empirically testable, and they do not appear to be relevant to understanding how Italian children acquire verb inflections (as distinguished from Italian words). For these reasons, we do not consider them any further.

The second prediction made by the stem parameter was that Italian children will learn the inflectional system or the affixes (Hyams, 1991, p. 2; 1992, p. 696) earlier than English children. Our findings do not support this prediction: Contrary to what has been claimed by Hyams (1986a, 1986b, 1991, 1992), Italian children do not master verb morphology at strikingly more precocious ages or stages than English children. Our children clearly had *not* "mastered the present-tense verb paradigm by age 2;0" and they did not control a significantly greater number of verb inflections than their English counterparts. With respect to the type and number of verb inflections controlled by English and Italian children it is appropriate, at this point, to discuss two proposals made by Hyams concerning the early mastery of the present progressive inflection in English and the present-tense person inflections in Italian.

Commenting on the difficulties English children seem to have with "verbal inflection in general" Hyams (1986a, pp. 2ff.) noted that "there is an apparent exception to this generalization; the present progressive morpheme -*ing* which Brown ranks as the first of the 14 morphemes to be acquired." Hyams (1986b, p. 7) further remarked that "the progressive verb is first used without the auxiliary *be*, suggesting that -*ing* is not a separate morpheme which is selected by the auxiliary, as is the case in the adult grammar. Instead, it may be that the child learns each progressive form as a distinct verb so that *hit* and *hitting*, for example, actually represent two distinct lexical entries. This hypothesis is supported by a second fact, noted by Cazden (1968) that unlike the verbal affixes -s and -ed, -ing fails to overgeneralize." Hyams then proposed that "if we credit the child with actually knowing the progressive morpheme only at the point at which it co-occurs with the auxiliary *be*, then its acquisition occurs significantly later."

This interesting proposal is certainly one possible reinterpretation of Brown's and Cazden's findings: It undoubtedly reconciles the actual data on the acquisition of English with Hyams' parameter-setting account. However, the evidence currently available is simply not sufficient to evaluate the plausibility of Hyams' proposal. A comprehensive reanalysis of the English data on the development of the present progressive would seem to be necessary. For example, in normal dialogues (especially in child–adult language), it may often be equally appropriate to use a progressive inflection with or without the accompanying auxiliary (e.g., in question and answer dialogues such as *What are you doing? Playing*). Considerations of this sort are apparent in Brown's (cf. 1973, pp. 259ff.) discussion of the contexts that define obligation for the use of this inflection in child's speech. On Hyams' account, these productions that have been considered appropriate by other investigators would all be discarded. In the present study, as shown by the comparative information provided in Table 6.4, we maintain the traditional (rather than Hyams') view of an early mastery of the English present progressive inflection.

To our knowledge, at the present there is no complete explanation for the earlier acquisition of the present progressive as compared with other verb inflections in English. However, some of the factors that are likely to facilitate its acquisition include the regularity of this inflection as compared with the more irregular patterns of the past tense and third-person singular inflections; the fact that in English the progressive may function as the most basic present tense in the deictic sense of immediate present, being associated initially with durative aspect (Berman, personal communication, July 1992; cf. also Bloom et al., 1980; Brown, 1973, pp. 315ff.); the high frequency of the inflection in parental input (cf. J. G. de Villiers & P. A. de Villiers', 1985, review of the relevant evidence on this topic).

Commenting on the findings reported by Pizzuto and Caselli (1991, 1992), and documented also in this chapter, Hyams (1991, 1992) proposed that the earlier mastery of the Italian first-, second-, and third-person singular present-tense inflections, as compared with the later mastery of the English third-person singular inflection '-s', should be interpreted as unequivocal evidence in support of the second prediction of the stem parameter. In addition, the scarce use of plural inflections by Italian children should not be considered as evidence that the children did not productively use plural forms. Hyams (1992, p. 699) proposed that "all we can conclude from the lack of plural inflections is that children do not like to talk about plural things. . . . This finding is interesting but hardly relevant to the question of children's morphological development."

We think that Hyams' proposal is questionable. First, as concerns the set of singular present-tense inflections, Italian and English children can be appropriately compared only with respect to the single inflection Italian and English have in common: the third-person singular present. Because the other person inflections are simply not represented in English, it cannot be plausibly stated that Italian children are more precocious than English children because they acquire "more" inflections—as implied by Hyams' proposal. Second, our findings on Italian children's control (and productive use) of singular and plural inflections (also supported by Caselli et al.'s study) result from the application of explicit acquisition criteria. Criteria of this sort are simply necessary methodological tools if we aim to conduct meaningful cross-linguistic comparisons among typologically different languages. By these criteria, in all but one case the Italian children examined in the present study did not use plural inflections productively.

How can the patterns we identified be accounted for within current models of language development? In our view, these patterns can be best described within more psychologically oriented models of language acquisition (e.g., Batcs & MacWhinney, 1982, 1989; Berman, 1981, 1982, 1991; MacWhinney, 1978, 1985; Maratsos, 1983; Maratsos & Chalkley, 1980; Slobin, 1973, 1982, 1985a) in which several different yet interrelated factors shape the course of development. These factors include cognitive abilities and learning mechanisms that enable children to exploit distributional regularities of a pragmatic, semantic, and morphophonological type in the input to which they are exposed. Cross-linguistic similarities and differences can be explained by similarities and differences in the nature of the child's linguistic input. A clearer understanding of the role that *these* factors play in development is a necessary, preliminary step in order to uncover language-independent, universal traits of development and to assess, on this basis, to what extent the universal factors implicated in the human "language making capacity" (Slobin, 1985a) are, or become, specific of the language domain, or belong to more general cognitive abilities.

Formal and distributional regularities appear to account for the most general trends in the children's production, where the least marked, more frequent, and more productive patterns appear earlier, and in some cases are also mastered, than the more marked and less frequent patterns (e.g., the indicative present vs. the past and future; the first conjugation vs. the second and third conjugation verbs; the singular vs. the plural forms). The gradual development of the various forms suggests that different morphological paradigms, or subparadigms, can be characterized as subdomains that may require the development of different abilities. For example, the greater productivity of person markers over tense/aspect markers indicates that, in Italian at least, and using the criteria of productivity we adopted in the present work, aspectual distinctions develop later than distinctions of person. Because tense/aspect markers are reported to be mastered fairly easily and early in agglutinative languages such as Turkish (Aksu-Koç & Slobin, 1985; Slobin, 1982), it is possible that the synthetic-fusional features of the morphology play some role in delaying the acquisition of these categories in Italian. Yet tense/aspect markers appear to be acquired with particular ease in other fusional inflecting languages such as Polish, where they are clearly and uniformly marked on finite and nonfinite verb forms (Smoczynska, 1985; Weist, Wysocka, Witkowska-Stadnik, Buczowska, & Konieczna, 1984). Considering the stem alternations that are implicated in conveying tense/aspect distinctions across languages, Bybee (Bybee, 1985; Bybee Hooper, 1979) showed that in many languages these distinctions are less marked and more basic than person distinctions, and this may promote an earlier development of tense/aspect, compared with person categories, in languages such as Brazilian Portuguese (Simões Perroni & Stoel-Gammon, 1979). Further research is certainly needed, along with a reassessment of some earlier findings reported on Italian by Antinucci and Miller (1976) and Volterra (1976), to clarify the reasons leading to such cross-linguistic differences, and the kind of knowledge that may be required to master tense/aspect distinctions in Italian.

General cognitive and pragmatic factors, and the greater salience of word-final, local obligatory cues, seem to be relevant to understanding the appearance and development of person marking on the verb, particularly as concerns the earlier appearance of first- and second-person singular compared with the later appearance of first-person plural inflections. This order of emergence of (subject-marked) person referring expressions is well documented in other languages, and especially in English, where the equivalent (and obligatory) subject pronouns *I, you,* and *we* are productively, and in most cases also correctly used by children at MLU Stage I (Brown, 1973; Chiat, 1986; Strayer, 1977; Valian, 1991). Consistent with previous findings on Italian and other Romance languages (Clark, 1985), our data indicate that learning to mark the category of person by obligatory word-alternation patterns is not significantly different from learning to mark these notions by obligatory lexical items—as in English. However, within Italian, the optional/obligatory distinction appears to play a role in the developmental process: The optional subject person pronouns appear and/or are acquired later than the corresponding verb inflections (Pizzuto & Caselli, 1992).

Productive use of some verb inflections for person does not necessarily imply that children control subject-verb *agreement*. In a recent cross-sectional study of 50 Italian children (age range: 3;0 to 9;0 years), D'Amico and Devescovi (1993), using acting-out tasks, explored the role of verb morphology (vs. other semantic and syntactic factors such as animacy, word order) in the comprehension of simple declarative sentences. They found that adultlike use of verb morphology (including third-person singular inflections) as a major device for sentence interpretation develops only around 7 to 9 years of age. These results further indicate how morphological development is a gradual process, with different functions being mastered at rather different ages.

Consider now some of the possible explanations that may plausibly account for the relatively early mastery of the third-person singular present indicative in Italian (or, conversely, the relatively late mastery of the third-person singular present in English).

The first explanation revolves around a juxtaposition of pragmatic and morphological factors. The Italian children produced pragmatically inappropriate utterances in which they referred to themselves using their own names and a third-person, rather than a first-person verb. Utterances of this kind have been well documented in the child language literature (Chiat, 1986; Simões Perroni & Stoel-Gammon, 1979; Strayer, 1977), and probably reflect the difficulty that children experience with shifting reference in the first and second person. Yet this third-person bias presents a very different problem for English and Italian children. Because English provides a "zero option" in verb marking, English children can refer to themselves by name and finesse the problem of verb conjugation that this presents by using an unmarked verb. Italian children have no zero option available: If they choose to refer to themselves in the third person (for pragmatic reasons), then they have to choose some kind of explicit verb suffix to go with their name. As we have shown, they typically choose the third person. In fact, they may be forced into an earlier mastery of this particular inflection as a way of dealing with the problem of shifting reference in the absence of a zero option for morphological marking.

This explanation is compatible with other reports in the literature demonstrating that pragmatic motives sometimes force children to attack a morphosyntactic problem earlier than they might have otherwise preferred. This point has been noted by Demuth (1989), who showed that Lesotho children make frequent and productive use of passives by 2 to 3 years of age—presumably because this is the only way to carry out the pragmatic function of topicalization in their language. In a similar vein, the surprisingly early appearance of tag questions in English-speaking children can be explained if we remember that tag questions require a response from one's conversational partner, providing the child with a strong tool for guaranteeing adult attention and acknowledgment (Bates, 1976).

A second reason that may facilitate acquisition is that, as noted, in Italian as in most other languages (but not in English), the third-person singular inflection can be considered the most neutral or least marked form of the verb (Benveniste, 1946; Bybee, 1985; Jakobson, 1957; Greenberg, 1966). The unmarkedness of the Italian inflection may be even more salient, and perhaps more readily detectable for children, than in other languages because in the largest verb classes (first and second conjugation), the verb stem is homophonous with the inflection (e.g., *parla, cade*). Some of our data are consistent with this hypothesis: The largest majority of the verbs that the children used with a third-person singular inflection belonged to the first and second conjugation, and the forms produced were thus homophonous with verb stems (*N* across children: 39 to 49, or 82% to 87% of all verb roots inflected for third-person singular, and 111 to 201 or 75% to 83% of all corresponding tokens).

Other factors may also influence the disparity between English and Italian children in mastery of the third-person singular, and thereby generate a developmental delay (cf. Brown, 1973, pp. 260–261, 339–340; Cazden, 1968) or an advantage in, respectively, English and Italian. These include:

1. The English third-person inflection is the only marked form in the conjugation of main verbs; this contrasts with the uniformity and regularity of the Italian verbal paradigm marking all six person/number inflections.

2. The redundancy of the English inflection as a person marking device. In English information on the person and number of the subject is encoded by the obligatory pronominal or nominal subject—the third-person singular inflection is always redundant. The opposite is true for Italian, where the obligatory verb inflection provides the most reliable information or "cue" on person and number, whereas the nominal or pronominal subject is commonly optional.

3. The complex interaction, in English, between verb inflections and the auxiliary (and modal) system, with the related variability this entails: The third-person singular is used in simple declarative sentences, but in interrogatives and negatives the markers for tense and person shift to the auxiliaries (e.g., *Claudia plays* vs. *Does Claudia play?* or *Is Claudia playing? Claudia doesn't play*). A very different condition holds in Italian, where the same inflection remains constant across sentence types (e.g., *Claudia gioca* vs. *Claudia gioca?* or *Claudia sta giocando? Claudia non gioca*).

4. The English inflection is a final consonant that may be subject to the process of final consonant deletion, whereas the Italian third-person singular is marked by a final vowel. Final consonants (but not vowels) are notoriously difficult for children in the early stages of development. Leonard et al. (1987) suggested that this difference may explain why some inflections are used more proficiently by Italian children with specific language impairment, than their English counterparts.

5. The overall frequency of the English third-person inflection also appears to be significantly lower than, for example, the inflections for the present progressive or also the regular past tense, at least in child–adult speech (cf. Brown, 1973; J. G. de Villiers & P. A. de Villiers, 1985). As Brown (1973, p. 261) observed, "The data points for -*s* are, therefore,

based on smaller frequencies than those for the other two verbal inflections, and it is likely that the points of acquisition are somewhat less accurately placed." The opposite seems to hold for Italian, where this type of inflection is significantly more frequent than others.

6. Due mostly to the complex interaction between the third-person singular inflection and the auxiliary/modal system, the scoring of this inflection is often particularly difficult in English, even at the two-word stage (cf. Brown, 1973, p. 261). This difficulty was not encountered in the Italian data, especially after the children had reached the two-word stage.

The advantaging factors listed earlier for the Italian third-person indicative present inflection can be easily extended to the other Italian verb inflections marking person and number at least in the indicative/imperative paradigm, and can account for the (relative) ease with which two of our subjects acquired some of them.

Primarily phonological and perceptual features, related with the syllabic and stress patterns of Italian verbs, can account for the errorless performance over first-person plural indicative/imperative inflections, which we noted in all three children. The -iamo inflection is bisyllabic, and receives primary stress: Both these features greatly enhance its perceptual salience, and can be assumed to play a major role in facilitating its acquisition (U. Bortolini, personal communication, December 1992). This is consistent with Leonard et al.'s (1987, 1992), and Pye's (1983) findings on the importance of phonological and intonational factors for morphological development. Our data also provide some indications on the different role of stress versus syllabic structure. If the bisyllabic structure of a given inflection were by itself a primary determinant for the order of acquisition of morphemes, we could have expected that other bisyllabic inflections be used productively or acquired at the same time, particularly within the relatively productive present-tense paradigm. On the contrary, within each child, and across children, we noted a correct and significantly more productive use of the stressed first-person plural, and a nonproductive, and in some cases erroneous use of the unstressed third-person plural inflection. This indicates that stress plays a greater role than the syllabic structure by itself.

The developmental patterns of different plural inflections also clarify that, contrary to Hyams' (1992) conclusion, the generally nonproductive use of plural inflections in the Italian children we studied cannot be attributed to their preference in talking, or not talking, about plural things. Some plural inflections are used, and more productively than others, and this appears to depend, at least in part, from the syllabic and stress features of the word-alternation patterns to be acquired.

In addition, we cannot dismiss the role that the frequency of each inflection in parental input may play in development. The first-person plural inflection is commonly used in child–adult interaction as a relatively unmarked verb form, especially in hortative/imperative and interrogative utterances (e.g., *dai, giochiamo* 'come on, let's play', or *mangiamo, adesso?* 'should we eat now?'). It is very likely that this inflection is used more frequently than other plural inflections, and this may in part explain not only its earlier appearance, but also the sparse use of third-person plural, and the virtual absence of second-person plural inflections in our children's repertoires.

It is of interest to mention that some of the regularities noted in the children's verb production have been recently identified in the language that the mother and other adults used in the corpus of Francesco, one of the subjects of present study. Analyses conducted by Tangorra (1990) and Pizzuto (1990) showed the following: In the adults' production, as in the child's, singular forms of verbs largely predominated over plural forms. The largest majority of verbs were finite, simple, mostly present-tense forms of main verbs; among these, the forms most frequently used were those inflected for third-person singular, and this was true especially in the samples corresponding to the child's youngest ages. This is particularly interesting if we recall that this inflection was also the first to be acquired by Francesco, and the one exhibiting the more regular developmental pattern across the three children. In addition, in referring to herself while playing the role of speaker the mother frequently used the expression for "mommy" and, concurrently, a third-person inflected verb, instead of a first-person pronoun and/or verb inflection. This "motherese" phenomenon was also observed, albeit to minor extent, in the other adults interacting with Francesco.

In sum, we find that no single, unifying explanation can be given for the developmental patterns we observed. A variety of concurring formal, distributional, phonological, pragmatic, and semantic factors seem to be involved. More generally, there is good reason to question the assumption that, in terms of learning processes, the richness of the Italian verb inflectional paradigm may render it harder to acquire, as for example hypothesized, or implicitly assumed by Hyams (1986a, 1992). If the information presented to the child is consistent, then more information (i.e., more consistent morphological contrasts) may actually decrease the difficulty of a learning task. This is compatible with the findings of several cross-linguistic studies as reported by Slobin (1982) (see also Johnston & Slobin, 1979; Slobin, 1973, 1985a; Slobin & Bever, 1982). These studies have explored the development of basic grammatical and semantic notions such as locative, patienthood, and possessive relations across different language types: languages with relatively simple inflectional systems such as English, languages with richer but relatively inconsistent inflectional morphology such as Serbo-Croatian, and languages with a very rich but highly regular and consistent inflectional system such as Turkish. Not surprisingly, the second language type results in the slowest rate of learning. However, the fastest rate of learning was observed not in the simple system, but in the system that presents the child with a larger number of consistent contrasts. It remains to be seen whether this phenomenon is a special characteristic of language learning, or a more general feature of learning mechanisms and processes that language shares with other cognitive domains.

ACKNOWLEDGMENTS

A version of this chapter was presented at the workshop on "Crosslinguistic and cross-populations contributions to theories of language acquisition," held at the Hebrew University of Jerusalem in June 1991. We would like to thank all the workshop participants for stimulating discussions over the ideas expressed. We are particularly indebted to Ruth Berman for many valuable, detailed comments and suggestions on an earlier draft. Comments and suggestions received from Elizabeth Bates, Cristina Burani, Margherita Orsolini, and Virginia Volterra are also gratefully acknowledged. All the errors and misunderstandings that remain despite their best efforts are entirely our own. Part of the data reported here have also been described, in a different form, in Pizzuto and Caselli (1992, in press). Partial financial support was provided by the CNR FATMA Project.

REFERENCES

Aksu-Koç, A. A. & Slobin, D. I. (1985). The acquisition of Turkish. In D. I. Slobin (Ed.), *The crosslinguistic study of language acquisition* (pp. 838–878). Hillsdale, NJ: Lawrence Erlbaum Associates.

Antinucci, F., & Parisi, D. (1973). Early language acquisition: A model and some data. In C. A. Ferguson & D. I. Slobin (Eds.), *Studies of child language development* (pp. 607–619). New York: Holt, Rinehart & Winston.

Antinucci, F., & Miller, R. (1976). How children talk about what happened. *Journal of Child Language, 3*, 169–189.

Bates, E. (1976). *Language and context: The acquisition of pragmatics*. New York: Academic Press.

Bates, E., & Carnevale, G. (1992). *Developmental psychology in the 1990s: Language development* (Tech. Rep. No. 9204). San Diego: Center for Research in Language, University of California.

Bates, E., Bretherton, I., & Snyder, L. (1988). *From first word to grammar: Individual differences and dissociable mechanisms*. Cambridge: Cambridge University Press.

Bates, E., & MacWhinney, B. (1982). Functional approaches to grammar. In E. Wanner & L. Gleitman (Eds.), *Language acquisition: The state of the art* (pp. 173–218). Cambridge, England: Cambridge University Press.

Bates, E., & MacWhinney, B. (1989). Functionalism and the competition model. In B. Mac-Whinney & E. Bates (Eds.), *The cross-linguistic study of sentence processing* (pp. 3–73). Cambridge: Cambridge University Press.

Benveniste, E. (1946). Structures des relations de personne dans le verbe. *Bulletin de la Société de Linguistique, 43*(1), 1–12.

Berman, R. (1981). Regularity vs. anomaly: The acquisition of Hebrew inflectional morphology. *Journal of Child Language, 8*, 265–282.

Berman, R. (1982). Verb-pattern alternation: The interface of morphology, syntax, and semantics in Hebrew child language. *Journal of Child Language, 9*, 169–191.

Berman, R. A. (1985). The acquisition of Hebrew. In D. I. Slobin (Ed.), *The crosslinguistic study of language acquisition* (pp. 255–371). Hillsdale, NJ: Lawrence Erlbaum Associates.

Berman, R. (1991). In defense of development. *Behavioral and Brain Sciences, 14*, 612–613.

Bloom, L., Lifter, K., & Hafitz, J. (1980). Semantics of the verbs and the development of verb inflection in child language. *Language, 56*, 366–412.

Bortolini, U. (1987, June). *Phonological development in Italian children.* Paper presented at the International Symposium on Language Acquisition and Language Impairment in Children, Salsomaggiore Terme, Italy.

Bortolini, U. (1993). Continuità fonetica fra "babbling" e prime parole. In M. Moneglia & E. Cresti (Eds.), *Ricerche sull'acquisizione dell'Italiano* (pp. 45–61). Roma: Bulzoni Editore.

Bortolini, U. (in press). *Lo sviluppo fonologico.* Padova: Libreria Progetto.

Bortolini, U., & Zampolli, A. (1979). Frequenza e distribuzione dei gruppi consonantici nella lingua italiana. *Acta Phoniatrica Latina, 2*, 195–206.

Brown, R. (1973). *A first language: The early stages* (2nd ed.). Cambridge, MA: Harvard University Press.

Bybee Hooper, J. (1979). Child morphology and morphophonemic change. *Linguistics, 17*, 21–50.

Bybee, J. (1985). *Morphology: A study of the relation between meaning and form.* Amsterdam: John Benjamins.

Caselli, M. C., & Casadio, P. (in press). Sviluppo lessicale e prima grammatica nel secondo anno di vita. *Età Evolutiva.*

Caselli, M. C., Leonard, L. B., Volterra, V., & Campagnoli, M. G. (1993). Toward mastery of Italian morphology: A cross-sectional study. *Journal of Child Language, 20*, 377–393.

Cazden, C. B. (1968). The acquisition of noun and verb inflections. *Child Development, 39*, 433–448.

Chiat, S. (1986). Personal pronouns. In P. Fletcher & M. Garman (Eds.), *Language acquisition: Studies in first language development* (2nd ed., pp. 339–355). Cambridge: Cambridge University Press.

Chilosi, A. M., & Cipriani, P. (1991). *Il bambino disfasico.* Pisa: Edizioni del Cerro.

Chomsky, N. (1981). *Lectures on government and binding.* Dordrecht: Foris.

Clark, E. V. (1985). The acquisition of Romance, with special reference to French. In D. I. Slobin (Ed.), *The cross-linguistic study of language acquisition* (pp. 687–782). Hillsdale, NJ: Lawrence Erlbaum Associates.

Clark, E., & Berman, R. A. (1984). Structure and use in the acquisition of word formation. *Language, 60*(3), 542–599.

Crain, S. (1991). Language acquisition in the absence of experience. *Behavioral and Brain Sciences, 14*, 597–650.

Dardano, M., & Trifone, P. (1985). *La lingua italiana.* Bologna: Zanichelli.

D'Amico, S., & Devescovi, A. (1993). Processi di comprensione nei bambini italiani: l'interpretazione della frase semplice. In E. Cresti & M. Moneglia (Eds.), *Ricerche sull'acquisizione dell'Italiano* (pp. 273–289). Roma: Bulzoni Editore.

Demuth, K. (1989). Maturation and the acquisition of the Sesotho passive. *Language, 65*(1), 56–80.

de Villiers, J. G., & de Villiers, P. A. (1973). A cross-sectional study of the acquisition of grammatical morphemes in child speech. *Journal of Psycholinguistic Research, 2,* 267–278.

de Villiers, J. G., & de Villiers, P. A. (1985). The acquisition of English. In D. I. Slobin (Ed.), *The cross-linguistic study of language acquisition* (pp. 27–139). Hillsdale, NJ: Lawrence Erlbaum Associates.

Dromi, E., & Berman, R. (1982). A morphemic measure of early language development: Data from Israeli Hebrew. *Journal of Child Language, 9,* 169–181.

Drozd, K. F. (1989). Language acquisition and the theory of parameters. *Language, 65*(2), 406–413.

Gordon, P., & Chafetz, J. (1990). Verb-based versus class-based accounts of actionality effects. *Cognition, 36,* 227–254.

Grant, J., & Karmiloff-Smith, A. (1991). Diagnostics for domain-specific constraints. *Behavioral and Brain Sciences, 14,* 621–622.

Greenberg, J. (1966). Language universals. In T. A. Sebeok (Ed.), *Current trends in linguistics* (Vol. 3, pp. 61–112). The Hague: Mouton.

Hickey, T. (1991). Mean length of utterance and the acquisition of Irish. *Journal of Child Language, 18,* 553–569.

Hyams, N. M. (1986a, October). *Core and peripheral grammar and the acquisition of inflections.* Paper presented at the 11th Annual Boston University Conference on Language Development, Boston.

Hyams, N. M. (1986b). *Language acquisition and the theory of parameters.* Dordrecht: Reidel.

Hyams, N. M. (1987). The theory of parameters and syntactic development. In T. Roeper & E. Williams (Eds.), *Parameter setting* (pp. 1–22). Dordrecht: Reidel.

Hyams, N. M. (1988). A principles-and-parameters approach to the study of child language. *Papers and Reports on Child Language Development, 27,* 153–161.

Hyams, N. M. (1991). *Comments on the paper by Pizzuto and Caselli.* Unpublished typescript circulated at the Workshop on cross-linguistic and cross-population contributions to theories of language acquisition, Jerusalem, Israel.

Hyams, N. M. (1992). Morphosyntactic development in Italian and its relevance to parameter-setting models: Comments on the paper by Pizzuto and Caselli. *Journal of Child Language, 19,* 695–709.

Jaeggli, O., & Safir, K. J. (1989a). The null subject parameter and parametric theory. In O. Jaeggli & K. J. Safir (Eds.), *The null subject parameter* (pp. 1–44). Dordrecht: Kluwer.

Jaeggli, O., & Safir, K. J. (Eds.). (1989b). *The null subject parameter.* Dordrecht: Kluwer.

Jakobson, R. (1957). *Shifters, verbal categories and the Russian verb.* Cambridge, MA: Harvard University Press.

Johnston, J. R., & Slobin, D. I. (1979). The development of locative expressions in English, Italian, Serbo-Croatian and Turkish. *Journal of Child Language, 6,* 529–545.

Karmiloff-Smith, A. (1979). *A functional approach to child language.* Cambridge: Cambridge University Press.

Karmiloff-Smith, A. (1991). Beyond modularity: Innate constraints and developmental change. In S. Carey & R. Gelman (Eds.), *Epigenesis of mind: Essays in biology and knowledge* (pp. 171–197). Hillsdale, NJ: Lawrence Erlbaum Associates.

Kuczaj, S. A. II. (1977). The acquisition of regular and irregular past tense forms. *Journal of Verbal Learning and Verbal Behavior, 16,* 589–600.

Lebeaux, D. (1987). Comments on Hyams. In T. Roeper & E. Williams (Eds.), *Parameter setting* (pp. 23–39). Dordrecht: Reidel.

Leonard, L. B., Bortolini, U., Caselli, M. C., McGregor, K. K., & Sabbadini, L. (1992). Morphological deficits in children with specific language impairment: The status of features in the underlying grammar. *Language Acquisition, 2*(2), 151–179.

Leonard, L. B., Sabbadini, L., Leonard, J., & Volterra, V. (1987). Specific language impairment in children: A cross-linguistic study. *Brain and Language, 32*, 233–252.

Lepschy, A. L., & Lepschy, G. (1988). *The Italian language today* (2nd ed.). London: Hutchinson.

Levy, Y. (1983a). The acquisition of Hebrew plurals: The case of the missing gender category. *Journal of Child Language, 10*, 107–121.

Levy, Y. (1983b). It's frogs all the way down. *Cognition, 15*, 73–93.

Loeb, D. F., & Leonard, L. B. (1988). Specific language impairment and parameter theory. *Clinical Linguistics and Phonetics, 2*(4), 317–327.

MacWhinney, B. (1978). The acquisition of morphophonology. *Monographs of the Society for Research in Child Development, 43*(1).

MacWhinney, B. (1985). Hungarian language acquisition as an exemplification of a general model of grammatical development. In D. I. Slobin (Ed.), *The cross-linguistic study of language acquisition* (pp. 1069–1155). Hillsdale, NJ: Lawrence Erlbaum Associates.

MacWhinney, B. (1991a). *The CHILDES project*. Hillsdale, NJ: Lawrence Erlbaum Associates.

MacWhinney, B. (1991b). Connectionism as a framework for language acquisition theory. In J. F. Miller (Ed.), *Research on child language disorders* (pp. 73–103). Austin, TX: Pro-Ed.

MacWhinney, B., & Leinbach, J. (1991). Implementations are not conceptualizations: Revising the verb learning model. *Cognition, 40*, 121–157.

MacWhinney, B., Leinbach, J., Taraban, R., & McDonald, J. (1989). Language learning: Cues or rules? *Journal of Memory and Language, 28*, 255–277.

MacWhinney, B., & Snow, C. (1985). The Child Language Data Exchange System. *Journal of Child Language, 12*, 271–296.

MacWhinney, B., & Snow, C. (1990). The Child Language Data Exchange System: An update. *Journal of Child Language, 17*, 457–472.

Maratsos, M. (1983). Some current issues in the study of the acquisition of grammar. In P. H. Mussen (Ed.), *Handbook of child psychology* (Vol. 3, pp. 707–786). New York: Wiley.

Maratsos, M. P., & Chalkley, M. A. (1980). The internal language of children's syntax: The ontogenesis and representation of syntactic categories. In K. E. Nelson (Ed.), *Children's language* (Vol. 2, pp. 127–214). New York: Gardner Press.

Matthews, P. H. (1974). *Morphology—An introduction to the theory of word structure*. Cambridge: Cambridge University Press.

Newmeyer, F. J. (1988). Extensions and implications of linguistic theory: An overview. In F. J. Newmayer (Ed.), *Linguistics: The Cambridge survey: Vol. 2. Linguistic theory: Extensions and implications* (pp. 1–14). Cambridge: Cambridge University Press.

O'Grady, W., Peters, A. M., & Masterson, D. (1989). The transition from optional to required subjects. *Journal of Child Language, 16*, 513–529.

Pizzuto, E. (1990, December). *Unpublished computerized analyses of patterns of correspondence between input and output in one child's acquisition of Italian verb morphology*. Institute of Psychology, CNR, Rome.

Pizzuto, E., & Caselli, M. C. (1991, June). *The acquisition of Italian morphology in a cross-linguistic perspective*. Paper presented at the Workshop on cross-linguistic and cross-population contributions to theories of language acquisition, Jerusalem, Israel.

Pizzuto, E., & Caselli, M. C. (1992). The acquisition of Italian morphology: Implications for models of language development. *Journal of Child Language, 19*, 491–557.

Pizzuto, E., & Caselli, M. C. (1993). L'acquisizione della morfologia flessiva nel linguaggio spontaneo: evidenza per modelli innatisti o cognitivisti? In E. Cresti & M. Moneglia (Eds.), *Ricerche sull'acquisizione dell'Italiano* (pp. 165–187). Roma: Bulzoni Editore.

Pizzuto, E., Caselli, M. C., & Tangorra, T. (1991, October). *The acquisition of Italian definite articles: Insights from the study of natural language and neural networks*. Paper presented at the 16th Annual Boston University Conference on Language Development, Boston.

Plunkett, K., & Marchman, V. A. (1990). U-shaped learning and frequency effects in a multilayered perceptron: Implications for child language acquisition. *Cognition, 38*, 1–60.

Pye, C. (1983). Mayan telegraphese: Intonational determinants of inflectional development in Quiché Mayan. *Language, 59*(3), 583–604.

Radford, A. (1990). *Syntactic theory and the acquisition of English syntax*. Oxford: Blackwell.

Rizzi, L. (1982). *Issues in Italian syntax*. Dordrecht: Foris.

Rizzi, L. (1986). Null objects in Italian and the theory of pro. *Linguistic Inquiry, 3*, 501–557.

Roeper, T. (1986). Preface. In N. M. Hyams, *Language acquisition and the theory of parameters* (pp. ix–xii). Dordrecht: Reidel.

Roeper, T. (1988). Grammatical principles of first language acquisition: Theory and evidence. In F. J. Newmayer (Ed.), *Linguistics: The Cambridge survey: Vol. 2. Linguistic theory: Extensions and implications* (pp. 35–52). Cambridge: Cambridge University Press.

Roeper, T., & Williams, E. (Eds.). (1987). *Parameter setting*. Dordrecht: Reidel.

Rumelhart, D. E., & McClelland, J. L. (1986). On learning the past tenses of English verbs. In J. L. McClelland, D. E. Rumelhart, & the PDP Research Group (Eds.), *Parallel distributed processing: Explorations in the microstructure of cognition* (Vol. 2, pp. 216–271). Cambridge, MA: MIT Press.

Scalise, S. (1990). *Morfologia e lessico*. Bologna: Il Mulino. (Original English ed. *Generative morphology*. Dordrecht: Foris, 1984).

Simões Perroni, M. C., & Stoel-Gammon, C. (1979). The acquisition of inflections in Portuguese: A study of the development of person markers on verbs. *Journal of Child Language, 6*, 53–67.

Slobin, D. I. (1973). Cognitive prerequisites for the development of grammar. In C. A. Ferguson & D. I. Slobin (Eds.), *Studies of child language development* (pp. 175–208). New York: Holt, Rinehart & Winston.

Slobin, D. I. (1982). Universal and particular in the acquisition of language. In E. Wanner & L. Gleitman (Eds.), *Language acquisition: The state of the art* (pp. 128–170). Cambridge: Cambridge University Press.

Slobin, D. I. (1985a). Crosslinguistic evidence for the language-making capacity. In D. I. Slobin (Ed.), *The crosslinguistic study of language acquisition* (pp. 1157–1249). Hillsdale, NJ: Lawrence Erlbaum Associates.

Slobin, D. I. (Ed.). (1985b). *The crosslinguistic study of language acquisition* (Vol. 1–2). Hillsdale, NJ: Lawrence Erlbaum Associates.

Slobin, D. I. (1988). Confessions of a wayward Chomskyan. *Papers and Reports on Child Language Development, 27*, 131–136.

Slobin, D. I. (1991). Can Crain constrain the constraints? *Behavioral and Brain Sciences, 14*, 633–634.

Slobin, D. I., & Bever, T. G. (1982). Children use canonical sentence schemas: A crosslinguistic study of word order and inflections. *Cognition, 12*, 229–265.

Smith, A. (1988). Language acquisition: Learnability, maturation and the fixing of parameters. *Cognitive Neuropsychology, 5*(2), 235–265.

Smoczynska, M. (1985). The acquisition of Polish. In D. I. Slobin (Ed.), *The cross-linguistic study of language acquisition* (pp. 595–686). Hillsdale, NJ: Lawrence Erlbaum Associates.

Strayer, E. (1977). *The development of personal reference in the language of the 2 year olds*. Unpublished doctoral dissertation, Montreal, McGill University.

Tangorra, A. (1990). *Input e output riconsiderati: Analisi computerizzate di alcune regolarità nell'acquisizione dell'italiano.* Unpublished doctoral dissertation, Rome, University of Rome "La Sapienza."

Valian, V. (1990). Null subjects: A problem for parameter-setting models of language acquisition. *Cognition, 35,* 105–122.

Valian, V. (1991). Syntactic subjects in the early speech of American and Italian children. *Cognition, 40,* 21–81.

Vincent, N. (1987). Italian. In B. Comrie (Ed.), *The world's major languages* (pp. 279–302). London: Croom Helm.

Volterra, V. (1976). A few remarks on the use of the past tense in child language. *Italian Linguistics, 2,* 149–157.

Weist, R. M., Wysocka, H., Witkowska-Stadnik, K., Buczowska, E., & Konieczna, E. (1984). The defective tense hypothesis: On the emergence of tense and aspect in child Polish. *Journal of Child Language, 11,* 347–374.

CHAPTER SEVEN

Developmental Perspectives on Transitivity: A Confluence of Cues

Ruth A. Berman

Tel Aviv University, Israel

The study argues for a developmentally motivated view of language acquisition, and for multiple mechanisms to account for the passage from entry to exit in the process. Linguistic knowledge such as transitivity marking is not acquired in a single step, but involves partial and piecemeal knowledge en route from initial to endstate mastery. And there is no strict dichotomy between the principled, rule-bound knowledge of syntax and idiosyncratic knowledge of lexical particulars. Rather, children rely concurrently on a "confluence of cues"—prosodic, semantic, syntactic, and lexical—to bootstrap into, and move across, acquisition of linguistic structure. This view is consistent with the idea of "multiple bootstrapping" suggested by Shatz (1987), but the notion of multiple cues applies beyond initial entry into a system, taking into account subsequent reconstruals across the developmental path.

In attending to these different cues, children are guided by different psycholinguistic factors (e.g., typological bias, rhetorical options, and levels of lexical productivity) and they have recourse to various acquisitional strategies (e.g., rote learning, avoidance, or overgeneralization), which interact in language learning and in language use.

The linguistic system analyzed in support of these claims concerns transitivity distinctions in Hebrew. I propose that knowledge of the major fact of transitivity, that predicates take one or more arguments, need not be learned. Relatedly, children do not need to learn that there are different kinds of verb-argument relations in the most general sense of people performing an activity on their own or in relation to some other entity as against something happening or being in a state. These universal distinctions are expressed from the time children produce clauselike utterances. The moment children start formulating clauses, they do so with all kinds of predicates (including existentials and possessives, which are not considered here), whatever their mother tongue. That is, there are two interrelated sets of universal semantic distinctions underlying children's acquisition of systems of transitivity: The major thematic roles such as the difference between doer and receiver or agent and undergoer, and the major types of predicates, such as the difference between activity, state, and event, between doing versus being or becoming. These are universal categories distinguished in the semantics of all natural languages, in line with Talmy's (1987, 1988) proposals concerning a universal set of conceptual systems, which are shaped by (and possibly also shape) human cognition, and are specialized for verbal expression by grammatical means (Slobin, 1991). This shared, basic set of distinctions sets constraints on the hypotheses children can construe about possible form–meaning relations in the mother tongue and hence are presumed accessible to children at the phase of early syntax.

Children do, however, need to learn the particular means employed for marking these distinctions by the syntax of their language, through the grammatical devices of constituent word order, case marking, and/or (classifier or inflectional) agreement. In Hebrew, as in other languages, this knowledge is mastered rapidly, by around age 2;6, as part of early grammatical development (section 1). Children also need to learn the morpholexical properties of transitivity marking specified by their native tongue. In Hebrew, as a Semitic language, valency distinctions are expressed by verb morphology, analogous to a few frozen alternations in Modern English (e.g., *rise* vs. *raise, sit* vs. *seat,* or *fall* vs. *fell*); in the Hebrew counterparts of these pairs, both verbs share the same root (*kam* vs. *hekim, yashav* vs. *hoshiv,* or *nafal* vs. *hipil,* respectively; section 2).[1] In general, English relies on other devices: idiosyncratic lexical alternation (e.g., *learn* vs. *teach, eat* vs. *feed*; cf. Hebrew *lamad* vs. *limed, axal* vs. *he'exil*); changes in syntactic configuration (*the boy broke the window* vs. *the window broke.* cf. Hebrew *shavar* vs. *nishbar*); or syntactic auxiliaries (e.g., *sicken* = intransitive inchoative *get sick* vs. transitive causative *make sick,* cf. Hebrew *xala* vs. *hexli*). As these examples

---

[1]Hebrew verbs are cited in the morphologically simple form of past-tense, third-person masculine singular, unless otherwise specified. The stops *p, b,* and *k* may alternate with the fricatives *f, v,* and *x* in different forms of verbs constructed from the same consonantal root.

suggest, children also need to learn the specific subcategorization properties of verbs and the membership of verb classes entering into different verb-argument relations, because these will differ from one language to another. For instance, the Hebrew counterparts of English verbs listed in Levin (1989, pp. 5–12) as sharing various transitivity alternations would fall into rather different groupings.

A number of interrelated claims about the nature of language development underlie my analysis of how children acquire the morphosyntax of transitivity in Hebrew (section 3). First, language acquisition is viewed as a stepwise progression from unanalyzed, rote knowledge of isolated forms to structure-dependent, rule-governed representations of individual systems, which are subsequently integrated by knowledge of conventions of language use and how these systems function in extended discourse (Berman, 1986b). Second, language acquisition is construed as starting out with shared, cross-linguistic principles and constraints, and as moving toward greater sensitivity to typologically relevant factors, eventually being narrowed down to a highly language-particular construal of linguistic structures (Berman, 1986a). Third, this narrowing down from most universal to most particular explains the relatively early mastery of the syntax of transitivity, before systematic morphological marking of this distinction, which in turn precedes specific lexical knowledge about conventions of usage, lexical exceptions, and incidental gaps (Berman, in press-a).

These developments converge as follows along three interrelated dimensions in acquisition of transitivity distinctions as well as of other domains of linguistic knowledge.

(1) a. Item-based > structure-dependent > usage-sensitive
    b. Language-shared > language type > mother tongue
    c. Simple-clause syntax > word-level morphology > vocabulary mastery

Morphology, or word structure, has a special status in this analysis, as a highly language-particular phenomenon, which typically formed the basis for traditional structuralist classifications of language types.[2] A central aim of this study is to examine how children proceed from a typological (Semitic) bias to language-particular form–meaning correspondences and eventual command of lexical specificity. The developmental pattern that emerges is accounted for by the interrelated factors of typo-

---

[2]Word formation also tends to be a particularly robust facet of language structure. Even where a language like Hebrew has undergone quite a radical typological change in the course of its history, its means for new word formation will remain relatively stable.

logically pervasive structures constraining early grammatical development, target language preferences determining the range of expressive
options available to children at different phases of development, and the
relative productivity of a given device in both structure and use (section
3.2). These factors also explain *when* children acquire transitivity marking
via the *binyan* verb patterns compared with other forms constructed
through the *binyan* system: (a) endstate resultatives and denominal verbs,
acquired in parallel with transitivity distinctions; and (b) syntactic passives and action nominals, which constitute later acquisitions (section 4.3).

1. SYNTACTIC TRANSITIVITY

Structural cues that contrast transitive with intransitive constructions include word order, case marking, and subject–verb agreement. Examples
(2) to (4) compare pairs of Hebrew sentences with (a) high and (b) low
transitivity (Hopper & Thompson, 1980; Slobin, 1985). The prepositional
et is the accusative object marker, and the letter *P* plus integer specifies
each of five verb patterns.[3] Agreement marking is noted for plural number (PL) and/or feminine gender (FM); masculine singular is taken as neutral, and not noted in the glosses.

(2) a. *Ron shafax* [P1] *et ha- mits.*
       Ron spilt   OM the juice

   b. *ha- mits nishpax* [P2]
      the juice spilt

(3) a. *ha- isha   horida   [P5]   et ha- yeladim (me ha- mita)*
       the woman took-down + FM OM the boys   (off the bed)

   b. *ha- yeladim yardu   [P1]   (me ha- mita)*
      the-boys   got-down + PL   (off the bed)

(4) a. *ha- yalda mesovevet [P3]   et   ha- matbe'ot (al ha- xut)*
       the girl   is-turning + FM OM the coins   (on the string)

   b. *ha- matbe'ot mistovevot [P4]   (al ha- xut)*
      the coins   are-turning + FM (on the string)

The transitive (a) sentences have the form Noun-Verb-Noun (NVN) corresponding to Subject-Verb-Object (SVO); the first noun is semantic agent
and the second is patient; the verb agrees with the first noun—its gram-

---

[3]These cover all five active and middle-voice patterns, but exclude the two patterns
of *pu'al* and *hof'al*, which function as passive-voice counterparts of P3 and P5 and as such
are rare in child language input as well as output (see discussion in section 4.2).

matical subject—in number and gender; and the second noun—the grammatical object—is marked by *et* as accusative. That is, word order, grammatical agreement, and case marking conspire to mark these sentences as transitive. In the (b) sentences, the grammatical subject is also sentence initial and governs number and gender agreement with the verb. As intransitives, they need have no second NP; when they do, its NP is obligatorily oblique, and takes a preposition other than accusative *et*, for example, *mi* 'from, off' or *al* 'on'. The (a) and (b) sentences also differ in verb morphology: (2a) and (2b) share the root sh-p-x 'spill', in two different forms—Trans(itive) P1 and Intr(ansitive) P2; (3a) and (3b) share the root y-r-d, again in two different patterns, but here P1 marks the intransitive version; and in (4), the root s-b-b 'turn, rotate' is used in two more patterns, Trans P3 and Intr P4 (see fn. 1).

Children's initial construals of transitivity are guided by canonical schemata, as argued for in comprehension studies by Slobin (1981, 1982) for English, Italian, Serbo-Croatian, Turkish, and also Hebrew, and by Hakuta (1982) for Japanese in contrast with English. Hebrew-speaking children demonstrate rapid and early acquisition of three structural cues to transitivity: word order, object case marking, and subject–verb number and gender agreement—typically in that order. This combination of cues gives them early and reliable recourse to a canonic sentence schema of the form shown in (5) as characteristic of all, though not necessarily only, transitive constructions.

(5) N_1 V   Pr N_2 =   S V O

N_1 stands for the grammatical subject, which has zero case marking, and governs number, gender, and person agreement on V; N_2 is a nominal complement, a nonsubject argument; and Pr is a case marking prepositional, which may but need not be the accusative object marker (OM) *et*, as in (6).

(6)	(i)	a.	*hu daxaf*	[P1] *et hakadur*	= He pushed OM the ball
		b.	*hu ba'at*	[P1] ***ba** kadur*	= He kicked at the ball
	(ii)	a.	*hu hika*	[P5] *et ha-xamor*	= He beat OM the donkey
		b.	*hu hirbits*	[P5] ***la** xamor*	= He hit to the donkey
	(iii)	a.	*hu nitseax*	[P3] *et ha-ax shelo*	= He defeated OM his brother
		b.	*hu hitgaber*	[P4] ***al** ha-ax shelo*	= He overcame on his brother
	(iv)	a.	*hu ahav*	[P1] *et ha- misxak*	= He liked OM the game
		b.	*hu nehena*	[P2] ***me** ha-misxak*	= He enjoyed from the game

Semantically, the same relations hold between the verb and the patient or object NP in the (a) and (b) sentences of each pair; but in the (b) sentences, the verb governs an object with prepositions other than *et* (*be, le, al, me*), which are both obligatory and nonalternating. Syntactically, the (b) sentences are less transitive; for instance, only the *et* marked verbs like those in (a) permit passivization and construct-state nominalization. But they are closely parallel in surface structure and thematic relations. That is, all the sentences in (6) obey the schema in (5).

Children acquiring Hebrew can thus rely on different structural cues to transivity: (a) *word order*—the surface array of argument nominals vis-à-vis the predicate; (b) *case marking*—zero versus accusative *et* or oblique prepositions; and (c) *verb inflections*—marking number and gender agreement between the subject nominal and the predicate verb. I argue that the unmarked, canonic SV(O) schema has such a privileged status that other word-order options are largely irrelevant to early acquisition of valency distinctions (section 1.1); the distinction between accusative versus nominative and other prepositional case marking is critical (section 1.2); and subject–verb agreement is a slightly later development that depends on command of the grammatical relations of subject and object (section 1.3).

1.1. Word Order: SV(O), VS, and VO

Basic word order of everyday Hebrew is clearly SV(O) in both structure and use, even though Hebrew also allows VS order (Givon, 1976). In structural terms, all three predicate types—transitive verbs, intransitive activity verbs, and intransitive change-of-state verbs or so-called "unaccusatives" (Borer & Grodzinsky, 1986; Perlmutter, 1978)—can take an initial subject, that is, occur in SV order; and SV but not VS constructions, allow either a lexical noun or pronoun, and both definite and indefinite NPs, as surface subject. Across a wide range of spoken corpora, including conversational usage and narratives of adults and children, we found very low occurrence of the VS option in either child input or output.[4] Strings of a lexical verb followed by a lexical subject accounted for

---

[4]The naturalistic materials relied on in this study include: (a) longitudinal corpora—a brother and sister in intermittent interaction with each other from ages 1;10 to 5;6 years of age, and another 3 girls and 1 boy starting around age 1;6, and going up to 3 years in interaction with their parents (Berman & Weissenborn, 1991); (b) cross-sectional speech samples of over 100 children from ages 1;6 to 5;6 (Dromi & Berman, 1986); (c) narratives based on a picture storybook elicited from preschoolers age 3 to 5 years, schoolchildren age 7 to 12 years, and Hebrew-speaking adults (Berman, 1988); and (d) a collection of over

at most 5% of all clauses analyzed, while obligatorily predicate-initial existential and possessive constructions came to another 5%. The bulk of all utterances were either SV subject-initial, both transitive and intransitive, or else subjectless, predicate-initial constructions, for example, impersonals and verbs marked inflectionally for first or second person (Berman, 1990a). Further evidence for the strong bias toward (S)VO order is the general avoidance of object-initial OSV or OVS options, and the very few dislocations and other types of noncanonic word order that we found in preschool children's input as well as output, even though Hebrew tolerates a range of left dislocations and topicalizations that move nonsubject arguments and adjuncts to utterance-initial position.

In sum, Hebrew child language input and output utterances are predominantly either SV or else lacking in a surface subject. Correlation of surface word order with the semantic distinction between actor-controlled activity versus patient-endured event or between different syntactic classes of intransitive constructions is thus not a reliable basis for children to acquire Hebrew transivity (despite certain formal claims to the contrary, as in Borer & Grodzinsky, 1986).

1.2. Case Marking and Grammatical Relations

In contrast to the lack of fit between surface word order and syntactic transitivity, the grammatical status of subject compared with direct and oblique objects provides a highly relevant cue to transitivity distinctions. An important surface feature of the grammatical subject in Hebrew, apart from its syntactically unmarked position as clause initial NP, is that it alone has no prepositional case marking, and it governs verb agreement. Initial word combinations, in Hebrew as in other languages, typically lack any grammatical marking of the subject relation, but by early in their third year, children no longer manifest indiscriminate subject omission in contexts that require a grammatical surface subject. From ages 1;9 to 2;4, six different children (see fn. 4) learned to use a surface subject as required by Hebrew grammar, with verbs in the third person and/or in present tense, and they also started to alternate null subjects with third-person pronoun and expletive subjects (Armon-Lotem & Kfir, 1990; Berman, 1990a). Their shared acquisitional pattern is charted in (7) for one highly precocious child (Smadar, a girl) and two others with more typical rates of language development (Hagar, a girl, and Leor, a slightly slower boy).

---

600 unconventional lexical usages collected from the 6 children in our longitudinal sample, from parental reports on another 10 to 12 children, and from published records of Hebrew children's coinages in the 1930s to 1950s (Berman & Clark, 1992).

(7) Steps in Early Acquisition of Grammatical Subject and Null Subjects:

0 *Pregrammatical*
Low MLU, no productive verb inflections
No surface subjects, no grammatical null subjects

I *Initial Acquisition: Restricted Subjects*
Some alternating verb inflections
Deictic *ze* 'it, this' or lexical subjects
Occasional grammatical null subjects
Smadar 1;6   Hagar 1;7   Leor 1;9

II *Main Acquisition: Personal Pronoun Subjects*
Productive verb inflection (all singular, some plural)
First and second person pronoun subjects, occasional third person (singular)
Past-tense verbs with and without grammatical null subject
Present tense with (ungrammatical) null subjects recoverable from context
Smadar 1;8   Hagar 1;10   Leor 2;0

III *Grammatical Subjects and Null Subjects Established*
Full use of third-person pronoun subject, as required in all tenses
First- and second-person pronoun used with present-tense verbs
Elsewhere, first and second pronoun subject reflects usage—typically dropped in past tense, and retained in future tense (nonimperatives)
Initial use of expletive *ze* 'it'
Smadar 1;10   Hagar 2;2   Leor 2;4

The developments set out in (7), coupled with the findings for word order (section 1.1), indicate that once children have established the notion of grammatical subject, they can reliably identify it with the utterance-initial NP.

Recognition of the grammatical relation of "object" depends on more than linear order, because postverbal NPs may take various kinds of complements or adverbial adjuncts, in addition to object-type arguments. The most critical cue in this context is the accusative marker *et*, required with definite NPs as the direct object of verbs that govern accusative case—shown in the (a) sentences in examples (1) to (3). Acquisition of this marker was analyzed for cross-sectional speech samples using picture-description tasks with children from 1;10 to 2;8 (Zur, 1983) in addition to our longitudinal corpora (see fn. 4). Children typically used the accusative marker *et* as required by age from 2;3 to 2;6. Relevant developments are shown in (8) for the same three children as in (7).

(8) Steps in Early Acquisition of Direct Object Marker *et*:

	0 No suitable context [no + def Object NPs]	I Omitted in context [except formulaic]	II Initial usage [sporadic]	III Well established [most oblig contexts]
Smadar	1;7	1;8	1;10	1;11
Hagar	1;10	1;11	2;0	2;1–2;2
Leor	2;0	2;1–2;2	2;3	2;5

Other, nonaccusative case markings are also potential cues to different degrees of transitivity. Acquisition of oblique nonnominative pronouns, obligatorily inflected for case marking, takes place at the phase of early grammatical development. By around age 2;6, children distinguish between nominative *hu* 'he' and accusative *oto* 'him', genitive *shelo* 'of him = his', or comitative *ito* 'with him', while dative pronouns such as *lo* 'to-him' contrasting with *la* 'to-her' or *li* 'to-me' are among the earliest of these forms to emerge (Berman, 1985, 1986b; Kaplan, 1983; Rom & Dgani, 1985). By this age, children use dative-marked constructions quite widely, of the kind that Borer and Grodzinsky (1986) termed "possessive datives," which I analyzed as serving to present an affectee rather than an agentive perspective on events (Berman, 1982a). For example, nominative-accusative SVO *ani shafaxti et ha-xalav / et ze* 'I spilt [P1] OM the-milk / OM it' alternates with nominative-dative *haxalav / ze nishpax li* 'the milk / it spilt [P2] to-me = went and got (itself spilt on me)', or with subjectless *nishpax li* 'spilt to-me' and, occasionally, with VS *nishpax li ha-xalav* 'got-spilt to-me the-milk'; and in place of nominative-accusative *hu pocec et ha-balon* 'he burst [P3] OM the-balloon' children, possibly adults as well, prefer the dative *ha-balon hitpocec lo* 'the-balloon burst [P4] to-him' or even verb-initial *hitpocec lo ha-balon*.

In sum, by around the middle of their third year, children manifest knowledge of the basic syntax of verb-argument relations within the simple clause, including: cognizance of the grammatical relation of syntactic subject, typically the initial NP in the simple clause; specification of direct-object NPs by the accusative marker *et*, generally in contexts that manifest high transitivity (inanimate, specific, and referential definite object NPs); appropriate use of verbs that govern other prepositions to form oblique objects, as in the examples in (6); and reliance on dative marking to reduce transitivity by referring to protagonists as affected-undergoers of events rather than as nominative agents of actions.

1.3. Morphological Marking of Agreement and Tense versus Predicate Transitivity

The distinction between subjects and nonsubjects is reinforced by children's increasing conformity to the rule that the subject noun triggers number and gender agreement on the verb (Levy, 1983a, 1983b). A range of sources—from spontaneous speech output in cross-sectional surveys (Kaplan, 1983; Maoz, 1989; Zur, 1983) and longitudinal studies (Berman, 1990a; Berman & Weissenborn, 1991)—reveal the following developmental sequence: Sentence initial Subject > *et* or other prepositional marking on Object > Subject–Verb agreement. These findings are confirmed by a careful elicited imitation study: Guri-Herling (1988) found that 3- and 4-year-olds (with a mean age of 3;3 and 4;3) both imitated and corrected input sentences in the form {S V *et* O} when presented with various types of NVN strings (e.g., they would change both bare {N V N} and {et N V N} to {N V *et* N}); older children, from age 5 years, like adults, took appropriate account of the accusative marker *et* in sentence-initial position in the contexts {et O S V} and {et O V S}, and they also paid increasing attention to markers of subject–verb agreement.

It seems hardly surprising, then, if a child of less than 3 years old uses the same verb form in both the following {N V Pr N} contexts, one well-formed and one ungrammatical:

(9) a.   *ha- tinok nafal* [P1] *me ha- kise*
          the baby fell   off the-chair

     b.   **ha- tinok nafal* [P1] *et   ha- kise*
          the baby fell   [sic] OM the-chair

          cf. *ha- tinok hipil* [P5] *et   ha- kise*
               the-baby made-fall OM the chair =
               knocked the chair over

Just such errors have been documented in the naturalistic speech output of different Hebrew-speaking children. This is shown by the examples in (10) from Hagar and Leor in the latter part of their third year at a point where, as outlined in (7) and (8), both already have command of the grammatical relations of subject and direct object.

(10) a.   Hagar, 2;8;10, talking about a rabbit in a storybook:
           ve hu nafal letox   bor . . . Yonatan *nafal oto—cf. P5 *hipil*
           and he fell into (a) hole. . .Johnny   fell   him

      b.   Hagar, 2;8;27, to her mother, who is rubbing lotion on her legs:
           at   nofelet   oti!   —cf. P5 *mapila*
           you + FM fall + FM me + ACC = 'You're falling me'

c. Hagar, 2;9;4, to her mother, who is trying to pick her up:
ima,   *lama **nafalt***   *oti?*   —cf. P5 *hipalt*
Mommy, why   fell + FM + 2nd   me? =
why did you push me down?

d. Leor, 2;9;30, to his aunt, wants her to come play with him on
the rug:
bo'i   *la-shevet ve*   *ani **yipol***   *otax*   —cf. P5 *apil*
come + FM to-sit   and I   will-fall you + FM =
'come and sit down . . .'

The utterances in (10) are grammatically well-formed and reveal command of basic clause structure in: word order, the accusative case form of the object pronoun, and subject–verb number and gender agreement. Other examples of such levelings of grammatically mandatory *binyan* distinctions from different children are analyzed in detail in section 3.4.2. Here, note that both Hagar and Leor have proceeded beyond the initial, prototypical past-tense (perfective) use of the very common early verb meaning 'fall' or intransitive 'drop' (the Pl form of the root n-p-l), as shown by the present- and future-tense forms in (10b) and (10d). This same verb occurs with high frequency in narratives elicited from 3- to 4-year-olds (see fn. 4): All 16 children used a past-tense form of Intr P1 *nafal* (or plural *naflu*) 'fell' to describe what happened to a boy (and his dog) in search of his missing frog; and over half of them also used the causative P5 form *hipil* 'make-fall, throw down' to describe what the animals they encountered did to the boy (Berman, 1988). That is, these somewhat older children did *not* misuse the intransitive form with a causative sense or in a transitive syntactic context.

Younger children, like Hagar and Leor, also know which thematic relations are involved in simple clause verb argument configurations—for instance, an animate patient to whom something happened and the locative source of that event in (10a), compared with the mother as an agentive actor who has done something to the child patient in (10b) and (10c), or the child who wants to perpetrate something to the adult in (10d). They also have command of the relevant syntax: SVO word order and locative compared with accusative case marking. What they do not yet know is the relevant verb morphology, which requires that the verb *nafal* 'fell' or *lipol* 'to-fall' from the root n-p-l can occur only with intransitive syntax; where it has a direct object, this verb must be morphologically transitive, in the P5 verb pattern, taking forms like past tense *hipil* 'made-fall, dropped, knocked down' or infinitive *le-hapil* 'to knock down' from the same root n-p-l. Consider, next, what kind of knowledge this entails.

2. LEXICAL MARKING OF TRANSITIVITY:
THE *BINYAN* VERB PATTERNS

The morphological verb patterns known as *binyan-im* "conjugations"
are outlined later with the aim of integrating syntactic, semantic, and lexical factors in a unified characterization, taking into account the task fac-
ing the language-acquiring child. (For a summary of other analyses, see
Junger, 1987). Three factors are analyzed as relevant to the acquisitional
task: *structural generality* along the transitivity axis—that is, the correlation between morphosyntactic alternations in the *binyan* patterns and
valency distinctions (section 2.1); *semantic regularity*—the extent of one-
to-one mapping between *binyan* form and semantic content in terms of
inherent verb semantics and the functional uniqueness of the verb-
argument relations expressed by each *binyan* pattern (section 2.2); and
lexical productivity compared with lexical convention—that is, the effect of processes for new word formation compared with knowledge of
the established lexicon (section 2.3). The developmental prediction
motivating this analysis is that generality of rule application and close-
ness of fit between form and function combine to facilitate and acceler-
ate acquisition in this as in other domains of language knowledge.

2.1. Structural Generality: Syntactic Correlates
of the *Binyan* System

The five patterns considered here (see fn. 3) display typical values for
syntactic transitivity, where [+ Transitive] verbs are narrowly defined as
occurring in SVO constructions and governing accusative case (i.e., the
object nominal takes *et*) and [− Transitive] means all the rest. Under this
strict definition, the patterns cluster as follows:

(11)	[− Transitive]		[+ Transitive]	
P1 - QAL:	*caxak*	laugh	*daxaf*	push
= PA'AL	*yashen*	sleep	*shavar*	break
	yarad	go down	*sagar*	open
P2 - NIF'AL:	*nishpax*	spill		
	nikra	tear		
	nivhal	get a fright		
P3 - PI'EL:			*tiken*	fix, mend
			nipeax	inflate, blow-up
			nigev	wipe
P4 - HITPA'EL:	*hitracex*	wash (oneself)		
	histovev	turn around		
	hitbayesh	be ashamed		

	[– Transitive]	[+ Transitive]	
P5 - HIF'IL:		*hixnis*	put-in, insert
		hidlik	light, ignite
		hirdim	put-to-sleep

Several properties relate syntactic transitivity and *binyan* verb morphology. (a) P1 is syntactically neutral, because it alone is equally available to both intransitive and transitive predicates. (b) Only, though not all, verbs in P1, P3, and P5 govern accusative case direct objects marked by *et*, as in the first sentence in each pair of examples in (2) through (4). (c) Verbs in P2 and P4 can be "loosely transitive" because they may require an object argument, for example, P2 *nixnas le* 'go in to', *nehena me-* 'enjoy from' or P4 *histakel be* 'look at', *hitgaber al* 'overcome on', but this will never be marked by *et*. And (d) verbs in the intransitive P2 and P4 patterns have no passive voice counterpart, in contrast to transitive verbs in P1, P3, and P5.

That is, children need to learn that verbs in P1 can be either transitive or intransitive, that verbs in P2 and P4 never govern accusative case, and that P3 and P5 are generally transitive and may, but need not, take direct objects. These are broad generalizations, however, rather than across-the-board rules of grammar, and they are not readily accessible to non-specialist native-speaking adults on the metalinguistic level of conscious awareness.

Another type of structural cue is provided by the fact that typical *patterns of alternation* hold between the five patterns. These are illustrated in (12), without regard for directionality, that is, the question of which patterns are "basic" and which are derived.

(12) Typical Interpattern Alternations:

a. P1	˜	P5	*caxak*	laugh	˜	*hicxik*	amuse
[– Tr]		[+ Tr]	*yarad*	go down	˜	*horid*	take down
b. P1	˜	P2	*sagar*	shut, close	˜	*nisgar*	get-shut
[+ Tr]		[– Tr]	*shafax*	spill	˜	*nishpax*	get-spilled
c. P2	˜	P5	*nivhal*	get-a-fright	˜	*hivhil*	frighten
[– Tr]		[+ Tr]	*nirdam*	fall asleep	˜	*hirdim*	put to sleep
d. P3	˜	P4	*nipeax*	blow up	˜	*hitnapeax*	swell up
[+ Tr]		[– Tr]	*nigev*	wipe	˜	*hitnagev*	wipe oneself

These alternations mean that any change in valency is marked by a morphological shift in *binyan* assignment. This is a more robust generalization than the distribution of transitivity distinctions set out in (11). There are only two classes of exceptions to this general rule of Modern Hebrew, both cases where a single P5 form can be either transitive or intransitive: (a) causative and inchoative versions of adjectives—for example, *hilbin* 'whiten' means both 'make white' and 'become white', *hivshil* 'ripen' means both 'make ripe' and 'get ripe'; and (b) aspectual verbs for phases in a process, particularly *hitxil* 'begin, start', which occurs only in P5 both in transitive and intransitive contexts (and, less normatively, *himshix* 'continue, go-on', which does have an intransitive P2 alternant). But these exceptions are marginal, and largely irrelevant to children's construal of the system. First, the intransitive inchoatives in P5 derive from Biblical Hebrew and are rare in everyday colloquial usage, where they are generally replaced by a periphrastic inchoative auxiliary plus adjective (e.g., 'turn white', 'become ripe') or by extension of the P4 intransitive pattern to nonnormative forms such as *hizdaken* 'grow old' [cf. *zaken* '(be) old'] *hitbashel* 'become ripe' (cf. *bashel* 'ripe'), and *hitlaben* 'turn white' (cf. *lavan* 'white'). Second, the verb 'begin' is used by children mainly in its transitive sense without any overt argument, in imperative *tatxil!* 'start, begin' analogously to P5 *tafsik!* 'stop!' (which does contrast with intransitive P1 *pasak* or P2 *nifsak*). These high-style, normative forms of inchoative adjectives, and an occasional aspectual verb, are the only instances that could provide learners with positive evidence for assuming that pattern switching is optional in Hebrew. The fact that valency alternation at the level of the sentence entails morphological alternation at the level of the verb can thus be considered part of the *grammar* of Modern Hebrew.

2.2. Semantic Regularity: Form–Meaning Relations and Functional Uniqueness

The learning process could also be facilitated by an invariant mapping between *binyan* form and semantic content. However, this does not hold at either of the levels of inherent verb semantics or of thematic verb-argument relations. There is, again, only a partial fit between *binyan* pattern and the presumably universal division of predicates into the four classes of Aktionsarten or aspectual semantics distinguished by Dowty (1979), and defined by Van Valin (1990) as follows: *State* predicates refer to an entity BEING in a given state of affairs; *activity* predicates refer to an actor DOING something, performing a (nontelic) activity; *accomplishment* predicates refer to an agent or actor CAUSING some entity to BE in a state or BECOME something; and *achievement* predicates refer to an entity BECOMING something, entering into or undergoing a change of state. Hebrew statives can take the form of adjectives (e.g., *xaxam* 'be wise'), verbs in P1 (e.g., *yada* 'know'), or in P5 (e.g., *hevin* 'understand'); activity verbs occur in P1 (e.g., *caxak* 'laugh'), P3 (e.g., *xiyex* 'smile'), or P5 (e.g., *hicbia* 'vote, raise one's hand); accomplishment verbs can occur in P1 (e.g., *daxaf* 'push'), P3 (e.g., *tiken* 'fix'), or P5 (e.g., *hirgiz* 'annoy'); and achievement predicates can occur in P1 (e.g., *kafa* 'freeze'), P2 (e.g., *ne'elam* 'disappear'), P4 (e.g., *hit'alef* 'faint'), and even P5 (e.g., *higia* 'arrive').

Again, children can rely on partial semantic generalizations, and on the partial interface between these and the structural distinctions noted in section 2.1: Statives and accomplishments favor the transitive patterns P3 and P5, intransitive activities favor P1, achievement verbs favor P2 and P4. However, as the preceding examples show, lexical mismatches occur across the board, and in both directions: One semantic verb type can occur in different *binyan* patterns and a single *binyan* is not exclusively used for one verb type. Thus, P1 has several achievement predicates, like those meaning 'freeze', 'boil', 'grow (bigger)', as well as the common children's verb *nafal* 'fall'; P2 has an activity predicate such as *nixnas* 'enter = go in, walk into' (also interpretable as achievement 'enter = get inside'); P3 has a largish group of activity verbs, including *tiyel* 'go for a walk', *sixek* 'play (games)', *ciyer* 'draw, paint'; P4 has a subset of iterative and other activity verbs—for example, *hitrocec* 'run around', *histakel* 'look'; and P5 has some achievement ("unaccusative") type verbs as well as the inchoatives of adjectives noted in the preceding section.

This bidirectional lack of functional uniqueness is also manifested in the type of predicate–argument relations expressed through the *binyan* patterns. For example, *endstate resultatives* can take one of three forms: the passive participial forms of CaCuC[5] (e.g., *shavur* 'broken', *hafux* 'inverted = upside-down'), meCuCaC (e.g., *mevushal* 'cooked, not raw', *mesudar* 'arranged, tidy'), and muCCaC (e.g., *murgash* 'sensed, tangible', *mudbak* 'stuck [on]'); and, relatedly (see, further, section 4.2), *passive voice* can be expressed by P2 *nif'al* (e.g., *nignav* 'be-stolen', *nilkax* 'be-taken'), by P3-ps *pu'al* (e.g., *tukan* 'be-fixed', *sudar* 'be-arranged'), and by P5-ps *hof'al* (e.g., *hudbak* 'be-pasted', *huva* 'be-brought'). Different subclasses of achievement predicates also have a mixed distribution, for instance, *reciprocals* are generally in P4 (e.g., *hitkatev* 'correspond, write one another', *hitnagesh* 'collide, clash'), but they may occur in P1 *rav* 'quarrel' or P2 *nifgash* 'meet (one another)'; and adjective-based change-of-state inchoatives may be in P1 (*xala* 'get-sick'), P2 (*nexlash* 'grow-weak'), P4 (*hit'ayef* 'grow tired'), or P5 (*hivri* 'get-well, become-healthy'), and their causative counterparts may also take different forms—as in P3 *iyef* 'tire, make-tired' or P5 *hexlish* 'weaken = make-weak'.

---

[5]These forms follow the convention of using uppercase *C* for root consonants and lowercase consonants and vowels for affixal elements in Hebrew derivational paradigms.

It follows that under this analysis, the *binyan* patterns are construed as associated with the lexicon. That is, they manifest the irregularities and accidental gaps typical of derivational compared with inflectional systems of morphology, and so constitute more of a learning burden than the latter. On the other hand, children can be aided by attention to structural generalizations about transitivity alternations and the partial syntactic regularities noted in the preceding section. These combine with the usage-related factors of lexical frequency and productivity to explain children's acquisition of this system as both relatively rapid and as staggered across different developmental phases.

2.3. Lexical Factors of Frequency and Productivity

The notion of "productivity" is applied here to explain children's acquisition of *binyan* alternations (like other aspects of new word formation in different languages, see Berman & Clark, 1992) in a rather different sense than what is commonly accepted in linguistics or child language research. In the former, productivity is generally defined in purely structural terms (e.g., Jensen, 1990; Matthews, 1991). For example, an inflection like English *-ed* is productive in that it applies to nearly all verbs to mark past tense, in contrast to a suffix like inchoative *-en*, which is not productive because it appears on only a small number of existing verbs. In general, inflections or grammatical affixes are regarded as fully productive, and derivational word formation affixes as less productive, because they are more limited in where they can apply.[6]

A rather different idea of productivity is adopted here, following on from earlier accounts of *speaker preferences* in the domain of innovative nouns and noun compounding in Hebrew (Berman, 1987a, 1987b; Berman & Ravid, 1986; Clark & Berman, 1984; and see, too, Clark & Clark, 1979, on productivity of new verb formation in English). In this sense, productivity is linked (a) to transparency of form–meaning relations in the lexicon (section 2.2) and (b) to the activity of a word form type for the expression of a meaning not yet represented in the conventional lexicon. This characterization involves interrelated distinctions between lexical frequency and productivity (section 2.3.1), on the one

---

[6]In the field of language development, the notion of "productivity" has been used in a rather different sense. It was originally intended to capture the progression in children's language use from an occasional word combination to producing five or more new ones in a single session (Brown, 1973). It also serves to characterize the move from item-based rote learning to rule-based knowledge of entire classes of items and constructions, for instance, from using an inflectional affix like *-ed* on a single verb, to using it on a small group of verbs, to general application on all possible verbs (e.g., Gordon & Chafetz, 1990; MacWhinney, 1978; Pinker, Lebeaux, & Frost, 1987).

hand, and between current processes of new word formation and the established lexicon (section 2.3.2), on the other.[7]

From an acquisitional point of view, children as well as adults are affected by the frequency of input forms in actual language usage. And children as well as adults are not necessarily able to distinguish on-line, novel coinages from established, conventional lexical items in their speech input and output. But adults have a very large conventional lexicon, whereas children know only a small subset of the total adult repertoire. As a result of this imbalance between endstate and developing knowledge of the lexicon, children are likely to be more affected by relative frequency of input items. They are also more likely to fill lexical gaps by new word coinage and reliance on unconventional forms of existing words, where adult usage conforms largely to the established lexicon.

2.3.1. Frequency versus Productivity: The Special Status of P1.
The preceding sections suggest that the P1 pattern enjoys a privileged status from several points of view: Semantically, it contains state, activity, and accomplishment predicates, as well as a few achievement verbs, including the highly salient verb *nafal* 'fall'; that is, P1 has no specific semantic or functional bias, and its verbs equally refer to durative activities or to states, with or without a specified patient or location. Syntactically, P1 is unique in that it includes strictly transitive verbs governing accusative *et*, weakly transitive verbs governing oblique objects, and intransitive verbs with no obligatory complement. P1 also enters into the most varied cluster of interpattern alternations: Intransitive activity verbs alternate quite regularly with P5 causatives (and some also have semantically specific or accomplishment counterparts in P3), whereas transitive P1 activity verbs have regular alternants in P2 achievement predicates or in P2 syntactic passives, and sometimes also in P4 reflexives.

From the point of view of *usage* (of the conventional lexicon), P1 verbs include most of the generic level, semantically basic and least specific verbs typical of young children's early verb usage—for example, the verbs meaning *come* and *go*; *sit* and *stand*; *give, put,* and *take*; *go up* and *go down*; as well as more specific but very common children's verbs like *eat* and *drink*; *want* and *see*; and *sleep, laugh,* or *cry*. Finally, P1 verbs have the highest *frequency* of occurrence across different registers of adult usage (Schwarzwald, 1981, p. 70); they account for over half the verbs, both in types and tokens, used by children in a variety of cross-sectional

---

[7]Most linguistic accounts of productivity fail to take explicit enough account of this distinction. Important exceptions in the domain of word formation are the line drawn by Aronoff (1976) between "new" versus "old" words and Andersen's 1985 discussion of the relative "activity" of word-formation processes.

studies of preschool and early school-age usage (Berman, 1982b; Berman & Dromi, 1984; Elath, 1989; Kaplan, 1983; Rabinowitch, 1985); and between 50% and 60% of the early verbs of the children we studied longitudinally (see fn. 4) were in P1, prior to productive mastery of verb inflection, up to age 2 years. The robustness of these findings is confirmed by the highly similar distribution of pattern usage for both verb types and verb tokens across all these different corpora, as follows: Twenty-five percent to 35% of the remaining verbs divide fairly evenly between the two [+Transitive] patterns P3 and P5, followed by the two [−Transitive] patterns P4 and P2, in that order, accounting for between 10% to 5% of all verbs.

As against this predominance in frequency of usage from the established lexicon, P1 is uniquely *not* exploited for new verb formation in current Hebrew. This is partly due to structural constraints on the morphophonological alternations involved by P1 compared with other verb patterns. But it also relates to the preference of adults and children alike for making specialized use of other patterns to coin new verbs in Hebrew (see, further, in section 2.3.2): P3 is favored for transitive and P4 for intransitive verbs based on existing nouns (whether native Hebrew or loan words) and P5 for coining verbs from other verbs or adjectives. Avoidance of P1 coinages is almost total across a wide variety of spontaneous verb innovations as well as in experimental studies (Berman, 1989, 1990b, and see fn. 4). The only exception is reported in a study where both 4-year-old and adult respondents quite often relied on P1 to change the transitivity value of verbs derived from innovative, nonexistent roots (Alroy, 1992). But this runs counter to normal processes of new verb derivation in Hebrew: New verbs are invariably formed from existing verbs (e.g., P5 *hishtil* 'implant' from P1 *shatal*), from existing Hebrew nouns or adjectives (e.g., P3 *shiped* from the noun *shipud* 'skewer'), or from loan nouns or adjectives (e.g., P4 *hit'aklem* 'be acclimatized' from *aklim* 'climate'). In these highly productive processes for new verb formation in Modern Hebrew, P1 plays no role, as children as young as age 3 already know.

These observations suggest that P1 verbs are learned, and used, as unanalyzed amalgams, with no reference to how they interact with transitivity. This is generally true for initial acquisition of all early verbs, irrespective of *binyan* pattern, but it does not apply to subsequent use of verbs in other patterns (section 3.1). P1 has a privileged status semantically, syntactically, and in frequency of usage. Yet it is the least productive in the *binyan* system as a whole: It is rarely used to coin new verbs or for innovative alternations along the axis of transitivity.

2.3.2. Three Levels of Lexical Productivity.   In earlier analyses, a distinction was drawn between structural productivity, defined as the formal options available to speakers through the grammar of their language, compared with colloquial or speaker productivity, characterized by contemporary preferences in choosing from the range of grammatical devices for specifying form–meaning relations. Here, I elaborate these distinctions to a three-way contrast between nonproductive, semi-productive, and actively productive sets of form–meaning relations in the lexicon. These three degrees of lexical productivity are critically affected by the distinction between the established lexicon, which includes all the items at the less productive end of the continuum, and processes for new word formation, which account for those at its more productive end.

1. *Nonproductive* form–meaning relations have become frozen or fossilized, and so need to be learned by rote. An example would be the small groups of causative verbs in English that are derived either by vowel apophany (e.g., *rise~ raise, lie~ lay, sit~ seat, fall~ fell*) or by lexical suppletion (e.g., *eat~ feed, learn~ teach, fall~ drop, see~ show*). In Hebrew, use of morphological marking of aspect by *binyan* is similarly frozen in history, for example, P1 to P3 intensive aspect (compare *shavar* 'break' ~ *shiber* 'shatter', *shalax* 'send' ~ *shileax* 'send away') and P1 to P4 iterative aspect (compare *halax* 'walk' ~ *hithalex* 'walk up and down', *rac* 'run' ~ *hitrocec* 'run around'). These play only a marginal role in marking the aspectual contours of events in extended narrative productions (Berman & Neeman, in press), and they are nonfunctional for purposes of new verb formation.

2. *Semi-productive* form–meaning relations are transparent, they are relatively easily recognizable by naive speakers, and they include larger numbers of items. They also tend to represent options that are preferred by language-policy institutions, lexicographers, school grammars, and other representatives of the official language establishment. Nonetheless, they constitute closed classes, because they are *not* favored as a current device for new word formation, and so lack genuine colloquial, speaker productivity. This category includes (a) processes that are lexically defunct, such as use of P5 *hif'il* in Biblical Hebrew for intransitive, denominated verbs indicating direction of movement (e.g., *lehasmil* 'go left' from *smol* 'left', *lehacpin* 'go north' from *cafon* 'north'); and (b) processes that have been replaced by some other productive device, for example, use of the same P5 pattern in Mishnaic Hebrew for indicating both the causative and the inchoative version of color and other adjectives (e.g., *lehalbin* 'whiten' from *lavan* 'white' means both 'make white' and 'become white'; *lehavshil* 'ripen' from *bashel* means both 'make ripe' and 'become ripe'), whereas today the inchoative sense is taken over either by intransitive P4 or by syntactic periphrasis (see section 2.1).

3. *Actively productive* form–meaning relations are also transparent,

but they are not lexically restricted like the previous category. They constitute open-ended classes, as demonstrated by the following properties: (a) Speakers rely on them in spontaneous coinages to fill gaps in the contemporary lexicon; (b) they are favored as a means of new word derivation in structured experimental settings; (c) they are the source for solecisms and deviations from normative requirements in lexical usage stipulated by the language establishment; and (d) they are indicative of ongoing processes of language change in the usage of two groups of non-literate, less educated, and less self-conscious speakers (i.e., adult speakers of nonstandard variants and young children). Three examples of such productive trends in the current lexicon of Hebrew for which both naturalistic and experimental data are available are: (a) reliance on P3 in coining new, denominal transitive-activity verbs, from native or loan-word sources; (b) use of P5 in coining causative verbs from adjectives and from existing verbs in P1; and (c) preference for the passive participial patterns meCuCaC or else CaCuc and rejection of the third option muCCaC for expressing resultative endstates.

Underlying this analysis is the assumption that language acquisition is directly affected by the kind of knowledge involved in items with different degrees of lexical productivity. In acquiring Type 1 nonproductive classes, children must learn the items by rote, then relate them to other associated forms (e.g., *eat* and *feed*), and eventually recognize what general semantic relationship obtains between them (e.g., that *feed* is to eat as *show* is to *see* or *bring* is to *come*). That is, item-by-item learning is the basis for gaining command of members of this class, both initially and subsequently. Eventually, however, they will be recognized as special instances of more general morphosyntactic classes and/or semantic classes, for example, causatives.

At the other end of the scale, command of Type 2 actively productive classes of form–meaning relations is more similar to acquiring command of grammatical rules. For instance, children need to recognize that P5 is a means of forming causative verbs in Hebrew, with intransitive verbs in P1 [e.g., P5 *lehaziz* 'move (something)' from P1 *lazuz* 'move'] and with adjectives (e.g., *lehartiv* 'make wet' from *ratuv* 'wet'). The prediction is that these active derivational processes will shape children's initial hypotheses, and enable them to extract relevant generalizations about the interrelation between syntactic transitivity, verb semantics, and morphological form. These alternations will be the basis for children's "creative errors," indicating that the child has the rule but lacks command of the conventional lexicon and of lexical exceptions. Such errors are evidence that these processes are in fact "active," and may suggest directions of possible language change.

In the middle lies learning that combines features of Type 1 item-based lexical learning and Type 3 rule-based structural learning. A later kind of knowledge are lexical conventions I have characterized as Type 2 "semiproductive." These may be anchored in processes that at an earlier stage in the history of the language were the canonic way for doing things, and hence are most often specified in schoolbooks and other normativist descriptions. But in contemporary usage, they are lexically restricted in unmotivated ways to a frozen set of items. This appears to be the case with English use of the suffix -*en* to produce inchoative verbs with causative counterparts from (generally Germanic) adjectives, for example, conventional *soften, whiten*, compared with the currently productive -*ize* suffix for producing (predominantly Romance-based) activity verbs like contemporary *finalize, definitivize*. Such partial generalizations often tend to belong to a higher register, which would provide another reason for their being acquired later than either the item-based nonproductive (Type 1) alternations or the more regular, fully productive (Type 2) processes.

Processes manifested within the *binyan* system of Modern Hebrew can now be reanalyzed as in (13), to distinguish between those that are (I) syntactically fully productive; (II) lexically fully productive or "active"; (III) lexically partially or semi-productive; and (IV) nonproductive, closed classes.

(13)	*binyan* Pattern	Transitivity Value	Semantic Class	Direction of Alternations		Degree of Productivity		
	P1	Basically, a "closed class" of verbs:						
		– Trans	Activity	>	P5 Causative	II	=	active
		+ Trans	Accomplish	>	P2 Achievement	III	=	semi
		+ Trans	Accomplish	>	P2 Passive	I	=	syntax
	P2	– Trans	Achievement	<	P1 Accomplish	III	=	semi
		– Trans	Achievement	~	P5 Causatives	III	=	semi
	P3	+ Trans	Accomplish			IV	=	closed
		+ Trans	Accomplish	<	Nouns	II	=	active
		+ Trans	Causative	<	Adjectives	III	=	semi
	P4	– Trans	Achievement	<	P3 + Trans	II	=	active
		– Trans	Reflexives, Reciprocals			III	=	semi
	P5	+ Trans	Causative	<	P1 – Trans	II	=	active
		+ Trans	Causative	<	P2 – Trans	III	=	semi
		+ Trans	Causative	<	Adjectives	II	=	active
		– Trans	Inchoative	<	Adjectives	III	=	semi

As shown in (13), each pattern can be analyzed as currently coopted for a particular lexically active process; all other, nonsyntactically governed form–meaning relations between verb content and verb morphology need to be learned piecemeal. The next section considers how children move into, and across, acquisition of this knowledge.

3. ACQUISITION OF BINYAN TRANSITIVITY DISTINCTIONS

What, then, underlies children's acquisition of a system in which syntactic transitivity, verb semantics, and lexical morphology interact in only partly systematic ways? Earlier studies on the acquisition of the *binyan* system yielded two main observations. First, early verb usage does not entail any systematic alternation in verb morphology (Berman, 1982b). Initially, children fail to use *binyan* patterns to express any or all of the following functions: Syntactic distinctions of transitivity; semantic notions such as causativity or reciprocality; and lexical processes of new word formation, for example, for denomination. Verbs are used by 2-year-olds as unanalyzed amalgams from these three points of view, even after children have command of the rich inflectional system of person, number, gender, and tense marking. Second, knowledge of the system emerges clearly after early grammatical acquisition, both syntactic and inflectional, and is reflected in "creative errors" (Berman & Sagi, 1981). These may violate lexical convention, but they are grammatically appropriate in terms of the transitivity values typical of the five *binyan* patterns (Berman, 1980).

These two observations are examined here in light of the reanalysis of the *binyan* system sketched in section 2, combined with more extensive findings from naturalistic speech output (see fn. 4) and more recent structured elicitation studies. As noted in the preceding discussion, children are assumed to start out with the knowledge that predicates may enter into different kinds of verb-argument configurations, and there are different semantic types of predicates. This forms the basis for acquisition of language-particular knowledge of form–meaning relations, along the following developmental route. First, children acquire what I term *syntactic transitivity*, expressed in Hebrew through SVO order and the distinction between the grammatical relations of subject, direct, and oblique objects, aided by inflectional marking of subject–verb agreement. Second, they recognize that the grammar of their language requires morphological marking of valency alternations, typically from around age 3, after basic clause structure is established. Next, they need to extract out subgeneralizations regarding how this is achieved through *binyan* pattern alternation, and this is accompanied, finally, by command of the numerous lexical exceptions and form–meaning mismatches that characterize the system.

This stepwise progression is motivated on the basis of a more general model of language development (section 3.1); factors impinging on acquisition such as typological imperatives, lexical productivity, and the difference between grammatical and lexical knowledge (section 3.2); and strategies employed by children in acquiring the system (section 3.3).

3.1. General Developmental Path

The acquisitional model adopted here views language acquisition as proceeding in three major phases from (I) item-based rote learning to (II) structure-dependent rule learning, followed by (III) discourse-sensitive language use. This entails the following stepwise progression for acquisition of the *binyan* system, as well as other areas of language knowledge and language use:

(14) I. a. Early verb-use is rote-learned, ·*item-based*
            b. *Initial alternations* based on familiar exemplars, lexically associated isolates

      II. c. Emergence of a *generalized knowledge* of the system, shown by lack of transitivity errors in choice of *binyan* forms and by juvenile interim strategies ("creative errors") in using verbs in nonprototypical contexts
           d. *Consolidated knowledge* of the system, shown by increased spontaneous use of alternating forms of the same verb and by success on structured elicitation tasks with both familiar and novel items

      III. e. *Adultlike command*, shown by mastery of lexical exceptions and partially productive lexical classes; by the ability to coin innovative transitivity switches in structured elicitations; and by flexible deployment of *binyan* alternation for alternating perspectives in extended discourse.

The progression delineated in (14) is consistent with MacWhinney's (1978, 1982) proposals for the acquisition of morphology and early word combinations, by the mechanisms of rote, analogy, and combination, but aims at a generally integrated developmental view, beyond these three processes. My model is closely allied to the developmental phases proposed by Karmiloff-Smith (1986, 1987), in characterizing knowledge acquisition as being initially bottom-up or data driven, then top-down procedurally driven, and eventually integrated within a systematic conceptual gestalt.

This developmental sequence was first proposed to account for the acquisition of inflectional and derivational morphology (Berman, 1986b), and has since been supported by findings in other areas: for example, the development of complex nominals (Berman, 1987a), narrative structure (Berman, 1988, 1993a), and subjectless constructions (Berman, 1990a). The same progression also holds for results of a recent study of *binyan* alternation in structured elicitation settings (Berman, 1993b). But this model fails to address two important developmental issues: the question of *transitions*, of how children move from Phase I to II and on to end-state Phase III knowledge; and the issue of *cross-system ordering* of acquisition, for example, why agreement inflections emerge earlier than *binyan* transitivity marking, or why causative-verb innovation is both earlier, and more widespread, in Hebrew child language than intransitive verb formation.

3.2. Developmental Factors[8]

To this end, and in keeping with the view of multiple bootstrappings and a confluence of cues proposed in the introduction, other factors need to be incorporated in this account of the acquisition process. The shift from Phase I to II is motivated by *typological bias* in the sense of the relative weight of particular structural properties of the target language (section 3.2.1); the relative order of acquisition within the *binyan* system is explained by the impact of *lexical productivity* and usage preferences (section 3.2.2); and the relative order across different linguistic domains—by the principled distinction between grammatical and lexical knowledge (section 3.2.3). Factors that motivate the shift from Phase II to III, such as lexical convention (Clark, 1983; Clark & Clark, 1979), and the impact of formal study and literacy are noted in section 4.

3.2.1. Typological Structure.   Verb usage in the longitudinal corpora of six children at Phase I, Step (14a), during the period of initial word combinations and early grammar, confirms findings of cross-sectional distributions (Kaplan, 1983) and diary reports (Berman, 1978; Dromi, 1986). Initially, children use verbs in all five patterns, but the same child will rarely use a single verb root in more than one *binyan* pattern. A similar initial lack of alternating forms, and the view of early acquisition as "item based" and "context bound," have been noted for inflectional morphology and early word combinations, explained by MacWhinney (1978, 1982) as early reliance on rote learning, and in causative verb usage attributed by Bowerman (1974, 1982) to learning based on unanalyzed amalgams.

A separate question, not addressed in the present context, is what factors determine *which* forms of verbs are favored in early use. For example, children tend to use intransitive P1 *axal* 'eat' and *raxav* 'ride' well be-

---

[8]I adopt the neutral term *factors* in preference to the theory-dependent use of the term *principle* in psycholinguistics, for example, Slobin's (1985) "operating principles" and Clark's (1983, in press) "acquisitional principles," and particularly the sense given this term in the context of the "principles and parameters" model of current generative linguistics.

fore P5 causative *he'exil* 'feed', *hirkiv* 'give a ride'; on the other hand, intransitive P2 *nishpax* 'be-spilt' or *nish'ar* 'stay, remain' are used long before their transitive counterparts, but some transitive P1 verbs like *sagar* 'shut' or *maca* 'find' occur *before* their P2 intransitive counterparts. In contrast, both P1 *yarad* 'go-down' and P5 *horid* 'take-down', both P2 *nixnas* 'go-in, get-into' and P5 *hixnis* 'put-in, insert' may be used at around the same time.

I argue that these highly familiar initial exemplars form the basis for eventual rule extraction (Step 14b). This assumption corresponds to what Ingram (1985) called the "lexical principle," by which children "learn individual paradigmatic alternations as separate lexical items . . . [and] first acquire(s) paradigmatic variants like 'cat, cats', 'dog, dogs' as separate words, and only later realize that there is a separable plural morpheme '-s' " (p. 65). At the phase of early grammar, around age 2, such alternations in the *binyan* system are few and far between. And there is as yet no evidence that children recognize that a more general relationship is encoded between, say, P2 *nishpax* as referring to a change-of-state (being spilled) and P1 *lishpox* as referring to someone's activity (spilling something), or between P1 *laredet* for their own going down and P5 *le-horid* for making something or someone else go down. Nor, as a result, are children yet able to extend these form–meaning alternations to other, less familiar instances.

Two facets of verb acquisition thus need to be reconciled. The evidence is overwhelming that from ages 1;6 to 2;6, children rarely use the same verb with more than one transitivity value; that is, the same verb root will generally occur in only one *binyan*. But this poses a problem for explaining eventual acquisition of Hebrew grammar, which stipulates that a change in syntactic transitivity requires a change in verb morphology. These facts are confirmed by results of two picture-based elicitation tasks (Berman, 1993b). Children age 2;6 to 3;0 (mean age 2;9), 3;6 to 4;0, and 7;6 to 8;7 were presented with sentences containing familiar Hebrew verbs, and were required to provide verbs of inverse transitivity, to yield two types of responses: (a) conventional, existing verbs and (b) novel, nonexistent items. On the (a) part, the 2-year-olds used the correct verb morphology to mark changes in transitivity only around one third of the time (37.5%), differing significantly from the 3-year-olds (66%), whereas the 8-year-old schoolchildren did significantly better than both younger groups (92%); and both younger groups did even better when their responses were rated as *appropriate* though not necessarily morphologically normative changes in transitivity—for example, morphologically acceptable but nonconventional forms, or suitable syntactic recastings of the input sentences—52% among the 2-year-olds, compared with 84% of the 3-year-olds. On the (b) part of the test, when required to coin novel items, 2-year-olds were able to produce an appropriate response about one quarter of the time (26%), 3-year-olds were successful 59% of the time, and 8-year-old schoolchildren responded like adults, giving morphologically normative coinages around 70% of the time. That is, children in the latter part of their third year manifest good knowledge of transitivity, by age 3 to 4 they can alternate morphology of input verbs most of the time, and by age 8 they can do so innovatively, much like adults.

The first factor invoked to explain how children move forward from occasional familiar exemplars to rule extraction (i.e., from Phase I to II) is the structural factor of "typological imperative." This underlies the sensitivity that develops in children around 2 to 3 years old regarding what is "relevant" in their language, the realization that certain constructions, or linguistic systems have a favored structural status (Berman, 1986a, 1993b). The recognition in question is the fact that it is unHebrew, hence from their point of view nonlanguagelike in general, to use the same form of a verb in both the contexts {S V *et* O} and {S V}. There is no communicative or semantic need to switch verb morphology in order to describe a situation as an intransitive event rather than a transitive action. Word order, case marking, and inflectional agreement markers will generally suffice. But a child must do so in order to be a Hebrew speaker. This exactly corresponds to the claim that gender or number agreement may not be necessary for communicative purposes, but is essential to and pervasive across Hebrew grammar. That is, following the initial rote use of verbs as individual items, extended by lexical learning of pairs of isolated alternations, children's verb usage becomes typologically driven to attend to the Hebrew-particular fact of how transitivity affects the morphological shape of verbs. In other words, typological biases trigger rule learning in the most general sense of recognizing that some general linguistic category requires some kind of formal marking.

3.2.2. Lexical Productivity and Expressive Options.

A second factor, interacting with target-language typology, is that of lexical productivity (section 2.3). This concerns a rather different kind of "bias," relating to factors of language *use* within the frame of typological structure. What I term *rhetorical bias* refers to the expressive options favored by speakers of a language (often at a given time in its history) for formulating certain relations of form and meaning. For instance, the relation of P1 transitive activity and P2 intransitive event verbs (cf. *li-shpox ~ nish-pax* 'spill') and between P1 intransitive activity and P5 causative verbs (*la-redet ~ le-horid* 'get down' versus 'take down') are highly "productive" alternations in current Hebrew. Experimental findings confirm this:

Of four types of alternations elicited from 2- and 3-year-old children, those between P1 Intr and P5 Trans and between P1 Trans and P2 Intr and between scored highest, followed by P4 Intr alternating with P3 Trans, and even less for P2 Intr switching with P5 Trans (Berman, 1993b). These contrasts were even more marked on the *innovative* part of the test, where respondents were required to fill lexical gaps by coining verbs of inverse transitivity from lexically established verbs. Here, children age 2, 3, and 8 years as well as adults did significantly better on coining novel causative verbs than on novel change-of-state intransitives. This is because causative predicates lack a periphrastic expressive counterpart in Hebrew, analogous to English *make swim, put to sleep, get to crawl*, whereas achievement predicates *do* have an expressive option with an auxiliary verb *ne'esa* or *nihya* 'get, become' and so do reflexive predicates with *self* pronominals.

Both naturalistic data and structured elicitations thus reveal that once children recognize the typologically motivated *structural* demand for switching verb patterns to mark transitivity, once they abandon earlier rote learning in favor of rule-bound assignment of morphological transitivity, the particular *lexical* solutions they seek will be affected by increasing familiarity with the conventional lexicon combined with the impact of currently favored processes for new word formation.

Processes that are more "productive" in the sense applied here aid children in recognizing certain alternations as expressing quite general form–meaning relationships in their language. And the factor of lexical productivity interacts with lexical familiarity and relative *frequency* of item use as follows: Productivity helps children extract generalizations, and frequency determines to which sets of items these generalizations are first applied. That is, children come to recognize the commonality of such early verbs as P1 *yarad* 'go down' and P5 *lehorid* 'take down' on the one hand and P1 *nafal* 'fall' and P5 *lehapil* 'make-fall, drop' on the other; only later will they extend this to more specific, less high frequency verbs such as P1 *avar* 'pass' versus P5 *leha'avir* 'make-pass, convey'; similarly, alternations between P2 intransitive versus P1 transitive verbs will start out with very familiar verbs like those meaning *break, spill, tear*; later they will be extended to less prototypical instances of such alternations, for example, the P2 unaccusative-achievement versions of P1 transitive activity verbs meaning *catch, throw, write*. Semiproductive alternations will also be mastered late, as part of the growing command of convention and the established lexicon.

3.2.3. Grammatical and Lexical Knowledge: Verb Tense versus Verb Transitivity.

Initial unanalyzed use of verbs is exactly analogous to what children earlier do with verb tense marking, in Hebrew as in other languages: To start with, most verb stems occur either in infinitive or imperative, or else either in past- or in present-tense forms—with past tense favored for telic achievement predicates (e.g., *nafal* 'fell', *nishbar* 'broke') and present tense for atelic activities (e.g., *boxe* 'cry', *yashen* 'sleep'). The earliest verbs to show alternation are the high-frequency, general purpose verbs such as the P1 verb with the root h-l-x 'go' [e.g., children might use both imperative *lex (mipo)!* 'go away from here' and past tense or perfective *aba (h)alax (la)'avoda* 'Daddy has gone to work'] or the verbs meaning *do, make,* and also *put, give,* and *take.* And this is followed by well-established command of the relevant distinctions between past, present, and future tense in forms and meanings (Berman & Dromi, 1984).

Yet the analogy between the two systems holds only so far, owing to critical differences between grammatical compared with lexical constraints. As noted, acquisition of morphological marking of transitivity through *binyan* alternations emerges later than verb tense marking, which is typically well established by around age 2;0 to 2;6 (see example 7). Compare, for instance, the sentence in (15a), produced by Smadar at age 2;3, with the required version in (15b).

(15) a.   *Miryam **overet** [P1] et kol ha-dapim*
             Miryam passes   OM all the-pages
             = Miryam goes over all the pages

    b. cf.   Miryam ***ma'avira*** [P5] *et kol ha-dapim*
              Miryam makes-pass   OM all the-pages
              = Miryam turns (over) all the pages

Example (15a) is ungrammatical because an intransitive verb form is used in a transitive context, but it can be interpreted as exactly what the child meant: She was complaining to her mother that Miriam (her older sister) kept turning the pages of the book, without giving her time to do so herself. Compare this to a hypothetical case where the child might have meant one of the following:

(15) c.   Miryam ***ta'avor*** [P1] *al yadi*
             Miryam will-pass   by-me

    d.   Miryam ***he'evira***   [P5]   *et kol ha-dapim*
             Miryam passed = turned   OM all the-pages

Both (15c) and (15d) are grammatically well formed; but if the child had intended to use present tense rather than future with the intransitive verb in (c) or rather than past with the transitive verb in (d), she would have been violating the temporal semantics of her entire utterance. In principle, children might use other cues for temporal marking of their utterances, such as adverbials like those meaning 'now', 'all the time', or 'the other day'. But in fact Hebrew-speaking children make minimal use of such options (Berman & Neeman, in press), so that the only indication of verb temporality within the simple clause remains verb morphology. Morphological neutralizations of valency distinctions, in contrast, impinge on the categorization of the verb alone, rather than on the semantics of the entire proposition, because this is derivable by other cues to its verb-argument configuration (word order, agreement, case marking).

A related difference between verb tense marking compared with verb-transitivity marking is its *obligatoriness*, because grammatical tense has no "expressive options" in the language. Hebrew speakers *must* assign a temporal value to each sentence through verb tense marking, either past, or present, or future, and this value must be consistent with the temporal content of the event described. In contrast, they can select to present the same real-world event from different perspectives, as transitive or intransitive; for example, (15a) could be reworded as intransitive 'all the pages are passing = are turning', just as Hagar could have said the equivalent of 'I fell (because of you)' or 'Why did you push me?' in place of (10b) and (10c). Transitivity marking thus represents a pragmatic, discourse-based choice for speakers, compared with the semantic necessity for specification of verb tense. Besides, as already noted, alternations in transitivity can be expressed by syntactic paraphrase, for example, use of an auxiliary-type verb to yield the equivalent of 'Miriam does so that all the pages turn [Intr]', or 'become old' rather than an inchoative verb, or use of pronouns meaning 'self' or 'one another' in place of morphological reflexives or reciprocals. Tense marking has no such options for semantic paraphrase in Hebrew.

A major reason why verb transitivity is acquired later than verb tense marking lies in the difference between lexical compared with grammatical knowledge involved by these two systems. Tense marking applies across the board, to all verbs that meet the syntactic criterion of being members of the major category V. Assignment of *binyan* marking depends on the particular class of lexical items to which a given verb belongs, and so applies less generally across the grammar of the language. As a result, *binyan* assignment can change across time without radically affecting the grammar of the language. But if tense/aspect systems change, the entire typological character of the language is bound to be affected (Givon, 1976). The limited productivity of the *binyan* system, in the sense of its functional nonuniqueness and the structural and semantic gaps and anomalies that it displays (sections 2.1 to 2.3), is a further factor. Command of *binyan* alternations requires command of a rich and varied vocabulary, before children can attend both to the general properties of the system and the many irregularities it manifests in the established lexicon.

These factors combine to explain why inflectional morphology is acquired before derivational and why in Hebrew, as in other languages, children generally make little use of derivational morphology for word formation during the period when they are gaining command of the syntax of simple clause structure. Not only do grammatical inflections express quite constant and regular relations—for example, singular versus plural, past versus present tense, first versus second person—even where there is no clear semantic basis (as in Hebrew gender agreement), a given structural process applies broadly across the lexicon. Early avoidance of derivational processes is particularly marked in Hebrew, where word-formation processes nearly all entail affixal morphology, in contrast to English. English-acquiring 2-year-olds take advantage of options such as zero derivation (without affixes) and they also coin words with certain derivational affixes that are morphologically and semantically transparent and do not demand any changes in the shape of the root or stem to which they are added (e.g., *-er* in *jump-er*). Yet in English, as in other languages, the period from around age 3 to 4 emerges as critical in the acquisition of word formation in general, and of verb-transitivity marking in particular (Berman & Clark, 1992; Clark, in press). These facts together explain why the 2-year-old quoted in (15a) marks her verb correctly for number, gender, person, and tense, but not for transitivity.

3.3. Acquisitional Strategies

The strategies children employ and the errors they make in acquiring the grammar of transitivity were analyzed in the context of: (a) their responses on the structured elicitation tasks described in the preceding section; (b) examples of unconventional lexical usage from parental reports and diary studies; and (c) longitudinal records of six children from around 1;6 to 3 years. These sources reveal relatively few errors in transitivity marking. Only 10% of the 2-year-olds' responses and 5% of those given by the older children were rated incorrect in transitivity on both the familiar and novel sections of the test described in the preceding section (Berman, 1993b). In conversational contexts, young children appear to avoid the problem of transitivity marking altogether; they typically do not go beyond a prototypical or favored verb-argument configuration for any given verb. For example, they will use P1 *yoshev* 'sit' a lot, but have no occasion to use a transitive counterpart, either P3 *yishev* 'settle' or

P5 causative *moshiv* 'seat', they use P1 *zorek* 'throw' often, but will rarely produce a context requiring intransitive P2 *nizrak* 'be/get thrown'. As noted, at most they will produce unanalyzed alternations of a few very common verbs.

Initial usage is thus constrained by the immature nonanalytical strategies associated with "pregrammatical" knowledge (section 3.1). Once children move into the grammar of transitivity, they adopt various strategies that reflect how they represent the system. Two main phases were identified in the process. During initial entry into the system, children resort to two kinds of avoidance strategies: Reliance on general purpose verbs like *make, do,* or *put* (section 3.4.1); and lexical overextension, yielding "neutralization" errors, where an intransitive verb is misused in a transitive context and vice versa (section 3.4.2). Later, when children have grasped the principle of transitivity marking in their language, but have not yet fully mastered the morpho-lexical alternations that this requires, they rely on different kinds of strategies, mainly syntactic paraphrase or lexical innovations in the form of "creative errors." (section 3.4.3).

3.3.1. Immature Use of General Purpose Verbs. Examples of this immature strategy were more common among the 2-year-olds than the older children in the transitivity test. For instance, in place of P5 *malbisha* = transitive 'dress', children said things like *sama lo mixnasayim* 'puts to-him = on-him trousers', *sama alav bgadim* 'puts on him clothes'; or for P3 transitive *mexasa* 'covers' – *sama la smixa* 'puts to-her (a) blanket'; for P5 *ma'axila* 'feed' children said things like *notenet lo le'exol* 'gives him to-eat', *notenet lo daysa* 'gives him porridge'; whereas for P2 *nishbar* 'got broken, broke', one child said *kibel maka* 'received a hit = got hurt'; or for transitive *melaxlex* 'dirty'—children said things like *zorek klipot* 'throws peels', *ose lixlux* 'makes = creates dirt'. These are all grammatically well formed, and represent felicitous though juvenile-sounding usages. Use of general purpose motion verbs— for example, *holex lemata* 'go downwards' for P1 *yored, hakelev holex haxuca* 'the dog goes outside' for P5 *moci et hakelev* 'takes-out the dog'—were very rare, showing that by the age of 2;6, Hebrew children are fully attuned to the typology of their language, as one that marks direction of motion lexically, within the verb (Talmy, 1985).

In principle, children could use the general activity verb *la'asot* 'do, make' to express causatives and other agentive activities, even though the Hebrew verb lacks the syntactic status of French *faire* or of English *make* in causative constructions. And it is in fact occasionally used in a way that points to early grasp of the causative notion; for example, when Hagar, age 2;4, is having salve smeared on a rash, she says *yesh li lixlux ba-beten. ima osa lixlux kaze* 'I've got dirt on my tummy. Mommy's *making* sort-of dirt' (to which her Mother replies, *lo, ani lo lixlaxti et ba-beten shel Hagari, ani maraxti aleha mishxa* 'No, I didn't *dirty* [P3] Hagari's tummy, I smeared salve on it'). A week or so later, telling her mother a story from *The Jungle Book*, she says *ima ze'eva asta bananot le-Mogli* 'Mommy Wolf *made* bananas for Mowgli', to which her mother responds with the lexical causative *hi he'exila bananot le-Mogli* 'she *fed* bananas to Mowgli'. Hagar, age 2;6, complains that *ha-naknik asa li* [P1] *ko'ev* 'the-sausage made to-me hurt' (cf. *hanaknik hix'iv* [P5] *li* 'hurt'); later in the same session, she pinches her mother, who yells *ay!* 'ouch!'; the child replies *tasi ay le-Hagari* 'make = do "ay" to Hagari', which her mother queries with the P5 transitive verb *lebax-iv le-Hagari at mit-kavenet?* 'to-hurt (to) Hagari you mean?'. But the very early, and semantically nonspecific activity verb *la'asot* is *not* commonly used with another predicate to express causation—in children's as in adult Hebrew. This syntactic option is strictly immature, and it is abandoned by children once they acquire the productive means for expressing causativity by verb morphology. That is, the factors of "productivity in use" and of favored expressive options (section 3.2.2) push children to *lexicalize* causatives in Hebrew.

Two-year-olds' limited use of general purpose verbs in place of transfer-of-location or causative verbs reflects a general lack of lexically specific verbs, as one facet of their inability to use morphology for alternating valency. Another such strategy takes the form of overextension of intransitive verbs to syntactically transitive contexts and vice versa.

3.3.2. Early Transitivity Errors: Lexical Neutralizations.

Early command of syntactic marking of transitivity was contrasted with use of the high-frequency P1 verb *nafal* 'fall' in example (10) and in the use of intransitive *over* 'pass' in a transitive context in example (15): These occurred not only in well-formed intransitive contexts, but also erroneously, in transitive constructions, in place of P5 *hipil* 'make-fall, drop, push down' and *ma'avir* 'make pass, cause to turn'. Such errors typically occur at a phase when children do not make corresponding errors in marking grammatical verb tense (see section 3.3), but they are nonetheless an *early* type of error, rare in the speech usage of children beyond ages 3 to 4. These errors, akin to Bowerman's (1974, 1982) causative overextensions in English, and to what I term *neutralizations* of transitivity distinctions (Berman 1980, 1982b), are of considerable theoretical interest, particularly in Hebrew, which disallows use of the same verb form in both intransitive and transitive contexts, apart from two marginal exceptions (section 2.1). Consider, first, the distribution of such transitivity "misassignments" across the database examined here.

The structured elicitation test yielded relatively few such errors across 32 items—20 requiring established verbs and 12 lexical innovations (Appendix I-1). They accounted for only 5% of total responses from the youngest children, age 2;6 to 3. At least one such error was made by 8 out of the 10 youngest children, compared with only two of the older children (Lital, age 3;7, and Liat, age 7;9), and theirs were all on the innovative part of the test, in the form of intransitive P1 verbs not being changed to novel transitive verbs in a causative context. These findings confirm that neutralizations are an early strategy, at a period when children have not yet recognized the typological imperative for alternating morphology along with syntax to mark transitivity changes. Fully half the errors were, as predicted, overuse of the basic P1, with no switch to causative P5—but these verbs all elicited innovative forms, a task that is in general beyond the abilities of children younger than 3. More errors were made by overextending intransitive to transitive contexts, seeming to confirm Bowerman's (1974, 1982) claims for English. The only exceptions were from a single child (Yasmin, 3;0) who used P3 transitives in place of P4: *ha-kadur megalgel* 'the ball rolls + Trans', *ze megahec levad* 'it irons alone = by itself'. Finally, on both this test and an earlier pilot study, children extended P4 *hitpael* verbs to transitive contexts with object marking *et* far more than with P2 *nif'al* forms.

Parental observations and longitudinal samples of spontaneous speech show identical patterns (Appendix I-2): Neutralization errors were made at least once by around 20 different children; over two thirds were intransitive verbs used in transitive contexts; well over half were neutralizations to P1; and direct objects case marked by *et* occurred far more often with intransitive verbs in P4 than in P2. These findings indicate a phenomenon that is sporadic and yet consistent, occasional and yet robust, across different elicitation settings and different children. The claim that 2- and 3-year-old children, in the period of early grammatical development, do not know how to alternate the transitivity value of the verbs they use seems strongly corroborated.

But how can these errors be explained? They are remarkable because, unlike the case for the analogous English errors documented by Bowerman, Hebrew grammar prohibits the same verb form from being used with both intransitive and transitive syntax. This means that Hebrew-acquiring children have no "positive evidence" for overextending the transitivity value of verbs.[9] Bowerman's (1978, 1982) account of this phenomenon

---

[9]An analogous problem was encountered by Gergely (1989) in Hungarian: His daughter sometimes omitted a required causative suffix, using intransitive verbs in a causative context. He explained this by a two-phase processing model: Children start out by using bare stems, by means of "affix-stripping," and later they realize affix attachment must be assigned wherever a verb is used causatively. Such a strategem also characterizes how some

in English as overgeneralization of a rule that applies to part of the verbs in the target language might be upheld in one of two ways. It could be argued that children *do* have positive evidence, from the two small classes of Hebrew verbs that allow the same form both in causative and inchoative adjective-based verbs, both in transitive and unaccusative process verbs (section 2.1). This must be rejected, because the P5 inchoative forms of adjectives meaning *become red, healthy, ripe, white,* are not found in 2-year-old Hebrew input or output, whereas the P5 verbs meaning *start* or *continue* typically occur with agent subjects but no surface object, for example, in sentences like "No, I won't begin," "You can go on." So it seems unlikely that children's overgeneralizations derive from these marginal exceptions to the rule that the same verb cannot occur with both transitive and intransitive syntax in Hebrew. A more motivated alternative relates to the special status of verbs in the P1 pattern, described as having a privileged status: It has the highest frequency of occurrence across child and adult Hebrew, it alone is made up equally of verbs that are canonically transitive and intransitive, and it is semantically most "basic" or nonderived (section 2.3.1). All neutralization errors in Hebrew would then take the form of P1: Intransitive P1 verbs used in place of causative P5 verbs, and/or transitive P1 verbs used in place of change-of-state P2 verbs. However, overextensions of P1 verbs account for only around half the examples listed in Appendix I. And the fact that different children do sometimes use the intransitive P4 and P2 patterns with a direct object still needs accounting for. Thus the nature of endstate Hebrew cannot account for these errors as overgeneralizations from input data.

Other solutions have since been proposed to account for these phenomena: Pinker (1989) suggested that children may initially assign erroneous argument structure to the verbs they learn, whereas Braine (1988; Braine, Brody, Fisch, & Weisberger, 1990) argued that new verbs are acquired with a default argument structure, so that initially, their lexicon lacks any specific argument structure. My explanation is rather different. Initially, children acquire verbs with one specific argument structure (unlike Braine), and that argument structure is correct for that verb (unlike Pinker). The overextension errors they make in a language like Hebrew are due to *lack* of a relevant linguistic generalization: Use of a verb in a different argument structure than the one in which it is acquired demands a morphological operation on the form of the verb. This

---

children first conceive Hebrew verb morphology, because their earliest verbs may take the form of (nonexistent) free stems stripped down from the normative infinitive or imperative forms with prefixes. But this is relevant to the acquisition of Hebrew *inflectional* morphology. Because this takes place much earlier, well before age 2, perceptual difficulties may indeed play a major role in early verb construals and omission of obligatory affixal inflections.

knowledge builds up as follows: (a) Each verb has a single argument structure. (b) A single verb form can be used with more than one argument structure. (c) When the initial argument structure of (a) is changed, the verb form must change. The precise synchronization and integration of knowledge components (b) and (c) will determine for individual children and individual verbs how often, if at all, the syntactic knowledge of (b) is applied without the language-particular morphological constraint of (c). Finally, knowledge-component (c) needs to be further constrained by (d) the principle of lexical productivity and (e) learning of lexical idiosyncrasies. The strategies deployed in moving across these phases are next reviewed.

3.3.3. Creative Errors and Other Later Strategies.

What strategies are adopted by children once they proceed beyond the knowledge previously defined in (b), that verbs can be used with more than a single argument structure? To answer this question, different kinds of later, "creative" errors documented in earlier work on acquisition of Hebrew verb morphology (Berman, 1980, 1982; Berman & Sagi, 1981) were extended to include the following categories: *Periphrastic syntactic* means may replace verb morphology; *lexical mismatches* arise through *pattern mixing*, nonconventional use of P2 or P4 for intransitives, and of P3 or P5 for transitives; *semantic overmarking* operates on P1 verbs to express inchoativity by P2 or P4 and causativity by P5; and *lexical innovation* serves to fill genuine gaps in the established lexicon.

Hebrew has two main ways of marking transitivity distinctions: *binyan* verb morphology and syntactic periphrasis. It transpires that children prefer the *first* option almost universally. The three main classes of intransitive predicates all have productive syntactic means of expression: *reflexives* by 'self' pronouns (e.g., *acmi* 'myself', *acmo* 'himself'); *reciprocals* by 'each other' pronouns (e.g., colloquial *exad et ha-sheni* 'one OM the-other'); and *inchoatives* by an auxiliary verb meaning 'become': *nihya*, the P2 form of the verb for 'be' or *na'asa*, the P2 form of 'make, do'. Detailed analysis of these constructions in children's Hebrew is beyond the present study. But there is evidence that children use reflexive pronouns from age 3; for instance, on the structured test described earlier, one child aged 3;0 said *megalgel et acmo* 'is-rolling OM himself' in place of expected P4 *mitgalgel*, and another age 3;9 said *mesareket et acma* 'is-combing + Fem OM herself' in place of P4 *mistareket*. These children are clearly beyond step (b), although they avoid verb morphology in these examples. A rather different picture emerges for syntactic constructions expressing reciprocals and inchoatives. I do not recall a single use of a reciprocal pronoun in all our extensive database; but there are several examples of morphological expression of reciprocality among older children who overextend P4 to express this notion, for example, a boy age 4;3 says *hayeladim kaxa **mitlaxamin** ba-gan* 'the kids kind-of *fight* at school', in place of conventional P1 *loxamin* or P2 *nilxamin*; a girl of 5;1 says *ani lo ohevet she **mitravim** kol hazman* 'I don't like (it) that (people) ***quarrel*** all the time (cf. established P1 *ravim*); and a 6-year-old describes a game by saying *ha-yetedot **mitpagshim** be'emca* 'the pegs ***meet*** in the middle' (cf. established P2 *nifgashim*). Similarly, to express inchoatives, preschool children rarely, if ever, use the auxiliary verbs meaning *become*; they do innovate inchoatives morphologically with P4, as in the following examples from different children age 3½ to 6: *hitrazet* 'you got thin' from 'thin' *raza*, *hitkatmu* 'got-stained' from *kétem* 'a stain', *hit'avek* 'got-dusty' from *avak* the noun 'dust', *hitparati* 'I got (my hair) untidy' from *parua* 'untidy', *mitxashex* 'getting dark' from *xoshex* 'dark' (cf. established P4 *hizdaken* 'grow old', *hit'ayef* 'get tired', *hitragez* 'get angry').

Children's "creative errors" in extending predicates to different syntactic contexts thus favor *binyan* morphology for marking reciprocality and inchoativeness. Reflexives alone alternate with the fully productive set of *self* pronouns, specified by Condition A of government and binding theory (Chien & Wexler, 1989; Kave, 1990). In Hebrew, these reflexive pronouns apply across the board, beyond the restricted set of syntactic accusatives and of semantic bodily activities such as washing, dressing, or drying oneself. In expressing reciprocals and inchoatives, by contrast, children prefer verb morphology by P4, both in normative and unconventional extensions.

An earlier study noted the importance of lexical mismatches in the form of "pattern mixing" (Berman, 1980), as evidence that once children recognize that morphological changes are required—that is, they reach step (c)—they may select the wrong pattern for a given verb, but this will not cross the bounds of transitivity. Instead, P2 and P4 forms will be reserved for intransitive predicates, and P3 and P5 for transitives (section 2.1). We recorded about 40 such P2/P4 intransitive switchings. For example, Daniel (3;5) uses P2 *niklaf* for P4 *hitkalef* 'peel off', and Ran (5;0) uses P2 *nexlaf* for *mitxalef* 'change, switch places'; whereas Nir (3;9) uses P4 *mitxankim* for P2 *nexnakim* = Intr. 'suffocate' and Sival (4;1) uses P4 *hit'alev* for P2 *ne'elav* 'be-offended'. As for the even commoner P3/P5 transitives, Asaf (3;10) says P3 *xibeti* for P5 *hexbeti* 'hid (something)', Anat (5;10) says P3 *mesaba'at* for P5 *masbi'a* 'satisfy = fill up with food', Ginat (4;6) says P5 *higdalti* for P3 *gidalti* 'raise, grow', and Shelly (4;8) says P5 *hicfifu* for P3 *cofefu* 'they-crowded'. Similarly, the syntactically productive passive participle resultant endstate forms alternate between the P1-derived CaCuC pattern and the P3-derived meCuCaC pattern, for example, Nir (3;7) uses *kamut* for *mekumat* 'crushed', Ido (5;0) says *mecuba* for *cavua* 'colored' (see, further, section 4.2). These errors manifest grammatical rule-bound knowledge, earlier defined as operating prior to command of lexical convention. And they support the claim that the factor of productivity precedes that of convention in the acquisition of word formation in general (Clark & Berman, 1984).

At this phase, a rather different strategy is revealed by semantic over-extension, in the form of overmarking of P1: Children turn P1 intransitives into nonoccurrent P2 forms to express inchoativity, or they turn P1 transitives into nonoccurrent P5 forms to express causativity. For example, the highly precocious 2-year-old Smadar describes entry into a state of pain by P2 *nik-av* 'got-hurt' (cf. P1 *ko'ev* 'be-hurt'), Sivan (3;7) uses P2 *nifxadeti* for 'get-scared' (cf. P1 *paxadeti* 'be-scared'), Rama (4;6) says that her ache P2 *ne'evar* 'passed, got-over' versus P1 *avar* 'be-over'. These children clearly distinguish between entering into and being in state, and they use unconventional verb morphology to mark this. Other instances of innovative P2 forms where the only conventional intransitive verb is in P1 show that children reject the basic P1 as a means of expressing unaccusative change-of-state predicates (noted as very rare in this form in Hebrew)— for example, Arik (5;2) *ninbal* for P1 *naval* 'faded, got faded' (of a flower that had withered), Anat (4;6) says the boy *nigdal* 'got-big' for P1 *gadal* 'grew', Ron (5;3) *nikpe'u* for *kaf'u*' froze = became frozen', and the same child also innovated P2 *niktan* 'got smaller, shrank', cf. *katan* 'small'.

A similar pattern is revealed when children change P1 transitive verbs to P5 to express high transitivity, even though these forms are syntactically unmotivated, because they fail to alter the surface verb-argument configuration. Thus, a 4-year-old girl demonstrating how she is turning her cardboard crown around to show the gold-painted side says *tir'i ex ani* **mahafixa** *et ha-keter* 'look how I am-making-invert [P5] OM the-crown' (cf. conventional [P1] *hofexet*); a 5-year-old boy brags he can un-lace his shoes by himself, saying *ani yaxol levad* **le-haxlic** *et ha-na'alayim* 'I can alone make-take-off [P5] my shoes' rather than established P1 *la-xloc*; and when Hagar is 4;1, her mother tells her not to stifle her baby sister with P1 *al* **taxneki** *et ha-tinoket*, to which she replies *ani lo* **maxnika** *ota* 'I'm not stifling [P5] her' (cf. P1 *xoneket*). There are other examples: Hagar (4;0) P5 *mashpixa* for P1 *shofexet* = Trans 'spill', Asaf (3;7) *mam-xik* for *moxek* 'erase', Rama (3;5) *madxifa* for *doxefet* 'push', Yael (3;4) *himriax* for *marax* 'smear, spread', Ginat (4;5) *masrif* for *soref* Trans 'burn'.

In modifying the basic, high-frequency P1 pattern, children are guided by productivity in current lexical usage and new word formation: P2 rather than intransitive P1 functions to express semantic change-of-states, and P5 rather than transitive P1 to mark an activity as highly agentive and causative in content. Children's construal of P5 as *the* means par excellence for expressing causativity is supported in several ways. First, they quite often use P5 for lexically missing causatives and so fill accidental lexical gaps by spontaneous coinages, for example, *meshin* (normative *moshin*) from P1 *yashen* 'sleep', *masxe* from P1 *soxe* 'swim', *maxrik* from P1 *xorek* 'creak'. Second, they almost never use available options for syntactic periphrasis with verbs meaning *make* or *cause*. And, third, on the structured elicitation task described earlier, they did much better on coining novel causatives than in producing other innovative forms. However, children's overextensions from P1 transitives to P5 causatives violate what was defined earlier as canonic, productive causative formation in current Hebrew: by P5 applied to P1 intransitive activity verbs and stative adjectives. The fact that children go beyond this to causativize P1 transitive-activity verbs could be symptomatic of a more general process of *language change* now under way in Hebrew: There is a tendency to extend P1 transitive verbs to P5 in colloquial usage (e.g., novel P5 *le-halxic* 'to make someone feel under pressure, put under pressure' versus P1 *li-lxoc* 'to press [on], *le-ha'aziv* 'cause to leave, fire' from *la'azov* 'leave'), as well as in specialized contexts (e.g., *le-hashtil* 'implant' from *li-shtol* 'to-plant', *le-hashgir* 'to-launch' from P3 *le-shager* 'send-off'). Moreover, colloquial usage avoids the classical morphological identification of P5 for both intransitive inchoatives and transitive causatives akin to English *harden, blacken, ripen* (section 2.1). Although children's nonnormative usages will not *cause* change in language, their more sophisticated, knowledge-based "creative" errors are indicative of quite general directions of ongoing processes of change.

In sum, the nonfelicitous immature errors as well as more creative later errors reviewed here support the developmentally constructivist view underlying this study. In learning how transitivity distinctions are marked in Hebrew, as in acquiring other systems of the grammar, children do not proceed from zero to endstate knowledge, from entry to exit in one single jump. They acquire partial, piecemeal knowledge, extended through varied strategies. The errors they make are evidence of reorganizations and reconstruals en route from initial to full mastery.

4. DISCUSSION: IN DEFENSE OF DEVELOPMENT[10]

An important criterion of language acquisition theory is how it explains the child's task in distinguishing between general and particular knowledge: general in the sense of common to all input languages com-

---

[10]The phrase "in defense of development" is the title of my commentary to Crain's article "Language Acquisition in the Absence of Experience" (Berman, 1991).

pared with the particular native tongue, on the one hand, and of rule bound and regular compared with idiosyncratic, on the other. I suggest that from the phase of early grammar, children become increasingly sensitive to the typological bias of their particular native tongue, which pushes them to recognize that Hebrew verb morphology is relevant to verb-argument configurations. However, they do not acquire this system in toto, by a one-step jump into full, endstate knowledge: As in other areas of the grammar, no knowledge gives way to partial knowledge, which is then extended and reorganized to encompass major and minor regularities (e.g., particular directions of *binyan* changes), and these in turn are constrained by detailed knowledge of particular subsystems and idiosyncratic groups of items.

Certain assumptions about the development of linguistic knowledge guide the following discussion of continuity (section 4.1), speed (section 4.2), and order (section 4.3) of development in this analysis. The same "operating principles" and processing explanations (Slobin, 1985), the same "acquisitional principles" (Clark, 1983, in press), and the same developmental factors (section 3.2) impinge both on how children move into new knowledge and how this knowledge changes and gets reorganized across time. However, such factors do *not* apply equally across the board by invariant, age-related stages, as within a Piagetian constructionist view; rather, they interact with developmental phases that recur at different periods of time in relation to different subdomains of linguistic (and other) knowledge (Karmiloff-Smith, 1986). Structurally equivalent linguistic subdomains do not emerge at the same time in all languages, as in a maturationist view of acquisition (Borer, 1991; Borer & Wexler, 1987); rather, acquisition of specific subdomains is affected by how these factors interact in the development of specific target languages (section 4.3).

4.1. Continuity in Development: Universal versus Particular

My analysis was based on the assumption that linguistic universals are accessible to children from the outset: Children do not need to learn that there are different semantic classes of predicates, that predicates can have one or more arguments, or that different types of propositions will entail different configurations of verb-argument relations. They do have to learn how these distinctions are specified in the surface morphosyntax of their native language. Such language-particular knowledge includes: (a) the subcategorization constraints that apply to specific verbs and verb classes—an issue not considered in the present context; for instance, in Hebrew the verb *use* governs an instrumental case-marking preposition, and the verb *want* can take an infinitival and a *that* complementizer (for English, see Fisher, L. Gleitman, & H. Gleitman, 1991, and for Japanese, Rispoli, 1991); (b) the system of case marking, by bound inflections, appositions, and so on, and how these markers are distributed in realizing predicate–argument relations; (c) possible correlates between predicate semantics, such as activity versus achievement and morphosyntactic realizations; and (d) the focus of this study: morpholexical correlates of different values for syntactic transitivity.

An earlier finding for which new evidence was marshaled in this study relates to this last issue, the occurrence of morphological "neutralizations" of the obligatory change in morphological form with a change in transitivity (section 3.3.2). Any account of acquisition must contend with children's espousal of rules, or of constructions, not available in the input (see, for examples, Borer's, 1991, study of Italian children's marking of participle agreement on the object of verbs that take *have* as well as those taking *be*). This issue can be accommodated within the general model I have proposed for language development as proceeding from pregrammatical to structure bound and on to conventions of language use (section 3.1). Early verb use of Hebrew-speaking children is definable as "pregrammatical": It does not violate universal constraints, because there are languages in which syntactic configurations suffice to indicate a change in transitivity values (e.g., the *break, change*, or *open* class of verbs in English); it does, however, violate the grammar of the input language, Hebrew. But this is exactly what one might predict, because the principle of *binyan* pattern alternation needs to be *learned*; it is simply not available to children at the pregrammatical phase of acquisition of language-particular markings of transitivity distinctions. This set of claims is consistent with what has been termed the "weak continuity" hypothesis: Early Hebrew, like early Italian or English, conforms with universal constraints on possible form–meaning matchings in natural languages, but not with all the particular manifestations of these relations in a given target-language.

4.2. Rate of Acquisition: The Developmental Paradox

The developmental thrust of this discussion follows from the assumption that in language as in other areas children do not proceed in a single jump from initial to endstate knowledge. This is shown by the different strategies and distinct types of unconventional, non-endstate usages of children at different phases in the development of *binyan* transitivity marking (section 3.3). The "developmental paradox" is that the rate of this development is both very rapid and long drawnout. Rapidity is demonstrated, for instance, by the brief duration of only a few months characterizing the stepwise developments sketched for acquisition of the grammatical relations of subject and object in examples (7) and (8) (section 1.2). Yet elsewhere I argue that such knowledge, too, is only partial, often confined to the domain of the simple clause. For instance, the knowledge that null subjects in Hebrew can occur in the syntactically inadmissible contexts of third person and present tense across strings of clauses, when discourse motivated by the need for topic elision, emerges much later than age 3, and is not fully commanded even by school-age children (Berman, 1990a).

Work in progress on the development of diverse structural domains (e.g., tense-aspect systems, relative clauses, and clause linkage) in narrative texts elicited from children at different ages in five different languages reveals the selfsame paradox (Berman & Slobin, in press). Three-year-olds may manifest near-complete mastery of the structural devices available to their native tongue. But they use them in very restricted contexts, from a syntactic and semantic as well as from a discourse point of view. For example, English -*ing* participles are used first without and later with auxiliary *be* as a deictic present tense, only later with *be* as a relative tense in past progressive or without *be* in complement constructions, even later as a major means of expressing attendant circumstances through nonfinite modifying clauses. That is, initial acquisition of this construction and errors in its grammatical form are shortlived, yet its full developmental path is staggered across different interrelated subsystems, across a long period of time. Acquiring command of Hebrew verb morphology, too, is both an early and a lengthy process, dependent on a complex interaction of the developmental factors delineated earlier.

4.3. Order of Emergence: Language Structure and Language Use

I have suggested that a "typological imperative" motivates Hebrew-acquiring children to recognize that they must mark the transitivity value of predicates by means of *binyan* morphology. I also argued that this knowledge emerges later than the highly pervasive or structurally "weighty" inflectional markings of subject–verb agreement, and of verb-tense inflections. The relatively later acquisition of *binyan* transitivity was explained as due to the more central structural status of inflectional compared with derivational morphology, of (simple-clause) grammar compared with lexicon. This is confirmed by research based on naturalistic data and structured elicitations showing that *binyan* verb morphology emerges at much the same time as *other* processes of Hebrew word formation. The age of 3 to 4 also proves to be critical for derivation of: (a) innovative nouns from familiar verbs (Clark & Berman, 1984);

(b) innovative denominal verbs from familiar nouns and adjectives (Berman, 1989); and (c) adjectival passives marking resultant endstates from familiar verbs in different transitive *binyan* patterns (Berman & Clark, 1992). Two-year-olds typically make errors in these areas, or else they avoid such formations altogether; from around age 3, children apply appropriate morphological modifications much of the time; 4- to 5-year-olds show good command of the structural properties of such alternations; and by early school-age, children conform increasingly to conventions of the established lexicon.

In marked contrast to these processes of word formation, three other areas of Hebrew morphology constitute much later developments: (d) noun compounds derived from the combination of two simplex nouns; (e) abstract verb-derived nominals based on the *binyan* distinctions; and (e) syntactic passives, derived from the finite forms of the three transitive *binyan* patterns (sections 2.2, 2.3.2). The later emergence of these constructions is explained in large part by the factor of "rhetorical bias," in the sense of the structural options preferred by speakers out of those available in their language in order to express different form–meaning relations and discourse functions. The idea of "rhetorical bias" is closely allied to the factor of relative productivity in current usage, as defined for new verb formation (section 3.2.2). It explains why it takes longer for children to acquire certain constructions that appear equally available for expressing the same semantic content.

Consider, first, the relatively late emergence of noun compounds in Hebrew. The morphological operations demanded by these constructions are in principle accessible to Hebrew-acquiring children from the rich bound morphology of the inflectional systems they master by age 3. And syntactically compounds are straightforward, because they follow the head-initial order of all noun-plus-modifier expressions in Hebrew (compare the compound noun-noun string *sixat telefon* 'conversation-telephone = phone conversation' with the noun-adjective *sixat telefonit* 'telephonic conversation', or the noun-demonstrative *sixa zo* 'this conversation', *sixa sheli* 'my conversation'). Nonetheless, children avoid these constructions until well beyond age 4, in contrast to their English-speaking peers (Clark & Berman, 1984). The reason lies in language usage rather than linguistic form. Colloquial Hebrew, which forms the input and output for children's acquisition, possesses other, equally productive *alternatives* for expressing noun-noun relations, using the genitive particle *shel* for possession or other prepositions for relations of containment, partitivity, and so on (Berman, 1987a). Compounding as a "productive" syntactic means for combining nouns is restricted to more normative literary usage and to formal expository style, of the kind largely irrelevant to children's construals of the language. And as a means for new noun formation, children like adults consistently prefer the morphological device of affixation to a consonantal root or bound stem rather than by juxtaposing two nouns as is common in Germanic languages.

An even later acquisition are action nominals, which correspond to both gerundive *breaking* and derived *breakage*, both *arriving* and *arrival* in English. Children age 5 and 7 years often appeared to understand sentences with these constructions, but they produced them in fewer than one third of the elicitation contexts, compared with 9-year-olds and 11-year-old sixth-graders, who gave 70% and 93% correct responses (Mayroz, 1988). In terms of form, these nominals are constructed by a quite regular set of derivational processes relating to the *binyan* membership of their source verbs. Yet they are consistently avoided by children, who can and do use other devices to express the same ideas: finite clauses subordinated by the Hebrew *that* formative; nonfinite infinitivals; or prepositional phrases. These latter options are more analytically transparent than the corresponding nominalizations (compare *hu shavar* 'he broke' vs. *shvirat-o* 'breaking-his', *hem higi'u* 'they arrived + PL vs. *haga'at-am* 'arrival-their'); and they are typically preferred in everyday spoken Hebrew, the input language most relevant to children well on through school-age.

The third, most pertinent, example is the avoidance of verbal or syntactic passives by Hebrew-speaking children, in contrast to the early acquisition of corresponding constructions in Sesotho (Demuth, 1988) or Quiche Mayan (Pye & Poz, 1988). Hebrew passive formation is structurally almost entirely productive for verbs that are semantically active, and that syntactically govern accusative case. And it is morphologically productive through the *binyan* system: P1 verbs like those for *give, push, steal* change to P2; P3 verbs change to the passive *pu'al* pattern (e.g., *tukan* 'was-mended', *ye-kuftar* 'will-be-buttoned'); and P5 change to their passive *hof'al* counterpart (e.g., *huram* 'was lifted', *yu-klat* 'will-be-recorded'). But in current Hebrew, syntactic passives occur mainly in the expository style of academic discourse and more formal media usage. Not only are syntactic passives relatively rare in colloquial Hebrew, it is hard to elicit them from young children by experimental procedures. Second-graders, age 7 to 8, gave passive-form responses to follow-up questions asking "What happened . . . ?" less than one third of the time, compared with around two thirds such answers from seventh-graders (age 13 to 14), and 75% from adults (Shani, 1990). And on a sentence-completion task, toward the end of first grade (age 6;8 to 7;6) children avoided using the *pu'al* and *hof'al* passive *binyan* forms almost entirely, compared with extensive use of these forms by both 12-year-old sixth-graders and adults: Total passive forms provided in obligatory contexts came to 97% of the responses from older children and adults, as against only 14% from

6-year-olds, and nearly all of the latter were in the *nif'al* P2 form, and not in the two strictly passive binyanim (Kenan, Nirpaz, & Dekel, 1988). This cannot be attributed to avoidance of *binyan* alternations, because on the same test, the 6-year-olds produced *causative* P5 *hif'il* verbs as required in 65% of their responses (12-year-olds and adults provided causatives to the same high extent as passives, in almost all obligatory contexts). Nor is this avoidance due to formal difficulty of morphological patterns with the uniquely passive-marking [u] element. As noted, children use passive [u]-marked participles (e.g., P1 *shavur* 'broken', P3 *metukan* 'fixed', P5 *muram* 'raised, heightened') in adjectival or lexical passive forms, to express the notion of resultant endstate, from an early age (around half the required responses from 3-year-olds and nearly 70% from 5-year-olds; Berman & Clark, 1992). Rather, passives are *marked* constructions in Hebrew, not only in morphosyntactic terms, but also in terms of rhetorical bias and usage preferences. Again, Hebrew speakers have several *alternative* ways of achieving the pragmatic discourse functions typical of passives: downgrading of the agent and topicalized focusing on the patient–undergoer element. One such option, common in Hebrew 2-year-old input and output, are subjectless impersonal constructions with third-person plural verbs (e.g., impersonal *lakxu oti* 'took + PL me' = 'I got-taken' versus passive *nilkax-ti*). Speakers can also use dative-affectee constructions for agency downgrading (section 1.2); and patient or undergoer thematic roles can be focused on by simple fronting operations or by use of middle-voice achievement predicates in P2 or P4. These options, favored in colloquial Hebrew, are accessible in both the input and output of 2- and 3-year-olds. It is not surprising, then, that they forego passive constructions well on through school-age.

The developmental route sketched here involves two complementary facets of the form/function relationship in language acquisition. Order of development across time (as with the English *-ing* forms in the preceding section) is determined by the development of more functions for a single form. Order of emergence (this section) is determined by the development of new forms for a particular function.

4.4. The Developmental Challenge: A Confluence of Cues

What emerges is that generalizations concerning order of acquisition will be typologically constrained by the particular target language from two points of view: structural and rhetorical. Certain construction types may emerge early or late in different languages depending on their typological "weight" in that language—for example, early emergence of lexicalized causatives and resultatives compared with verbal passives in Hebrew, and early emergence of passives in Sesotho and Quiche Mayan compared with English or Hebrew; perfect aspect in American versus British English (Slobin, 1987) and nominalizations or relative clauses in Turkish compared with European or Semitic languages (Slobin, 1988, 1991).

There is obviously a close correlation between frequency of input occurrence and both rate and order of language acquisition and language development. But input frequency alone does not explain children's *selectivity*. After all, young children do encounter instances of other usages, including Hebrew compound nouns, nominalized forms, and syntactic passives, as well as VS word order. Children from middle-class backgrounds, like those who provided the database for our studies, have considerable exposure to the rather formal and archaic style of much children's literature from as early as age 2. Rather, as Slobin (1987) pointed out, "frequency reflects function," in the sense that children are sensitive to the preferred options for expressing particular semantic content and discourse functions from an early age. The fact that certain forms are favored in everyday usage defines the particular dialect to which children are initially peculiarly attuned, prior to the addition of more specialized varieties, such as narrative or academic discourse. The latter are critically affected by factors such as linguistic convention, literacy, and formal study, and they are thus particularly suited to school-age acquisition and usage.

Finally, this chapter has noted several factors involved in the multiple bootstrapping at emergence, and confluence of cues in development, of verb transitivity in Hebrew. The challenge for a theory of language development is to articulate precisely how these and other factors interact with one another, in relation to different subsystems of different target languages. This can be illustrated by a topic relevant to acquisition of transitivity distinctions, not as yet analyzed for Hebrew (or, as far as I know, for other languages): What constitutes a "basic form"? The question is still open as to which form of a given predicate children initially prefer, transitive or intransitive, activity or achievement. Nor is it clear what motivates the choice of early verbs from these points of view. Different explanations might be sought which, in keeping with the general thrust of this chapter, I would consider to be interactive rather than mutually exclusive. Relevant factors might include: (a) formal morphophonological simplicity, although this tends to account more for accuracy rather than extent of production (Clark & Berman, 1987); (b) input frequency, which as noted is at best a partial explanation, because some motivation must exist for why some forms are more common in input than others; and adults probably use alternating forms of the same verbs from the time children are very young; (c) the pragmatics of "prototypical activity scenes" (Slobin, 1985), such that certain situations are basically viewed and hence described in early child language input and output as change-of-state events, and so would initially favor P2 or P4 intransitive predicates, whereas others might be prototypically actor–activity-type events, favoring P1 intransitive or P3 intransitive activity verbs with animate subjects; whereas (d) the impact of discourse constraints, such as appropriate alternating of perspectives on a given scene, may constitute a later development in general (Berman, 1993a).

This chapter has aimed at pointing to some directions that might profitably be pursued in the interests of formulating an integrative theory of both the emergence and development of knowledge, of both linguistic structure and language use. Attempts to isolate out one specific variable of the many involved in such a task may provide strongly predictive theories. But they run the risk of not accounting for many of the facts.

ACKNOWLEDGMENTS

Collection and analysis of the database for early grammatical development was supported by grant no. 1-11-070:4/87 from the German-Israel Foundation for Scientific Research and Development (GIF). Research on lexical usage and innovations was supported by grant no. 87-00015/1 from the United States–Israel Binational Science Foundation (BSF). Transcription of longitudinal data was facilitated by funding from the Child Language Data Exchange System, Carnegie-Mellon University, Pittsburgh. I am indebted to Eve Clark for helpful comments on an earlier draft, and to Clifton Pye for his meticulous review of the version prepared for the workshop on Cross-Linguistic and Cross-Population Contributions to Language Acquisition Theory, Institute for Advanced Studies, Hebrew University, Jerusalem, June 2–6, 1991.

REFERENCES

Alroy, O. (1992). *Causativity marking in the Hebrew* binyan *system: A study of children and adults*. Unpublished master's thesis, Tel Aviv University.
Andersen, S. (1985). Typological distinctions in word formation. In T. Shopen (Ed.), *Language typology and syntactic description* (Vol. 3, pp. 150–201). Cambridge: Cambridge University Press.
Armon-Lotem, S., & Kfir, Y. (1989). *Surface subjects in early child Hebrew*. Language Acquisition Project Working Paper, Tel Aviv University.
Aronoff, M. (1976). *Morphology in generative grammar*. Cambridge, MA: MIT Press.
Berman, R. A. (1978). Early words: How and why a child uses her first verbs. *International Journal of Psycholinguistics, 5*, 1–25.
Berman, R. A. (1980). Child language as evidence for grammatical description: Preschoolers' construal of transitivity in the Hebrew verb system. *Linguistics, 18*, 677–701.
Berman, R. A. (1982a). Dative marking of the affectee role. *Hebrew Annual Review, 6*, 35–59.

Berman, R. A. (1982b). Verb-pattern alternation: The interface of morphology, syntax, and semantics in Hebrew child language. *Journal of Child Language, 9*, 169–191.

Berman, R. A. (1985). Acquisition of Hebrew. In D. I. Slobin (Ed.), *Crosslinguistic study of language acquisition* (Vol. 1, pp. 255–371). Hillsdale, NJ: Lawrence Erlbaum Associates.

Berman, R. A. (1986a). The acquisition of morphology/syntax: A crosslinguistic perspective. In P. Fletcher & M. Garman (Eds.), *Language acquisition* (2nd ed., pp. 429–447). Cambridge: Cambridge University Press.

Berman, R. A. (1986b). A step-by-step model of language learning. In I. Levin (Ed.), *Stage and structure: Re-opening the debate* (pp. 191–219). Norwood, NJ: Ablex.

Berman, R. A. (1987a). A developmental route: Learning about the form and use of complex nominals. *Linguistics, 27*, 980–1007.

Berman, R. A. (1987b). Productivity in the lexicon: New-noun formation in Modern Hebrew. *Folia Linguistica, 21*, 425–461.

Berman, R. A. (1988). On the ability to relate events in narrative. *Discourse Processes, 11*, 469–497.

Berman, R. A. (1989, October). *Children's knowledge of verb structure: Data from Hebrew.* Paper presented at Boston University Conference on Language Development, Boston.

Berman, R. A. (1990a). On acquiring an (S)VO language: Subjectless sentences in children's Hebrew. *Linguistics, 28*, 1135–1166.

Berman, R. A. (1990b, February). *On new-root formation in Hebrew: A psycholinguistic view.* Paper presented at Workshop on Modern Hebrew, Israel Theoretical Linguistics Society, Hebrew University, Jerusalem.

Berman, R. A. (1991). In defence of development. Commentary on Stephen Crain: Language acquisition in the absence of experience. *Behavioral and Brain Sciences, 14*, 612–613.

Berman, R. A. (1993a). The development of language use: Expressing perspectives on a scene. In E. Dromi (Ed.), *Language and cognition: A developmental perspective* (pp. 172–201). Norwood, NJ: Ablex.

Berman, R. A. (1993b). Marking of verb transitivity by Hebrew-speaking children. *Journal of Child Language, 20*, 1–28.

Berman, R. A. (in press). Crosslinguistic perspectives on native language acquisition. In K. Hyltenstam & A. Viberg (Eds.), *Progression and regression in language: Sociocultural, neuropsychological, and linguistic perspectives.* Cambridge: Cambridge University Press.

Berman, R. A., & Clark, E. V. (1992). *Lexical productivity in child and adult.* Final Report to U.S.–Israel Binational Science Foundation (BSF), Jerusalem.

Berman, R. A., & Dromi, E. (1984). On marking time without aspect in child language. *Papers & Reports on Child Language Development, 23*, 23–32.

Berman, R. A., & Ravid, R. (1986). Degree of lexicalization of noun compounds. *Hebrew Linguistics, 26*, 5–22.

Berman, R. A., & Sagi, Y. (1981). Word-formation and lexical innovations of young children. *Hebrew Linguistics, 18*, 31–62.

Berman, R. A., & Slobin, D. I. (in press). *Relating events in narrative: A crosslinguistic and developmental study.* Hillsdale, NJ: Lawrence Erlbaum Associates.

Berman, R. A., & Weissenborn, J. (1991, May). *Acquisition of word-order and early grammatical development.* Final Report to German-Israel Foundation for Research and Development (GIF), Jerusalem.

Borer, H. (1991, May). The *maturational agenda.* Paper presented at symposium on the Spectrum of Mind: Cognitive Studies of Language Use, Tel Aviv University.

Borer, H., & Grodzinsky, Y. (1986). Lexical cliticization vs. syntactic cliticization: The case of Hebrew dative clitics. In H. Borer (Ed.), *Syntax and semantics* (Vol. 19, pp. 123–172). New York: Academic Press.

Borer, H., & Wexler, K. (1987). The maturation of syntax. In T. Roeper & E. Williams (Eds.), *Parameter setting* (pp. 123–172). Dordrecht: Reidel.

Bowerman, M. (1974). Learning the structure of causative verbs: A study in the relationship of cognitive, semantic, and syntactic development. *Papers and Reports on Child Language Development, 8,* 142–178.

Bowerman, M. (1982). Evaluating competing linguistic models with language acquisition data: Implications of developmental errors with causative verbs. *Quaderni di Semantica, 3,* 5–65.

Braine, M. D. S. (1988). Modeling the acquisition of linguistic structure. In Y. Levy, I. M. Schlesinger, & M. S. S. Braine (Eds.), *Categories and processes in language acquisition* (pp. 217–260). Hillsdale, NJ: Lawrence Erlbaum Associates.

Braine, M. D. S., Brody, R. E., Fisch, S. M., & Weisberger, M. J. (1990). Can children use a verb without exposure to its argument structure? *Journal of Child Language, 17,* 313–342.

Brown, R. (1973). *A first language: The early stages*. Cambridge, MA: Harvard University Press.

Chien, Y-C., & Wexler, K. (1989). Children's knowledge of locality conditions in binding as evidence for the modularity of syntax and pragmatics. Unpublished manuscript.

Clark, E. V. (1983). Convention and contrast in acquiring the lexicon. In T. B. Seiler & W. Wannenmacher (Eds.), *Concept development and the development of word meaning* (pp. 67–91). Berlin: Springer-Verlag.

Clark, E. V. (in press). *The lexicon in acquisition*. Cambridge: Cambridge University Press.

Clark, E. V., & Berman, R. A. (1984). Structure and use in the acquisition of word-formation. *Language, 60,* 542–590.

Clark, E. V. & Berman, R. A. (1987). Types of linguistic knowledge: Interpreting and producing compound nouns. *Journal of Child Language, 14,* 547–567.

Clark, E. V., & Clark, H. H. (1979). When nouns surface as verb. *Language, 55,* 767–811.

Demuth, K. (1988). Maturation and acquisition of the passive in Sesotho. *Language, 66,* 56–80.

Dowty, D. (1979). *Verb meaning and Montague grammar*. Dordrecht: Reidel.

Dromi, E. (1986). *Early lexical development*. Cambridge: Cambridge University Press.

Dromi, E., & Berman, R. A. (1986). Language-general and language-specific in developing syntax. *Journal of Child Language, 14,* 371–387.

Elath, K. (1989). *Distribution of* binyan *patterns by type and token at different age-groups*. Seminar paper, Tel Aviv University.

Fisher, C., Gleitman, L., & Gleitman, H. (1991). On the semantic content of subcategorization frames. *Cognitive Psychology, 23,* 331–392.

Gergely, G. (1989, July). *Erroneous causative verb formation in the acquisition of Hungarian*. Paper presented at the Fifth International Congress for the Study of Child Language, Budapest.

Givon, T. (1976). On the VS order in Israeli Hebrew: Pragmatics and typological change. In P. Cole (Ed.), *Studies in Modern Hebrew syntax and semantics* (pp. 153–192). Amsterdam: North-Holland.

Gordon, P., & Chafetz, J. (1990). Verb-based versus class-based accounts of actionality effects in children's comprehension of passives. *Cognition, 36,* 227–254.

Guri-Herling, N. (1988). *The relative weight of word order, accusative marking, and gender number agreement in specifying semantic relations*. Unpublished seminar paper. Tel Aviv University.

Hakuta, K. (1982). Interaction between particles and word order in the comprehension of simple sentences in Japanese. *Developmental Psychology, 18,* 62–76.

Hopper, P., & Thompson, S. A. (1980). Transitivity in grammar and discourse. *Language, 56,* 251–299.

Ingram, D. (1985). The psychological reality of children's grammars and its relation to grammatical theory. *Lingua, 66,* 79–103.

Ingram, D. (1989). *First language acquisition: Method, description, and explanation.* Cambridge: Cambridge University Press.

Jensen, J. T. (1990). *Morphology: Word structure in generative grammar.* Amsterdam: Benjamins.

Junger, J. (1987). *Predicate formation in the verbal system of Modern Hebrew.* Dordrecht: Foris.

Kaplan, D. (1983). *Order of acquisition of morpho-syntactic elements by Hebrew-speaking children aged 2–3 years.* Unpublished master's thesis, Tel Aviv University.

Karmiloff-Smith, A. (1986). Stage/structure versus phase/process in modelling linguistic and cognitive development. In I. Levin (Ed.), *Stage and structure: Re-opening the debate* (pp. 164–190). Norwood, NJ: Ablex.

Karmiloff-Smith, A. (1987). From meta-processes to conscious access: Evidence from children's metalinguistic and repair data. *Cognition, 23,* 95–147.

Kave, G. (1990). The influence of reflexive action on children's performance on Condition A. Unpublished seminar paper, Tel Aviv University.

Kenan, A., Nirpaz, A., & Dekel, N. (1988). *Passivization, transitivity, and lexical innovations: Verb-pattern alternations of children compared with adults.* Unpublished seminar paper, Tel Aviv University.

Levin, B. (1989). *Towards a lexical organization of English verbs.* Evanston, IL: Northwestern University Department of Linguistics.

Levy, Y. (1983a). The acquisition of Hebrew plurals: The case of the missing gender category. *Journal of Child Language, 10,* 107–121.

Levy, Y. (1983b). It's frogs all the way down. *Cognition, 12,* 75–93.

MacWhinney, B. (1978). Processing a first language: The acquisition of morphophonology. *Monographs of the Society for Research in Child Development, 43* (Serial No. 174).

MacWhinney, B. (1982). Basic syntactic processes. In S. Kuczaj (Ed.), *Language development: Vol. 1. Syntax and semantics* (pp. 73–136). Hillsdale, NJ: Lawrence Erlbaum Associates.

Maoz, T. (1989). *Acquisition of grammatical agreement by Hebrew-speaking children.* Unpublished seminar paper, Tel Aviv University.

Matthews, P. H. (1991). *Morphology: An introduction to the theory of word-structure* [2nd ed.]. Cambridge: Cambridge University Press.

Mayroz, Ora. (1988). Acquisition of action nominals in Modern Hebrew. Unpublished masters' thesis in Hebrew, Tel Aviv University.

Perlmutter, D. (1978). Impersonal passives and the unaccusative hypothesis. *Fourth Annual Meeting of the Berkeley Linguistics Society,* 157–189.

Pinker, S. (1989). *Learnability and cognition: The acquisition of argument structure.* Cambridge, MA: MIT Press.

Pinker, S., Lebeaux, D. S., & Frost, L. A. (1987). Productivity and constraints in the acquisition of the passive. *Cognition, 26,* 165–197.

Pye, C., & Poz, Q. P. (1988). Precocious passives and antipassives in Quiche Mayan. *Papers and Reports in Child Language Development, 27.*

Rabinowitch, S. (1985). Hebrew language proficiency of English–Hebrew bilingual preschoolers compared with their monolingual peers. Unpublished doctoral dissertation, Tel Aviv University.

Rispoli, M. (1991). The acquisition of verb subcategorization in a functionalist framework. *First Language, 11,* 41–64.

Rom, A., & Dgani, R. (1985). Acquiring case-marked pronouns in Hebrew. *Journal of Child Language, 12,* 61–78.

Schwarzwald, O. (1981). *Grammar and reality in the Hebrew verb*. Ramat Gan: Bart-Ilan University Press.

Shani, R. (1990). *Schoolchildren's construction of reversible and irreversible passives*. Unpublished seminar paper, Tel Aviv University.

Shatz, M. (1987). Bootstrapping operations in child language. In K. Nelson & A. van Kleeck (Eds.), *Children's language* (Vol. 6, pp. 1–22). Hillsdale, NJ: Lawrence Erlbaum Associates.

Slobin, D. I. (1981). The origins of grammatical encoding of events. In W. Deutsch (Ed.), *The child's construction of language* (pp. 185–199). New York: Academic Press.

Slobin, D. I. (1982). Universal and particular in the acquisition of language. In E. Wanner & L. Gleitman (Eds.), *Language acquisition: The state of the art* (pp. 128–172). Cambridge: Cambridge University Press.

Slobin, D. I. (1985). Crosslinguistic evidence for the language-making capacity. In D. I. Slobin (Ed.), *The crosslinguistic study of language acquisition* (Vol. 2, pp. 1157–1256). Hillsdale, NJ: Lawrence Erlbaum Associates.

Slobin, D. I. (1987, January). *Frequency reflects function*. Paper presented at Conference on the Interaction of Form and Function in Language, University of California, Davis.

Slobin, D. I. (1988). The development of clause chaining in Turkish child language. In S. Koc (Ed.), *Studies in Turkish linguistics* (pp. 27–54). Ankara: Middle East University.

Slobin, D. I. (1991). Learning to think for speaking: Native language, cognition, and rhetorical style. *Pragmatics, 1*, 7–26.

Talmy, L. (1987). The relation of grammar to cognition. In B. Rudzka-Ostyn (Ed.), *Topics in cognitive linguistics*. Amsterdam: Benjamins.

Talmy, L. (1988). Force dynamics in language and cognition. *Cognitive Science, 12*, 49–100.

Van Valin, R. (1990). Semantic parameters of split intransitivity. *Language, 66*, 221–260.

Zur, B. (1983). *Acquisition of definiteness by Hebrew-speaking children*. Unpublished masters' thesis, Tel Aviv University.

APPENDIX
EXAMPLES OF "NEUTRALIZATION" = TRANSITIVITY MISASSIGNMENTS

(1) STRUCTURED ELICITATION TEST (Berman, 1993b)

P1 Intransitive ipv P5: [ipv = in place of]

1. *aba soxe oto*	– Daddy swims him	[Guy 2;6]	– NOVEL
2. *soxe oto*	– swims him	[Moran 2;7]	– NOVEL
3. *soxe et hayam*	– swims OM the sea	[Rotem 2;7]	– NOVEL
4. *aba colel oto*	– Daddy dives him	[Guy 2;6]	– NOVEL
5. *aba colel oto*	– Daddy dives him	[Yasmin 3;0]	– NOVEL
6. *aba colel oto*	– Daddy dives him	[Lital 3;7]	– NOVEL
7. *colel et hayeled*	– dives OM the boy	[Liat 7;9]	– NOVEL
8. *zoxelet oto*	– crawls + Fem him	[Rotem 2;7]	– NOVEL
9. *zoxElet et hayeled*	– crawls OM the boy	[Liat 7;9]	– NOVEL
10. *yoshEnet et hatinok*	– sleeps OM the baby	[Liat, 7;9]	– NOVEL

P4 Intransitive ipv P3

11. *mistovev oto*	– turns – itself him	[Hila 2;9]	
12. *mitraxecet oto*	– washes + herself him	[Hila 2;9]	
13. *mitraxecet oto*	– washes + herself him	[Matan 3;0]	
14. *mitpocec et habalon*	– bursts – Intr OM the balloon	[Matan 3;0]	
15. *aba mitgalech et hayeled*	– Daddy slides – Intr OM the boy	[Lika 2;6]	– NOVEL

(Continued)

P2 Intransitive ipv P1

16. *nishbar et ha'ec*	– got-broken OM the tree	[Hila 2;9]
17. *nishpax et hakaze*	– got-spilt OM that thing	[Matan 3;0]

P3 Transitive ipv P4:

18. *hakadur megalgel*	– the-ball rolls + Trans.	[Yasmin 3;0]
19. *ze megahec levad*	– it irons alone = by itself	[Yasmin 3;0]

(2) SPONTANEOUS SPEECH DATABASE—DIARY RECORDS AND LONGITUDINAL SAMPLES:

1) INTRANSITIVE FORMS [Px] USED IN PLACE OF REQUIRED TRANSITIVE [Py]

1.1 P1 Intr. [usually Unergative Activity] ipv P5 Causative:

1. #151 – Miryam *overet* et kol hadapim	– cf. *ma'avira* [Smadar 2;3]
2. #199 – ani tekef *ola* et hasefer.	– cf. *ma'ala* [Ronit 3;0]
3. #200 – hem *yardu* et ze kvar.	– cf. *horidu* [Asaf 3;0]
4. #208 – nu matay kvar *ya'axlu* oti!	– cf. *ya'axilu* [Asaf 3;5]
5. #214 – efshar *lehikanes* kan bubot.	– cf. *lehaxnis* [Asaf 3;3]
6. #225 – aba *yilbash* li pijama.	– cf. *yalbish* [Amiram 2;10]
7. #205 – at *takumi* oti.	– cf. *takimi* [Nir 4;6]
8. #473 – ima, *tin'ali* oti	– cf. *tan'ili* [Hagar 2;8]
9. #476 – ani *eshev* oto.	– cf. *oshiv* [Hagar 2;8]
10. #403 – ima *teshvi* oto.	– cf. *toshivi* [Hagar 2;9]
11. #474 – at *nofelet* oti kaxa.	– cf. *mapila* [Hagar 2;8]
12. #505 – hu *nafal* oto.	– cf. *hipil* [Hagar 2;8]
13. #405 – ima lama *nafalt* oti?	– cf. *hipalt* [Hagar 2;9]
14. #406 – aba *tered* oti.	– cf. *torid* [Hagar 2;9]
15. #407 – *xazarti* ota.	– cf. *hixzarti* [Hagar 2;9]**
16. #447 – *ra'iti* et haciyurim le aba	– cf. *her'eti* [Shelly 2;7]
17. #510 – *er'e* lax mash(eh)u, tov?	– cf. *ar'e* [Shelly 2;8]
18. #448 – Lidya, ima *oxelet* oti hayom	– cf. *ma'axila* [Shelly 2;6]
19. #511 – she aba *yoxal* oti axshav	– cf. *ya'axil* [Shelly 2;10]
20. #449 – ima, *zuzi* li et hakise.	– cf. *tazizi* [Zivit 3;2]
21. #509 – ani *epol* otax.	– cf. *apil* [Leor 2;9]
22. #217 – *tazuzi* et hataxat shelax.	– cf. *tazizi* [Ginat 4;7]
23. #229 – *razati* oti [sic]	– cf. *herzeti et acmi* [Ginat 4;7]

**Hagar 2;10–2;11: Gives no evidence of either this type of misassignment or of productive causatives, uses P5 verbs *lehavi* 'bring', *lehadlik* 'light', *lehar'ot* 'show', which have intransitive alternants, also *lehazmin* 'invite'; Hagar age 3;3 has more P5 verbs, e.g., *lehaxin, leharim*, and very advanced syntax, but shows no evidence of productive causatives.

1.2 P2 Intr [Unaccusative] ipv P5 Causative:

1. #196 – *kansi* oti at [= Activity]	– cf. *taxnisi* [Sivan 3;9]
2. #204 – yeladim ra'im *ne'elmu* et hacaacu'im	– cf. *he'elimu* [Asaf 2;6]
3. #223 – *tesha'ari* et ze kan.	– cf. *tash'iri* [Ginat 4;7]

(Continued)

1.3 P1 Intr. ipv P3 Causative ~ Transitive Activity:

1. #206	– carix *ligdol* oto basade.	– cf. *legadel* [Sivan 3;7]
2. #202	– ma, at yoda'at *lilmod* lisxot?	– cf. *lelamed* [Asaf 4;0]

1.4 P4 Intr [Unaccusative or Reflexive] ipv P3 [or P1 ~ P5] Transitive Activity:

1. #38	– le'an hem holxim kshe hu *mitgaresh* otam?	– cf. *megaresh* [Sivan 3;7]
2. #209	– ani lo roca she *yistapru* oti	– cf. *yesapru* [Sivan 4;4]
3. #310	– boi boi *nistorek* otax axshav	– cf. *nesarek* [Leor 2;9]
4. #503	– ani *histarakti* oto	– cf. *sirakti* [Hagar 2;9]
= 5. #409	– hine *histarakti* oto.	– cf. *sirakti* [Hagar 2;10]
6. #450	– anaxnu lo *mishtatfim* ota bamisxak	– cf. *meshatfim* [Dalit 3;9]
7. #451	– boi *titnadnedi* oti axshav	– cf. *tenadnedi* [Shelly 2;11]
8. #221	– *itraxaci* oti ima!	– cf. P1 *tirxeci* [Ginat 4;7]
9. #203	– ima *titlabshi* oti!	– cf. P5 *talbishi* [Ziva 3;6]

2. TRANSITIVE FORMS [Px] USED IN PLACE OF REQUIRED INTRANSITIVE [Py]

2.1 P1 Transitive [Activity] ipv P2 Intransitive [Unaccusative, Passive]

1. #452	– tiri ex kol haxalav *shapax*	– cf. *nishpax* [Shelly 2;11]
2. #453	– lama hadelet lo *potaxat*?	– cf. *niftaxat* [Ori Degan 2;4]
= 3. #197	– lama shamanu et hadelet *potaxat*	[Asaf 3;11]
4. #207	– ze lo *lo'es* oti [sic]	– cf. *nil'as li* [Asaf 2;7]
5. #212	– eyx *osim* acuvim?	– cf. *na'asim* [Sivan 3;10]
6. #218	– hem yihyu giborim lo'olam ve	– cf. *yehargu* [Sivan 5;6]
	bamilxamot lo *yahargu* afpaam	
7. #23	– kol hanyar *zarak* lasal	– cf. *nizrak* [Uri K. 2;5]
8. #20	– baybay, *gamar* ner	– cf. *nigmar* [Leor 2;0]
9. #156	– hakaseta *shabar* [sic]	– cf. *nishbar(a)* [Leor 2;5]
10. #198	– hagvina *marax* [sic] al haricpa	– cf. *nimrax(a)* [Or 2;6]
11. #224	– hapcacot *gamru* li	– cf. *nigmeru* [Ginat 4;6]

2.2 P3 Transitive [Activity] ipv P4 Intransitive [Unaccusative, Reflexive]

1. #189	– hen *mixacxecot* levad	– cf. *mitcaxcexot* [Rama 3;6]
2. #193	– ze lo *misader*	– cf. *mistader* [Varda 2;2]
3. #219	– ze *mekamet* kaxa	– cf. *mitkamet* [Ginat 4;7]
4. #222	– hacamid *minadned* li	– cf. *mitnadned* [Ginat 4;7]
5. #17	– hu *yedabek* kaxa	– cf. *yitdabek* [Ginat 4;6]

2.3 P5 Transitive [Causative] ipv P2 Intransitive [Unaccusative]

1. #482	– ze lo *madbik* levad	– cf. *nidbak* [Naama 2;5]

(Continued)

SUMMARY DATABASE NEUTRALIZATIONS

		Smad	Hag	Leo	Asa	Siv	Shel	Gina	Oth	Tot	
Trans > Intr	P1 ipv P5	1	8	1	4		4	2	4	24	
	P2 ipv P5				1	1		1		3	
	P1 ipv P3				1	1				2	
	P4 ipv P3		2	1		2	1	1	2	9	= 38
Intr > Trans	P1 ipv P2	-	-	2	2	2	1	1	3	11	
	P3 ipv P4		-	-	-	-	-	3	2	5	
	P5 ipv P2								1	1	
											= 17

Out of total 516 unconventional lexical usages:

V > V:	NZ	= "neutralization"	39 + 17	=	55
	PM	= "pattern mixing"	95 [excluding 20 Resultatives]	=	75
	GA	= "gap filling"	33 [including OM, EX]	=	33
N > V:		= denomination		=	70
		Total innovative, unconventional verb forms		=	233

NZ accounts for about one quarter of the unconventional verb forms recorded

CHAPTER EIGHT

A Cross-Linguistic Approach to the Causative Alternation

Clifton Pye
University of Kansas

One of the bedrocks of current linguistic investigation is that there is a fairly direct mapping between thought and language. There is an assumption that at some level of the grammar—whether it is d-structure (Chomsky, 1981), argument structure (Grimshaw, 1990), or lexical conceptual structure (Hale & Keyser, 1986)—there is a tie between language structure and a more universal cognitive perception of events. Perlmutter and Postal's (1984) universal alignment hypothesis (UAH) and Baker's (1988) uniformity of theta assignment hypothesis (UTAH) are concrete expressions of this assumption. These hypotheses, with Chomsky's (1981) projection principle (or its extended variants) impose meaningful constraints on verb argument structures. A universal or uniform association of thematic roles to syntactic positions would eliminate cross-linguistic variation in verb argument structures.

Ideally, children would be able to use such principles in constructing their initial lexical entries for verbs and so avoid confusion from hearing well-formed sentences with null arguments or ill-formed sentences with missing arguments. On hearing a sentence such as 'The stick broke,' the UAH or UTAH would tell a child that the NP 'the stick' was in the direct object position at some level of the syntactic derivation because it bears the thematic role of theme. The linguistic principles in combination with the primary linguistic data would provide the child with all the information necessary to construct a syntactic derivation for the sentence.

Things are not quite this simple. Some recent work has explored the implications of Perlmutter's (1978) unaccusative hypothesis for the UAH and UTAH. The unaccusative hypothesis claims that it is necessary to distinguish between intransitive verbs such as *run*, *jump*, and *arrive*, which are unergative, and intransitive verbs such as *melt*, *slide*, and *roll*, which are unaccusative. A host of tests in many languages suggest that unergative and unaccusative verbs have different initial argument alignments. If the UAH and UTAH are correct, then all languages should classify the same verbs as unergative or unaccusative. Since Rosen's initial survey (1984), linguists have debated the degree of cross-linguistic uniformity among intransitive verbs (Grimshaw, 1990; Levin & Rappaport Hovav, 1992; Perlmutter, 1989; Van Valin, 1990). Certain subclasses of verbs (e.g., psych verbs and verbs for bodily processes) exhibit more cross-linguistic variation in argument structure than other subclasses (e.g., motion verbs), but a final assessment of the degree of cross-linguistic variation is not available.

Another problem is that languages commonly employ one or more processes that alter the argument structure of verbs. Examples of such processes include the passive, antipassive, causative, dative, locative, conative, middle, and applicative alternations (cf. Baker, 1988). If such processes worked in a uniform manner they would not create a problem because a child would have direct evidence of how each process affected verb argument structure. Passives, for example, eliminate the direct expression of agent roles at the level of syntax, whereas antipassives eliminate the direct expression of theme roles at the syntactic level. The problem is that there is a great deal of cross-linguistic variation in the productivity of each process.

Every language contains verbs that do not undergo a particular process. The verbs *have*, *resemble*, and *want* cannot be passivized in English, for example. Children could solve this problem if the lexical exceptions to a process involved a small set of thematic roles or semantic features (Green, 1974). Pinker's (1989) criterion-based hypothesis applies such a procedure to account for the acquisition of the passive, causative, locative, and dative alternations in English. Such solutions, though, call for cross-linguistic study of argument structure alternations. The lexical exceptions to argument-changing processes should fall within discrete subclasses of verbs across languages. These subclasses, in turn, would provide useful data for determining the relevant restrictions on the operation of the argument-changing processes.

1. THE CAUSATIVE ALTERNATION

In this chapter I show that detailed cross-linguistic data provides an insight into the manner in which the structure of the verb lexicon affects the acquisition of transitivity alternations. I pay particular attention to the causative alternation. Many verbs alternate between intransitive and transitive syntactic forms to indicate the cause of a patient argument's change of state. The mystery is that not all intransitive verbs alternate in the same way. Bowerman (1974) pointed out that children learning English sometimes extend the causative alternation to verbs that alternate in other ways. Thus, Bowerman reported such examples as Christy (2;9) saying 'I come it closer so it won't fall' instead of 'I made it come closer' or 'I moved it closer.' My own son has produced several of these errors, including 'Mommy has to talk the king' for 'Mommy has to make the king talk' (at age 3;7).

Pinker (1989) underlined the dilemma such constructions raise for language acquisition theories. Once children determine that a particular transitivity alternation is productive they may extend the alternation to new verbs. Such extensions are unacceptable for English verbs like *come*, but there is no record of parent tutorials correcting children who produce these forms. There is no other obvious means that children could rely on to cut back unacceptable extensions. Thus, there is no logical procedure children can use to acquire the causative alternation.

Pinker outlined three possible sources of children's errors. They could be applying a lexical rule too broadly, and fail to notice narrow-based semantic constraints that restrict the lexical rule. Alternatively, children may retrieve the wrong verb stem under pressure from the discourse. A third possibility is that children have not yet acquired an adult semantic representation for some verbs and thus misuse these verbs. Pinker felt that children stop producing causative errors when they learn the meaning of each verb, when they are better at retrieving verbs, and when they learn the proper restrictions on the causative alternation.

This chapter reports the results of a pilot elicitation study that I conducted with K'iche' Maya children from the Western Highland region of Guatemala. The K'iche' children showed a different pattern of causative alternations than their English-speaking peers, which indicates that language-specific structures influence the acquisition of the causative alternation more than the semantic structure of individual verbs. The following section sets out the system of causative alternations found in the K'iche' language. The next section presents acquisition data on the K'iche' causative from a longitudinal study of children. I then present the results of an elicitation study on the causative alternation and discuss its findings. In the last section I discuss the implications of this study for different theoretical proposals concerning the acquisition of the causative alternation.

2. THE CAUSATIVE ALTERNATION IN K'ICHE' MAYA

K'iche' is a Mayan language spoken by a million inhabitants of the Western Highlands of Guatemala. K'iche' has an agglutinating morphology that reflects the distinction between transitive and intransitive verbs in several respects (see example 1). The language has an ergative cross-referencing system on the verb, so intransitive verb subjects and transitive verb objects are marked with an absolutive marker whereas transitive verb subjects receive a distinctive ergative marker. All verbs also require a special clause-final termination, which distinguishes between transitive and intransitive verb stems (Pye, 1983a).[1] Intransitive verbs in simple, declarative sentences have the clause-final termination /-ik/, "root" transitive verbs in the same sentences have the termination /-oh/ or /-uh/ and "derived" transitive verbs have the termination /-Vj/ where V may be either /i, e, a, o, u/.

(1) Transitive verbs   Intransitive verbs
  a. k-at-inw-il-oh   c. k-at-b'e:-ik
     INCOMP-2A-1E-see-TTV   INCOMP-2A-go-IV
     'I see you.'   'You are going.'

  b. k-Ø-a-kuwi:-j   d. k-Ø-taq'en-ik
     INCOMP-3A-2E-hurry-TV   INCOMP-3A-PROGRESSIVE-IV
     'You are hurrying.'   'It is-ing.'[2]

---

[1]All K'iche' words are shown in the practical orthography developed by the Proyecto Lingüístico Francisco Marroquín (Kaufman, 1976) with a single exception: I use < ' > rather than <7> for the glottal stop. The other orthographic symbols have their standard IPA values except: <tz> = /ts/, <ch> = /tʃ/, <b'> = /ɓ/, <tz'> = /t͡sʼ/, <ch'> = /t͡ʃʼ/, <x> = /ʃ/, <j> = /X/. I use the colon <:> to indicate long vowels.

I have also used the following morphological abbreviations: COMP = completive aspect; INCOMP = incompletive aspect; 1A, 2A, 3A = first-, second-, third-person singular absolutive person markers (what Mayanists refer to as "set B"); 1E, 2E, 3E = first-, second-, third-person singular ergative person markers (or 'set A'); CAUSE = the causative morpheme; ABS = the absolutive antipassive; TV = the affix marking derived transitive verbs; TTV = the clause-final termination marker for root transitive verbs; IV = the clause-final termination marker for intransitive verbs.

[2]This verb serves as an overt marker of the progressive aspect in K'iche'. K'iche' speakers frequently shorten the verb to *taq'en* or even *q'en*.

K'iche' uses the suffix /-**isa**/ to derive the causative form of intransitive verbs. Examples of this causative construction are shown in (2). In K'iche' the causative suffix can only be added to intransitive verb stems, unlike Berber, Japanese, and Korean where it is also possible to add a causative affix to transitive verb stems.

(2) K'iche' causative verbs with /-**isa**/

Intransitive Form	Causative Form
a. k-∅-poqow-ik	k-∅-a-poqow-**isa**:-j
INCOMP-3A-boil-IV	INCOMP-3A-2E-boil-**CAUSE**-TV
'It is boiling.'	'You are boiling it.' (= cause to boil)
b. q'alaj	k-∅-in-q'alaj-**isa**:-j
clear	INCOMP-3A-1E-clear-**CAUSE**-TV
'It is clear.'	'I will clarify things.' (= cause to be clear)

Although the causative construction is very productive in K'iche' it is not completely so. There are two classes of intransitive verbs in K'iche' that do not take the causative affix. The first of these exceptional classes uses another means of deriving a transitive verb stem. I refer to this class of verbs collectively as the "zero class," although the examples in (3) show that this set of verbs uses several different derivational processes. The transitive verb in (3a) has a polysyllabic stem and so takes a "derived" transitive termination marker /-j/.[3] Its intransitive counterpart deletes the final vowel from the stem and changes the final consonant before adding the intransitive termination. The verb pair in (3b) simply switch termination markers without changing any other part of the verb stem, while the intransitive verb in (3c) adds the intransitive termination to the whole transitive verb, including its derived transitive termination as part of the intransitive stem. I group these verbs together because they share the feature of alternating between intransitive and transitive verb forms by a derivational process that is distinct from the regular affixal causative process (c.f. Dayley, 1985).

---

[3]Mayan linguists analyze the transitive verb form as containing the causative suffix in an underlying level of the derivation. Because Mayan verb roots are monosyllabic, all derivational processes that yield transitive verb stems produce polysyllabic stems. In this case the underlying form of the transitive verb would be *qa-isa-j*. The initial vowel of the causative affix /i/ is lost through a regular process of vowel merger and the final consonant /j/ of the intransitive stem would be added by epenthesis. I have included the verb in the zero derivation category because the processes of vowel merger and epenthesis obscure the relation between the intransitive verb form and the output of the affixal causative derivation. I also do not want to assume that this relation is apparent to children learning K'iche'.

(3) K'iche' zero class verbs

Transitive verbs	Intransitive verbs
a. k-Ø-in-qasa:-j	k-in-qaj-ik
INCOMP-3A-1E-go__down-TV	INCOMP-1A-go__down-IV
'I am taking it down.'	'I am going down.'
b. x-Ø-in-tzaq-oh	x-in-tzaq-ik
COMP-3A-1E-drop-TTV	COMP-1A-fall-IV
'I dropped/lost it.'	'I fell.'
c. x-Ø-a-tzali:-j	x-at-tzalij-ik
COMP-3A-2E-return-TV	COMP-2A-return-IV
'You returned it.'	'You returned.'

I dub the remaining set of exceptional intransitive verbs the periphrastic class. This set of verbs does not permit any derivational process to produce a simple transitive verb stem. The only way to express a transitive notion with the members of this set is to use a complex sentence that contains a verb like -b'an 'do/make'. Examples of periphrastic verbs are shown in (4).

(4) K'iche' periphrastic verbs

Intransitive verbs	Periphrastic constructions	
a. k-in-pet-ik	k-Ø-in-b'an	k-at-pet-ik
INCOMP-1A-come-IV	INCOMP-3A-1E-do	INCOMP-2A-come-IV
'I am coming.'	'I will make you come.'	
b. k-in-muxan-ik	k-Ø-in-b'an	k-at-muxan-ik
INCOMP-1A-swim-IV	INCOMP-3A-1E-do	INCOMP-2A-swim-IV
'I am swimming.'	'I will make you swim.'	

The K'iche' causative alternation is further complicated by one additional factor. Transitive verbs may lose the direct object with the addition of an absolutive antipassive affix. K'iche' speakers use the absolutive antipassive to emphasize an action rather than a result (Mondloch, 1981). With many verbs, the antipassive acts like an anticausative. Two examples of the absolutive antipassive alternation are shown in (5).

(5) The K'iche' absolutive antipassive

a. k-Ø-u-chaku:-j	k-Ø-chaku-n-ik
INCOMP-3A-3E-work-TV	INCOMP-3A-work-ABS-IV
'He/she is working it.'	'He/she is working.'
b. x-in-a-tze'-j	x-at-tze'-n-ik
COMP-1A-2E-laugh-TV	COMP-2A-laugh-ABS-IV
'You made me laugh.'[4]	'You laughed.'

---

[4]The translation of such verbs presents immense difficulties for linguistic theories that seek a uniform mapping relation between semantic and syntactic components. The K'iche'

To put it mildly, the combination of productive causative and antipassive alternations plus a good number of lexical exceptions should create considerable problems for any child so unfortunate as to be faced with the prospect of learning K'iche'.[5] Such complexity provides the perfect testing ground for competing hypotheses about the sources of children's derivational rules. If children are conservative learners, they should be unwilling to produce a causative alternation until they have learned the proper lexical form. In this case their language productions should be error free (Baker, 1979). Another possibility would be that children adopt a simple lexical schema as a ready-made means of producing the causative alternation (Braine, Brody, Fisch, & Weisberger, 1990). Such a schema would result in a multitude of overgeneralization errors for K'iche', such as using simple intransitive verb stems in transitive sentences. Finally, children might rely on some type of semantic classification when applying the causative alternation (Green, 1974; Pinker, 1989; Slobin, 1985). In this case K'iche' children should initially behave like children learning English and have difficulty with similar ranges of semantic subclasses of verbs.

3. ANALYSIS OF K'ICHE' LANGUAGE SAMPLES

Spontaneous language samples suggest that the causative derivation is a relatively late acquisition for K'iche' children. I have found that by age 2;10 the children are beginning to produce examples of causativized verbs (Pye, 1992). Children learning English begin to produce examples of causativized verbs around 2;2, whereas children learning Turkish apparently begin producing causativized verbs around 2;3 (Aksu-Koç & Slobin, 1985). The K'iche' children's causativized verbs alternate with the intransitive verb forms, sometimes in the same session. Their alternations are evidence that the children apply a productive morphological alternation rather than using the same verb form in transitive and intransitive contexts. However, the children do not use the causative affix very frequently in the spontaneous data. My three primary subjects produced a total of 24 affixal causativized verb tokens in 20,103 utterances. The children also used intransitive and transitive verbs from both the zero and periphras-

---

verb *tze'* might also be translated as 'amuse', but the choice between 'laugh' or 'amuse' would have to be made on a semantic basis. To use verb transitivity as a basis for translation would lead to a circular argument that verb meaning determines verb argument structure and verb argument structure determines the translation of verb meaning (Pye, 1993b).

[5]I do not examine antipassive forms of causativized verbs or the causative forms of antipassive verbs here. Both occur sporadically in K'iche'.

tic verb classes without adding the causative affix to them. They did not add the causative affix to any transitive verb stems.

I have found two examples in which one of the children failed to produce the causative affix. The first occurred when Al Cha:y was 2 years and 10 months old and had a mean utterance length of 1.92 morphemes. Her older sister told her to tell me to turn on my tape recorder using a verb that requires the causative affix in this context. Al Cha:y produced this utterance as **k'at e laya** (= *chak'atisaj le: aradio*). Al Cha:y's production lacks the causative affix and literally means 'Your radio is burning.' The causativized form of this verb undergoes a semantic shift from 'burn' to 'turn on.' Two weeks later my assistant and I were picking the girls up and swinging them around. We had just done this with Al Cha:y's sisters and Al Cha:y wanted to be next. In this context she produced the utterance **lij in** (= *kinawalijisaj in*). If she wanted to be picked up she should have used the verb with the causative affix (**walij-isa-j**). Her utterance literally means 'I am going up,' which is a possible, though less likely, interpretation in this context. Later in the same tape Al Cha:y succeeded in producing a verb with the causative affix (**paw'ixaj chik** = *kinapaqilisaj chik* 'Pick me up again').

This result agrees to some extent with acquisition data from other languages. Bowerman (1974) provided many examples of such causative overgeneralizations in English, and Berman (1982) noted examples from the initial stage of learning Hebrew. The number of examples these authors cited lead one to believe that causative overgeneralizations are fairly common in the initial stage of language acquisition. Unfortunately it is impossible to calculate base rates of overgeneralization on the basis of the data provided. My finding of 2 overgeneralizations in 20,103 utterances is comparable to Maratsos' (1979) estimation that Bowerman's 100 or so examples were culled from approximately 750,000 utterances. However, it would be more accurate to use the number of transitive contexts in which affixal causative verbs appear rather than the total number of utterances to calculate overgeneralization rates. For the K'iche' samples, the finding of 2 overgeneralizations in 26 contexts increases the rate of overgeneralization to 8%. This rate suggests that K'iche' children have an accurate knowledge of verb transitivity that is susceptible to occasional lapses in performance (cf. Pye, 1987). The verb argument structures in their verbal lexicon are essentially correct.

4. AN EXPERIMENTAL STUDY

Experimental studies provide the best means of estimating overgeneralization rates and thereby children's knowledge of the causative alternation. Such studies provide a convenient way to collect information on a large number of causative verb forms in a short amount of time. An experimental study of the K'iche' causative alternation provides the best way of collecting information on children's knowledge of all three verb categories as well as a way to determine whether children make the same types of overgeneralizations with the verbs in each category. One drawback to such a study might be that it would induce children to make more than the usual number of overgeneralizations. A control for this problem is to test older subjects. If the experiment induces adult subjects to overgeneralize then it is not looking at lexical competence. If there is a gap between the children's rate of overgeneralization and that of the adults, then one can estimate the degree of priming the experiment is creating and eliminate that from the estimation of the children's overgeneralization rates. I put together a pilot test of the K'iche' causative alternation using verbs from all three groups. The verbs are shown in (6).

(6) K'iche' verbs from causative elicitation study

Morphological		Zero-derivation verbs		Periphrastic verbs	
xojow-isa	dance-CAUSE	qaj-ik	go_down-IV	muxan-ik	swim-IV
aq'an-isa	climb-CAUSE	sutin-ik	turn-IV	wakat-ik	walk-IV
ch'aqt-isa	wet-CAUSE	el-ik	leave-IV	pet-ik	come-IV
noj-isa	full-CAUSE	wul-ik	destroy-IV		
atin-isa	bathe-CAUSE				

5. METHOD

Our initial pilot testing had shown that we could induce children to produce more causative forms if we began with some familiar causativized verbs. Therefore, we began the test by eliciting the causative forms for the verbs *xojow* 'dance' and *aq'an* 'climb'. Thereafter we alternated between the different classes of verbs. We used the same order for each child (*xojow* 'dance', *aq'an* 'climb', *ch'aqt* 'wet', *qaj* 'go down', *sutij* 'turn', *wul* 'destroy', *pet* 'come', *noj* 'full', *atin* 'bathe', *el* 'leave', *muxan* 'swim', and *wakat* 'walk'). We used a set of plastic farm animals as our stimulus items, primarily a mother pig and two baby pigs. For example, our protocol for the verb *xojow* 'dance' went:

'Kaxojow ri: aq i'. Kawiloh? Kaxojowik. Ma kaxojow taj le: jun aq chik. Kara:j na luna:n kaxojow le: ra:l y ku'an le: ri ri'. Jas ku'an le: nan che le: ra:l?'

'This baby pig is dancing. See? It's dancing. The other baby pig is not dancing. Its mother wants her baby to dance so she goes like this. What is she doing to her baby?'

If a child failed to respond, we would repeat the action and again ask what the mother was doing to her baby. If a child responded that the baby was dancing, we would draw the child's attention to the mother's action and again ask what the mother was doing to her baby. If the child still could not say what the mother was doing, we would record the response as a refusal and go on to the next item. I was surprised to find that we had very little difficulty eliciting transitive verbs from even our youngest subjects in this manner. While one of us manipulated the animals and delivered the monologue, the other would transcribe the children's responses. In addition, all sessions were audio-recorded.

6. RESULTS

Table 8.1 shows what an ideal response pattern would look like. Children should use the morphological form of the causative with morphological causative verbs, the zero form with zero derivational verbs, and the periphrastic form with periphrastic verbs. Anything else would count as an overgeneralization.

We elicited quite a range of responses from our subjects. Besides the expected (adult) responses, the children used other transitive verbs, other causativized verbs, periphrastic responses, the intransitive verb form, or another intransitive verb. Their responses are shown in Table 8.2. I calculated the percentage of overgeneralizations based on the types of errors for each class of verbs. For the morphological causative, only the use of a zero form would count as an overgeneralization. For the zero verb class, only the use of a causative affix /-isa/ would count as an overgeneralization, and for the periphrastic verbs, the use of either the causative affix or a zero derivation would count as an overgeneralization.

7. DISCUSSION

Our most significant finding is that we actually succeeded in eliciting some causative overgeneralizations from the children. We have had some difficulty eliciting passive sentences from K'iche' children in previous

TABLE 8.1
Ideal Response Pattern

	Type Used		
Type	Morphological	Zero	Periphrastic
Morphological	X		
Zero		X	
Periphrastic			X

TABLE 8.2
Causative Data

	4,5,6,7 years (N = 11)			8,9,10,11 years (N = 62)			12,13 years (N = 7)		
	Morph	Zero	Other	Morph	Zero	Other	Morph	Zero	Other
Morphological									
xojowisa:j	11			58		4	7		
atinisa:j	11			55		7	6		1
aq'anisa:j	11			42		20	4		3
nojisa:j	8		3	36		26	6		1
ch'aqtisa:j	1		10	32		30	3		4
Percent	0	(0/42)		0	(0/223)		0	(0/26)	
Zero									
qasa:j	3	4	4	12	31	19	1	4	2
suti:j		11		4	55	3	1	6	
esa:j		8	3		46	16		2	5
wuli:j		3	8		16	35		1	6
Percent	10	(3/29)		10	(16/164)		13	(2/15)	
Periphrastic									
muxanik	1	7	3	1	28	33	1	1	5
wakatik	1		10	3	1	58		1	6
petik			3			23			5
Percent	35	(9/25)		24	(33/139)		16	(3/19)	
Total Percent	10	(11/107)		8	(49/575)		8	(5/63)	

studies (Pye & Quixtan Poz, 1988), so I was relieved to find that it was fairly easy to get the children to talk about causative actions. Some children added the causative affix to the zero class verbs *qajik* 'go down' and *sutinik* 'turn', as well as the periphrastic class verbs *muxanik* 'swim' and *wakatik* 'walk'. It was also a surprise to see that the children applied the zero derivation to verbs in the periphrastic class as well as using the regular causative derivation. For *muxanik* 'swim' their favorite zero derivation was *muxa:j*, whereas their zero derivation for *wakatik* 'walk' was *wakati:j*.

I was not prepared to find the children overgeneralizing these verbs so frequently. I had expected the children to overgeneralize in 8% to 10% of their responses based on my previous estimation from longitudinal samples and reports in the literature (Cazden, 1968). Experimental studies such as this one seem to elicit higher rates of overgeneralization. Maratsos et al. (1987) reported a mean overgeneralization rate of 26%, and a recent study by Braine et al. (1990) found their subjects overgeneralized the English causative alternation to intransitive verbs in 39% of the trials. Seventy-three percent (8/11) of the youngest K'iche' subjects extended the causative to the verb *muxanik* 'swim', and 43% (3/7) extended the morphological causative to the verb *qajik* 'go down'. Only 33% (2/6) of the oldest subjects extended the causative to the verb *muxanik* 'swim'.

There is no indication of an order effect in the children's responses. The final verbs on the test *muxanik* 'swim' and *wakatik* 'walk' had a large number of overgeneralizations, but the verb that immediately preceded them (*elik* 'leave') was not overgeneralized by any of the children. The children produced overgeneralized forms of two of the verbs in the zero class (*qajik* 'go down' and *sutinik* 'turn'), which were the fourth and fifth items on the test. However, none of the children overgeneralized the sixth and seventh items on the test (the verbs *wulik* 'destroy' and *petik* 'come'). These trends suggest that the children's responses reflected the state of their knowledge of the individual lexical items rather than a simple priming effect from the order of elicitation.

I was especially surprised that we succeeded in eliciting causative overgeneralizations from 13-year-olds. An assumption has crept into the literature that all the interesting developments in syntax occur before 5;0. Pinker (1989, p. 289) stated that Christy made such overgeneralizations over a period of 6 years, from 2;1 to 7;11. Braine et al. only tested 2- and 4-year-olds in addition to adults. The K'iche' data shows that the acquisition of lexical alternations is not completed in all languages by 8;0. This, of course, raises the learnability issue of exactly what mechanism would operate over such an extended period of time. The slow rate of progress rules out a maturational or grammatical change because such changes would lead to more abrupt "across-the-board" restrictions on the causative.

There was a striking difference in the children's willingness to produce transitive versions of individual verbs. The children were quite happy to supply causativized versions of the verbs *xojow* 'dance', *aq'an* 'climb', and *atin* 'bathe', but had real trouble finding a way to causativize *ch'aq* 'wet' and to a lesser extent *noj* 'full'. This result shows that our experiment was not equally successful in eliciting the causative forms of all the verbs. Subjects often responded to probes on *ch'aq* 'wet' with the causative form of *atin* 'bathe' because bathing someone is more typical than wetting them.

Even more striking was the difference in the children's overgeneralizations of the verbs in each class. Three of the youngest subjects overgeneralized the verb *qajik* 'go down' and eight children overgeneralized the verb *muxanik* 'swim'. None of them overgeneralized the verbs *sutinik* 'turn', *elik* 'leave', and *petik* 'come'. In fact we stopped using the verb *petik* 'come' in our experiment because the K'iche' children were unwilling to causativize it and it seemed to lead to more frustration on their part when we kept probing for it.

This data suggests another important difference between children learning K'iche' and those learning English. Pinker (1989, p. 303) reanalyzed Bowerman's (1982) data and found that children learning English most frequently causativized the verbs *come*, *go*, *fall*, *rise*, and *drop*. The K'iche' children did their best to avoid causativizing the verb *petik* 'come' while most frequently overextending the causative derivation to the verbs *qasaj* 'go down', *muxanik* 'swim', *sutinik* 'turn', and *wakatik* 'stroll'. Berman (1982) reported that Hebrew-speaking children overgeneralize the intransitive forms of the verbs *see*, *eat*, *move*, *sit*, *hurt*, *go down*, *get up* (p. 179) and Aksu-Koç and Slobin reported errors with the Turkish verbs *burn* and *get up* (1985, p. 849). The data suggests significant cross-linguistic differences in the verbs children overgeneralize.

One possible explanation for these cross-linguistic differences would be a difference in input frequencies. If frequencies of the verbs differed significantly in the input languages, they might underlie differences in the children's knowledge of each verb and therefore differences in the overgeneralization rates for each verb. Children should find more evidence for a verb's argument structure if that verb is frequently produced by parents. Children might produce more causative overgeneralizations with verbs that are less frequent in the input.

I examined this issue by counting the different verbs in the speech of the mothers in my spontaneous samples of K'iche'. I had previously selected samples in which the mothers did a lot of the talking to estimate the frequency with which the mothers used various morphemes. I counted the number of times the mothers used each of the verbs from the causative experiment. For a comparison with English I counted the number of times Adam's mother and Eve's mother used the English equivalents of the K'iche' verbs in their first samples (Brown, 1973).[6] I used the Pye Analysis of Language (PAL) computer program to extract the verbs from the mothers' language samples (Pye, 1987). The results are shown in Table 8.3.

I included tokens of both transitive and intransitive uses of the verbs in my count. Thus, I counted uses of both *pet* 'come' and *k'am* 'bring' for the K'iche' mothers and their equivalents for Adam's and Eve's mothers. I also excluded uses of the English verbs that fell outside the range of meaning of the K'iche' verbs. Adam's and Eve's mothers tended to use the verb *leave* more frequently with a meaning of 'let it stay' rather than 'go out of some place'. I only included the latter use in my count.

---

[6]I used the first sample of Adam's speech (Adam01.chi) from the Childes database for this estimate (Brown, 1973).

TABLE 8.3
Token Frequency of Experimental Verbs in Speech to Children

Verbs		K'iche' Mothers			English Mothers	
		Al Tiya:n	Al Cha:y	A Carlos	Adam	Eve
xojow	'dance'					3
aq'an	'climb'				2	1
ch'aq	'wet'		2			
qaj	'go down'	1				
sutij	'turn'		2			6
wulin	'destroy'					
pet	'come'	23	32	5	3	16
noj	'fill'					
atin	'wash'	1			1	
el	'leave'	3	5	2	2	4
muxan	'swim'					1
wakat	'walk'				3	
Total verb types		58	88	36	82	74
Total verb tokens		285	417	290	523	789

These samples may not be large enough to provide incontrovertible evidence of a difference in input frequency between K'iche' and English, but they are robust enough to rule out a simple correlation between input frequency and causative overgeneralizations.

There is a fair degree of consistency between the K'iche' mothers, which derives from their frequent use of the verbs *pet* 'come' and *el* 'leave' and their transitive counterparts *k'am* 'bring' and *esa:j* 'take out'. It is also true that the K'iche' subjects in my experiment did not overgeneralize the causative with these verbs. However, the K'iche' children did not overgeneralize the causative with the verb *wulin* 'destroy' either, despite its infrequency in the input. Adam's and Eve's mothers both used the verb *come* the most frequently. This finding is at odds with English-speaking children's frequent overgeneralization of the causative alternation with *come*. It seems as though differences in input frequencies will not account for the cross-linguistic differences in children's willingness to overgeneralize the causative with certain verbs, although this issue should be pursued further with larger samples of parental speech to children.

Interestingly, the children did not overgeneralize the intransitive verb forms to transitive contexts. The classic observation from Bowerman is that children use intransitive forms in transitive contexts—for example, Christy (2;9) said 'I'm gonna just fall this on her.' In fact, this is the phenomenon that Braine and Maratsos succeeded in eliciting from their subjects. Berman (1982, p. 179) reported that this is a relatively frequent error for Hebrew-speaking children and Aksu-Koç and Slobin (1985, p. 849) provided an example of this type of error in Turkish. Even though

I found two examples of such an error in my spontaneous K'iche' data, we did not elicit a single example of this sort from our K'iche' subjects. We did elicit a few intransitive verbs from the children, but in these cases it is clear that the children were using the verbs as intransitives. The verbs have an intransitive morphology, and more telling, the children only used these verbs with one argument.

One 7-year-old boy, for example, produced the sentence in (7a). His sentence only contains one argument ('the little pig') and the verb uses the regular third-person absolutive subject marker and the intransitive verb termination /-ik/. For the trial with *pet* 'come' this same boy produced the sentence in (7b). In this example the boy retains a transitive relation by using the transitive verb *yo'* 'scold', and manages to convey the right motion by adding an extra clause with the intransitive verb *pet* 'come'. He displays his control of the verb morphology in switching between an ergative subject marker on the transitive verb *yo'* 'scold' and an absolutive subject marker on the verb *pet* 'come'. The verbs also have the correct termination markers. I think the discrepancy in the types of causative overgeneralizations produced in my spontaneous and experimental studies might stem from the ages of the subjects in the two studies. I plan to work with younger subjects in a future experiment on the causative to see if they will use intransitive verb forms in transitive sentence contexts.

(7) a. kamuxanik le: wich' aq
   k-Ø-muxan-ik
   INCOMP-3A-swim-IV the little pig
   'the little pig is swimming.'

   b. kuyo'oj b'ik eh kapetik
   k-Ø-u-yo'-oj   b'i-k   eh   k-Ø-pet-ik
   INCOMP-3A-3E-scold-TV there-T and INCOMP-3A-come-IV
   'She scolds him and he comes.'

8. THEORETICAL IMPLICATIONS

I think this data, admittedly preliminary, supports a number of conclusions about the process of acquiring the causative alternation. Both the spontaneous and experimental data confirm observations from English that children will overgeneralize the causative alternation in ways that violate adult usage. This finding disconfirms Baker's (1979) hypothesis of conservative learning. Unfortunately, this finding also raises the learnability paradox discussed so extensively in Pinker (1989). What mechanism can children rely on to learn the adult restrictions on lexical alternations like the causative?

Braine et al. (1990) proposed a competition between the verbs' argument structure and canonical sentence schemas to account for children's causative overgeneralizations. This is essentially identical to Pinker's hypothesis that children first construct a broad-based rule as the basis of the causative alternation. It is important to recognize that the alternation takes place in both directions, as Braine et al. demonstrated (see also Aksu-Koç & Slobin, 1985, p. 848; Berman, 1982, p. 180; Lord, 1979). Children could apply such a rule without changing the lexical entries of verbs. However, some additional mechanism is needed to explain why adults do not use canonical sentence schemas as often as children. The fact that the K'iche' children in the experimental study never used an intransitive verb in a transitive argument frame suggests that they have extracted more than a simple alternation between argument structures. They have mastered the morphological changes associated with the changes in verb transitivity in K'iche' (cf. Pye, 1985).

Pinker (1989) proposed that children come to rely on narrow range semantic verb classes to acquire the adult restrictions on lexical alternations like the causative. Pinker derived the narrow semantic verb classes on the basis of his Grammatically Relevant Subsystem Hypothesis (1989). He stated that

> for it to be true, there would have to be a single set of elements that is at once conceptually interpretable, much smaller than the set of possible verbs, used across all languages, used by children to formulate and generalize verb meanings, used in specifically grammatical ways . . . , and used to differentiate the narrow classes that are subject to different sets of lexical rules. (p. 169)

He failed to show that the set of elements he used to characterize the causative alternation in English has cross-linguistic validity or guides children in restricting the causative alternation to specific narrow verb classes.

The form of Pinker's hypothesis creates a dilemma. If the set of semantically relevant elements is too small, the degree of cross-linguistic variability is overly restricted. It follows that all languages would differentiate pretty much the same narrow verb classes. If the set of elements is too large, it will allow for more cross-linguistic variation, but at the cost of becoming nothing more than an extremely complex feature notation. Unfortunately, it is difficult to tell how Pinker intended to use his semantically relevant elements because many of his semantic representations contradict his definitions of the semantic elements. He represented the verb *support* as a STATE incorporating an ACT (p. 201). Earlier he stated that ACTs have the feature $< +\text{dynamic}>$ and STATEs are $< -\text{dynamic}>$ (p. 195). Feature clashes of this sort usually lead to ill-formed structures.

Another example of his flexibility in applying the basic semantic elements occurs in his discussion of the cross-linguistic differences that exist with respect to the unergative/unaccusative distinction. By and large, unaccusative verbs causativize whereas unergative verbs do not. There is considerable cross-linguistic variation in the unaccusative distinction, however (Rosen, 1984). Pinker solved this problem by hypothesizing that in some languages ambiguous verbs "may be expressed as a kind of ACT, in others as a kind of GO or BE" (p. 225). Such flexibility indicates that Pinker's elements do not have an independent conceptual interpretation; they can be attached to any verb as a diacritic of its ability to causativize. This imprecision makes it impossible to empirically test Pinker's theory in its current form.

Apart from these definitional problems, Pinker's theory cannot account for the findings from the experimental study. His theory does not predict cross-linguistic differences in which verbs children will be prone to overgeneralize. All children learning a particular verb should have the same difficulty in learning the semantic elements associated with the verb's meaning. Pinker's narrow range semantic constraints hypothesis cannot explain why K'iche' children show such reluctance to causativize the verb *petik* 'come', whereas English-speaking children causativize the verb *come* with relative abandon. The meaning of these verbs is as similar as verb meanings can be in different languages, thus some factor beyond verb meaning must affect children's tendency to causativize verbs.

Another difficulty with Pinker's theory is that it is not compatible with the extended period of time children require to develop causative restrictions. Thirteen-year-olds should have a fairly accurate representation of the meaning of *muxanik* 'swim' and *sutinik* 'turn' as well as a basic understanding of which narrow range semantic classes these verbs belong to. Although Pinker is not specific about the length of time children need to establish the narrow range restrictions on lexical rules, such a process should not require the better part of a decade. The semantic elements that are basic to Pinker's acquisition mechanism should be readily accessible to children because they constitute a small set of universally relevant semantic features.

The preceding arguments suggest that lexical retrieval processes may be the primary determinant of children's causative errors. I think it is best to view the problem in the general perspective of choosing a suitable verb on any given occasion. Children are learning the difference between the verbs *come* and *go*, *bring* and *take*. The causative alternation requires that they also appreciate the difference between the verbs *come* and *bring* as well as *qajik* and *qasa:j*. Several studies have suggested that children do not always succeed in retrieving the proper word (Hoek, Ingram, & Gibson, 1986). The retrieval process is especially indicated in children's failure to select a suppletive alternate. They may lack this alternate or not be able to retrieve it as readily as the other form. The availability of suppletive forms provides children with positive evidence for the appropriateness of the different verbs. Thus acquiring lexical alternations is no different from acquiring irregular inflections. Pinker stated that such suppletive alternations account for 77% of Bowerman's data.

Another finding in favor of the retrieval process is that it explains why children only produce causative errors intermittently. If children actually did have an immature semantic representation of a verb's meaning, they would use the verb incorrectly every time they met a suitable occasion. Instead, children only produce causative overgeneralizations in extraordinary circumstances (such as elicitation experiments), and then only in a certain percentage of instances. The retrieval explanation would account for the individual differences between children in the verbs they overgeneralize as well as the frequency with which they overgeneralize them. Each child's history of encounters with verbs would lead to individual developmental profiles. The retrieval process would also become better with time as children added suppletive forms to their lexicon and strengthened their access to individual verbs. This would be compatible with the extended developmental time frame seen in the data.

I have mentioned before that another factor seems to be affecting the children's access to particular verbs. The best example of this is the difference between the K'iche' and English-speaking children's willingness to causativize the verb for *come* in their languages. K'iche' children would be able to use the monosyllabic form of the verb stem as additional information about the verb and its possibilities for participating in a transitivity alternation. There is a basic split in the K'iche' language between monosyllabic and polysyllabic verb stems. Monosyllabic stems are underived transitive or intransitive stems. They only alternate with the addition of an affix. Most polysyllabic verb stems are derived from some other type of root. They are more likely to alternate in transitivity with a simple affix change. The K'iche' children could use the monosyllabic status of the verb *pet* to infer that it was an underived intransitive verb and only alternate it when they encountered positive evidence in their input.

The K'iche' children show further evidence of this sensitivity to the derived/underived verb distinction in their willingness to overgeneralize the causative alternation to the verbs *muxanik* 'swim' and *wakatik* 'stroll'. Their tendency to overgeneralize the verb *muxanik* is especially pronounced and may stem from the misinterpretation of the /n/ in the stem as an absolutive antipassive affix. Verbs with the antipassive have a straightforward transitive form, and if *muxanik* was an antipassive form, its transitive equivalent would be *muxa:j*. This is indeed the form supplied most frequently by the K'iche' children, and thus striking evidence that the children have extracted the underlying distinction between derived and underived verb stems.

I think there is support for this position in the results Berman (1992) reported on verb-pattern alternation in Hebrew. Recall that Hebrew children use intransitive verb forms in transitive contexts in the same way English-speaking children do. They also make the reverse error, as Lord (1979) reported for English. Hebrew employs a complex system of stem changes to encode the causative alternation. Verb stems generally fall into a set of five patterns that constitute the Binyan system of alternations. Most of the verbs in pattern one (e.g., *katav* 'write') have a causative form in pattern five (e.g., *hixtiv* 'dictate'). Some pattern one verbs (e.g., *lamad* 'learn') have causative forms in pattern three (e.g., *limed* 'teach'). Reflexive verbs (e.g., *mitracex* 'wash') in pattern four have a transitive form in pattern one (e.g., *roxec*) and inchoative verbs retain their pattern five form in causative contexts (e.g., *yavri* 'become healthy'). A few process verbs also have the same pattern five form in intransitive and causative contexts (e.g., *hitxil* 'start').

This is a complex system and, not surprisingly, it takes many years before children learn it completely. I think the interesting feature of the Hebrew Binyan system is the extent to which the first pattern contains many transitive and intransitive verbs. Berman stated that pattern one is used for the transitive actions *make = do, give, eat, drink, build*, for statives such as *like, want, see*, and for intransitives like *go, sleep, run, jump*, and *sit*. Thus, unlike the situation in K'iche' where there is a clear morphological distinction between transitive and intransitive verbs, children learning Hebrew have plenty of evidence that pattern one contains both transitive and intransitive verbs. I think this is the primary reason why they use the verbs in different contexts without making the necessary morphological changes.

My last conclusion would be that children may never entirely succeed in accessing the correct verbs all of the time. I have received written responses in my university classes from undergraduates who have overgeneralized verbs. One such example is "These changes don't deteriorate the language." Even the 1991 Stanford child language conference abstracts contains the example, "When encountered with sentences. . . ." Thus the retrieval process becomes essentially error free in adults for core verbs, but remains susceptible to intrusions in the case of low frequency verbs.

ACKNOWLEDGMENTS

Preliminary versions of this chapter were presented at the 1990 Mid-America Linguistics Conference, November 7, 1990, the 1991 Stanford Child Language Research Forum, April 7, 1991, and the workshop on

Cross-linguistic and Cross-population Contributions to Theories of Language Acquisition, June 6, 1991, Jerusalem. I thank all of these audiences for their suggestions, especially Ruth Berman, Paul Bloom, Charles Ferguson, Jess Gropen, Teun Hoekstra, David Ingram, and Dan Slobin. In addition, Jess Gropen responded to a preliminary version with an extensive and helpful set of comments. None of these people are responsible for the way I have incorporated their suggestions in this version. Once again I must also acknowledge the support my research receives in the Zunil community, which always makes fieldwork in Guatemala highly productive and extremely enjoyable. I would hope that Zunil has recovered from the devastating 1991 explosion that occurred as a result of geothermal exploration.

Pedro Quixtan Poz has taught me much about when it is possible to causativize K'iche' verbs and was instrumental in refining our experimental techniques. My fieldwork in Guatemala was supported by NSF grant No. BNS-8909846.

REFERENCES

Aksu-Koç, A. A., & Slobin, D. I. (1985). The acquisition of Turkish. In D. I. Slobin (Ed.), *The crosslinguistic study of language acquisition: Vol. 1. The data* (pp. 839–878). Hillsdale, NJ: Lawrence Erlbaum Associates.

Baker, C. L. (1979). Syntactic theory and the projection problem. *Linguistic Inquiry, 10*, 533–581.

Baker, M. (1988). *Incorporation: A theory of grammatical function changing*. Chicago: University of Chicago Press.

Berman, R. A. (1982). Verb-pattern alternation: The interface of morphology, syntax, and semantics in Hebrew child language. *Journal of Child Language, 9*, 169–191.

Bowerman, M. (1974). Learning the structure of causative verbs: A study in the relationship of cognitive, semantic and syntactic development. *Papers and Reports on Child Language Development, 8*, 142–178.

Bowerman, M. (1982). Evaluating competing linguistic models with language acquisition data: Implications of developmental errors with causative verbs. *Quaderni di Semantica, 3*, 5–66.

Braine, M. D. S., Brody, R. E., Fisch, S. M., & Weisberger, M. J. (1990). Can children use a verb without exposure to its argument structure? *Journal of Child Language, 17*, 313–342.

Brown, R. (1973). *A first language*. Cambridge, MA: Harvard University Press.

Cazden, C. B. (1968). The acquisition of noun and verb inflections. *Child Development, 39*, 433–448.

Chomsky, N. (1981). *Lectures in the theory of government and binding*. Dordrecht: Foris.

Dayley, J. P. (1985). *Tzutujil Grammar*. Berkeley, CA: University of California Press.

Green, G. M. (1974). *Semantics and syntactic regularity*. Bloomington, IN: Indiana University Press.

Grimshaw, J. (1990). *Argument structure*. Cambridge, MA: MIT Press.

Hale, K., & Keyser, J. (1986). *Some transitivity alternations in English*. (Lexicon Project Working Papers 7.) Cambridge, MA: MIT Center for Cognitive Science.

Hoek, D., Ingram, D., & Gibson, D. (1986). An examination of the possible causes of children's early word extensions. *Journal of Child Language, 13*, 477–494.

Kaufman, T. (1976). *Proyecto de alfabetos y ortografías para escribir las lenguas mayances.* Guatemala: Ministerio de Educación.

Levin, B., & Rappoport Hovav, M. (1992). The lexical semantics of verbs of motion: The perspective from unaccusativity. In I. M. Roca (Ed.), *Thematic structure: Its role in grammar* (pp. 247–269). Berlin: Mouton de Gruyter.

Lord, C. (1979). "Don't you fall me down": Children's generalizations regarding cause and transitivity. *Papers and Reports on Child Language Development, 17*, 81–89.

Maratsos, M. P. (1979). How to get from words to sentences. In D. Aaronson & R. Reiber (Eds.), *Psycholinguistic research: Implications and applications* (pp. 285–353). Hillsdale, NJ: Lawrence Erlbaum Associates.

Maratsos, M. P., Gudeman, R., Gerard-Ngo, P., & DeHart, G. (1987). A study in novel word learning: The productivity of the causative. In B. MacWhinney (Ed.), *Mechanisms of language acquisition* (pp. 89–113). Hillsdale, NJ: Lawrence Erlbaum Associates.

Mondloch, J. L. (1981). *Voice in Quiché-Maya.* Unpublished doctoral dissertation, State University of New York, Albany.

Perlmutter, D. (1978). Impersonal passives and the unaccusative hypothesis. In *Proceedings of the Fourth Annual Meeting of the Berkeley Linguistics Society* (pp. 157–189). Berkeley: University of California.

Perlmutter, D. (1989). Multiattachment and the unaccusative hypothesis: The perfect auxiliary in Italian. *Probus, 1*, 63–119.

Perlmutter, D., & Postal, P. (1984). The one-advancement exclusiveness law. In D. Perlmutter & C. G. Rosen (Eds.), *Studies in relational grammar* (Vol. 2, pp. 81–125). Chicago: University of Chicago Press.

Pinker, S. (1989). *Learnability and cognition: The acquisition of argument structure.* Cambridge, MA: MIT Press.

Pye, C. (1983). Mayan telegraphese: Intonational determinants of inflectional development in Quiché Mayan. *Language, 59*, 583–604.

Pye, C. (1985). The acquisition of transitivity in Quiché Mayan. *Papers and Reports in Child Language Development, 24*, 115–122.

Pye, C. (1987). The Pye analysis of language. *Working Papers in Language Development, 3*, 1–37.

Pye, C. (1992). The acquisition of K'iche' Maya. In D. I. Slobin (Ed.), *The crosslinguistic study of language acquisition* (Vol. 3, pp. 221–308). Hillsdale, NJ: Lawrence Erlbaum Associates.

Pye, C. (1993a). Breaking concepts: Constraining predicate argument structure. Unpublished manuscript, University of Kansas.

Pye, C. (1993b). *Language acquisition as "radical translation."* Unpublished manuscript, University of Kansas.

Pye, C., & Quixtan Poz, P. (1988). Precocious passives (and antipassives) in Quiché Mayan. *Papers and Reports on Child Language Development, 27*, 71–80.

Rosen, C. (1984). The interface between semantic roles and initial grammatical relations. In D. Perlmutter & C. Rosen (Eds.), *Studies in relational grammar* (pp. 38–77). Chicago: University of Chicago Press.

Slobin, D. I. (1985). Crosslinguistic evidence for the language-making capacity. In D. I. Slobin (Ed.), *The crosslinguistic study of language acquisition* (Vol. 2, pp. 1157–1249). Hillsdale, NJ: Lawrence Erlbaum Associates.

Van Valin, R. D., Jr. (1990). Semantic parameters of split intransitivity. *Language, 66*, 221–260.

CHAPTER NINE

Structural Dependency
and the Acquisition
of Grammatical Relations

Matthew Rispoli
Department of English
Northern Arizona University

The acquisition of grammatical relations (GRs) is central to the study of language acquisition. Perhaps the major impediment to our theoretical attempts to explain how children acquire GRs has been the cross-linguistic variability of the GRs themselves. This is a problem for theory building, but not necessarily for the child acquiring a first language. The primary goal of this chapter is to set out some observations concerning just what children find difficult and what they find easy when they acquire case and agreement systems, those systems most intimately related to GRs. The plan of this chapter is to outline two opposing theoretical approaches to the acquisition of GRs, and to synthesize a cross-linguistic review of data from four languages that will help us better understand just what is and is not difficult in the process of acquiring GRs.

1. APPROACHES TO THE ACQUISITION OF GRs

Networks, prototypes, and coalitions have found their way into theoretical discussions of the acquisition of GRs, largely as an attempt to deal with cross-linguistic variability in GRs. Assume for the moment that GRs are best treated as abstract symbols in an autonomous module of syntactic representation. Pinker (1984) asked the question, if GRs are abstract, how does the child recognize examples of a GR in an input sentence? As an answer to this question, bootstraps were proposed that would

265

signal valid instantiations of GRs to the language acquisition device. One example of a bootstrap was the semantic role of agent. When a child encounters an agent-action-object sentence, then the child's language acquisition device would recognize the agent as the subject GR.

However, there are no universally constant bootstraps for a GR-like subject (Foley & Van Valin, 1977; Keenan, 1976). A bootstrap sufficiently powerful to engage a GR has the flaw of enabling a child to erroneously identify a GR when learning a language in which that particular bootstrap is not valid. Pinker (1987) addressed this problem by proposing that bootstraps to GRs enter into networks of rules that refer to a particular GR. As Pinker (1987) explained, "Each network consists of a set of unmarked, default, or prototypical rules referencing a common substantive universal (e.g., SUBJ, N)" (p. 422). Networks cohere because they refer to a common GR symbol. Here is an example, paraphrased from Pinker (1987, p. 423), of the rule network referencing subject: (a) subject precedes object in phrase structure, (b) subjects are agents in the basic lexical entry of a transitive verb, (c) subject is the theme in a passive, (d) verbs agree with subject, (e) subject takes nominative case, (f) subject nouns are more likely to be uninflected by case markers, (g) subjects can be omitted in pro-drop languages, (h) control verbs control the subjects of complement clauses. The effect of such networks on the acquisition of GRs is to allow the child to be more tentative about identifying GRs in the input, until a maximally parsimonious hypothesis has been reached within the limits of the rule network.

Pinker (1987) was led to the position that, in the final state of adult grammars, the "naturalness" of grammatical relations will differ as a function of the language acquired: "In the present model one can, of course, compare the 'goodness' of subjects in one language to that in another. For example, English might be said to have more prototypical subjects than Dyirbal" (p. 436). A person having acquired English has acquired a more natural subject, and so Pinker's (1987) position sounds anglocentric. However, even in Pinker's (1987) model the child acquiring Dyirbal is not at a disadvantage, for the constraint satisfaction network surrounding subject ensures that the child will eventually acquire the Dyirbal subject. The model seems close to being unfalsifiable.

Bates and MacWhinney's (1987) "competition model" incorporated prototypes and coalitions in a prominent manner. They spoke of a natural coalition of two functions that prototypically cooccur: topic and agent (p. 166). Parallel to this functional coalition, they posited a structural coalition of preverbal position and verbal agreement (p. 166). Bates and Mac-Whinney called this combination of functional and structural coalitions "the organization of 'sentence subject' " (p. 166). Unlike Pinker's prototype, which is a priori, the Bates and MacWhinney (1987) prototype is a posteriori: "Our knowledge of a 'prototypical subject' is the emergent property of a great many weightings between individual forms and functions. It is the result of a lifetime distributional analysis" (p. 168).

Are these a posteriori prototypes and coalitions truly necessary for the acquisition of GRs in every language? Consider the Bates and MacWhinney (1987, 1989) treatment of topicality and case in Italian. They pointed out that topics are designated by word order, and that nominative case (which they called "agent") is signaled by verb agreement (for person and number). In their view, topicality and agency is a prototypical functional coalition; "the correlation between agent and topic reflects a high-probability tendency for speakers of all cultures to talk about their own activities and the actions of those who are near and dear to them" (Bates & MacWhinney, 1989, p. 49). Preverbal position and verb agreement is a prototypical structural coalition for the encoding of subject. The entire set of structural and functional correlations is organized together into complex super-block "grammogens," such as the one they described connecting topic and agent (Bates & MacWhinney, 1989, pp. 47–51). When, in Italian, an accusative case argument (which they called "patient") is topicalized, it appears in a preverbal position. To Bates and MacWhinney this represented a dissection of the prototypical structural coalition for subject, or what they termed a "divide the spoils" strategy. According to Bates and MacWhinney (1987), "The set of surface devices comprising 'subject' is simply split to separate elements. . . . The highly correlated subject devices in English tend to be assigned as a block, while the lower correlations among the same devices in Italian permit the coalition to be split up for non-prototypical situations" (p. 168). But what are these coalitions like such that they are so easily split apart? The separability of such coalitions suggests that, in Italian, the structures encoding topic (stress and preverbal position) and the structures indicating nominative case (verb agreement) never truly coalesce over the course of development.

Some linguists have claimed that there is an unmarked or normative relationship between the actor and the unasserted part of the sentence, and conversely between the object and the asserted part of the sentence (Du Bois, 1987; Lambrecht, 1987). But these are normative relations in discourse, and are not the reflection of the child's a priori grammatical knowledge. Functional and structural coalitions may play a causal role in the formation of GRs, that is, the social and historical process of grammaticization (Du Bois, 1987; Silverstein, 1976). It is not apparent, however, that this sociolinguistic, diachronic process is the same as the developmental process by which an immature speaker acquires the GRs of their language. Because prototypes and coalitions are not a priori, and because some languages do not require the formation of functional coalitions in the process of acquiring a language-specific set of GRs, proto-types and coalitions do not seem to be a necessary component of the acquisition of GRs.

Both Pinker (1987) and Bates and MacWhinney (1987, 1989) agreed that it is impossible to define subject with uniquely sufficient properties. Pinker (1987) claimed that the GRs of English are highly prototypical and the difference between languages matters little because acquisition is only the adjustment of rule networks that reference GRs. Such a claim may be impossible to test. Bates and MacWhinney (1987) claimed that GRs emerge from acquiring numerous mappings between structures and functions. They also claimed that there are prototypes for GRs. But, on closer examination, it turns out that such prototypes or coalitions are easily decomposed, and not necessary for the acquisition of language-specific GRs. In addition, despite that fact that we have full-blown theories of the acquisition of GRs, two basic empirical questions have yet to be pursued systematically with cross-linguistic comparisons: (a) When do children find structures that encode grammatical relations difficult to acquire, and conversely, (b) when do they find these structures easy to acquire? In our examination of cross-linguistic data, I believe there is little evidence for prototypes of either the a priori or a posteriori kinds. The data are drawn from a body of research that has accumulated in the area of the cross-linguistic study of language acquisition spearheaded by Slobin (1985). The cross-linguistic study of language has revealed a complex picture of errors, interim strategies, and competent behaviors, which are evidence for hypothesis formulation and testing in the systematic study of the acquisition of GRs.

2. GRAMMATICAL FRAMEWORK

Before we can proceed to a review of developmental data, it is necessary to introduce the theoretical framework in which this data is viewed. For this purpose I have chosen Role and Reference Grammar (RRG), because it is the only grammatical framework in which GRs are treated as decomposible, construction-specific relations between a noun phrase (NP) and its clause. This synopsis of pertinent aspects of RRG can only serve as an introduction to the larger theoretical framework (Foley & Van Valin, 1984; Van Valin, 1990, 1993). Here we review four basic components of RRG's decomposition of GRs: logical structures, macroroles, case systems, and pragmatic distinctions.

2.1. Logical Structures

RRG's representation of semantic roles and their interface with syntax begins with the logical structure of a predicate, a theory of lexical representation based on Dowty (1979), which in turn is based on the Vendler (1967) Aktionsart classification of predicates. This classification recognizes four types of predicate: states, achievements, accomplishments and activities, displayed diagrammatically in Table 9.1. There are two basic operators in logical structures, BECOME and CAUSE. The operator BECOME is a symbol for the fact that achievements are telic. Activities are atelic actions, and therefore do not have the BECOME operator in their logical structure. Accomplishments are decomposable into predicates connected symbolically by the CAUSE operator. CAUSE and BECOME differ in the following way: CAUSE symbolizes the interconnectedness of two predicates, whereas BECOME does not; CAUSE in itself does not symbolize telicity, whereas BECOME does.

The logical structures outlined here provide information for the first step in determining thematic roles for a given predicate. Activities are dynamic and can have an effector role, for example, *the wheel is rotating, the flag is waving*. If the effector is an animate being, acting intentionally it is an agent, for example, *the man is waving goodbye*. An

TABLE 9.1
Predicate Class and Logical Structure in RRG

Predicate Class	Logical Structure
State	predicate' (x) or (x,y)
The clock is broken.	**broken**' (clock)
John is a lawyer.	**be**' (John, [**lawyer**'])
Achievement	BECOME predicate' (x) or (x,y)
The clock broke.	BECOME **broken**' (clock)
John became a lawyer.	BECOME **be**' (John, [**lawyer**'])
Activity	do (x) [predicate' (x) or (x,y)]
The children cried.	do (children) [**cry**' (children)]
Larry ate fish.	do (Larry) [**eat**' (Larry, fish)]
Accomplishment	@ CAUSE %
	(where @ is an activity, and % is an activity or accomplishment).
The child broke the clock.	[do (child)] CAUSE [BECOME **broken**' (clock)]

Note: Adapted from "Semantic Parameters of Split Intransitivity" by R. Van Valin, 1990, *Language, 66*, p. 224. Copyright © 1990 by the Linguistic Society of America. Adapted by permission.

animate being, acting unintentionally is just an effector, for example, *The child sobbed* (uncontrollably) (Holisky, 1987; Van Valin, 1990). States cannot have effectors associated with them. Single argument states, for example, *The clock is broken* can have patients as their sole arguments. In contradistinction, activities can never have a patient argument.

Other thematic roles, corresponding to a variety of perceptual and psychological features, are found in Fig. 9.1. We have already outlined the status of agent, effector, and patient. Locative can be broken down into the familiar goal, source, and recipient roles: for example, *She entered the theatre*, *He left the building*, and *She gave Tom a book*. The role theme refers to any entity, intentional or unintentional, that moves with reference to a background. The role experiencer must refer to an animate being that is capable of psychological experience.

Logical structures represent the number of thematic roles associated with a specific predicate. The roles stipulated in the logical structure are termed *core arguments*. For example, the predicate *send* stipulates three core arguments, an effector, a recipient goal, and a theme, as in the sentence *Wilma sent Fred a pterydactl*. We call the core argument that ranks lowest on the thematic role hierarchy the lowest ranking core argument (LRCA).

2.2. Macroroles

Before we can approach the question of how case systems are structured, a second tier of semantically motivated roles, *macroroles*, are posited in RRG. There are two macroroles, *actor* and *undergoer*. Thematic roles are mapped into these macroroles in interaction with Aktionsart. An agent of an activity predicate will always be an actor; a patient in a state predicate will always be an undergoer. The arguments of the English verbs

```
Actor ------------------------------>

Agent Effector

             Experiencer Locative

                           Theme Patient

             <--------------------------- Undergoer
```

FIG. 9.1. Thematic role hierarchy for assignment to macrorole status. *Note.* '---->' refers to increasing markedness of realization of thematic role as a macrorole. Adapted by the author from ''Semantic parameters of split intransitivity,'' by R. Van Valin, *Language, 66*, p. 226. Copyright © 1990 by the Linguistic Society of America. Adapted by permission.

fear and *frighten* seem to be the same. However, *fear* is a state, whereas *frighten* is an accomplishment (roughly, "*x* causes *y* to fear"). In (1a) the simple nonpast form of the verb *fear* can have a present-tense reading, and in (1b) the progressive is peculiar with *fear*. In contrast the progressive with *frighten*, in (2a) is normal. Moreover, an agent is possible with *frighten* but not with *fear*, as can be seen by comparing (2a) and (2b).

(1) a. Bill fears John.
    b. *Bill is fearing John.
(2) a. John is deliberately frightening Bill.
    b. *Bill deliberately fears John.

In (2a) *John* is assigned an actor macrorole, because, as stated earlier, the intentional effector is always assigned the actor macrorole. In (1a), however, *John* is not an effector at all, because *fear* is not dynamic. In the RRG framework it is considered a theme and is outranked by an experiencer for eligibility to the actor macrorole (see Fig. 9.1). The experiencer, *Bill*, is linked to the undergoer macrorole when the predicate is an accomplishment, as in (2a), but when the predicate is a state, the experiencer is linked to the actor macrorole, as in (1a). As with other English state verbs, such as *see* and *know*, the experiencer takes the actor macrorole. In sum, macroroles are not merely a partitioning of thematic roles, they are the result of an interaction of Aktionsart and thematic roles.

The number of macroroles a predicate has is equal to or less than the number of core arguments, and there are never more than two macroroles in a clause. Thus, in a sentence like *Wilma sent Fred a pterydactl*, there are three core arguments, but only two macroroles: *Wilma* is the actor and *Fred* is the undergoer.

2.3. Case Systems

Case systems are sets of structures motivated by macrorole assignment. Case systems come in three major varieties: *nominative/accusative*, for example, English; *ergative/absolutive*, for example, Yidin (Dixon, 1979); and *active/stative*, for example, Acehnese (Durie, 1988). Case systems all have one characteristic in common. In multiple argument accomplishment predicates (more familiarly called transitive predicates), actors and undergoers are treated as different roles. Nominative, ergative, and active cases encode actors, whereas accusative, absolutive, and stative cases encode undergoer. Each of the case systems orients single argument predicates differently, the implications of these different orientations is now well discussed in the language acquisition literature (Bowerman, 1985; Maratsos, 1989; Pye, 1990). Single arguments in nominative/accusative languages receive nominative case, and in ergative/absolutive languages receive absolutive case. In active/stative systems, actor arguments of intransitives are given active case, the same case as actors in transitive predicates. Undergoers in intransitives are given stative case, the same case given to undergoers in transitive predicates.

None of these systems are considered especially marked or unusual because all of these systems are adapted to the basic task of encoding the actor/undergoer distinction. In contrast to Pinker's (1987) position, it is consistent with the RRG framework to expect that all three case orientations are equally acquirable by the child.

2.4. Pragmatic Distinctions

RRG recognizes not only semantic motivations for GRs but also pragmatic motivations. These motivations are a collection of factors, each separable in theory. Each may have an independent relationship to the GRs of a particular language. The first of these factors is information structure. Every sentence has information structure (Lambrecht, 1987). The motivating force behind information structure is the pragmatic distinction between presupposition and assertion. Those constituents of a sentence that are not presupposed are eligible to become part of a sentence's focus. Lambrecht (1987) treated focus as a "formal scope indicator, i.e., as a grammatical signal indicating the scope of the assertion expressed by a sentence or proposition" (p. 374). Marking the breadth of focus in a sentence has morphosyntactic consequences, and such consequences are of concern in RRG. In English, the scope of focus is expressed by stress. Thus, (3) and (4) are a proper question and answer pair, but (3) and (5) are not. Stress is signaled by caps.

  (3) Who bought a new car?
  (4) TOM bought a new car.
  (5) *Tom bought a NEW CAR.

Beyond narrow scope single NP focus, there are broader focus types, predicate focus, and full sentence focus. Once again, let us turn to question–response pairs to see the difference. Question (6) is a predicate focal question, where the queried constituent is encoded by the word *how*. Once again stress is signified by caps.

  (6) How's your neck?
  (7) My neck HURTS.

(8) It HURTS.
(9) *MY NECK hurts.

The responses to (6) must be predicate focal, and either (7) with a repetition of the full lexical NP or (8) with an anaphoric pronominal reduction of the NP are possible. Sentence (9) is ungrammatical as a reply to (6) because the focus of the sentence, as signaled by stress, is off the predicate *hurts*.

The scope of focus may be coextensive with the entire sentence. This occurs when all the elements of a sentence are part of the assertion. The stress pattern for sentence focal sentences is distinct from that of predicate focal sentences. Example (10) is a sentence focal question, and as such (11) is a grammatical response. In contrast, (12), which is identical with (7), is an ungrammatical response.

(10) What's the matter?
(11) My NECK hurts.
(12) *My neck HURTS.

In Japanese this set of distinctions in the breadth of focal scope motivates the NP postpositional distinction between *wa* and *ga*. Sentences (13) and (14) are translations of (7) and (11), respectively.

(13) *kubi wa   ita-i*
     neck TOP hurt-NON PAST[1]
     (My) neck HURTS.

(14) *kubi ga   ita-i*
     neck FOC hurt-NON PAST
     (My) NECK hurts.

Sentence (13) is an example of what Kuno (1973) called a topic–comment structure in Japanese, with *wa* marking the topic NP. The focal scope of sentences like (13) cannot include the NP marked by *wa*, but rather

---

[1]The abbreviations for grammatical morphemes used in this chapter are as follows: A = actor (Georgian), ABS = absolutive, ACC = accusative, AGR = agreement (Sesotho), AOR = aorist aspect (Georgian), DAT = dative case, DEF = definite conjugation (Hungarian), ERG = ergative, EMPH = emphatic sentence final particle (Kaluli), EVID = evidential verb form (Kaluli), F = feminine (Italian), FOC = focus, FUT = future tense, IMP = imperative, INDEF = indefinite conjugation (Hungarian), LOC = locative, M = mood (Sesotho), M = masculine (Italian), NOM = nominative, NON PAST = Nonpast tense (Japanese), P = plural, PASS = passive, PAST = past tense, PRES = present tense, PROG = progressive aspect, PRT = participle, RECP = recipient verb inflection (Georgian), REFLEXIVE = reflexive pronoun (Italian), SG = singular, TOP = topic, U = undergoer (Georgian), 1 = first person, 2 = second person, 3 = third person, ? = question.

is limited to the predicate *ita-i* 'hurts' (Lambrecht, 1987). Topic in the RRG framework is a pragmatic function assigned to an element or elements of a clause that are outside the scope of focus. Sentence (14) has two possible information structures. The NP marked by *ga* may be the sole focal element in the sentence, a narrow scope single NP focus, or the entire sentence may be focal in what Lambrecht (1987) termed a "sentence focus" construction for Japanese. In either case, the NP marked by *ga* is within focal scope. Like topic, focus in the RRG framework is a pragmatic function assigned to an element or elements of a clause.

The second major factor in the pragmatic motivation of GRs is the discourse–pragmatic status of an NP. Consider two statuses that will figure into our discussion of acquisition. *Definiteness* is the status given an NP when the speaker believes that the hearer "already knows and can identify the particular referent" that the speaker has in mind (Chafe, 1976, p. 39). Thus, definiteness reflects the pragmatic accessibility of an NP's referent. It becomes evident that this particular distinction plays a role in the encoding of GRs in Hungarian. *Anaphora* is the use of a pronoun or zero to signal a definite referent that is given in discourse. While anaphors are definite, definite NPs need not be given, but rather, only "identifiable" (Chafe, 1976). In sentence 15, *the moon* is definite, although it need not be given in discourse. As there is only one moon possible in the context, the referent is clearly identifiable. In (16), the replacement of the erstwhile definite NP with *it* sounds quite strange, leaving the listener without clear reference for the anaphor.

(15) I took a walk outside. The moon shone brightly.
(16) ??I took a walk outside. It shone brightly.

In the following section on the acquisition of the Italian passato prossimo we see that NP anaphoricity can have an impact on GRs and that acquiring anaphoric pronouns can have an effect on the child's acquisition of GRs.

The roles of information structure and NP discourse–pragmatic status in motivating GRs are related, but they are by no means identical. A grammaticized topic structure, such as that found in Japanese, is motivated by information structure, not by discourse–pragmatic status. However, eligibility for topichood is based on the pragmatic accessibility of the NP referent (Lambrecht, 1987). If one asks a predicate focal question, such as in (17) (same as 6), one establishes a topic. To reply, the topic may be repeated as a full lexical, definite NP, or as an anaphor (see 7 and 8) but not as an indefinite NP, as in (18).

(17) How's your neck?
(18) *A neck HURTS.

It has been observed that an NP marked by *wa*, the topic marker of Japanese, must be construed as either a definite NP, or an NP in a generic, timeless sentence, for example, *neko wa doobutsu desu* '(a) cat is (an) animal'. In contrast, an NP marked by *ga* can be construed as either a definite or indefinite NP (Kuroda, 1979). The pragmatic accessibility of a referent is necessary for eligibility as a topic, but pragmatic accessibility is not sufficient. The topic NP cannot fall under the scope of focus. We need to take into account both information structure and discourse—pragmatic status if we are to understand the pragmatic motivations for language-specific GRs.

By recognizing two different functional domains, semantic and pragmatic, RRG can easily capture GRs that are actually defined as intersections of features from both domains. As an example, consider Sesotho, a Bantu language. Sesotho has "a constraint on subjects which restricts them to being highly topical, old, given information" (Demuth, 1989, p. 67). In Sesotho active voice, transitive sentences, the verb agrees with the actor. Therefore, when a transitive verb agrees with the actor, the actor is topical, old, or given information. (19) is an active sentence, the verb agrees with the actor, which is the preverbal argument. Note that it has the pragmatic status of definite, because Thabo is a person's name. The postverbal argument is the undergoer *lijo* 'food'. Note that it can be construed as either definite or indefinite.

(19) *Thabo o-phehil-e   lijo.*
Thabo AGR-cooked-M food.
Thabo cooked the / some food.

When the actor is focal, a passive must be used (Demuth, 1989). Sentence (20) shows the correct form of an actor focal question in the passive. Sentence (21) answers the question in (20). As such, it is an actor focal sentence and must be passive. In these passive sentences, the verb agrees with *lijo* 'food', which is moved to preverbal position. As the preverbal argument *lijo* 'food' can only be construed as definite.

(20) *lijo   li-phehil-o-e   ke mang?*
food   AGR-cooked-PASS-M by who?
The / *some food was cooked by who?
(= Who cooked the food?)

(21) *lijo li-phehil-o-e   ke Thabo.*
food AGR-cooked-PASS-M by Thabo
The / *some food was cooked by Thabo.
(= THABO cooked the food.)

Sentence (22) is an ungrammatical attempt to form an actor question in the active voice, analogous to the English gloss. Transitive verbs cannot agree with focal actors.

(22) *Mang o-phehil-e lijo?*
who AGR-cooked-M (the) food?
Who cooked the / some food?

These constraints are easily stated in the RRG framework: (a) the preverbal argument agreeing with a transitive verb must be pragmatically accessible, (b) the focal actor of a transitive verb will appear in the *ke* phrase of a passive. Interestingly, Demuth (1989) argued that the semantic and pragmatic content of these structures leads to the early acquisition of the passive in Sesotho.

3. DEVELOPMENTAL HYPOTHESES

We have outlined a theory of linguistic representation that decomposes GRs into semantically and pragmatically motivated structures. It is important to keep in mind that semantic and pragmatic motivations are not merely constraints on the use of a structure. They are features of the content of the linguistic representation of these structures. There are semantic distinctions: thematic role distinctions, macrorole distinctions, and predicate class distinctions. There are also pragmatic distinctions: information structure distinctions and distinctions in the discourse–pragmatic status of NPs. It is expected that the number of these distinctions is finite.

We now turn to the question of how a system of GRs is acquired. The basic unit of a system of GRs is the encoding of distinction by morpheme or structure. Let us call those morphemes and structures "exponents." The acquisition of an exponent as a basic step in the process of acquiring a system of GRs. The number of semantic and pragmatic distinctions that can underlie GRs is finite, so the intersection of motivating distinctions encoded by the exponents is in principle discoverable in the finite amount of time a child has to acquire a system of GRs.

GRs are not simple reflections of the underlying semantic and pragmatic distinctions. The process of acquiring a language-specific system of GRs is complicated by the degree and type of structural dependency that exists between exponents. In this chapter we limit our attention to two types of structural dependency: *neutralization* and *globality*. Here we introduce a series of hypotheses about the relative difficulty for the learner when encountering these structural dependencies.

Hypothesis 1: The encoding of a distinction is easiest to acquire when the exponents encoding the opposing values of the distinction are complementary structures.

Hypothesis 2: A multidimensional exponent is not in itself difficult to acquire, if the exponent encodes the intersection of a pragmatic dimension and a semantic dimension for the same argument.

Hypothesis 3: The antithesis of complementary exponents (Hypothesis 1) is a global case-marking system. Global case marking has been discussed at length by Silverstein (1976), and occurs when a single morpheme encodes semantic or pragmatic characteristics of both the actor and undergoer of a clause. Global case marking is difficult to acquire because it forces the child to search for the characteristics of both the actor and the undergoer that both jointly motivate a given structure.

Hypothesis 4a: All oppositions between exponents are neutralizable. Neutralization occurs when a semantic or pragmatic distinction is signaled by two exponents, A and B. In certain definable conditions, the distinction is no longer signaled, that is, the distinction is "neutralized," and the exponent A is always used in these specially definable circumstances. There is nothing inherently difficult in acquiring a pattern of neutralization, but children must learn the conditions under which neutralization occurs. Difficulty may arise because the conditions on the neutralization are not recognized. At present, the question of why some conditions are more easily recognized than others is unanswered. The following are two preliminary suggestions:

Hypothesis 4b: If the conditioning factor makes the opposition irrelevant, the neutralization will be easily acquired. The most profound example of this is the neutralization of the actor/undergoer distinction for intransitive verbs that occurs in many languages. Intransitive verbs take only one macrorole, and so the marking of the actor/undergoer distinction is irrelevant for intransitives.

Hypothesis 4c: If the conditioning factor is only indirectly related to the motivating distinction, then children are less likely to recognize the conditioning factor quickly.

Hypothesis 5: The same distinction may be encoded by multiple sets of exponents, and each set of exponents may have a different pattern of neutralization. If the sets of exponents encoding these two different neutralization patterns are structurally distinct (structural independence), then the acquisition of one pattern of neutralization will not affect the acquisition of the other pattern of neutralization.

Keeping these hypotheses in mind, let us move on to acquisition data from four languages: Kaluli, Hungarian, Italian, and Georgian. In each of the following sections, part of the system of GRs in that language is described. Attention is drawn to structural dependency: the presence of neutralization and globality. Structural independence, the presence of opposing case orientations comingling in the same grammar, is also examined.

4. CROSS-LINGUISTIC DATA

4.1. Kaluli

Kaluli has three structures encoding case and information structure distinctions: (a) verb agreement for person and number with nominative case, (b) specialized pronoun forms for first and second person, and (c) postpositions for lexical NPs (Schieffelin, 1981, 1985). In this section we consider the relationship between the acquisition of the case system and the acquisition of the agreement system. Sentence (23) has a transitive verb agreeing with a first-person actor, and (24) has an intransitive verb agreeing with the single macrorole of an intransitive verb. This is a pattern of agreement with nominative case.

(23) *ne adam-ɔ   sulɔl-o*
 I   guava-ABS pick:1:PRES-EMPH
 I'm picking guava. (Schieffelin, 1985, p. 549)

(24) *ne yɔl*
 I   come:1:PRES
 I am coming. (Schieffelin, 1985, p. 569)

Among the first- and second-person pronouns the basic distinction is between the ergative and absolutive case, but the actor in transitive sentences is further broken down into focal and nonfocal actor. Sentences (23) and (24) have the first-person nonfocal pronoun *ne*. This pronoun is used for the single macrorole of intransitive sentences and for the actor of transitive sentences when the actor is nonfocal and both the actor and undergoer are overt. The specialized first- and second-person pronouns interact with word order, which signals information structure distinctions, where the immediate preverbal position is focal (Schieffelin, 1985, pp. 543–546). In transitive sentences with both actor and undergoer overt, the specialized focal actor pronouns must be placed in the immediately preverbal position. The conversation in (25) gives examples of transitive sentences in which the actor is focal. In fact, in the reply (25b) the actor is not only focal, it is also contrastive.

(25) a. *yagan-ɔ   ni diɛnɔ*
     cucumber-ABS I take:1:FUT
     I will take the cucumber.

   b. *a! yagan-ɔ   nisa   diɔl.*
     No! cucumber-ABS I (not you) take:1:PRES
     No! I'M taking the cucumber. (Schieffelin, 1985, p. 544)

The postpositions have an ergative/absolutive orientation, but the actors of transitive sentences are further divided into focal and nonfocal. Once again, word order interacts with the encoding of the case distinction. In undergoer-actor-verb (UAV) sentences, that is, actor focal transitives, the actor is marked by the ergative case postposition. When the actor is not in focus, as in actor-undergoer-verb (AUV) sentences, the actor is marked by the absolutive postposition. In (26), the actor, *Abi* is the focal macrorole and receives the ergative case marking. In (27) the undergoer, an inanimate NP, *bɔn mogago* 'bad water' is in focal position, and as a result both macroroles receive the absolutive case marking.

(26) *sɔlu-wɔ Abi-yɛ   nɛlab.*
     salt-ABS Abi-ERG eat:3:PRES
     Abi keeps taking salt. (Schieffelin, 1981, p. 107)

(27) *Abi-yɔ   bɔn   mogago-wɔ nab.*
     Abi-ABS   water bad-ABS   drink:3:PRES
     Abi drinks bad water. (Schieffelin, 1981, p. 108)

Kaluli children acquire several aspects of the Kaluli system of GRs with apparent ease. A few of the nonoccurring or highly infrequent errors were the following: (a) Kaluli children do not mark the single macrorole argument of intransitive verbs with ergative case marking (Schieffelin, 1985, p. 559), or use the specialized actor focal pronoun forms of the first and second person with intransitive verbs (p. 554). This supports Hypothesis 4b because intransitivity, based on the logical structure of the predicate, makes the actor/undergoer distinction superfluous. (b) When first and second pronouns were used for actors in AUV transitive sentences by the children, only nonfocal pronouns were used (pp. 551, 554). This provides partial support for Hypothesis 2. Recall that Hypothesis 2 regards the multidimensional nature of exponents: The intersection of a semantic and pragmatic dimension does not in itself make acquisition of an exponent difficult. (c) When the children produced UAV sentences with third-person lexical NPs as actors, they almost never used the absolutive postposition. It is reported that there was only one such error out of 77 tokens (Schieffelin, 1985, p. 560). The absence of errors here suggests that the children were aware that the immediately preverbal position in UAV sentences was for focal actors, once again supporting Hypothesis 2. (d) The nominative verb agreement suffixes are acquired independently of the ergative–absolutive postposition system. Kaluli children did not confuse the orientation of NP postpositions with the orientation of verb agreement (Schieffelin, 1985, pp. 574–575). This supports Hypothesis 5, namely that the antagonistic orientations of case and agreement systems do not interfere with one another in acquisition, if these orientations apply to different structures. The relationship between the nominative-oriented agreement system and the absolutive-oriented case-marking system of Kaluli is an example of antagonistic case orientations that are segregated into distinct subsystems. They are displayed in Fig. 9.2. The possible lines of overgeneralization are suggested in Fig. 9.2 by the arrows. The lack of overgeneralization in acquisition is symbolized by the vertical double bar, separating the two arrows.

4.2. Georgian

Georgian has both verb agreement and case marking. There are two series of verb agreement affixes that can be used simultaneously with a single verb. The two sets are called the *v*- and *m*- sets after the prefixes used in each set to cross-reference first person (Tuite, 1987). Examples (28) and (29) are of a transitive verb *ch'am* 'eat' and the verb *nax* 'see'

(28) *v-ch'am-e*
1A-ate-AOR
I ate it.

(29) *m-nax-a*
1U-saw-3SG AOR
He/She/It saw me.
(examples taken from Aronson, 1982, p. 172)

In addition to these agreement inflections on the verb, third-person NPs are marked for case. For example, the noun stem *kal* 'woman' has the forms *kal-i* 'nominative', *kal-ma* 'ergative', and *kal-s* 'dative', and the noun stem *xe* 'tree' has the forms *xe* 'nominative', *xe-m* 'ergative', and *xe-s* 'dative'. Pronouns of first and second person do not have distinctive nominative, ergative, and dative forms.

The assignment of case to NPs is determined by their thematic roles,

Macrorole

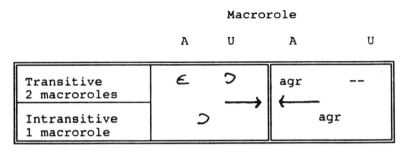

FIG. 9.2. Kaluli case postpositions & verb agreement. *Note*. agr = agreement, ɛ = ergative postposition, . = absolutive postposition. Horizontal double lines intervening between two arrows represents nonoccurring overgeneralization.

predicate class, and the "series" of the sentence. Georgian has three series: present-imperfective, aorist, and perfect-evidential (Holisky, 1981, p. 4). These series have semantically based differences and are morphologically distinguished by a combination of verb prefixes and suffixes that create verb stems (Holisky, 1981, pp. 3–13). The present series can be used to express nonpast tenses and imperfective aspect. The aorist series is used to express completive aspect. The perfect series is used to express a perfect aspect associated with a noneyewitness evidential stance. We are concerned with only the present-imperfective (henceforth present) and aorist series. The perfect series does not figure prominently in the early phase of acquisition to be reviewed here, which does not seem strange considering its function to signify noneyewitness evidential status. In this sense, the later acquisition of the perfect in Georgian resembles the relatively late emergence of the evidential function of the verb suffix *mIs* in Turkish (Aksu-Koç & Slobin, 1985). Sentences (30) and (31) serve to show a single verb root *ts'er* 'write' in both the present tense, which is part of the present series and the aorist aspect, which is part of the aorist series.

(30) *ts'er-s*
      write-3SG PRES
      He/she/it writes (it)

(31) *da-ts'er-a*
      preverb-write-3SG AOR
      He/she/it wrote (it)

There are four predicate classes in Georgian, referred to simply by number (Harris, 1981). In RRG these four predicate classes are identified with the four Aktionsarten. Class 1 are accomplishment predicates, Class 2 are achievement and state predicates, Class 3 are activity predicates, and Class 4 are state predicates (Van Valin, 1990).

Table 9.2 presents the system of case marking for NPs in the present and aorist series. The person agreement markers *v-* and *m-* are shown beneath the case used for NPs. These are the agreement affixes that cross-reference the NPs. Parentheses indicate that an argument of that case can appear with a predicate of a given class and series, but that not all such predicates take the parenthesized arguments.

Examples (32) and (33) are of verbs in both present and aorist series with the accompanying case switch. In (32a) and (32b), the verb *t'ok'* 'jerk' is shown, an intransitive verb of Class 3. In (34a) and (34b) the verb *achven* 'show' is used, a ditransitive Class 1 verb.

(32) a. *lek'v-i   t'ok'-av-s*
   puppy-NOM jerk-PRES-3SG
   (The) puppy jerks.

   b. *lek'v-ma   i-t'ok'-a*
   puppy-ERG preverb-jerk-3SG AOR
   (The) puppy jerked.
   (examples from Holisky, 1981)

(33) a. *nino achven-eb-s   surat-eb-s   gia-s*
   Nino show-PRES-3SG picture-P-DAT Gia-DAT
   Nino is showing pictures to Gia.

   b. *nino-m   achven-a   surat-eb-i   gia-s*
   Nino-ERG show-3A AOR picture-P-NOM Gia-DAT
   Nino showed the pictures to Gia.
   (examples from Van Valin, 1990)

Imedadze and Tuite (1992) note a sequence of phases in the acquisition of case assignment. At first, all NPs are produced in the unmarked form. Then dative case *-s* appears for recipients, which it consistently marks regardless of series in adult Georgian. Soon thereafter, dative case is produced for undergoers in the present series, whereas the nominative is being used for undergoers in the aorist series. Sentence (34) is an example given by Imedadze and Tuite (1992) of a child, age 2;6, producing the proper case switch within the same utterance.

(34) *mama, buti   mi-k'id-e!*
   father, ball-NOM 1RECP-buy-IMP

   me mi-k'id-ep   buti-s?
   I   1RECP-buy-FUT ball-DAT?
   Father, buy me a ball! Will you buy me a ball?

TABLE 9.2
Case Marking and Agreement Patterns in Georgian

Predicate Class	Series	
	Present	Aorist
1. Accomplishment	Nom—Dat	Erg—Nom
	V M	V M
2. Achievement, State	Nom—(Dat)	Nom—(Dat)
	V M	V M
3. Activity	Nom—(Dat)	Erg—(Nom)
	V M	V M
4. State	Dat—(Nom)	Dat—(Nom)
	M V	M V

Note: Nom = nominative case, Dat = dative case, Erg = ergative case, V = *v-* set of agreement inflections, M = *m-* set of agreement inflections. Adapted from "Semantic Parameters of Split Intransitivity" by R. Van Valin, 1990, *Language, 66*, p. 240. Copyright © 1990 by the Linguistic Society of America. Adapted by permission.

After the dative is used for undergoers in the present series, the ergative case is produced for actors in the aorist series only. Imedadze and Tuite (in press) offered (35) as an example of a child, age 2;10, producing the ergative case.

(35) *am   bavshv-am ga-lax-a   da,*
      this child-ERG   preverb-beat-3SG AOR and

      am-am   i-t'ir-a.
      this one-ERG   preverb-cry-3SG AOR
      This child beat (him) up and this one cried.

What is remarkable about this sequence of development is its conservatism. Georgian children never collapse the case-marking pattern of the present series and the aorist series. The children Imedadze and Tuite (in press) reported on did not use the dative *-s* for undergoers in the aorist series. This might be expected because they do use the dative for those same arguments in the present series. Once the children began to use the ergative *-m*, they used it only in the aorist series and did not overgeneralize it to the present series. The children closely observed the series restrictions on case marking, providing support for Hypothesis 5. Antagonistic case orientations do not interfere with one another in acquisition. As in Kaluli, we have reason to consider these orientations as applying to different structures. The relationship between the case systems is displayed in Fig. 9.3. Possible lines of overgeneralization are indicated by arrows. The lack of overgeneralization in acquisition is symbolized by the vertical double bar, separating the two arrows.

Predicate Class	Present		Aorist	
	Actor $\longrightarrow$	Undergoer	Actor $\longleftarrow$	Undergoer
1. Accomplishment	nom	dat	erg	nom
2. Activity	nom		erg	nom
3. Achievement, State	nom		nom	
4. State		dat		dat

FIG. 9.3. Acquisition of Georgian case marking. *Note.* nom = nominative case, dat = dative case, erg = ergative case. Horizontal double lines intervening between two arrows represents nonoccurring overgeneralization. Arrow crossing dotted line represents attested overgeneralization.

The acquisition of Georgian case assignment is not completely without error. Georgian children do overgeneralize the ergative case marker, but in a highly limited manner. After the first use of the ergative case, Georgian children occasionally mark actors of Class 2 verbs in the aorist series with the ergative case marker, rather than using the grammatical nominative case (see Fig. 9.3). Tuite (1986, p. 232) gave (36) as an example of a child age 2;9 using the ergative case with a Class 2 verb in the aorist.

(36) * . . . *k'at'a-m xe-ze   a-vid-a,   da . . .*
          cat-ERG   tree-LOC   preverb-go-3SG AOR, but
          . . . (the) cat climbed on the tree, but . . .

The overgeneralization is limited to the aorist series and never extends to the present series. The overgeneralization itself may be based on actorhood or Aktionsart; Imedadze and Tuite found evidence for both. In the former case such errors would be the result of basically the same mechanism for similar agency-based errors found by Mithun (1991) in the acquisition of Mohawk verb agreement. The important point is that even when children err, they respect the difference between the present and aorist series, supporting Hypothesis 5.

4.3. Italian

Italian is a nominative/accusative language in which the verb agrees with the nominative argument for person and number. We focus on the structures of the passato prossimo, a compound tense composed of an auxiliary, either *essere* 'to be' or *avere* 'to have', and a past participle. The auxiliary agrees with the nominative case argument. Activities take *avere* as their auxiliary. The past participle does not agree with any argument of the predicate, ending in a neutral, unchanging suffix -*o*. Sentences (37a) through (39a) serve as examples. The logical structures of the predicates in these sentences are set out in (37b) through (39b). Sentence 40 has a transitive verb *mangiato* 'eaten'. The nonactor argument of this predicate, *pizza*, is an indefinite mass noun, giving the sentence an activity Aktionsart (Dowty, 1979). In RRG this nonactor argument is considered a core argument of the predicate, but it is not an undergoer, because activities cannot have undergoers (Van Valin, 1990). This argument, *pizza*, in (40b) is still the lowest ranking core argument (LRCA).

(37) a. *Maria ha   corso   per un' ora.*
     Maria have:PRES:3SG run:PAST PRT for an hour.
     Maria ran for an hour.

   b. DO (Maria, [**run**' (Maria)])

(38) a. *Maria ha   dormito   molto ieri.*
     Maria have:PRES:3SG sleep:PAST PRT a lot yesterday.
     Maria slept a lot yesterday.

   b. DO (Maria, [**sleep**' (Maria)])

(39) a. *Anna ha   mangiato   pizza.*
     Anna have:PRES:3SG eat:PAST PRT pizza:FSG.
     Anna ate pizza.

   b. DO (Anna, [**eat**' (Anna, pizza)])

State, achievement, and motion accomplishment predicates take *essere*. Note that achievements and motion accomplishment predicates have state predicates embedded within their logical structures (see Table 9.1). The following examples are taken from Centineo (1986): (40a) is an achievement, (41a) an accomplishment, and (42a) a state predicate, as can be seen in the logical structures given in (40b), (41b), and (42b) respectively. Note that in all three examples the past participle agrees in number and gender with NPs that are arguments of state predicates at the level of their logical structures. If the state predicate takes two arguments as in (42a) and (42b), the past participle agrees with the LRCA (see Fig. 9.1).

(40) a. *La   lettera   è   arrivata*
     the:FSG letter:FSG be:PRES:3SG arrive:PAST PRT:FSG
     ieri.
     yesterday.
     The letter arrived yesterday.

b. BECOME **be here**' (lettera)

(41) a. *Il   cane è   corso   a casa.*
the:MSG dog be:PRES 3SG run:PAST PRT:MSG home.
The dog ran home.

b. [DO (cane, [**run**' (cane)])]
CAUSE [BECOME **be at**' (cane, casa)]

(42) a. *A Carlo è   piacuta   la*
to Carlo be:PRES:3SG like:PST PRT:FSG the:FSG

mostra.
exhibit-FSG.
Carlo liked the exhibit.

b. **like**' (Carlo, mostra).

Participial agreement is also mandatory in standard Italian when undergoer of a two macrorole accomplishment is realized as a clitic pronoun (Parisi, 1976, pp. 99–104). The clitic pronouns are anaphoric, as the English gloss of (43a) indicates. The reference of the clitic must be definite, established, or implicated in prior discourse, or readily accessible from the immediate nonlinguistic context. Example (43b) is the logical structure of (43a).

(43) a. *Manfredi l'   ha   letta*
Manfred it:FSG have:PRES:3SG read:PAST PRT:FSG.

[la   lettera].
[the:FSG letter:FSG]
Manfred read it [the letter].

b. [DO (Manfredi)] CAUSE [BECOME **read**' (lettera)]

In standard Italian the participle of the passato prossimo will agree only with the clitic pronoun: There is no agreement with the undergoer of a transitive (two macrorole) accomplishment when the argument is lexical (Centineo, 1986). An example of a standard Italian transitive predicate with a lexical NP is given in (44). Here we see that the distinction between two argument transitives and two argument activities is neutralized when the LRCA is lexical, as opposed to clitic. Compare (44) with (39a), which is repeated here as (45) for convenience. In (45), the activity, *pizza*, is an indefinite mass noun (not an undergoer but an LRCA), and in (44), an accomplishment, *la tazza*, is a definite singular count noun (both an undergoer and an LRCA). The lexical status of the LRCA is not diagnostic of the Aktionsart, because in both sentences the LRCA is a lexical NP. The relationship between lexicality and Aktionsart is only indirect.

(44) *Fabio ha   rotto   la   tazza.*
Fabio have:PRES:3SG break:PAST PRT the:FSG cup:FSG.
Fabio broke the cup.

(45) *Anna ha   mangiato   pizza.*
Anna have:PRES:3SG eat:PAST PRT pizza:FSG.
Anna ate pizza.

To summarize, past participles agree with the undergoer of state, achievement, and motion accomplishment predicates. Past participles also agree with the undergoer of two macrorole accomplishments when that argument is a clitic pronoun. In standard Italian, agreement is blocked when the undergoer is not represented as a clitic pronoun. In such cases the participles are marked with the neutral *-o* ending, and are formally identical to the past participles of activities. That is, the morphological distinction between activities and accomplishments is neutralized based on the lexicality of the LRCA.

The acquisition of this agreement pattern has been documented by Antinucci and Miller (1976) and Volterra (1976). When Italian children raised in families speaking standard Italian first acquire the passato prossimo, they begin to produce participial agreement for both achievement and accomplishment predicates. Sentences (46) and (47) are examples of a children's achievement predicates in this initial phase of acquisition.

(46) *Sono   caduti   per terra*
be:PRES:3P fall:PAST PRT:MP on the ground
i   braccialetti.
the:MP bracelet:MP.
The bracelets fell on the ground.
(Antinucci & Miller, 1976, p. 177; child age 2;0)

(47) *Si   e   rotta.*
REFLEXIVE be:PRES 3SG   broken:PAST PRT:FS
It's broken.
(Volterra, 1976, p. 152; child age 1;9)

During this period participial agreement of accomplishments is found in sentences without clitics. Examples (48a–b) are two examples of this phenomenon.

(48) a. *La   signora   ha   chiusa
       the:FSG woman:FSG have:PRES:3SG close: PAST PRT:FSG
       la   porta.
       the:FSG door:FSG.
       The woman closed the door.
       (Antinucci & Miller, 1976, p. 171; child age 1;10)

    b. *Dove   hai   messa   la   sedia?
       Where have:PRES:2SG put:PAST PRT:FS the:FS chair:FS.
       Where have you put the chair?
       (Volterra, 1976, p. 154; child age 1;6)

The sentences in (48) are starred because they are not, strictly speaking, grammatical. These sentences lack clitics. Were these adult sentences with clitics, the clitics would appear immediately before the auxiliaries *ha* 'has' and *hai* 'have'. The fact that in this early phase of acquiring the passato prossimo, Italian children produce agreement for both achievements (47) and accomplishments (48) is consistent with the RRG theory of the lexical semantic representation of predicates: Accomplishments may contain achievements in their logical structures (Table 9.1). This strongly suggests that there are lexical-semantic distinctions accessible to the child, other than transitivity. Volterra (1976) suggested that during this phase of acquisition the children treated the past participles "as if they were adjectives, that is simply as expressing a state in their argument" (p. 151). It is not clear on what basis this observation was made, but such a description is understandable, given that the logical structure of an accomplishment may contain not only an embedded achievement, but also a state embedded within that achievement (Table 9.1). All in all, the marking of states (embedded in) achievements and accomplishments by the same agreement pattern makes sense based on RRG's theory of logical structures.

Perhaps more interesting is the way Italian children handle the neutralization of the distinctions based on logical structure. Recall that a neutralization of the accomplishment/activity distinction occurs when the undergoer of the accomplishment is not a clitic (i.e., when it is lexical) (cf. 44 and 45). From the RRG perspective, this neutralizing condition is only indirectly related to the Aktionsart distinction otherwise encoded by participle agreement and we might well expect Italian children to have some difficulty in grasping these neutralizing conditions. Empirical support for this hypothesis comes from errors reported by Volterra (1976), one of which is repeated here as (49). In this child sentence we see the clitic realized immediately preceding the auxiliary, and the undergoer clearly of feminine gender. According to the grammar of standard Italian,

the participle should be feminine as well, but instead the child produced
the participle with the gender neutral -o suffix.

(49) *Mamma te   l'   ha   dato   la tua.*
     Mother   you it:FS have:3S give:PAST PRT the:FS yours:FS
     Mother gave you yours.
     (Volterra, 1976, p. 156; child age 2;0)

Further evidence that the neutralizing conditions are difficult for the child
to master come from the fact that this same child was observed, apparently in the same observational session, to produce participial agreement
in the correct conjunction with the clitic. Sentence (50) is an example.

(50) *Mamma te   l'   ha   data*
     Mother   you it:FS have:3S give:PAST PRT

     la tua   pistola.
     the:FS your:FS gun:FS
     Mother gave you your gun.
     (Volterra, 1976, p. 156; child age 2;0)

The research of Antinucci and Miller (1976) and Volterra (1976) suggested the following: The Italian children readily pick up on the semantic regularity of participle agreement, which from the RRG perspective
is based on the logical structures of the predicates. However, the Italian
children found opaque the conditions that blocked agreement in transitive (two macrorole) accomplishments, which is based on the lexical status of the undergoer. Figure 9.4 displays the distribution of participial
agreement across predicate types and levels of lexicality for the undergoer (clitic/lexical). The arrows indicate the Italian child's confusion concerning participial agreement dependent on the undergoer's level of
lexicality.

4.4. Hungarian

In Hungarian, verbs agree with the nominative argument in person and
number. Nominative NPs are unmarked and accusative NPs are marked
with the accusative case suffix. Hungarian has both definite and indefinite
articles that are placed at the beginning of an NP. When an accusative
argument is definite, a special set of agreement markers are suffixed to
the verb (Moravcsik, 1984). Examples (51) and (52) are representative conversations in Hungarian. In the conversation in (51) the verb *lát* 'see' is
used in the indefinite conjugation. In the conversation in (52) the same

Undergoer	Activity	Accomplishment	Achievement	State
Clitic	-o ↑	agr ↓	agr	agr
Lexical	↑ -o	↓	agr	agr

FIG. 9.4. Italian participle agreement in the passato prossimo. *Note.* Arrows crossing dotted lines represents attested overgeneralizations.

verb is used in the definite conjugation. The definite undergoer in (52a), *kép* 'picture', is marked as definite by the definite article *a*, therefore the conjugation of the verb is changed to definite. Note that in the reply, (52b), the definite undergoer is understood, an example of zero anaphora (examples taken from Bánhidi, Jókay, & Szabó, 1965).

(51) a. *jól   lát-sz?*
        well see-2SG:PRES:INDEF ?
        Can you see well?

     b. *jól   lát-ok.*
        well see-1SG:PRES:INDEF
        (yes) I can see well.

(52) a. *lát-od   a   kép-et?*
        see-2SG:PRES:DEF   the picture-ACC?
        Can you see the picture?

     b. *lát-om*
        see-1SG:PRES:DEF
        I see (it).

Hungarian conjugation is even a bit more complex. The accusative of personal pronouns in the first and second person take the indefinite conjugation, despite the fact that first and second referents always have the discourse–pragmatic status of definite. In addition, a special suffix is used on transitive verbs when the actor is first person and the undergoer is second person, as in (53).

(53) *Lát-lak.*
      see-1SG:PRES:2
      I see you.

The Hungarian conjugation of transitive verbs forms a global case-marking system (Silverstein, 1976), because these suffixes agree with the actor in number and person, with the third-person undergoer in definiteness, and additionally for the person of the undergoer, if the actor is first person.

Hungarian children have been observed to use the indefinite conjugation with transitive verbs in sentences that had definite accusative arguments, and to use the definite conjugation in sentences where the indefinite conjugation would be appropriate. Both of these errors occur with roughly the same frequency (MacWhinney, 1974, 1976). Sentences (54–56) are examples of errors made by children at approximately the second birthday. Sentence (54) is an example of the use of the indefinite conjugation in a sentence with a definite accusative argument, and (55) is an example of the use of the definite conjugation in a sentence with an indefinite accusative argument. Sentence (56) is an example of the use of the definite conjugation with a first-person undergoer pronoun.

(54) *megszur-t*   *a*   *fá-t.*
pierce-3SG:PAST:INDEF   the   tree-ACC
Pierced the tree. (MacWhinney, 1974, p. 531)

(55) *szed-tük*   *kavics-ot*
gather-1P:PAST:DEF gravel
We gathered gravel. (MacWhinney, 1974, p. 534)

(56) *keres-d*   *engemet.*
seek-2SG:IMP:INDEF   me
Seek me. (MacWhinney, 1974, p. 534)

The bidirectionality of these errors suggests that neither conjugation has any dominance and the alternation between conjugations is not well controlled in production. However, Hungarian children do seem sensitive to the fact that intransitive verbs should appear in the indefinite conjugation (logically because intransitives do not take accusative case, undergoer arguments). The erroneous use of the definite conjugation with intransitive verbs seems to be very rare (MacWhinney, 1974, pp. 529–535). This is consistent with the interpretation that a global case-marking system is at the heart of the Hungarian child's troubles, because global case marking is only a factor in transitive sentences. Therefore, in Hungarian we find support for Hypothesis 3. The global system is presented schematically in Fig. 9.5. The columns stand for the person of the actor macrorole. This is a simplification, because the Hungarian verb agrees with both the person and number of the actor. The rows stand for characteristics of the undergoer: definiteness (for NPs), and person (first and second person). The arrows represent the major lines of overextension for which we have evidence.

Undergoer	Actor		
	1st person	2nd person	3rd person
Definite	A	B	C
Indefinite	D	E	F
1st person	D	E	F
2nd person	G	E	F

FIG. 9.5.   Acquisition of Hungarian verb agreement. *Note.* Arrows crossing dotted lines represents attested overgeneralizations.

4.5. Kaluli Revisited

We noted in our first look at the acquisition of Kaluli that children acquiring Kaluli do a remarkable job of maintaining the ergative/absolutive case system and the nominative-based agreement system separate from each other (Schieffelin, 1985). However, this is not to say that acquisition is errorless. Kaluli children do have some trouble with the case system, but I argue that the difficulty is in no way due to the influence of the agreement system. Rather, the errors are due to the global nature of the case system.

Recall that the case postpositions, like the first- and second-person pronouns, have an ergative/absolutive orientation, but that word order interacts with case. In undergoer-actor-verb (UAV) sentences, that is in information structure terms, actor focal transitives, the actor is marked by the ergative case postposition. When the actor is not in focus, as in actor-undergoer-verb (AUV) sentences, the actor is marked by the absolutive postposition. There is one exception. The ergative case marker can be used with an actor that is not in narrow scope NP focus, but only if both the actor and undergoer NPs are either proper nouns or kinterms. In such AUV sentences the ergative marker will appear on the first NP if it is an actor, despite the fact that it is not in focus. Sentence (57) is an example. Here, the ergative casemarker is actually encoding aspects of the actor and undergoer globally: The actor is a proper noun or kinterm and the undergoer is also either a proper noun or kinterm (Silverstein, 1976).

(57) *Abi-yɛ   Suela-yɔ   sandab*
Abi-ERG Suela-ABS hit:3:PRES
Abi hits Suela. (Schieffelin, 1985, p. 557)

There is an additional restriction on the use of the ergative postposition. When a third-person actor appears as the only overt macrorole with a transitive verb, it must take the ergative postposition and should never appear with the absolutive postposition (p. 561). This is another example of global case marking. Here, the ergative case suffix is signaling the fact that the erstwhile undergoer has the lexical status of zero. This is what is called *surface intransitivity*, and it may arise when the undergoer is represented by zero anaphor or when the undergoer is nonspecific, as in (58) (cf. 51b and 52b).

(58) *do-wɛ*   *samɛib*
    my father-ERG   speak:3:FUT
    My father will speak / say (something).
    (Schieffelin, 1985, p. 562)

There were two major errors observed in Kaluli. The first major error was that the Kaluli 2-year-olds added the ergative postposition to sentence-initial actors in AUV sentences, even when the undergoer was neither a proper noun nor a kinterm (Schieffelin, 1985, p. 558). An example is found in (59).

(59) **do-wɛ*   *sɔlu diab.*
    my father-ERG   salt   take:3:PRES
    My father takes (the) salt. (Schieffelin, 1985, p. 558)

This is a clear example of global case marking (Silverstein, 1976), and according to Hypothesis 3 this pattern should be difficult for the child to acquire. When Kaluli children used the first- or second-person pronouns for actors in AUV sentences, they always used the nonfocal forms. The first- and second-person pronouns are not globally sensitive to the semantic characteristics of the undergoer. This suggests that the global case-marking system was the source of difficulty.

    The second major error was that the absolutive postposition was erroneously used with actors in actor-only transitive sentences, as in (60) (Schieffelin, 1985, pp. 561–563). This error was not categorical because the children mixed the absolutive and ergative case marking in this environment.

(60) **Abi-yɔ*   *dilɔb.*
    Abi-ABS   take:PAST:EVID
    Abi took. (Schieffelin, 1985, p. 561)

It would seem that Kaluli children overgeneralized the marking of actors with true intransitive verbs to cases of surface intransitivity. If such was the case, they overextended the absolute case marking on the basis of surface characteristics of the sentence only. Once again we can analyze this error as arising from the global case-marking system involved. In actor-only transitive sentences such as (58), the ergative postposition encodes actorhood, and also the fact that the undergoer is represented by zero, so that in actor-only sentences the same exponent, the case-marking postposition, simultaneously identifies the actor and encodes something about undergoer.

The case-marking system of Kaluli is responsive not only to macro-role choice, but also, as with the Hungarian agreement system, inter-relationships between the actor and undergoer of a given sentence. The global conditioning of the marking of actor is schematically displayed in Fig. 9.6. The horizontal axis represents the focal and nonfocal distinction possible for the actor. The vertical axis represents the transitive/ intransitive distinction, with the transitive sentence category being further subdivided by the semantic and structural status of the undergoer: whether the undergoer is a kin term or proper noun, a lexical NP, or represented by zero. The arrows in Fig. 9.6 show the lines of over-extension for case-marking postpositions exhibited by Kaluli children, according to Schieffelin's papers (1981, 1985). They are (a) the overex-tension of the ergative postposition to AUV transitive sentences in which the undergoer is neither a kin term nor a proper noun, and (b) the over-extension of the absolutive postposition to actor-only transitive sentences. The first overextension seems to have a semantic basis, whereas the second seems to have a surface structure basis. I maintain that both errors are due to the inherent difficulties of acquiring a global case-marking system.

		Actor	
Predicate Type	Undergoer	Focal	Non-focal
Transitive	Kin Term / Proper Noun	ε	ε
	Lexical NP	ε ⟶	ɔ
	Zero	ε ↑	ε
Intransitive		ɔ	ɔ

FIG. 9.6.   Kaluli case marking of the actor. *Note.* Arrows crossing dotted lines represents attested overgeneralizations.

4.6. Summary

We have considered developmental data from Kaluli, Hungarian, Italian, and Georgian. For each language we have asked the following two questions: (a) When do children find structures that encode GRs difficult to acquire, and conversely, (b) when do they find these structures easy to acquire? We have approached the question with a particular grammatical framework in mind, RRG, and with a set of hypotheses concerning the demands that structures, such as neutralization patterns and global case marking, put upon the learner. Let us review the evidence for these hypotheses.

Hypothesis 1: The encoding of a distinction is easiest to acquire when the exponents encoding the opposing values of the distinction are complementary structures. Support for Hypothesis 1 comes from Turkish, and has been discussed at length in Rispoli (1991). Therefore, Hypothesis 1 has been treated more as an assumption here.

Hypothesis 2: A multidimensional exponent is not in itself difficult to acquire, if the exponent encodes a pragmatic dimension and semantic dimension of the same argument. Support for Hypothesis 2 comes from Turkish (Rispoli, 1991) and Kaluli. In Turkish, specific + undergoer seems to be a readily acquirable combination of pragmatic and semantic features. In Kaluli, the combination of focal + actor (in transitive predicates) for first- and second-person pronouns seems to be readily understood.

Hypothesis 3: The antithesis of complementary exponents is a global case-marking system. Global case marking is difficult to acquire. Support for this hypothesis is found in Hungarian and Kaluli. Hypotheses 2 and 3 stand in direct contrast. The child has little problem with a multidimensional exponent encoding semantic and pragmatic information about the same argument, but the child has difficulty with a single exponent encoding features of two different macroroles, the actor and undergoer.

Hypothesis 4a: All oppositions between exponents are neutralizable. There is nothing inherently difficult in acquiring a pattern of neutralization, but children must learn the conditions under which neutralization occurs. Difficulty may arise because the conditions on the neutralization are not recognized.

Hypothesis 4b: If the conditioning factor makes the opposition irrelevant, the neutralization will be easily acquired. It has been argued throughout that the neutralization of the actor/undergoer distinction that occurs for intransitive predicates is extremely easy for children to acquire because of the fact that there is only a single core argument specified in LS, thus making the actor/undergoer distinction irrelevant.

Hypothesis 4c: If the conditioning factor is only indirectly related to the motivating distinction, then children are less likely to recognize the conditioning factor quickly. In Italian a distinction in Aktionsart is signaled by participle agreement and is neutralized by the difference between a full NP and an anaphoric pronoun, a dimension that is clearly independent of the Aktionsart distinction. In Kaluli, the focal/nonfocal distinction for actors is neutralized by surface intransitivity, a factor that is independent of the neutralized distinction.

Hypothesis 5: The same distinction may be encoded by multiple sets of exponents, and each set of exponents may have a different pattern of neutralization. If the sets of exponents encoding these two different neutralization patterns are structurally distinct, then the acquisition of one pattern of neutralization will not effect the acquisition of the other pattern of neutralization. Support for this hypothesis comes from the remarkably conservative behavior exhibited by children acquiring Kaluli and Georgian. In Kaluli, children are faced with an agreement system that is nominative/accusative in orientation, and a case-marking system that is ergative/absolutive. Kaluli children do not try to reorient the agreement pattern toward the case-marking pattern, or the case-marking pattern to the agreement pattern. In Georgian, the same case suffixes mark different roles across the present and aorist series. In the present series, nominative marks actor while the dative marks undergoer. In the aorist the ergative marks actor and the nominative marks undergoer. Georgian children do not overgeneralize the use of these cases across series boundaries. That is, despite the fact that Georgian case has a nominative/accusative orientation in the present series and an active/stative orientation in the aorist series, these orientations are not confused.

The picture that emerges is one in which the acquisition of GRs begins at a local level, where the child acquires morphemes or morphosyntactic patterns that act as exponents of semantic and pragmatic oppositions, such as the actor/undergoer distinction, predicate class distinctions, and sentence focus distinctions. These morphemes and morphosyntactic patterns are the basic building blocks of the system being constructed. The oppositions are most easily acquired when they are structurally independent (as in the Georgian case systems). The antithesis of structural independence is global case marking and agreement, as found in the Kaluli case system and the Hungarian system of conjugation. In order to acquire a language-specific set of GRs, patterns of neutralization must be acquired. The most common neutralization found is the neutralization of the actor/undergoer distinction for intransitive predicates resulting in either a nominative/accusative or ergative/absolutive case system. Children seem to acquire this sort of neutralization pattern quickly and easily. Each pattern of neutralization can be acquired independently of every other pattern of neutralization, just as long as the patterns of neutralization affect different case or agreement systems. That is, multiple neutralizations can be acquired easily if the neutralizations are structurally independent. The acquisition of Georgian and Kaluli, with their case-marking splits, provide evidence of this localized, structure-dependent, conservatism in acquisition. It is only when the conditions of neutralization are unrelated to the opposition that the child has a hard time acquiring the neutralization. An example of this comes from Italian, in which a basic, readily acquired opposition between states, achievements, and accomplishments on the one hand, and activities on the other, is masked when the undergoer of an accomplishment is lexical. This overall picture of the acquisition of grammatical relations, beginning with the local subsystems, proceeding by the addition and joining of further subsystems, the neutralization of basic oppositions and the ability to handle global case marking, has been termed elsewhere the "mosaic" acquisition of GRs (Rispoli, 1991).

5. DISCUSSION

The fact that Kaluli children and Georgian children do not confuse the mutually incompatible coexisting case and agreement systems in their languages is evidence against the notion of a pervasive, a priori rule network that should bias the child toward a prototypical GR (Pinker, 1987). Moreover, the fact that children are sensitive to structure, argues that something affects the child's acquisition of GRs beyond the statistical factors that figure so prominently in the competition model (Bates & MacWhinney, 1987, 1989).

If, as in Pinker's (1987) view, the variety of structures we have examined all refer through networks to discrete abstract symbols such as "subject" or "object," with certain universal biasings embedded a priori into the networks, then we would expect the grammatical relations in some languages to be more natural than in others. For example, consider the split case-marking system in Georgian, which follows a nominative/accusative orientation in the present series and an active/stative orientation in the aorist series. In Pinker's (1987) rule network referencing "subject" (p. 423), agents in transitive sentences are subjects. If rule networks were operative that defined natural GRs, then one might expect replacement of the nominative forms in the present series by the ergative case marking from the aorist series. In the acquisition of Kaluli, where the verb agrees with nominative case, but actors of transitive sentences are marked (often) by ergative case, we might expect children to attempt to bring these mismatched subsystems into a common alignment. None of this happens. Instead, what we see is remarkable conservatism.

Turning to the competition model, we should note that there are instances in which the mosaic model and the competition model will make similar predictions (Bates & MacWhinney, 1987, 1989). This should not be surprising, because the semantic and pragmatic distinctions that RRG uses to decompose GRs have been adopted by the competition model. For example, the competition model would probably account for the difficulty in the acquisition of the restrictions on the ergative postposition in Kaluli AUV sentences in the following way. The ergative postposition is a totally reliable cue to the actor of transitive sentences. As a result, 2-year-old Kaluli children overgeneralize it to AUV sentences. At this point, certain semantic features of the undergoer in AUV sentences still are not strong enough to inhibit the production of the ergative postposition. From the RRG perspective, Kaluli employs a global case-marking system. As a result, the child must learn that the ergative case postposition not only encodes actor, but also encodes something about the undergoer. This will cause difficulty because global case marking is the antithesis of what the child finds easiest to acquire: complementary exponents for actor and undergoer.

There are predictions that the competition model cannot make without first importing a functional theory of grammar, such as RRG, on which the mosaic model is based. Consider how the competition model might account for the acquisition of the agreement pattern in the passato prossimo of Italian. In general, the fact that neutralizations may cause difficulty is explained by the notions of cue availability and reliability (Bates & MacWhinney, 1989, p. 41). The unmarked exponent of the opposition, the *presence of gender–number agreement*, is a reliable cue for states, achievements, and accomplishments. If the participle agrees, the predicate belongs to one of these three classes. The marked exponent in the opposition, *the nonagreeing suffix -o* is a somewhat reliable cue to activities. How would the competition model account for the ease with which Italian children seem to acquire the basic opposition involving predicate types? It could be argued that it is relatively simple to import predicate classes and logical structures into the competition model. A complication in the course of acquisition arises because the nonagreeing suffix -o is also an unreliable cue to accomplishments: When the undergoer of an accomplishment is lexical, rather than a pronominal clitic, the nonagreeing suffix -o appears. This is a pattern of neutralization, which is unrelated to the predicate class distinction signaled by the opposition between gender–number agreement and the nonagreeing suffix -*o*. How would the competition model account for the confusion Italian children show in acquiring this pattern of neutralization? One could argue that it is relatively simple to set up the competition model such that the lexicality of the undergoer is only indirectly related to the predicate class distinction. In this way one could predict that Italian children would waffle in their use of agreement and the nonagreeing -*o* for accomplishment predicates. But plainly, in so doing, the explanatory power of the competition model would rest on a functionalist linguistic theory, such as RRG, not on the constructs of cue availability and reliability. The competition model must import a model of grammatical subsystems that dissociates lexicality from predicate type. Further, this dissociation must be a priori to the acquisition of the passato prossimo. In short, the competition model must import a priori grammatical structure. Whether the competition model will ever recognize its need for grammatical subsystems is not the main issue. The main point is this: A cursory look at the competition model shows that the content of most of the competition model's representational schemas, their "grammogens," include such terms as topic, agent, definiteness, transitive, and intransitive (Bates & MacWhinney, 1987, 1989). These terms are not defined by the competitional model. They are defined by functionalist linguistic theory.

After our examination of the acquisition of case marking and agreement phenomena in four languages, and our comparison of three approaches to the acquisition of GRs, one point should be exceedingly clear. The empirical evidence that will clarify this developmental psycholinguistic question will come from cross-linguistic comparison. Research in the competition model has conducted the most extensive set of cross-linguistic comparisons to date. However, this research has been aimed largely at the development of sentence processing; how children come to decide "who did what to whom" when they are parsing a sentence. This research asks how children decide which NP in a sentence is the actor and which is the undergoer. However, this is a very different question from the sort investigated here. The competition model assumes as given that case and agreement are cues in parsing. This chapter has focused its attention on a logically prior question: How does the child acquire case and agreement patterns in the first place? Pinker's (1987) model attempted to explain how the child can cut through individual language variations and arrived at a "best match" to universal prototypes for the subject and object. But this model failed to make concrete predictions about either the errors that children will make or the conservatism that children will exhibit in the process of acquiring two subsystems intimately related to the a priori GRs: case marking and agreement. Moreover, based on the evidence evaluated in this chapter, there is little evidence for such a priori prototypes. The mosaic model is an attempt to evaluate a wide range of data from a variety of languages. The framework on which the mosaic model is based, RRG, allows for language-specific variation, because it does not posit *subject* and *object* as elements of UG. Rather, it decomposes GRs into their more elemental parts, positing semantic and pragmatic distinctions as part of UG. The mosaic model holds that the difficulties children should experience are those that stem from structural dependencies that interfere with the smooth construction of language-specific GRs.

REFERENCES

Aksu-Koç, A., & Slobin, D. (1985). The acquisition of Turkish. In D. Slobin (Ed.), *The cross-linguistic study of language acquisition: Vol. 1. The data* (pp. 839–878). Hillsdale, NJ: Lawrence Erlbaum Associates.

Antinucci, F., & Miller, R. (1976). How children talk about what happened. *Journal of Child Language, 3*, 167–189.

Aronson, H. (1982). *Georgian: A reading grammar*. Columbus, OH: Slavica.

Bánhidi, Z., Jókay, Z., & Szabó, D. (1965). *Learn Hungarian*. Budapest: Tankonyvkiado.

Bates, E., & MacWhinney, B. (1987). Competition, variation, and language learning. In B. MacWhinney (Ed.), *Mechanisms of language acquisition* (pp. 157–193). Hillsdale, NJ: Lawrence Erlbaum Associates.

Bates, E., & MacWhinney, B. (1989). Functionalism and the competition model. In B. MacWhinney & E. Bates (Eds.), *The crosslinguistic study of sentence processing* (pp. 159–193). Cambridge: Cambridge University Press.

Centineo, G. (1986). A lexical theory of auxiliary selection in Italian. *Davis Working Papers in Linguistics, 1*, 1–35.

Chafe, W. (1976). Giveness, contrastiveness, definiteness, subjects, topics, and point of view. In C. Li (Ed.), *Subject and topic* (pp. 25–55). New York: Academic Press.

Demuth, K. (1989). Maturation and the acquisition of the Sesotho passive. *Language, 65*, 56–80.

Dixon, R. (1979). Ergativity. *Language, 55*, 59–138.

Dowty, D. (1979). *Word meaning and Montague grammar*. Dordrecht: Reidel.

Du Bois, J. (1987). The discourse basis of ergativity. *Language, 63*, 805–855.

Durie, M. (1988). The so-called passive of Acehnese. *Language, 64*, 104–113.

Foley, W., & Van Valin, R. (1977). On the viability of the notion of "subject" in universal grammar. *Berkeley Linguistics Society, 4*, 293–320.

Foley, W., & Van Valin, R. (1984). *Functional syntax and universal grammar*. Cambridge: Cambridge University Press.

Harris, A. (1981). *Georgian syntax*. New York: Cambridge University Press.

Holisky, D. (1981). *Aspect and Georgian medial verbs*. Delmar, NY: Caravan Press.

Holisky, D. (1987). The case of the intransitive subject in Tsova-Tush (Batsbi). *Lingua, 71*, 103–132.

Imedadze, N., & Tuite, K. (1992). The acquisition of Georgian. In D. Slobin (Ed.), *The cross-linguistic study of language acquisition* (Vol. 4). Hillsdale, NJ: Lawrence Erlbaum Associates.

Keenan, E. (1976). Towards a universal definition of "subject." In C. Li (Ed.), *Subject and topic* (pp. 303–334). New York: Academic Press.

Kuno, S. (1973). *The structure of the Japanese language.* Cambridge, MA: MIT Press.

Kuroda, S. (1979). *The 'w'hole of the doughnut: Chap. 1. The categorical and thetic judgement.* Ghent: E. Story-Scientia.

Lambrecht, K. (1987). Sentence focus, information structure, and the thetic-categorical distinction. *Berkeley Linguistics Society, 13,* 366–382.

MacWhinney, B. (1974). *How Hungarian children learn to speak.* Unpublished doctoral dissertation, University of California, Berkeley.

MacWhinney, B. (1976). Hungarian research on the acquisition of morphology and syntax. *Journal of Child Language, 3,* 397–410.

Maratsos, M. (1989). Innateness and plasticity in language acquisition. In M. Rice & R. Schiefelbusch (Eds.), *The teachability of language* (pp. 105–125). Baltimore: Brookes.

Mithun, M. (1991). Active/agentive case marking and its motivations. *Language, 67,* 510–546.

Parisi, D. (1976). The past participle. *Italian Linguistics, 1,* 78–106.

Pinker, S. (1984). *Language learnability and language development.* Cambridge, MA: Harvard University Press.

Pinker, S. (1987). The bootstrapping problem in language acquisition. In B. MacWhinney (Ed.), *Mechanisms of language acquisition* (pp. 399–441). Hillsdale, NJ: Lawrence Erlbaum Associates.

Pye, C. (1990). The acquisition of ergative languages. *Linguistics, 28,* 1291–1330.

Rispoli, M. (1991). The mosaic acquisition of grammatical relations. *Journal of Child Language, 18,* 517–551.

Schieffelin, B. (1981). A developmental study of pragmatic appropriateness of word order and case marking in Kaluli. In W. Deutsch (Ed.), *The child's construction of language* (pp. 105–120). New York: Academic Press.

Schieffelin, B. (1985). The acquisition of Kaluli. In D. Slobin (Ed.), *The crosslinguistic study of language acquisition: The data* (pp. 525–593). Hillsdale, NJ: Lawrence Erlbaum Associates.

Silverstein, M. (1976). Hierarchy of features and ergativity. In R. Dixon (Ed.), *Grammatical categories in Australian languages* (pp. 113–171). Canberra: Australian Institute of Aboriginal Studies.

Slobin, D. (1985). Why study acquisition crosslinguistically? In D. Slobin (Ed.), *The crosslinguistic study of language acquisition: The data* (pp. 3–24). Hillsdale, NJ: Lawrence Erlbaum Associates.

Tuite, K. (1986). Some remarks on the acquisition of split-ergative patterning. *University of Chicago Working Papers in Linguistics, 3,* 227–236.

Tuite, K. (1987). Indirect transitives in Georgian. *Berkeley Linguistics Society, 13,* 296–309.

Van Valin, R. (1990). Semantic parameters of split intransitivity. *Language, 66,* 221–260.

Van Valin, R. (1993). A synopsis of role and reference grammar. In R. Van Valin (Ed.), *Advances in role and reference grammar.* Amsterdam: Benjamins.

Vendler, Z. (1967). *Linguistics in philosophy.* Ithaca, NY: Cornell University Press.

Volterra, V. (1976). A few remarks on the use of the past participle in child language. In V. Lo Cascio (Ed.), *Italian linguistics: Vol. 2. On clitic pronominalization* (pp. 149–157). Lisse: Peter De Ridder.

PART THREE

PATHOLOGY

CHAPTER TEN

The Place of
Linguistic Theory in the
Theory of Language Acquisition
and Language Impairment

Thomas Roeper
Harry N. Seymour
University of Massachusetts

1. DESIDERATA

Our focus falls on the manner in which children learn the intricacies of formal grammar and its implications for communication disorders. We begin, however, with a statement of broad principles that both seeks to justify this approach and to address the sometimes hidden philosophical queries that lie within many of the debates about the value of highly formal theories in the applied domain. These questions come from both practitioners and theoreticians, but our effort is to articulate them, as far as possible, from an applied point of view.

In an easy programmatic way, many people seek to account for everything in general, but often very little in particular.[1] For instance, when children fail to comprehend complex sentences, the explanation is either a lack of knowledge about complex sentences or "performance factors" associated with lapses in attention and/or memory. Yet, neither memory nor attention tells us specifically why the same children are capable of understanding and even producing an endless series of "and's," and cannot understand a short sentence with a relative clause. How is one long sentence harder for memory than a shorter one? What exactly is the difference between a conjoined sentence and a relative clause such that one is more difficult than another?

---

[1]Portions of the opening section are drawn from a panel debate at the 20th anniversary of the Stanford Child Language Conference (1988).

There is a technical answer to this question (which we treat in greater depth later): The tree structures in the phrase-structure system involve different attachment sites for conjoined clauses and relative clauses. But why should one attachment site be harder to "remember" than another, or more difficult to acquire? An assertion that proclaims relative clauses to be more complex than conjunctions is an inadequate explanation as it stands. We must find statements in linguistic theory that translate naturally into a performance theory that, in turn, projects relative difficulty.

In general, broad cognitive explanations are neither true nor false; they are woefully imprecise and help neither the theoretician nor the applied professional. The concept of memory for language or attention for memory must be translated into precise linguistic terms if we are to know what they mean. In sum, if we have no deductive structure within linguistic theory but only programmatic nonlinguistic accounts, then little scientific progress will be possible and the rule nature of language impairment will remain a mystery.

The goal here is to present a set of theoretically derived theses on acquisition and language impairment so narrowly that it beomes absolutely clear that no approach, unlinked to linguistic theory, can possibly lead to an adequate account of the phenomena, that is, the details, variation, and nonvariation in child language.

(A) The concept of language changes as new data comes to light. Most core ideas in linguistics are formulated in terms of concepts discovered in the last decade.

Chomsky (1986) suggested that there may be no systematic definition or model of language at all, but only a systematic account of grammar. Numerous nongrammatical influences affect language—every aspect of cognition—while grammar remains a skeleton, hard and distinct, within a notion of language whose character is diverse and in some ways as squishy as flesh. If we can isolate grammatical factors, then nongrammatical factors should also become precise, just as the isolation of the notion of gravity allowed insight into the obscure domain of friction in physics. Every science that seeks to find fundamental explanatory theories tends to focus on unusual and rare facts as sources of unique insights. The common facts generally have too many potential explanations. We argue that remote or marginal facts discussed in linguistic theory may provide core insights into grammatical performance.

Consider now these two unusual facts about question formation:

(1) what did you file____without reading____

The first sentence depicts a "parastic gap" construction (1), where one *what* seems to come from two different positions in the deep structure of this sentence—that is, *You filed what without reading what*. So, one gap (what) is, metaphorically speaking, parasitic on the other. Parasitic gaps were unknown until Chomsky (1982) explored the phenomenon in depth. It has played a central role in the development of new theories.

Equally important (Huang, 1982) is the discovery of sentences that are ungrammatical (represented throughout this manuscript with *)—such as (2a), which contrasts with (2b).

(2) a. *who bought a house why
     b.   who bought what

Here there are two distinct forms of wh-words, an argument and an adjunct. An argument is an obligatory element in a sentence required for grammaticality. An example would be the object of the verb (bone) in *He took the bone yesterday*. Contrastingly, an adjunct is a nonobligatory element of the verb. In the previous example, *yesterday* would be an adjunct. In both (2a) and (2b) there is an argument wh-word, required by the verb, which can be left in its original position and appear with another wh-word. However an adjunct wh-word, like *why, when, how*, cannot be left in the verb phrase and must appear sentence-initially.[2] How does a child know that (2a) is impossible? We certainly cannot ask about its frequency of nonappearance. The frequency of appearance of the alternative, though, is very low. In the Adam corpus (CHILDES Corpus available through Carnegie Melon), for instance, there appear to be no instances of (2b) under 3½ years for the child or adult speaking to the child. Only experimentation can reveal if such structures are in a child's grammar.

The recent discovery of these sentences changed the boundaries of grammar and changed what a theory of grammar must explain. Suddenly the interaction of multiple wh-words produced patterns of grammaticality that before had not been realized. What principle excludes *why* at the end of a sentence but not *what*? Such questions have created the need to redefine the connection between syntax and semantics.

One important role of linguistic theory is to uncover new data like (2). The extent to which such data become observable depends on the power of theories. Indeed, linguistic theory is a complex data-generating device; the new data remain like rocks. They must be explained by any theory. However, one can ignore or dislike linguistic theory; it seems impossible to justifiably ignore the data that it brings into existence. If other

---

[2]In Asian languages there are important variations: A wh-word can be left in its original position, but similar restrictions apply.

nontheoretical approaches avoid these data, then we proceed from different assumptions about what language is. It follows that we do not agree on what has to be explained.

(B) One crucial question for acquisition is not how the child learns which sentences are syntactically grammatical, but which interpretations are excluded.

For instance, there is a difference between (3a) and (3b):

(3) a. whose shoes did he tie
    b. who tied his shoes

In (3b) we have a set of paired readings.[3] There are various ways to define bound variables in logic, whereas in syntax, the phenomenon of paired readings simply refers to the following interpretation. Possible answers to the question in (3b) include: *John tied John's shoes*, *Bill tied Bill's shoes*, and so on. The linguistic literature refers to this type of answer as a "paired reading" because individuals act on themselves. Although it is possible in (3a) for John to tie his own shoes, it is not possible for the answer to be a paired reading. This is both a very refined and a very clear distinction. How does a child know that the first sentence cannot refer to bound variables (paired readings)? In fact Roeper, Rooth, Akiyama, and Mallis (1985) showed that very young 3-year-olds do not give paired readings to (3a). At the same time their evidence showed that in long distance environments, a paired reading was available where it should not be, in (4b):

(4) a. who thinks he has a hat (paired reading)
    b. who does he think has a hat (no paired reading)

Roeper et al. (1985) found that children allowed a paired reading for both (4a,b) to the age of 7.[4] The question then arises: How do children eliminate one possible reading for (4b)? Note that the presence of nonpaired readings for (3a) and (4b), where someone ties another person's shoes (3a) and someone else has a hat (4b), says nothing about whether the paired reading is possible. How and when do children know this when

---

[3]There is debate in the literature over whether "paired" readings should be captured in the notation of bound variables. In the syntactic literature such relations are generally noted by co-indexation of subscripts. In semantic theories they are roughly represented as: For every X, X tied X's shoes.

[4]See J. de Villiers, Roeper, and Vainikka (1990) for further discussion of these issues; see also Thornton (1990).

they are never told that it is so. Hence, another fundamental claim of acquisition is involved:

(C) The child cannot receive significant negative evidence.

Negative evidence is any explicit or implicit correction of the grammaticality of a child's utterance. A most common example would take the form of overt correction. It is logically impossible for a child to receive negative evidence about an excluded optional reading. For example, if in the child's grammar there is the option to apply a paired reading to (4b), but there is never exposure to a correction of this option, how is knowledge acquired to exclude it? Moreover, a child's exposure to paired reading interpretations such as (4a), provide no evidence for excluding such readings for (4b). If a child were describing a paired situation and said "who does he want to put on his shoes" and the teacher said, "no you mean 'who wants to put on his shoes,' " the child would have no idea what exactly was being corrected. This issue has nothing to do with the explicitness of syntax. The existence of one possible reading does not eliminate another optional reading. The fact that *who likes his hat* can mean "his own hat" does not eliminate the possibility that it can mean "someone else's hat" as well. No frequency measure of possible readings is relevant to rare structures.

It is perhaps worthwhile to demonstrate the point that many grammatical structures are rare. In all of the Adam corpus we found only 16 examples of clear long distance movement like *What he went to play with*. There were only 11 instances of the expression *whose* from Adam over 3 years; there were 35 for his mother. Yet it is clear from context in the few instances where it is used, that the child and mother both understand the possessive *whose*.

Consider another example. It is implausible that frequency is relevant to permissible and impermissible interpretations of rare structures like those in: (1) what did you file *t* without reading *t*. These observations can be summarized in a question: How does a child acquire what we can call "invisible" information? This includes excluded interpretations and "traces" of transformational movement. In theory, traces are unpronounced elements of a sentence, such as noun phrases, reflected in a sentence's deep structure, as marked by *t* in (1). This is the heart of the acquisition problem. If we redefine the question in terms of observable phenomena, that is, spoken sentences, we are likely to overlook the question of how the child limits the interpretations of those sentences.

Consider the acquisition of the past-tense *-ed* form, which has been discussed by Rumelhart and McClelland (1987). Their observation of where and when it occurs in child and adult language is a simplified gloss on a complex aspect of syntax. First of all, the past tense is ambiguous with the participle *-ed* (as in 5b). How does the child know differences in meaning carried by each (illustrated later)?

It is not surprising that there is a relation in frequency of gross appearance of *-ed* among adults and use among children, as Rumelhart and McClelland pointed out. It may be frequency that, in a sense, brings a construction to the attention of a child. Frequency provides, however, no analysis. Much less does it explain the invisible features of meaning that the affix carries. Consider this example:

(5) a. the plant dropped
    b. the dropped plant[5]

Both instances of (5) could refer to a situation in which an agent is present. We might say something like "the plant dropped when he let go of it." However sentence (5a) does not refer to that agent; sentence (5b) contains an invisible reference to an agent, an implicit agent. Sentence (5b) can be seen as a passive derivative. Passives (unlike 5a) also have implicit agents:

(6) the plant was dropped.[6]

How does the child know, and when, that (5a) has no agent, whereas (5b) and (6) can have an implicit agent? It is the meaning differences of seemingly identical objects (*-ed* participles and *-ed* past tense) that provide the greatest challenge to an acquisition theory. Therefore the crucial question around the acquisition of the *-ed* suffix concerns the acquisition of these subtle features. We can get the most insight into the acquisition process by looking at the structures that seem as if they should be the most difficult to acquire, that is, those that are the most obscure to the adult speaker.

The problem is very real because in fact children do allow excluded interpretations and we do not know how they eliminate them. For instance, Roeper et al. (1981) assembled evidence that 3- to 4-year-old children allow the elephant to be an agent in (7) (the elephant pushes something):

(7) the elephant is pushable.

---

[5]The progressive patterns the same way as the participle: We find both *the leaves are dropping* and *the dropping leaves*.

[6]See Jaeggli (1986), Roeper (1987), and Baker, Johnson, and Roberts (1989) for theoretical discussion of the passive and implicit agents.

Children were shown two pictures: one where an elephant pushes something else and another where a man pushes an elephant. The children readily allow the elephant to be the pushed. It is something about the systematic nature of language that tells the child, at some later point, that the subject reading is excluded for (7). In other words, the elimination of an interpretation can be accomplished only by application of a principle, not exposure to data. Once again, we do not know how to state the principle perfectly in theoretical terms, the fact that -*able* must be passive, so *elephant* cannot be the subject. It is still clear that there is no simple pragmatic reason why there is a difference between *the elephant is able to push* and *the elephant is pushable*. So there must be a principled reason. No pragmatic situation can convey that principle, so therefore the child must have inner access to it. We now turn to a more extensive discussion of passive.

2. PASSIVE AND CROSS-MODULAR TRIGGERS

We outline a solution to the problem of how the passive form is acquired (see Berwick & Weinberg, 1986; Borer & Wexler, 1987) and then use our example as a model on which to evaluate a number of explicit and implicit proposals about constraints on an acquisition mechanism.

It is widely assumed that a "logical approach to language acquisition" must find triggering structures that are unambiguous as structures (see Lightfoot, 1987). However Chomsky explicitly argued that the acquisition process succeeds via "triggering experience." Now we can ask: What is the difference between triggering structures and triggering experience? The difference is precisely that we can make an assumption about a connection to experience, namely context,[7] which will guarantee a particular interpretation of an intrinsically ambiguous structure. We must first digress to introduce the passive and putative acquisition schemes before the relevance of the "triggering experience" concept becomes clear.

There is a well-known distinction between an adjectival passive and a verbal passive. The distinction can be captured in the following examples:

(8) John was shaven
(9) a. John was shaved
    b. John was being shaved

---

[7]See Roeper, Bing, Lapointe, and Tavakolian (1981) for discussion of these contextual assumptions. See also Wexler and Culicover (1980) for a similar assumption about deep structure.

In (8) the word *shaven* operates exactly as if it were an adjective like *big* and may be represented in a mental lexicon as an adjective as well. In (9a) *shaved* retains (or can retain) its verbal origins, one can even say (9b). In addition, (8) refers to a state, and (9) refers to an activity with a "disjoint agent" (someone else is shaving John—he is not shaving himself). What can the child use to trigger the difference? We consider a variety of possibilities.

   a. the phonetic difference between *-en* and *-ed* does not work as a diagnostic for the child because there are adjectival passives that have *-ed*, and verbal passives which have *-en* (*given*).

   b. It cannot be the implicit agent that triggers the notion of the passive because there are implicit agents that appear in prenominal position, a classic adjectival position:

   (10) the bounced ball = = a ball which was bounced by someone
        = / = a ball which bounced

   c. It is believed that adjectives are stative and passives are active. But the distinction is not always clear:

   (11) John was liked

No action occurs, but a passive is possible. And we find adjectives that designate a fixed (stative) property that are consistent with a scene of activity:

   (12) John was active

   d. It is sometimes assumed that a by-phrase (13) can trigger the passive, but this is not true. One finds forms of the following kind where it is clear that an adjective is involved, but a by-phrase is still possible:

   (13) learnable by machine, untouched by human hands, unseen by anyone, etc.

We know that *untouched* is an adjective because we cannot use a verbal version as in **John untouched Mary*.

   Not all potential evidence is ambiguous: It is clear in English that there must be a verbal passive if we look at very complex clauses. For instance, it is possible to passivize from the object of a complex cause. We can take the object of the infinitival verb *choose* and move it to being the subject of the passivized verb *believe*:

(14) was believed [t [to have been chosen *John* president]] =
      < = = = = =   < = = = = = = = = = =
    John was believed to have been chosen president.

This kind of long-distance passive relation does not occur with adjectives. In fact, we would have nonsense if we put real adjectives where the passive verbs are (*believed, chosen*):

(15) *was unhappy was sad [John president] = >
    *John was unhappy to be sad president

However, sentences of this kind (14) are fairly rare and, though not impossible, they seem unreliable as a trigger for the notion that a long-distance transformational operation must have occurred in passives.[8]

In Roeper et al. (1981) it is argued that the dative passive (as in 16b) was the one form that was clearly verbal and it was not acquired until children were 7 or 8 years old.

(16) a. the rat gave the dog a cat
     b. the dog was given a cat
     c. *the dog was generous the cat

It is impossible for an adjective to have an object (16c), and therefore (16b) must involve a verb that can take an object (*a cat*). In particular, in a variety of experiments on 60 children, it was found that children learned the relation between the double-object dative and the dative passive at the same moment.

Until 7 to 8 years, the children consistently interpreted these sentences as *the rat gave the dog to the cat* and *the dog was given to the cat*. It is conceivable that children would use the secure perception of a sentence like (16b), where they were in a context that they knew required the dog to be a recipient in order to generate a grammar in which the *dog* was linked to a trace in the verb phrase (VP) (a dog_i was given t_i a cat).

However, it seems very unlikely that no verbal passive is controlled until this late point, even if the rather unusual dative passive is only learned later. Deng (1991) argued for a different kind of trigger: an instrumental (the object used to perform an action). The trigger has a special feature: It requires an unambiguous context. She pointed out, first, that instrumentals only occur with transitive sentences, which in effect, means a sentence with a clear agent and object (17b) and not (17a):

---

[8]See van Riemsdyk and Williams (1986) for standard accounts of such grammatical phenomena.

(17) a. *the performance pleased the crowd with a somersault
     b. the performer pleased the crowd with a somersault

Therefore (17a) is unacceptable because an instrumental occurs without an agent: The sentence (17a) is an "experiencer" sentence (the perceiver of an event is *the crowd*) where the theme (*performance*) is in subject position. Now the instrumental prepositional phrase (PP) is not uniquely linked to a agentive verb phrase in all sentences. There are apparent instrumentlike PP's with experiencer verbs and also with adjectives. Consider the sentence:

(18) John is happy with two hands

It is an adjective with a PP that applies to the subject. The PP is the same as the instrumental-PP but no action is implied. Because this kind of subject-oriented PP is also possible with passives, we cannot consider the PP (with two hands) to be a diagnostic of a passive by itself. In (19) the PP naturally associates with the subject (*John has a hat*).

(19) a. John was seen with a hat
     b. John was seen with two hands
     c. John was seen with two eyes

In (19b) the sentence is technically ambiguous, either John or an implicit agent has two hands, but it is pragmatically impossible to see with your hands. In (19c) we have a truly ambiguous sentence: The two eyes could belong to either John or the implicit agent (an unmentioned seer). Therefore the presence of a PP- phrase of this kind is not a sure diagnostic that *seen* should be considered a verb rather than an adjective like *happy*. Suppose now a child heard the sentence:

(20) "John was pushed with two hands"

This sentence, under an adjectival analysis, could receive the interpretation that *pushed* is an adjective and the two hands belong to *John*. Therefore the structure that the child receives remains compatible with an adjectival reading. We are now stumped again: A further stipulation is needed in order to make a sentence like (20) an effective trigger for passive.
Suppose now that a child witnessed the following:

(21) (a one-handed person [John] being pushed by a two-handed person)
     John was pushed with two hands

The argument is yet more complex. It is possible for adjectives to entail agents, as in *the dropped ball*. And it is possible for nonverbal adjectives to have *with* phrases that are not instruments but might seem to be instruments: *John is active with his walking stick*. But it is not possible to get a connection between such an inferred instrumental use (*you use your walking stick to walk*) and an implicit agent. The inference is possible in the *performance pleased* sentence, but the sentence (17a) is still ungrammatical. It is only when the passive has applied that there is a trace and a syntactically live agent, that the instrument refers to the agent. In other words, the trigger must refer to all of these dimensions and therefore is complex. This example reveals that not only structural information but a contextually linked interpretation—that is, "triggering experience" in Chomsky's terms—is needed for acquisition. If we assume a set of connections, just the kind of connections assumed in parametric theory, the passive can be triggered:

(22) Assumption: contextual interpretation = syntax
                   = implicit agent has two hands

    a. instrumental implies a transitive sentence[9]

    b. a transitive sentence in passive syntax implies an object trace: $John_i$ was pushed t_i

    c. passive syntax allows an implicit agent on the participle: $pushed_{ag}$

    d. the implicit agent is syntactically active and therefore can be referred to by the instrumental:

    e. therefore, the implicit agent, not John, has the two hands[10]

Sentences of this kind, where there is an instrument that refers unmistakably to an implicit agent, are readily available (the room can be swept with a broom = / = the room with a broom should be swept). Therefore it is a plausible trigger. Note now that several linguistic components are involved:

(23) a. thematic roles
    b. traces of movement
    c. morphology (-ed)
    d. semantics of context

---

[9]Borer (personal communication, 1991) pointed out that it is an interesting fact that adjectives exclude instrumental PPs, except as we note, by inference (*he is especially powerful with a heavy bat/he is very threatening with a gun*). Presumably the theory of *event* structure explains these facts.

[10]Of course, John could also be the subject of the instrumental phrase, but we must account for the adult's intuition that the implicit agent can be the subject.

This example therefore is consistent with the view that it is "experience" and not simply "structures" that are crucial. The solution to this problem indeed involves a pragmatic assessment of the situation. This means that several distinct features of grammar, known as "modules" are involved in triggering: syntax of passive, thematic roles of verbs, and pragmatics. This argument shows that inherently diverse elements contribute to acquisition, but that insight comes when we can state precisely how they interact.

3. A DIRECT RELATION BETWEEN LINGUISTIC THEORY AND CHILD LANGUAGE

In the following discussion we proceed from a simple but very strong premise: All children's language, including that of impaired children, is directly relevant to linguistic theory. According to the strongest version of this premise: Acquisition data provides the most direct insight into core features of universal grammar, stronger than intuitional data. To sustain such a perspective, one must believe that so-called performance factors, and other mental capacities, do not distort the picture we have of children's grammar. For instance, although it is intuitively clear that a child, over 10 min, may lose attention, it is not clear that a child can lose attention in 500 ms during the length of a sentence. We are unaware of any research that shows such subtle attentional effects.

We follow the history of linguistics in our mode of argument. It has often been pointed out that, in principle, one needed a theory of what grammaticality judgments are before one can be sure that they pertain to linguistic theory. Early attacks on transformational grammar often had the form of attacking obscure features of intuition. For instance, it is not clear whether grammaticality judgments involve grammaticality, acceptability, stylistic effects, speech register effects, or misperception of degrees of grammaticality, or if there was always reliable uniformity across speakers. These arguments were never refuted. Instead, linguistic theory simply showed how much success could be achieved by assuming the direct relevance of grammaticality judgments. We argue, in the same vein, that one should assume the direct relevance of child language of every kind. We provide one pragmatic example and then discuss a syntactic case in depth.[11]

---

[11]Here is another example. The fact that *-ed* overgeneralizes in acquisition ("goed") but internal vowel modification rarely does ("think," "*thank") supports the distinction between marked and unmarked morphology in a way that is not so readily perceived in the adult language.

It is often suggested that a child may misinterpret a sentence on seemingly pragmatic grounds. Sinclair-de-Zwart (personal communication, 1972) reported that children will interpret the sentence *he hit her foot* to mean *he hit his foot*. This is not straightforwardly a grammatical phenomenon, and it seems to violate Universal Grammar (UG) because, although *he* can be taken as generic, it must agree with the possessive in Universal Grammar. One might say simply that the child pragmatically prefers self-reference and ignores grammar. Or one might claim that an auditory problem made the child fail to hear the difference between "her" and "his." Our view would force a different perspective: The child has the capacity to impose bound-variable readings on pronouns, and abstract away from their gender characteristics. This perspective reflects properties of UG, which allow bound-variable readings on a variety of pronouns. In other words, *he* is a combination of *he* and *she* and therefore can refer to either possessive.

To buttress this approach we have chosen an extreme example. We consider in this chapter a case study of a child that has been diagnosed as disordered. Our discussion is intended to suggest (a) that sophisticated aspects of linguistic theory may be crucial to the correct diagnosis of children with disorders; (b) that children with certain deficits provide unique or decisive insight into the formulation of what the acquisition problem in general is, as well as the particular problem of the language disordered child; and (c) that such deficits in turn reflect on the formulation of linguistic constraints themselves.

4. WH-MOVEMENT AS A DIAGNOSTIC INSTRUMENT

A major thrust of acquisition research over the past 5 years has centered on how children grasp wh-movement and its many special constraints (see, e.g., Maxfield & Plunkett, 1991). Some of us who have been involved in this research have extended it to include deaf speakers (J. de Villiers, P. de Villiers, & Hobin, in press) and those clinically defined as exhibiting language disorders (Seymour et al., 1992). How do they perform? First we need an introduction to wh-movement.

Chomsky's book *Barriers* (1986) provided a subtle redefinition of what is traditionally known as "island" phenomena: the fact that wh-question extraction cannot occur from certain domains. For instance, relative clauses cannot be extracted from:

(24) (John found a boy downtown. Bill saw him in the hospital.)
    a. where did Bill see the boy that John found
       = where-see, not where-John-found

The question can refer to where Bill saw the boy but not where John found him. If it is a complement clause, then both long and short extraction are fine:

> b. where did Bill say that John found the boy = >
>   where-found or where-say
>   long   short

Here we can refer to either where Bill said it or where John found him. Chomsky made this general observation far more subtle by observing that there is a contrast between optional elements (adjuncts) and obligatory ones (arguments). Arguments are those constituents that are lexically required, for instance, the direct object [make *a boat*]. Thus we find long distance (LD) extraction of arguments (*what*) works (25a) where adjuncts (*how*) do not move (25b) over wh-barriers:

> (25) a. How did you say what to make = > how-say, *how-make
>   b. What did you say how to make = > what-make

In intuitive terms, we know from the fact that the verb *make* is transitive in (b) that the wh-word must come from the object of the verb.

We represent long and short readings by a series of traces:

> c. How did you say to make it = > how-make
> d. How$_i$ did you say [t$_i$ to make it t$_i$]

The middle trace in (25d), in effect, is blocked by *what* if *what* is present as in (25a). This blocking effect is, in a sense, circumvented in transitive sentences where the verb requires an object. Verbs never require a manner phrase. That is, *what* is required by the final verb (as in make *what*), unlike *how* (make something [somehow]). Do children know this distinction between adjuncts and arguments (only recently articulated within linguistic theory)?

Our evidence, from several hundred children in six languages, indicates that the barrier effect is obviously comprehended. Children of 3½ years were exposed to sentences like those in (25), with stories, in minimal pairs, to determine if a question word in the middle would prevent an LD extraction from the subordinate clause. The contexts, in a pragmatic sense, in fact favored a subordinate-clause reading, because how one does something is almost always more salient than how one says something. Most researchers have implicitly or explicitly assumed that pragmatics would overpower grammar in these environments. That is, the child would associate the *how* with whatever verb interested them the most.

This never occurred. Here is one example from several hundred in which verbs, wh-words, stories, have all been systematically varied:

> This boy loved to climb trees in the forest.
> One day he slipped and fell down.
> He picked himself up and went home.
> That night, when he had a bath,
> he found a big bruise on his arm.
> He said to his Dad "I must have
> hurt myself when I fell this afternoon."

(26) a. When did he say he hurt himself = > afternoon, that night
     b. when did he say *how* he hurt himself = > that night

Either of these questions was asked in a counterbalanced framework. The results from normal children on this contrast were as follows (from J. de Villiers & Roeper, 1991): (Response percentage refers to subjects' responses to initial wh-word.)

(27) a. When did he say he hurt himself?
                    = Adjunct (when)—Blank (= nothing
                    in middle)
         When say   vs.   When hurt
          50%   44%
     b. When did he say how he hurt himself?
                    = Adjunct (when)—Adjunct (how)

         When say   vs.   *When hurt
          48%   6%

(28) a. How did the father say___ to cook the pie___
                    = Adjunct (how)—Blank
         how-say   how-cook
          23%   77%
     b. How did the girl decide___ what to wear___
                    = Adjunct (how)—Argument (what)
         how-decide   how-wear
          72%   5%
     c. When did the boy say___ how he fell down___ (= [27b])
                    = Adjunct (when)—Adjunct (how)
         when-say   when-fell
          48%   6%

    d. Who did the boy ask____ how to help____
                    = Argument (what)—Adjunct (how)
          who-ask   who-help
            63%   32%

Note the sharp contrast between (a) and (c), a shift from 77% long distance to 6%. The case (c) merits further discussion. Children answered the middle question rather than the initial question 40% of the time (*how he fell down*). That is, they virtually never answered how LD, but would answer the medial *what* that comes from the lower clause.

This result has led to a series of other experiments, reported in J. de Villiers, Roeper, and Vainikka (1990) and Maxfield and Plunkett (1991). In brief, it was shown that the medial response does not occur with a yes–no question (*Does he know what to wear*) where there is no *how* indicates the scope of the question. This type of response is identical to what one finds for German, where questions of the form *what did he say how to bake a cake* are answered as if *how* were the question ("with baking powder"). Therefore we argue that a special kind of question format exists for children at a certain age that happens to match adult German. These responses are also found in the data reported here but they are not the special focus of this discussion.

In a second series of experiments, the same approach was taken with a group of children diagnosed as disordered. In the domain of communication disorders a further pragmatic hypothesis exists: Children who lack syntactic skills will focus even more on pragmatics. This then becomes a further question in our work: Will children with diagnosed disorders be more likely to ignore a subtle syntactic cue in favor of a pragmatic one? The primary findings reveal that these children have the same profile with one notable exception: the treatment of relative clauses.[12] We present here a case study.

J.G. is a 4½-year-old boy who attends a school specializing in the treatment and education of children with moderate to severe language disorders. Crucial features of his diagnosis included these observations about production and comprehension: (a) does not use "why," "how," or consistently perform auxiliary inversion, and (b) does not respond to "what" questions with a verb answer, or to "if-what" questions ("if you fell down. what would you do"). A clinical profile with standardized test results is included in the appendix.

On the wh-tests we found a stark contrast. In Table 10.1 the full range of responses are noted. The profile is much like the normal children, except for a somewhat high number of unclear cases: Of the 24 responses

---

[12]See Seymour et al. (1992).

TABLE 10.1

Summary of J.G.'s Responses to Wh-Tasks Involving Adjunct-Adjunct Copy (Adj-Adj Cop), Adjunct-Adjunct Different (Adj-Adj Dif), Adjunct-Argument (Adj-Arg), Adjunct-O j (Adj-O), Adjunct-Relative Clause (Adj-Rel Cl), Argument-Adjunct (Arg-Adj), Argument-Argument (Arg-Arg), and Argument-O (Arg-O).

Category		Stimuli	Response	*Resp. Type	*Constituent
1. Adj-Adj Cop	1.	How did the brother say how to clean up?	fast (pointed to dog)	Med Dn	ADV
	2.	Where did the mother say where she dressed the boy?	on the porch	Med Dn	PP
	3.	How did the little girl say how to save the cat?	on the ladder	Med Dn	PP
2. Adj-Adj Dif	1.	How did the girl ask where to ride?	please	Unclear	V
	2.	When did the man say how he hurt his foot?	by his shoe fall off	Med Dn	ADVP
	3.	When did the boy say how he hurt himself?	on the tree	Med Dn	PP
3. Adj-Arg	1.	How did Rover learn what to catch?	the ball	Med Dn	Det + N
	2.	How did the mommy learn what to bake?	on TV	Sht Dist	PP
	3.	How did Big Bird ask who to give the medicine?	called him	Sht Dist	VP
4. Adj-O	1.	How did the dad say to cook the pie?	with fire	Lng Dist	PP
	2.	How did the fireman decide to get the cat down?	poured the milk to get him down	Lng Dist	VP
	3.	How did Kermit tell big Bird to draw Cookie Monster?	with blue	Lng Dist	PP
5. Adj-Rel Cl	1.	How did the dog climb up who barked?	climbed with kitten, pointed to	Sht Dist	VP
	2.	How did the woman swim who knitted?	pointed	Unclear	VP
	3.	How did the man talk who changed the baby?	I don't know	Unclear	PP
6. Arg-Adj	1.	Who did the little girl ask how to see?	brother	Lng Dist	VP
	2.	Who did Big Bird ask how to help?	Bert	Lng Dist	N
	3.	Who did Big Bird ask how to dress?	I don't know	Unclear	No Resp
7. Arg-Arg	1.	Who did the girl ask what to throw?	her dad	Sht Dist	Det + N
	2.	Who did the boy ask what to bring?	bologna	Med Dn	N
	3.	Who did the girl ask what to make?		Unclear	No Resp
8. Arg-O	1.	Who did the policeman help call?	the guy	Sht Dist	Det + N
	2.	Who did the girl ask to help?	her (pointing to mother)	Lng Dist	N
	3.	Who did the boy ask to call?	grandmother	Lng Dist	N

*Response type: Sht = short; Lng = long; Med Dn = medial down; Dist = distance. Constituent: ADV = adverb; ADVP = adverbial phrase; PP = prepositional phrase; NP = noun phrase; N = noun; VP = verb phrase; V = verb; and Det + N = determiner + noun.

by J.G., 7 were long distance, 5 were short distance, 7 were medial answers, and 5 were unclear. More important is the fact that none of the "long distance" answers occurred in the set of 15 (1, 2, 3, 5) where there was a barrier to long interpretation of an adjunct. Seven of nine responses were long distance in sentences (4, 6, 8), showing that he knew that where two clauses are involved, the wh-word is moved through a middle position. If that middle position is filled, then only a short distance upper clause response is possible.

Here are the central contrasts:

(29) a. how_1 . . . . . . what . . . . . $*t_1$
     b. how_1 . . . . . . $_{t_1}$ what

The *what* blocks the connection between *how* and the trace in (29a), forcing a short distance reading in (29b). We return to a discussion of the remedial implications of these results, after we provide a more detailed discussion of special features.

J.G.'s responses to our experiments are not identical to the normal children, although the crucial abstract barrier features for complex sentences are in place. Here is a typical story:

A man went to stay with a Daddy who had a very little baby.
In the middle of the night the baby cried and needed changing.
The man said "I can change him" and he put on some big rubber gloves.
The Daddy called out "How are you doing?" and the man said
"Not very well" with his hand over his nose!

(30) How did the man talk who changed the baby?

We find an unusual difficulty with relative clauses. J.G., like a number of others in a larger study, tends to simply omit a relative clause.[13] For instance, in the following story, the restrictive character of the content of the relative clause is completely ignored by many children in answering the question. That is, they replied about how either man spoke and not just the one "who changed the baby." J.G. just said "I don't know." We find, in fact, a very large number of "I don't know" or unclear responses just to relative clauses among disordered children in forthcoming work.

What does this mean? Why is one kind of complex sentence properly understood, whereas another causes problems? Such surprising observa-

---

[13]Omission of relatives was also reported among normal children in Solan and Roeper (1978).

tions make it necessary to built a theory to explain. We expect it to be the result of highly complex activities, following simple principles that are not open to view. In principle, our task is like lifting a car hood with the notion of "combustion" as a general hypothesis and trying to find a carburetor within a large array of other devices. We have the principle of cyclic movement that must be located in a complex linguistic domain which is further complicated by cognitive and neurological factors. According to our hypothesis, we have located the carburetor and we can now ignore the rest of the motor, not to mention the wheels and the road (which is like purpose and pragmatics).

We might add at this point that normal children use certain kinds of relative clauses before they use sentences with two question words. In general they begin with object relatives (*here is the boy I like*), then *that* relatives, and finally *who or which* relatives.[14] We can begin to ask, however, what feature of wh-relatives might be involved that causes difficulty.

In virtually all complex sentences, the subordinate clause is projected by features of the matrix clause, either through direct obligatory semantics, as in a sentence like *I know that* . . . or by virtue of a manner adverbial adjunct. Thus we have:

(31) a.   John got better by drinking a glass of water
     b.   *John is better by drinking a glass of water

We find that *is* does not take a manner adverbial. Relative clauses are unusual in that they are adjoined without any projection from a noun phrase. If we say *John decided*, then we can infer that he decided something in some way. If we say *the rat chased the cat* there is no grammatical necessity, or implication, that a relative clause is necessary. Although they are very productive, and semantically restrict nouns, relative clauses are not syntactically required. This is still an undeveloped idea, but we think it points in the right direction.

In a general way, then, relative clauses are like conjunctions that involve very little syntactic connection between the parts:

(32) John went outside and the king declared war

In fact there is evidence and arguments to the effect that they are literally treated as if they were conjunctions (Tavakolian, 1978). A special problem may exist in taking an independent clause and attaching it at a low point in a sentence, below an NP. This is reflected in the behavior

---

[14]See Ingram (1989) or Goodluck (1991) for overview on relatives.

of normal children who delete the relative clause in certain contexts.

(33) The cat put the rat that hit the dog in the barn

They forget about the phrase "that hit the dog." Thus normal children and J.G. exhibit the same general sort of behavior: They delete relative clauses in comprehension tasks. J.G. does this for any relative clause as far as we can tell. The normal children do it when the verb is complex (*put* + locative).

New work on second language acquisition also points to the idea that relative clauses are analyzed in a significantly different way from other complements. Li (1992) showed that in learning English, Chinese speakers clearly prefer extractions from noun complements (34b) over extractions from relative clauses (34a), although both are traditionally regarded as ungrammatical in adult English:

(34) a.   **What did that man buy a hat that matches____ in our store.

    b.   *What does John believe the story that Mary saw____ last night

She found that 155 of 180 (86.1%) Chinese speakers consider (34a) ungrammatical, whereas only 104 of 180 (57.8%) consider (34b) ungrammatical. This is a very subtle context and the fact that there is a significant difference among L2 learners indicates that this form of experimentation is able to tap a significant level of linguistic variation—a level of subtlety not widely recognized in intuitional work.

How is this difference to be accounted for? Because linguistic theory is rich with technical devices, it is not difficult to develop one that will produce a difference. The deeper challenge is to find the notation that correctly captures an idea of the difference. Intuitively, the idea is that in a sequence like *the story that Mary saw (something) last night* the complement clause is equivalent to—the same thing as—the story. On the other hand, the sequence *the hat that matches (something)* involves a clause that modifies the *hat* but is not equivalent to it. If we translate the relation into a copula, the difference is clear. *The story is that Mary saw something*, but the hat is not "that matches something."

We can translate this relation into the difference between a sisterhood structure and a nonsisterhood structure, following Li (who follows Radford, 1988). There are a variety of technical means to state this relation. The intuitive idea is that equivalence (of story and its content) involves a parallel structure in structure (i.e., both *story* and *that Mary saw something* are at the same level). Relative clauses are attached lower, but higher than the noun they modify, as in (b):

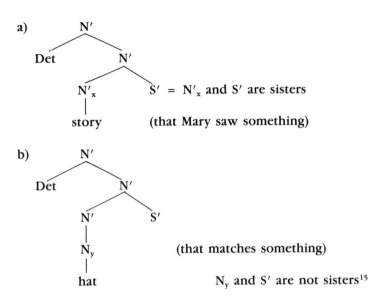

a)
N'_x = story
S' = N'_x and S' are sisters
(that Mary saw something)

b)
N_y = hat
(that matches something)
N_y and S' are not sisters[15]

This is a technical mode of execution. The core notion is the idea of relatedness discussed earlier.[16]

Lebeaux (1988), Chomsky (1992), and Speas (1990) sought to execute the same intuition in a different way. They suggested a constructivist approach to the creation of sentences, which means that two parts may be generated in tandem and connected afterward. This is the core notion behind the concept of "generalized transformations" and it is intuitively captured by thinking of conjoined clauses that could, in a sense, be independently created and then linked by an "and." The problem comes in (35) when one whole new sentence (who John likes) has to be added in before another is finished (. . . was pushed by him). That is the special feature of relative clauses:

(35) the boy [who John likes t] was pushed by him

The relative clause is added on before the higher sentence is finished. Even if it occurs at the end of the sentence, the two clauses bear only a minimal connection. This is intuitively why relative clauses are more difficult. It is acquisition data from both L1 and L2 that points most distinctly to the importance of this contrast.

---

[15]If the two nodes are sisters, then there is a possible relation of lexical government between N_{9x} and S_9, which makes the higher N_9 a non = barrier under Chomsky's definition of *Barrier* (1986).

[16]See Boyd (1992) for relevant discussion of extraction from relative clauses and conditions under which it can occur.

J.G.'s behavior on these questions does not show that the test is completely unrevealing. Such children are referred to clinics because some real problem exists and that real problem is reflected in various symptoms in the diagnostic process. But what is the real problem? We are not in a position to answer that question in general. Our results, however, begin to point at specific issues rather than a global characterization. Moreover, without the wh-test it would not have been evident at all that certain features of the relative clauses posed a particular problem.

In sum, our detailed analysis of one language-impaired child converges with abstract theory at an important point. Long distance question formation and relative-clause formation are quite different in the child's grammar. This distinction correlates with sophisticated facts from intuitional studies discussed by Lebeaux (1988) and Chomsky (class lectures),[17] but it is arguably clearest in data of this kind. It is not clear exactly what the remedy for such a deficiency is, but it is clear that linguistic theory has begun to fulfill its promise: to provide an analysis of language that captures the true representations that we use.

Finally, we have argued that (a) language-impaired children may have much more sophisticated knowledge of complex syntax than many diagnostic procedures reveal, (b) that, in particular, knowledge of universals that apply to complex syntax are evident, and (c) that for structures involving subtle variations, such as relative clauses and verb complements, these procedures may reveal some distinctions between normal and impaired language. Much, of course, remains to be explored in seeing the implications of normal acquisition for impaired populations and, equally important, vice versa.

5. IMPLICATIONS
FOR COMMUNICATION DISORDERS

Linguistic theory has illuminated much, but most of its claims are not fully articulated. Nonetheless, it is extremely important in evaluating children that we see their difficulties as accurately as possible and we use the insights we have available. Any vagueness in our characterization will overstate a child's problems, perhaps endanger their dignity, and work as a detriment to them and their treatment. For instance, a statement that a child lacks complex sentences is halfway to a statement that a child cannot think complex thoughts. But a statement that a child does not control tense agreement in complex clauses is more like saying that someone needs a splint for a fractured elbow rather than saying that the child no longer understands what arms are because he cannot move a broken one.

---

[17]The discussion turns on what are known as "reconstruction facts." We do not discuss them here.

We must also add a caveat about misleading implications of a detailed description of linguistic inability. Possibly, the remedy should be as detailed as the description. This does not necessarily follow. If a child exhibits an inability to process relative clauses, then drills on the relative clause may not be appropriate. It may be, as whole language theorists advocate, that promoting self-expression in general is the remedy.

Once again we believe[18] that it is very important not to overstate the problem, because an overstatement of the problem diminishes the children and may give anyone who works with them an unfairly negative view.

ACKNOWLEDGMENTS

Thanks to Jill de Villiers, Clifton Pye, and Yonata Levy for their editorial comments.

APPENDIX

CASE DATA

J.G. is a 4½-year-old, language-impaired, male child who attends a school specializing in the treatment and education of children with moderate to severe language disorders. The school provides diagnosis in areas of speech and language, cognition and psychology, occupational, and academic skills. The following description summarizes J.G.'s formal evaluation in each of these areas of assessment.

Speech and Language

J.G. was considered to have a receptive communication age of 3 years, 0 months. The following represent the kinds of tasks he had difficulty performing on norm-referenced standardized tests:

- following commands involving two or more objects;
- following commands involving two actions and two objects;
- identifying coins; and
- responding to "number" requests to give three, four, and six items.

J.G.'s expressive skills ranged from 2 years, 8 months to 3 years, 3 months on formal test measures. Test results indicated that he:

---

[18]Based on the second author's 20 years of clinical experience with disordered populations.

- does not use question transformations consistently;
- could not repeat three digits or unrelated words, or sentences of over four words;
- does not use "why" questions;
- did not use prepositions "on," "under," or "beside";
- did not respond to "if-what" questions as in "If you fell down, what would you do";
- did not respond to "what" questions requiring a verb answer; and
- does not use "how" questions.

A spontaneous language sample indicated a mean length of utterance (MLU) of 3.57, which compares J.G. with norms of children about 3 years, 3 months of age. J.G. used mostly sentence fragments and no complex sentences. His phonology was characterized by numerous misarticulations as measured by a formal articulation test, and was even more severe in connected speech.

Academic-Educational

Reading readiness was assessed in three areas: alphabet knowledge, comprehension, and conventions of reading. Results indicated an age equivalence of 2 years, 4 months. This equivalency measure placed J.G. in the third percentile for his age.

Psychological

Based on formal cognitive testing J.G. scored in the low average range of intelligence.

Occupational

J.G. showed no gross motor difficulties. However, in fine motor area, he performed at about a 36-month level, as indicated by inconsistency in crossing his midline during table-top activities. He demonstrated an immature prehension when using a crayon and a pencil. He was unable to use scissors correctly, in that he held them with both hands and was not able to use them for cutting. J.G. performed at an age equivalence of 3 years, 11 months in visual motor skills.

REFERENCES

Baker, M., Johnson, K., & Roberts, I. (1989). Passive revisited. *Linguistic Inquiry*.

Berwick, R., & Weinberg, A. (1986). *The grammatical basis of linguistic performance*. Cambridge, MA: MIT Press.

Borer, H., & Wexler, K. (1987). The maturation of syntax. In T. Roeper & E. Williams (Eds.), *Parameter setting* (pp. 123–172). Dordrecht: Reidel.

Boyd, J. (1992). *Extraction and referentiality*. Unpublished doctoral dissertation, University of Massachusetts.

Chomsky, N. (1982). Some concepts and consequences of the theory of government and binding. *Linguistic Inquiry Monograph, 6*. Cambridge, MA: MIT Press.

Chomsky, N. (1986). *Barriers*. Cambridge, MA: MIT Press.

Chomsky, N. (1992). A minimalist program for linguistic theory. *MIT Occasional Papers in Linguistics, 1*.

Deng, Xiaoping (1991). The acquisition of passive with instrumental prepositional phrases in English. In B. Plunkett (Ed.), *University of Massachusetts occasional papers, 15* (UMOP). Amherst, MA: Graduate Linguistic Students' Association, University of Massachusetts.

de Villiers, J., de Villiers, P., & Hoban, E. (in press). The central problem of functional categories in the English system of oral deaf children. In H. Tager-Flusberg (Ed.), *Theoretical approaches to atypical language*. Hillsdale, NJ: Lawrence Erlbaum Associates.

de Villiers, J., & Roeper, T. (1991). Introduction. In T. Maxfield & B. Plunkett (Eds.), *University of Massachusetts occasional papers in linguistics: Special Issue on the Acquisition of Wh-* (pp. 1–18). Amherst, MA: Graduate Linguistic Students' Association, University of Massachusetts.

de Villiers, J., Roeper, T., & Vainikka, A. (1990). The acquisition of long distance rules. In L. Frazier & J. de Villiers (Eds.), *Language acquisition and language processing* (pp. 257–297). Dordrecht: Kluwer.

Engdahl, E. (1983). Parasitic gaps. *Linguistics and Philosophy, 6*, 5–34.

Goodluck, H. (1991). *Language acquisition*. Cambridge, England: Cambridge University Press.

Huang, J. (1982). *Logical relations in Chinese and the theory of grammar*. Unpublished doctoral dissertation, MIT.

Ingram, D. (1989). *First language acquisition*. Cambridge, England: Cambridge University Press.

Jaeggli, O. (1986). Passive. *Linguistic Inquiry, 17*, 587–622.

Lebeaux, D. (1988). *Language acquisition and the form of the grammar*. Unpublished doctoral dissertation, University of Massachusetts.

Li, X. (1992). *Constraints on wh-long distance movement in adult Chinese for L2 acquisition and the implication for L2 teaching*. Unpublished doctoral dissertation, University of Massachusetts, School of Education.

Lightfoot, D. (1987). The child's trigger experience: Degree-O learnability. *Behavioral and Brain Sciences, 12*, 2.

Maxfield, T., & Plunkett, B. (1991). *Acquisition of wh-movement*. Special issue of University of Massachusetts occasional papers. Amherst, MA: Graduate Linguistic Students' Association, University of Massachusetts.

Radford, A. (1988). *Transformational syntax*. Cambridge: Cambridge University Press.

Riemsdyk, H., & Williams, E. (1986). *Introduction to the theory of grammar*. Cambridge, MA: MIT Press.

Roeper, T. (1987). Acquisition of implicit arguments. In B. MacWhinney (Ed.), *Mechanisms of language acquisition* (pp. 267–310). Hillsdale, NJ: Lawrence Erlbaum Associates.

Roeper, T., Bing, J., Lapointe, S., & Tavakolian, S. (1981). A lexical approach to learning passive. In *Language acquisition and linguistic theory*. Cambridge, MA: MIT Press.

Roeper, T., Rooth, M., Akiyama, S., & Mallis, L. (1985). *The problem of empty categories in language acquisition*. Unpublished manuscript, University of Massachusetts.

Rummelhart, D., & McClelland, J. (1987). Learning the past tense of English verbs: Implicit rules or parallel processing. In B. MacWhinney (Ed.), *Mechanisms of language acquisition*. Hillsdale, NJ: Lawrence Erlbaum Associates.

Seymour, H., Bland, I., Roeper, T., de Villiers, J., & Champion, T. (1992, November). *Long distance wh-movement in children of divergent language backgrounds*. Paper presented at American Speech-Language-Hearing Association (ASHA) convention, San Antonio, TX.

Solan, L., & Roeper, T. (1978). Children's use of syntactic structure in interpreting relative clauses. In H. Goodluck & L. Solan (Eds.), *Papers in the structure and development of child language* (pp. 105–127). University of Massachusetts occasional papers. Amherst, MA: Graduate Linguistic Students' Association, University of Massachusetts.

Speas, M. (1990). A comparison of Chomsky and Lebeaux's approach to generalized transformations. Unpublished manuscript, University of Massachusetts.

Tavakolian, S. (1978). *Structural principles in the acquisition of complex syntax*. Unpublished doctoral dissertation, Graduate Linguistic Student Association, University of Massachusetts, Amherst.

Wexler, K., & Culicover, P. (1980). *Formal principles of language acquisition*. Cambridge, MA: MIT Press.

Williams, E. (1980). Predication. *Linguistic Inquiry.*

CHAPTER ELEVEN

Theoretical Implications
of Inherited Dysphasia

Myrna L. Gopnik
McGill University, Montreal

1. INTRODUCTION

The aim of this book is to look at the ways in which evidence from different populations can provide insights into the theory of language acquisition. The population discussed in this chapter is children who have specific problems with the acquisition of language but who are otherwise unimpaired. In particular, the chapter will present data from a large family that exhibits a specific language disorder. There is evidence that this developmental disorder has a genetic etiology associated with an autosomally dominant gene. This evidence will be used to discuss both the way in which linguistic theory influences the characterization of this disorder and the way in which the existence of this genetic language disorder has consequences for the metatheoretical properties of language. This disorder constitutes a natural experiment that can provide direct evidence about the heritability of language. Fundamental assumptions about language provided by theories of language and theories of the acquisition of language necessary for any serious characterization of this disorder are presented. It is shown that present accounts of specific language impairment often ignore these fundamental linguistic principles and therefore misinterpret some aspects of the problem. In addition, the significance of this genetic disorder for metatheoretic issues such as innateness, species specificity, and modularity are discussed.

That language is a consequence of the biological endowment of human beings, rather than merely an arbitrary learned skill, is now well accepted. The precise content of this endowment is still the subject of much lively debate. It has been argued that there is continuity between apes and humans with respect to language as evidenced by the apes' ability to learn symbol manipulation tasks that share certain properties with human language. Therefore, because other species can learn some language-like skills, the argument goes, language must be the result of the evolutionary forces working on already established capacities. The opposite position is taken by Pinker and Bloom (1990) who argue that language evolved more recently, after the evolutionary line of species that lead to the great apes separated from the line that lead to humans. They show that the properties of human language are distinct from those of other species and that, because systems with these properties convey advantages, the normal processes of natural selection could have worked evolutionarily to produce a separate species with a unique capacity for human language. Even if language is the result of a recent evolutionary development, it would not necessarily be the case that language is autonomous from other cognitive processes. A more powerful general cognitive capacity could have evolved and then been available for learning many complex systems including language. The opposite hypothesis, that language constitutes a separate and autonomous module, is argued for by Fodor (1983). Language is seen to be the result of an innate language-specific system that analyzes incoming data from the peripheral processors according to principles specific to language and organizes this data by means of rules designed specifically to construct grammars.

All sides of these questions have been claimed to be supported by philosophical arguments, by data from the grammars of various languages, from patterns of language acquisition, and from the effect of injury to this system. Though it has been inferred from all of these sources of evidence that the species specificity and modularity hypotheses are true or not true, depending on the theoretical school, none of the arguments have been able to present evidence from an innate, genetic mechanism that would directly address the issue.

The biological and genetic mechanisms that underpin natural selection in general are known, at least in part. In a sense then, all of the pieces of the puzzle are available: We can infer that there must be innate mechanisms that control and constrain the acquisition of language, we have some notion about what some of the properties of these constraints must be, and we believe that these kinds of innate mechanisms must be governed by the same sort of genetic principles that govern other innate properties. We can now even gather evidence about the neurological structures that appear to be specific for language.

2. DYSPHASIA

Unfortunately, the clinical diagnosis of dysphasia is a diagnosis by exclusion. Children so diagnosed do not follow the normal course of language development but they appear to be normal in all other respects: They are not retarded, deaf, blind, or psychotic. The lack of specificity necessary for clinical diagnosis results in a heterogeneous population that exhibits a wide range of other symptoms and outcomes. For example, it is estimated that as many as half of the children diagnosed as dysphasic have no residual language problems as they get older and the other half persist in having problems with language. There is an equivalent diversity of terms used to refer to this population: *dysphasic, specific language impaired, developmental aphasic, developmental language impaired*. It can be expected that this heterogeneous clinical population will turn out to consist of several subpopulations. Nevertheless it is clear that there is a group that shares many properties. Typically these children do not start to speak at as young an age as other children do and when they do begin to use language it is phonologically and grammatically impaired. Moreover, the deficit persists, even in adulthood, despite intensive therapy. Though there has been speculation about the origins of this disorder, it is only recently that several different studies provide evidence that a genetic pathway is implicated.

2.1. The Genetic Evidence

There is now evidence from single family studies, statistical studies of familial aggregation, and twin studies that taken together argue that at least some cases of dysphasia are genetic in origin. (This evidence is reviewed in more detail in Gopnik & Crago, 1991).

2.1.1. Single Family Studies. There are recent reports of single family studies in which there is clear evidence of familial aggregation of dysphasia. A very large multigenerational family that exhibits a clear pattern of familial aggregation of dysphasia is reported on by Gopnik (1990a, 1990b); and by Hurst, Baraitser, Auger, Graham, and Norell (1990). J. Hurst (Hurst et al., 1990), a geneticist, concludes that "inheritance in this family is autosomally dominant, and chromosome analysis of one of the affected members was normal. Its importance seems to be that there is a single gene coding for a pathway which is fundamental for developing intelligible language" (p. 354). See Fig. 11.1. Samples and Lane (1985) report on another family study in which six siblings, ranging in age from 11.9 years to 5.2 years, in a single family all have specific language

F(74) * - M(deceased)

F(46)* -husband   M -wife   F(43)* -husband   M(40)*-wife   F (38)* -husband

f   (17) *   m (20)   f (21)   m (10)   m   (17) *
m   (16) *   f (18)   f (17)   f   (7) *   m (15) *
f   (12) *   f (12) *   f   (5) *   m   (14) *
m   (8) *   f (11) *   f (2) ? *   f   (12) *
                                      m (7)   m   (10) *
                                                                                m   (8) *
                                                                                f   (7) *
                                                                                m   (6) *
                                                                                f   (6) *

FIG. 11.1. The 16 members of the family that are underlined were
diagnosed as dysphasic by the school system and all of them have received
some kind of speech therapy except the grandmother, because such therapy was not available when she was in school. (The 2-year-old has been
only tentatively diagnosed as dysphasic because of her late onset of language.) The 22 members indicated by **bold and asterisk** were actually
studied. The spouses have never been diagnosed as having any problem
with language and the family reports that they do not have such problems.
The age of the subject at the time of testing is given in parentheses. The
two youngest members of the family of nine children are fraternal twins.

learning disorders. They conclude "that a genetic component contrib-
utes to the disorder" (p. 25).

2.1.2. Statistical Studies of Familial Aggregation. Tallal, Ross,
and Curtiss (1989a, 1989b) studied 112 4-year-olds, 62 language impaired
and 50 controls, and concluded that "the results demonstrate highly significant differences in the incidence of reports of positive family histo-
ries for first-degree relatives between the families of language-impaired
and control children" (1989a, p. 172) and that "the pattern of familial
aggregation, if genetically influenced, would be compatible with autosomally dominant transmission, with greater penetrance through the
mothers than through the fathers" (1989b, p. 994). Tomblin (1989)
reports a similar pattern of familial aggregation in a study of 203 children ranging in age from 7 to 9, 51 language impaired and 152 controls.
He concludes that "the possibility that one or several paths exist between
genetic characteristics, neural development and/or function, and ultimately language learning must be considered as plausible" (p. 293).

2.1.3. Twin Studies. Borges-Osorio (Borges-Osorio & Salzano,
1985), a geneticist, reports on several aspects of language in three sets
of monozygotic twins and purports that his data show that "genetic factors in the etiology of language is now clearly established, although the

details of the gene-environmental interaction in the different categories of such defects are far from being elucidated" (p. 99). Tomblin (1991) reported that a study of the language therapy history of 80 sets of male twins found that if a twin was language impaired and was reported to be monozygotic, then the probability that the other twin was also language impaired was over 80%; if the language impaired twin was reported to be dizygotic, then the probability that the other twin was also language impaired dropped to 35%. The findings for the dizygotic twins are consistent with the results for male siblings reported in Tomblin (1989) discussed later.

Though a marker for this gene is being sought, as yet there has been no success with finding one, which is not in itself surprising. The techniques for the identification of genes are not yet very precise. For example, researchers have known for 10 years that the gene for Huntington's disease is on chromosome 4, but no one has yet determined its precise location on that chromosome. Though there is no physical evidence of a marker for this gene, geneticists nevertheless believe that the pattern of occurrence of this disorder in families as evidenced by single family studies, statistical studies, and by twin studies is sufficient to support the hypothesis that the dysphasia in these families is genetic in origin.

2.2. Alternate Environmental Explanations

Though geneticists regard these patterns of familial aggregation as typical of those caused by genetic factors, it has been suggested by others that there might be an environmental explanation for the familial aggregation of dysphasia. For example, it has been argued that this pattern of language deficit in families might be the result of caregivers providing impoverished linguistic input to the children. Because the input is impoverished, the children build impoverished grammars. There are several cogent reasons that make the familial environment unlikely to be the explanation for this pattern of occurrence. If dysphasia in families is caused by the way in which the caregivers speak to the children, then one would expect that either all of the children be equally affected or at least that they all be affected to a greater or lesser degree. But that is not what happens. In these families, some of the children are severely affected whereas the other children in the family appear to have no linguistic deficit. Furthermore, if we study the pattern of distribution of the affected and unaffected children in the families, it can be seen that this distribution of affected and unaffected children occurs in a pattern typical of an autosomal dominant gene. It is this study of the patterns of distribution in his large sample that led Tomblin to conclude that "the data from this study do not provide support for the environment as a principal mechanism'' (1989, p. 293).

There are theoretical problems, in addition to the distributional ones, with the hypothesis that the caregivers' linguistic input causes the language disorder in the child. Underlying any such explanation is the hypothesis, not altogether false, that there is some direct relationship between the caregiver's language and the grammar built by the child on the basis of this input. In order for this explanation to hold, it would have to be shown that there is some principled relationship between the linguistic structure of the caregiver's language and the linguistic properties of the child's deficit. In the family that we have examined in detail, some of the children are impaired and others are not. Therefore, if the disorder is the result of the linguistic input provided by the caregivers, it has to be the case that the caregivers systematically provided the correct linguistic data for the unimpaired siblings and impaired input to the disordered siblings. It is not impossible that caregivers speak differently to different children in the same family. However, when the nature of the linguistic deficit is looked at in more specific detail, such an explanation seems unlikely. For example, one of the many problems that dysphasics can be shown to have with language, which will be discussed in detail in a later section of this chapter, is that they do not use the grammatical category TENSE correctly either with respect to the temporal context of the action or with respect to agreement with other elements in the sentence; the unimpaired children in the same family acquire TENSE with no problem. In order for this deficit to be caused by the way the caregiver speaks to the child, it would have to be the case that the caregiver would have to produce a language that was impaired with respect to the category TENSE when talking to the dysphasic children and unimpaired for TENSE when talking to the nondisordered children. Although it is reasonable to believe that people can control their language for vocabulary and some kinds of syntactic complexity, it is inconceivable that such control could be exercised over an unconscious, automatic feature such as TENSE. It can be seen, therefore, that the plausibility of the hypothesis that the caregivers' language is a causal factor in the language deficit depends directly on the linguistic characterization of the deficit. If the deficit involves a part of language that can be under the control of the speaker, such as the level of the vocabulary to be used, then such a hypothesis may be true. However, if it can be shown that the deficit is in a part of language that is part of the automatic processes of language, such as the marking of TENSE, then such a hypothesis is very unlikely to be correct.

It is interesting to note that some children raised by a dysphasic parent with other dysphasic children are able to learn language normally.

They must be able to filter out the aberrant data provided to them by their dysphasic relatives and attend only to the correct data being supplied by the unimpaired speakers in the family. This is evidence that unimpaired children must have some expectations about what a grammar should look like and are able to select the data that is consistent with their expectations about the kinds of rules that are likely to exist in language.

2.3. Neurological Evidence

There is very recent evidence about the neurological consequences associated with familial dysphasia. The interpretation of data about neurological structure is somewhat controversial, but it raises interesting interim hypotheses. Plante et al. (1990; Plante, Swisher, & Vance, 1991) examined the neurological structure of the brains of four boys who had been diagnosed as dysphasic. Evidence from magnetic resonance imaging (MRI) demonstrate that "atypical perisylvian asymmetries [are] linked to the language disorder" (Plante et al., 1991, p. 52). These MRI findings agree with an autopsy report on a dysphasic child (Cohen, Campbell, & Yaghmai, 1989), which also finds such atypical asymmetries. In these subjects, instead of the normal cerebral asymmetries that one would expect, the right and left perisylvian region are both within the range of the left hemisphere region in normals. These subjects have symmetry where one would expect asymmetry. Though in some of the subjects these unusual symmetries occur in other areas of the brain, the only area that is impaired in all of the dysphasic subjects is the perisylvian region. This occurrence of impairment in other regions of the brain might account for these cases of dysphasia in which other cognitive abilities, such as the ability to visualize spatial relationships, can be shown to co-occur with dysphasia. The abnormality in the neurological substrate would therefore be the common cause of both the cognitive and the linguistic disorder, though neither of them would be causally related to each other. It may be the case that the gene in question controls not for language in particular, but rather for the construction of cerebral asymmetries. If this were the case then one could expect that the same gene might account for cases of familial aggregation for other cognitive disorders. However, even if this were true it would still be the case that the specific problems with language would not be causally connected to these other cognitive disorders. The specificity of the atypical asymmetries in the perisylvian region appear to be the proximate cause of dysphasia. The crucial question is what the particular consequences of these changes in brain structure have for the development of language.

2.4. Inferences From Impaired Populations

Underlying this study is the assumption that data from impaired populations can give insights about the normal system. If it can be demonstrated that certain parts of a system can be impaired while other parts remain
intact, then one may infer that these parts constitute significantly different constituents in the normal system. Another way to look at this is that
the organization of a system constrains the way in which that system can
go wrong. Grodzinsky (1990) argued cogently that evidence from acquired disorders of language have the potential for providing insights
about normal grammars. Marshall (1989) argued that the way in which
dyslexia, both developmental and acquired, can impair the ability to read,
can give us insights into the organization of reading in the normal population. Both of these scholars have emphasized that there is an interaction between linguistic theory and language disorders. The basic concepts
of *disorder* and *error in language* must be seen to be relative to a particular theoretical framework, whether or not explicitly acknowledged. This
obligatory framework guides the selection of the data that is considered
to be relevant to the disorder and specifies the theoretical variables that
describe this data. A particular theoretical description can be said to be
insightful, or perhaps even right, if the patterns of ability and impairment
in the language of the subject can be accounted for in terms of the distinctions among variables established by the theory. If the breakdown
of language can be shown to occur at just those places where the theory
says that there is a joint between two different systems, then this data
from the disorder can be seen to verify the distinction made within the
theory. Therefore, it seems reasonable to suppose that the normal course
of language development can be illuminated by studying those cases in
which this normal development goes awry.

3. DYSPHASIC LANGUAGE

The very fact that there is a genetic basis for language development is,
in itself, important, but the crucial question that must be addressed is
just what consequences dysphasia has for language. Does this disorder affect language in particular, or are the problems that occur in dysphasic language merely epiphenomena of some more general nonlinguistic
problem? If it could be shown to be the case that the genetic disorder
directly affects some basic property of the linguistic system itself, then
the hypothesis that language is autonomous would be strengthened. On
the other hand, if it could be demonstrated that the apparent problem
with language is, in fact, caused by some more general perceptual or

cognitive deficit, then the evidence from dysphasia could not be said to support the modularity hypothesis. In order to address this question in a serious way, it is absolutely necessary that there be a clear and detailed account of dysphasic language.

Providing such an account of dysphasic language in itself requires a commitment to some basic theoretical assumptions about the nature of language. Any adequate description of this language must be based on the fundamental principles that must guide the description of any language. It is only when such a principled description is available that one can evaluate proposed explanations for dysphasia. Any explanation of dysphasia, whether it is constructed in terms of a theory of auditory perception or cognitive processing or parental influence or underlying grammars, must demonstrate that the abstract variables within the higher level theory are necessary and sufficient to account for the properties of the grammar that can be shown to produce dysphasic language. This account of dysphasic language must in itself be based on fundamental theoretical principles of linguistic description if it is to provide the database for the construction of causal arguments about the disorder. Therefore dysphasia interacts with linguistic theory in two different ways. In the first place the evidence from dysphasia provides evidence for some fundamental linguistic hypotheses. Secondly, other fundamental assumptions about language must guide the description of dysphasic language.

3.1. Some Principles That Must Guide the Characterization of Dysphasic Language

Because characterizing dysphasic language in itself involves a commitment to fundamental linguistic principles, it is important that these principles be explicitly stated so that the terms of the subsequent discussions can be clear. These principles are not specific to any particular theory of grammar, but rather are general principles about the nature of language that have been articulated as far back as Panini (600 B.C.). First, speakers of a language have an internalized set of abstract rules that guide their explicit linguistic utterances. The actual utterances produced by speakers, the surface forms, may constitute evidence about the properties of these abstract rules, but these empirically occurring utterances do not, in themselves, constitute language. It is the set of abstract rules, the grammar, that produces these utterances that constitutes language and therefore it is this grammar that must be characterized if we want to understand any language, including dysphasic language. Any analysis of the surface forms alone is necessarily incomplete and therefore inadequate. Second, these abstract rules organize individual forms into more complex constituents. It is not the succession of individual forms that constitutes language, but rather the organization of these individual forms into larger constituents that are themselves organized into more abstract, hierarchically ordered constituents. A description of individual forms without an account of how these forms participate in larger constituents is also an inadequate analysis. Third, individual surface forms underdetermine the form of the underlying grammar. It is only by considering the system as a whole that the abstract representations underlying the surface forms and the rules operating to construct larger constituents can be determined. It follows that two forms produced by two different speakers may be identical in their surface form and yet may come from two different underlying representations via two different rules. An example of this is that an abstract marker in the underlying grammar, e.g., "singular" in English, may be realized in the surface form by the absence of any overt marking.

Although most linguists would agree that any adequate account of language must adhere to at least these few fundamental principles of linguistic analysis, these principles have not informed all of the reports in the literature about dysphasia. The typical report about dysphasic language examines the empirically occurring utterances produced by the dysphasic and provides an enumeration of the individual forms that are different from those in the normal language. These forms are termed *errors* and the forms that the dysphasic produces that are the same as those in the normal language are treated as "correct." In many cases an item-by-item comparison of the dysphasic's utterances with same age or same MLU controls is provided. These item-by-item comparisons obscure the fact that these individual forms are part of an integrated linguistic system. It is only by considering the interaction of all of the forms that the linguistic system as a whole can be characterized. These analyses of individual surface forms do not relate these data to other surface forms in the sentence that form constituents, nor do they provide any description of the abstract underlying rules that produce these surface forms. And because only surface forms are dealt with, any grammatical marker that is realized on the surface by zero is not recognized as occurring.

Subjects are typically reported to have difficulty with plural and past, but, in English, because there is no explicit marker for singular or present, the unmarked forms that the dysphasics produce for singular and present are not reported as errors. Although such a description may be accurate in terms of the surface forms, it is clearly not interpretable in terms of an underlying system. If they do not have plural then there is no warrant for establishing the abstract category NUMBER at all. A more careful analysis of the data shows that they do not have problems with plural at all, if what is meant by plural is the ability to mark a given lexical entry with the appropriate marker for plural for that particular lexical item. They do, however, have a serious problem with reliably matching the NUM-BER marker on the lexical item with the number of objects in the refer-ent. They are also reported to have difficulty with articles as well as with plurals but these two facts are reported as if they were independent and therefore the observation that they have difficulty with number agree-ment among constituents in the sentence is almost never drawn. Another difficulty with the data about dysphasia as it is typically reported is that the occurrence of a marked form in the surface language is treated as evi-dence that the subject has gotten it "correct," and therefore has normal language in this respect. But such an inference is unwarranted. It must be demonstrated that this form is not only similar in surface form, but is derived from the same underlying rules. When the language of adult dysphasics is examined, it can be shown that though they often produce the "correct" form, further analysis of their performance in other respects shows that the rules governing this form in their grammar is not the same as in unimpaired speakers.

The data from adult dysphasics is important, not only in what it can tell us about the final state grammar that these individuals can achieve, but also because it can help us to understand the way in which language is acquired by children with this impairment. The child's task in learning language is to construct a grammar that will allow the child to produce new grammatical utterances. This is a difficult job and all children do this imperfectly at first. Children refine the initial simple grammars to more complex grammars until their grammars converge on the adult gram-mar. The task is complicated by the fact that children only hear a small, finite set of utterances and there are very many different grammars that are formally adequate to represent any such finite set of data. Children, therefore, must have some way of constraining the grammars that they construct. It has been assumed within current linguistic theory that the initial genetic endowment of the child constrains the kinds of grammars that will be constructed. In our genetically impaired population, these normal innate constraints cannot be a priori assumed to hold. Another kind of constraint that can be imposed on hypotheses about children's interim grammars is that these grammars must be converging on the adult form of the grammar that can be assumed to be the final state that the normal child will achieve. This is not the case for language-impaired chil-dren because the data from the adult dysphasics provides evidence that the grammars that underlie their production of language are very differ-ent from normal grammars of English. Therefore the transitional gram-mars that younger dysphasics are constructing in their developing language must be constrained by the properties of the final state dysphasic grammar that they can be expected to achieve.

GOPNIK

4. DATA

This chapter is intended to concentrate on the theoretical implications of genetic dysphasia, so only the broad outlines of the data are discussed here, though much more data is available.

Certain facts about the language of dysphasics in English and in German seem to be quite clear and widely reported in the literature. In this section a brief overview of these properties of the language of dysphasics is provided. More importantly an account is given that integrates these individual descriptions into a coherent system of abstract of rules that conforms to the principles of linguistic description already discussed. Detailed analyses of spontaneous speech and test results that support this principled linguistic description have already appeared (Clahsen, 1989; Crago & Gopnik, in press; Gopnik, 1990b; Gopnik, 1992; Gopnik, submitted; Gopnik & Crago, 1991). These data are reviewed briefly here. The statistical results of some of the analyses of the English data, discussed in detail in the previously cited works, is provided here in parentheses. Dysphasics do not have a problem with plural when plural is understood to mean putting the appropriate plural marker on the appropriate lexical item. This effect is particularly striking in German where plural marking is more complex than it is in English. Young German dysphasics are the same as unimpaired children in their ability to assign the correct plural marker to the correct lexical item. Whereas dysphasics can mark plural correctly, they cannot control NUMBER in NPs. In dysphasics, number marking on nouns does not reliably agree with the number of objects that the noun is meant to refer to and there is no NUMBER agreement among the constituents in the sentence. Though it is often reported that English dysphasics are poor at plural, the observations and tests that support this description, such as picture description tasks, really assess the ability of the dysphasics to produce a word marked for plural in a context in which the intended referent is more than one object. These tests do not assess the ability to produce the correct plural marker, but rather what they are really reporting on is the dysphasics deficit in NUMBER. Dysphasics also make errors on articles and on third-person singular /s/ on verbs, which is additional evidence of their difficulty with NUMBER agreement. All of these results are consistent with the hypothesis that dysphasics can construct lexical entries for plural on the basis of semantic correlates in the world, but they cannot construct the abstract feature NUMBER in their grammar.

A similar picture emerges with respect to verbs. In English, dysphasics do not know that all main verbs must obligatorily be marked for TENSE. This is evidenced by the absence of past marking in contexts in which the event clearly took place in the past both in spontaneous speech and in written notebooks. In spontaneous speech, the dysphasics produce past tense marking in only 64.4% of the obligatory contexts whereas their nonimpaired relatives mark tense in 99.3% of the obligatory contexts. In the notebooks, kept by dysphasics during a year, only 53% of regular verbs are written with -ed, though throughout the notebooks the teacher corrects these errors by writing in the -ed. It is also evidenced by the significant difference between the nondisordered members of the family and the dysphasics in their ability to perform tasks that require them to change TENSE on a sentence to accord with the event-time being referred to (out of 10 items the mean for controls = 9.17; mean for dysphasics = 3.83). In German the fact that they do not mark verbs for finiteness can be easily seen by the errors that they make in the placement of the verb. The fact that some of the impaired individuals sometimes do produce a word that is identical in surface form to the marked past tense forms produced by nonimpaired speakers does not necessarily mean that the forms produced by the impaired subjects are really marked for past. These forms can be simply stored, unanalyzed lexical items that carry the meaning of "pastness" as part of their meaning.

In addition to the problems with NUMBER and TENSE, dysphasics also have problems with consistent marking of ASPECT, with pronoun deletion, with regular case marking in German, and with auxiliaries. All of these errors are consistent with a deficit in their ability to control morphological features in the syntax.

Though adult dysphasics in English are not significantly different than controls in their knowledge that the s-marked plural forms of familiar words refers to plural referents (out of 10 items, mean controls = 9.17; mean dysphasics = 8.67), they cannot productively use the plural formation rule to mark /s/ on nonsense words that refer to plural referents (out of 6 items, mean controls = 5; mean dysphasics = 3). New data from ranking tests on verbs, done in collaboration with S. Pinker, show that though adult dysphasics are not significantly different from controls in preferring the marked form of the regular past (mean controls = 18; mean dysphasics = 14.2), they are significantly different in their ranking of the unmarked forms (where 1 is defined as unacceptable and 7 as perfectly acceptable):

ranking of unmarked form of regular verbs in past contexts:
mean controls = 1.22; mean dysphasics = 4.19

This difference in performance is consistent with a model in which the controls know that there is an obligatory rule in the syntax that requires TENSE to be marked, but the dysphasics do not have such a rule. If the word exists in the language they will accept it even if it is not marked for past in a past context.

These results all demonstrate that the underlying grammar that the dysphasics construct differs from the normal grammar in linguistically significant ways. The question that must now be posed is whether these facts can be shown to be an epiphenomenon of a deficit in some other nonlinguistic system. If this pattern of deficits can be accounted for by variables independent of language, then it might be supposed that the gene, mediated by neurological processes, that causes dysphasia does not really affect the language faculty directly, but rather interferes with some other perceptual or cognitive system that is necessary for language to be established. If, however, it can be shown that no such nonlinguistic variables are adequate to account for the data and that any account of the deficit in dysphasic language must include variables that range over specific linguistic properties, then it can be hypothesized that the gene in question controls for a property of language.

5. ALTERNATIVE EXPLANATIONS

One kind of argument that has been used to support a nonlinguistic cause for dysphasia is that although the diagnosis of dysphasia definitionally excludes serious auditory, cognitive, neurological, psychological, or social problems, low-level difficulties in these nonlinguistic domains have been found in some subjects. The fact that some low level difficulties in nonlinguistic domains occur in some of these subjects cannot, in itself, be accepted as evidence for a nonlinguistic cause for dysphasia. The question that must be asked about these associated disorders is what their causal relationship is to the specific problems that these subjects have with language. For example, an analysis of the familial patterns of dysphasia, and our knowledge of which features of language can be brought under conscious control, makes it much more likely that caretakers simplify the language that they direct to dysphasics because the dysphasics are producing impaired language, rather than that the simplified linguistic input causes the dysphasia. Moreover, in cases of genetic dysphasia it may be that the two disorders are both caused by some other problem at a totally different level. For example the genetic determinants of x and y may be close together on a chromosome and may therefore tend to be selected together. Or, even if they are both allied to a single gene, it may be the case that the neurological consequences of this gene tend to affect several parts of the brain independently.

Alternative explanations for dysphasia will have to provide a theoretical framework that connects the variables in the nonlinguistic domain with the observed variation in dysphasic language. For example, it would have to be shown that the deficits in the nonlinguistic domain can account for the specific deficits in abstract morphology that can be shown to characterize dysphasic language.

5.1. Auditory Hypotheses

One group of hypotheses that have been proposed to account for dysphasia claim that it is caused by a deficit in the ability to perceive or process acoustic input. Because dysphasics have a problem in perceiving or processing incoming data, the information available to them from the language that they hear is not the same as that available to unimpaired speakers with the same input. Because these two groups have different available linguistic input, they construct different grammars. Under this hypothesis the language faculty is intact; it is the perceptual system that is impaired. The primary direct support cited for these hypotheses is that both otitis media and low level auditory processing problems have been observed in some dysphasics. Tallal, Stark, Kallman, and Mellits (1980) proposed that the disorder is in the peripheral auditory processing system. The data from dysphasic language that such theories account for is that dysphasics sometimes do not mark plural with /s/ and past tense with /ed/ in English. Because these sounds require fast auditory transitions, it is argued that the dysphasics do not produce them because they cannot hear them.

In such explanations the assumption is made that there is a direct route from the auditory input to the articulatory output. It is assumed that if it can be shown that there is an impairment that interferes with the full analysis of the surface properties of the acoustic signal, and there is an impairment in the production of a surface form, then the auditory disorder must be the cause of the linguistic disorder. Generally speaking, these sorts of explanations relate the empirically observed phonetic form of the input to the empirically observed phonetic form of the output. They do not assume that there is any intermediate abstract representation in terms of an underlying phonological system or grammar. As a consequence of this position, there is no way for such an explanation to distinguish among surface forms that, within other explanatory models, are generated from different underlying representations. For example, in English there are at least four different sources for the surface form /s/: it can occur within the lexical representation itself, it can be added to a lexical representation by the rule plural → /s/, it can be added by third person present-tense rule, and it can be added to a lexical representation by the rule that rewrites genitive case as /s/. The surface forms generated from these four underlying representations are identical. Therefore any explanation that maps surface input to surface output has to treat all of these forms as equivalent. Within the Tallal et al. model, the processing of final /s/ involves fast auditory transitions of the kind that dysphasics cannot process. Therefore they cannot extract this information from the input signal and this results in their not producing /s/ in their output. Such an explanation correctly predicts that words are often produced without the /s/ and /ed/ that marks plural and tense. What this explanation does not account for is that there is a difference in the behavior of dysphasics that depends on the underlying source for the /s/. For example, the data show that the impaired subjects do not have any problems with the /s/ in monomorphemic words that have these same sounds (Gopnik, 1993; Leonard, Bortolini, Caselli, McGregor, & Sabbadini, 1992).

5.2. Auditory Salience

A somewhat different hypothesis has been proposed by Leonard et al. (1989, 1992). He claims that the perceptual and articulatory characteristics of English grammatical morphemes make specific language impaired (SLI) children's task of morphological paradigm building especially difficult. This hypothesis asserts, as opposed to Tallal et al. (1980), that the primary problem is not with the first stages of the auditory processing of the incoming acoustic signal, but at higher levels of auditory processing where the differences in sound, for example between *kick* and *kicks*, are perceived but are not salient, therefore the dysphasic cannot use this auditory information to construct the general paradigm saying, for example, that plural is marked in English by adding /s/ to the root noun. Under this hypothesis the underlying grammar that constructs these rules is unimpaired. However, because the sounds that encode the distinction have "difficult surface characteristics," the intact grammar has no evidence that a marker for past or a marker for plural exists.

One major problem in evaluating this hypothesis arises because of the concept of *salience*. Leonard et al. (1992) recognized that a more precise explication of the construct "difficult surface characteristic" is needed. However the problem is not merely that more precision is needed in delimiting an otherwise clear construct. It is the very concept of "difficult surface characteristic" itself that is problematic. It is not clear whether this concept is defined over acoustic, phonetic, or phonological sequences, therefore there is no way of predicting which sounds do and do not have difficult surface characteristics. Does *salience* involve properties of the surface acoustic signal that can be expected to hold in the same way for all language learners or is it a deeper problem with the language specific phonological system that the dysphasic constructs? It is not unlikely that fundamental properties of the phonological system could have direct consequences of this type. One such constraint might be that morphological markers could not be eliminated if the resultant form was not a possible phonological word in the language. However, even if such a definition were able to be provided it would still have to be demonstrated that the dysphasics, in fact, had the impairment in the acoustic, phonetic, or phonological domain in question.

If the dysphasics really can be shown to have problems with plural /s/ and the past /ed/, and if all of their problems in language are of this sort, then an auditory salience explanation, although inadequate in its present form, might be salvageable. But, as the account of their language given earlier shows, it is not true that they have the problems that Leonard et al. (1992) claim or that all of their problems are accountable in terms of the surface properties of the sounds that encode the morphemes.

In the first place, it is not true that dysphasics have problems with attending to and representing the plural marker. A wide range of data show that dysphasics can and do produce and distinguish marked plural forms (Clahsen, 1989; Gopnik, 1990b; Gopnik & Crago, 1991; Leonard et al., 1992). The problem is that they cannot control for NUMBER in the syntax in general, whether it is marked or unmarked. The data presented in Leonard analyzes errors as if they resided in a particular individual surface form and not at the more general level of the constituent. For example, we are told that:

> Some of the errors observed are:
> Articles: *a bees*
> Plurals: *this one cats*
> Third singular: *I draws*
> Copula: *trees is big*

If it is true (as proposed earlier) that the agreement rule for NUMBER is missing from dysphasic grammars, then what is described by Leonard et al. as four different and independent errors can be more parsimoniously accounted for by a deficit in a single rule that operates, not on the surface forms, but on their abstract representations. Our data show that adult dysphasics who do often produce the marked forms cannot make reliable grammaticality judgments about these forms (of 30 items: mean controls = 27.5; mean dysphasics = 17.17) although they are not significantly different from controls in their ability to make reliable grammaticality judgments about errors in argument structure (of 12 items: mean controls = 10.17; mean dysphasics = 9.83).

In addition to the data from Leonard et al. involving explicit morphological marking there is other data, all of which can not be reviewed here, that does not involve explicit morphological marking and can be accounted for only by an explanation referring to the abstract representation of the forms. For example, adult dysphasics do not appear to have problems with exophoric pronouns that refer directly to objects in the world. They are not significantly different from controls on tasks that require them to point to pictures that are distinguishable on the basis of such pronouns [such as "She holds him." versus "He holds them." (mean controls = 3.83; mean dysphasics = 3.67)] yet they are significantly different from controls in using full noun phrases instead of anaphoric pronouns in the construction of spoken narratives (mean controls = 55%; mean dysphasics = 91.2%). Both tasks involve the use of the same pronouns in the surface utterances; they differ, however, at a more abstract level. Exophoric pronouns can be represented in the grammar by specifying the semantic content of the pronoun in the lexicon. The anaphoric use of the pronoun in the construction of a narrative requires that there be agreement between abstract features marked on the pronoun and the same features on its antecedent. Therefore these data can be accounted for within the agreement deficit hypothesis but not within the auditory salience hypothesis.

Dysphasics also make errors in marking progressive aspect, animacy, mass/count, pronoun deletion, and in derivational morphology. Let us look in more detail at aspect marking. Aspect in English is marked by two different forms, a form of *to be* before the verb and /ing/ added to the verb. Dysphasics do produce the /ing/ progressive aspect marker on the verb and do produce forms of *to be*. This would be expected by the auditory hypotheses because these forms are not dependent on fast auditory perception and are presumably salient. However, when all of the evidence is considered the situation is not so simple and direct. Although dysphasics do produce these surface forms, they do not consistently produce both forms together, as is required in marking progressive. The data show that they produce three different versions of progressive, one with both *be* and /ing/, one with just *be* and a third with just /ing/:

Carol is cry in the church.
I walking down the road.
Anne is fighting.

Any analysis that considers just the surface forms must conclude, as does Crystal, that although they are able to produce the form they do not always use it correctly: "The profile chart is confusing with approximately equal numbers of correct vs. incorrect uses of the auxiliary and *ing*" (1987, p. 117). Such data cannot be accounted for in terms of a deficit in the input. However, these variations in surface forms are predictable from the assumption that the dysphasics do not have agreement rules. It has been proposed for other reasons having to do with normal language

(Travis, 1984) that "be" and "ing" are both independently generated and each is marked with the feature progressive. An agreement rule checks to see that both parts of the verb phrase have this feature progressive. It follows that all three forms that are observed to be produced by dysphasics would be predicted to occur as they do, if it is assumed that they do not construct such agreement rules.

Moreover, as we have already discussed briefly with respect to both NUMBER and TENSE, not only are the surface forms produced by dysphasics different, but the kinds of abstract rules that they construct to produce these forms also appear to be different from those constructed by controls. Therefore, even when they do produce the same surface form, as for example a marked past form, it is not reasonable to conclude that it is equivalent to the normal form because it is produced in a very different way than the normal form.

A principled linguistic analysis of the data, both in English and German, show that it is the features and agreement rules that guide the construction of the surface grammatical morphemes that are missing in these subjects, and not merely the surface forms themselves. However, it is still not clear what causes this inability to construct such rules. It is not impossible that one of the factors involved is an interaction between the way in which the dysphasics represent the incoming acoustic information in their phonological system and the way in which this information is available to them to construct their underlying grammar, but the principles that underlie this interaction must be more complex than those so far suggested. The data show that any adequate account of dysphasia cannot be framed in terms of phonetic or phonological variables alone, but must include variables that refer to abstract rules of grammar. In order to address this issue, there must be a careful and detailed analysis of the phonological systems that they actually construct and an analysis of the consequences of this phonological system on categories in the syntax. Such analyses are not yet available, but they are presently being undertaken.

5.3. Cognitive Explanation

Cognitive explanations begin with the assumption that the underlying properties of mind that give rise to language are the same as those that determine other cognitive processes. It follows, therefore, that dysphasia should be able to be demonstrated to be the consequence of a more general cognitive deficit. Such explanations hypothesize that dysphasics have a deficit in their general cognitive abilities that does not allow them to construct cognitive rules of a particular kind. This approach specifically challenges the hypothesis that language constitutes a separate and

autonomous module in the mind. If it can be shown that the disorders
of language manifested in dysphasia are in fact particular to language then
this would constitute supporting evidence for the linguistic modularity
hypothesis. The primary argument that has been advanced with respect
to the cognitive hypothesis consists of the conviction, based on some
facts about normal acquisition, that language is governed by general cognitive rules and evidence that disorders in various levels and kinds of cognitive function have been found to exist in dysphasic subjects. It is
concluded therefore that because dysphasic subjects sometimes exhibit
difficulties in other cognitive domains, as well as linguistic disorders, that
the cognitive disorder must cause the linguistic disorder. It should be
remembered, however, that definitionally, subjects are not diagnosed as
dysphasic if they present with major cognitive dysfunctions. Moreover,
there are subjects who have severely impaired cognition, yet appear to
have relatively intact language (Yamada, 1990). In addition, the neurological data from Plante et al. (1991) show that atypical asymmetries can
occur in parts of the brain known to be associated with cognitive processes other than language, for example spatial reasoning. There is, therefore, a plausible mechanism that can account for the cognitive deficits,
such as spatial reasoning, that have been reported to sometimes co-occur
with specific language deficits. In order for a cognitive hypothesis to be
convincing, mere co-occurrence of cognitive and language disorders
would be inadequate. A more complex pattern of evidence would be required. First it would have to be demonstrated that there is a general cognitive model that exhibits the same formal properties as the model
necessary for characterizing abstract morphology. Second, the particular nonlinguistic cognitive consequences of this model would have to be
described in enough detail so that information about the subjects' ability
to perform these tasks could be assessed in a way that did not depend
on their ability to use language. Third, the linguistic deficit in dysphasia
would have to be shown to be a deficit that could be accounted for by
an inability to perform this specific cognitive task. And lastly, the subject would have to be shown not to be able to perform this cognitive
task in all of the other domains in which it was manifested.

So far arguments at this level of specificity have not yet been constructed. The extent and precise nature of the cognitive deficits claimed to cause
dysphasia have varied widely from an inability to handle hierarchical relationships to a reduced amount of symbolic thought. Cromer (1978), for
example, claimed that some dysphasics also have difficulties with hierarchical processing. Because language is presumed to involve hierarchical processing, the disorders in dysphasic language must be a consequence
of a more extensive cognitive inability on the part of dysphasics to handle these hierarchical relationships. If it could be shown that dysphasics

in general have a problem with hierarchical relations, and, further, that all and only hierarchical relationships in language are affected, then such an explanation would be likely. However, neither is the case. Dysphasics that have serious problems with language can be unimpaired, or even talented, with respect to mathematical ability, which would indicate that they are able to process hierarchical relationships. In fact, one of the subjects that we have studied in detail (Gopnik, 1990b), and who is still severely dysphasic even at eighteen, is reported by his teachers to be the best student in his class at mathematics and routinely writes programs for his computer, which certainly requires the ability to manipulate hierarchically ordered values. Moreover, a careful study of the language disorders in dysphasia does not support a hypothesis that all hierarchical relationships in language are impaired. The data cited previously show that though dysphasics are not able to construct abstract rules for agreement of categories such as NUMBER and TENSE, they do not seem to be impaired in handling the underlying rules governing argument structures that are equivalently hierarchical. It can be argued that the dysphasics in fact do use their general cognitive abilities for learning and remembering and constructing semantic interpretations for symbols in order to learn certain aspects of language. This general cognitive strategy, however, results in a grammar that is quite different from that produced by normals.

Whereas Cromer's cognitive hypothesis is reasonably clear and therefore testable, some of the other cognitive hypotheses do not have this character. Although the coincidence of the occurrence of the linguistic disorder and the cognitive disorder is noted, the properties of the causal connection hypothesized to exist between the purported disorder in the cognitive system and the disorder in the linguistic system is usually not provided, and when it is, it is metaphoric at best. For example, it has been noted that dysphasic children do not indulge in as much symbolic play as other children (Udwin & Yule, 1983). However, no serious causal relationship between symbolic thought and the well-documented deficits in language, for example, morphological number marking, is suggested.

Although any simple auditory hypothesis can be shown to be inadequate in principle by the evidence from dysphasia demonstrating that any explanation of dysphasic language must have reference to abstract representations, there can be no such evidence that refutes, in principle, the possibility of finding a cognitive explanation. Both cognitive and linguistic explanations have reference to abstract rules. The difference between these explanations is the specificity that is assumed to hold for these rules. The linguistic explanation presumes that these rules are specifically linguistic rules; the cognitive explanation presumes that all linguistic rules are derivable from more general cognitive rules. The only way to resolve this is to have a careful and detailed description of the dysphasic deficit in terms of abstract rules, which, in the first instance, must be phrased in terms of rules of language. Even if a complete account of dysphasia in terms of linguistic rules is possible, it still may be that these deficient rules can be shown to be subsumable under some more general cognitive deficit. However, in advance of such evidence, and in light of the neurological evidence that suggests an alternative explanation, there is no warrant at the moment for supposing that dysphasia is cognitive in origin.

5.4. Linguistic Explanations

Linguistic accounts of dysphasia propose that the cause of dysphasia is a disorder in the language-specific module that constrains the construction of grammars from the incoming linguistic data. The linguistic hypothesis cannot assume merely that grammar be rule governed. If that were the case there would be no way of distinguishing this hypothesis from the general cognitive hypothesis, which also can account for rule-governed behavior. The linguistic hypothesis must go further and provide specific constraints on both the formal and the substantive content of these rules. For example, a model that specifies a hierarchy of constraints at different levels of the grammar would predict that one part of the grammar could be selectively impaired. In order for this hypothesis to be testable, conditions similar to those that were argued to hold for cognitive hypotheses must also be met. In the first place, the variables that operate within the linguistic module must be described in enough detail so that specific linguistic hypotheses can be tested. Second, it must be shown that the deficits that are exhibited by dysphasics can in fact be accounted for in terms of these specific grammatical variables. There are current linguistic models in which rules that control agreement of abstract features are distinguished from rules that govern argument structure. The variables specified in this model appear to accord with those variables that are needed to provide a comprehensive account of the language produced by dysphasics.

One model of normal language acquisition (Pinker, 1984) suggested that children use the data from the lexical items they hear to construct hypotheses about the underlying rules of language that can be expected to apply to all of the language and not just to the particular items they have already encountered. The child acquiring language treats the incoming linguistic data not as significant in and of itself, but significant insofar as it provides evidence for general rules that can produce an infinite set of similar items. The problem for the child is to figure out these general rules from the individual items they hear. An analysis of dysphasic language suggests that they use a totally different strategy in learning language. The evidence indicates that the dysphasics actually do try to learn language from the surface data as they encounter it. They do not construct underlying recursive rules that can then be applied to all new cases, rather they learn language by learning the individual lexical items. Such an approach results in a final state grammar that produces surface strings that look very like the surface strings produced by other speakers. It is only by looking at the longitudinal development of this language and reconstructing the kinds of rules producing these surface forms that insights into the true nature of this disorder can be gained.

5.5. Conclusion

At the beginning of this chapter it was argued that if it could be shown that a specific disorder in the development of language was genetically inheritable, then this phenomenon would provide a direct natural experiment relevant to three fundamental hypotheses about language: innateness, species specificity, and modularity. It has been shown that evidence from a significant variety of sources strongly supports the hypothesis that some specific developmental disorders of language are genetic in origin and perhaps associated with an autosomally dominant gene. The neurological data cited provides a mechanism by means of which this is accomplished. A natural experiment, therefore, is available that can tell us something about the interaction of genes, brain structure, and the development of language. It has been argued further that the properties of dysphasic language can be fully understood only if the analysis of this language obeys certain very fundamental theoretical properties of linguistic analysis. A linguistic analysis based on these principles reveals that the disorder in dysphasia involves not merely the inability to produce surface forms, but a deeper inability to construct underlying abstract rules, including feature agreement rules. The question then is, what are the implications of this data for the theoretical hypotheses?

5.5.1. Innateness.　It would seem undeniable that the existence of a genetic deficit that interferes directly with the development of language strongly supports the hypothesis that the development of language is dependent on some innate properties of mind. Other evidence suggests that this gene controls for the development of neurological asymmetries and, if the appropriate asymmetries in the perisylvian region are not constructed, then normal language development cannot take place. It may very well be that this gene does not directly encode any properties of language, but rather controls for cerebral asymmetry in particular

regions of the brain. The data show clearly, however, that not all cerebral asymmetries need be equally impaired. In particular, the perisylvian region, and consequently language, may be selectively impaired in some individuals. It may be that a similar etiology underlies diverse cognitive disorders, from the development of language to the ability to visualize spatial relationships. However, even if it were true that other cognitive functions could be affected by this gene, it would still be the case that some specific aspects of normal language development could be shown to be under genetic control and therefore innate.

5.5.2. Species Specificity.
The relevance of this data to the species specificity hypothesis is both empirical and theoretical. An empirical approach to test the species specificity hypothesis has been to see if great apes could be taught a languagelike system. There has been vigorous debate about both the theoretical assumptions on which these experiments are based and the reliability and validity of these experiments themselves. But even if we credit the claims that have been made, the variables they have investigated may not be relevant to the species specificity hypothesis. The ape language studies have primarily concentrated on teaching the animals lexical reference and simple order constraints. It has been claimed that the animals can learn to use individual symbols to refer to objects and further that they can learn to construct ordered sequences of these symbols. Some have argued that the ability of the animals to learn these tasks shows that language in humans (which, it is claimed, involve these same tasks) must be continuous with the abilities in apes. The evidence from genetic dysphasia shows that the normal development of language involves the ability to construct rules of a very different kind from any that have been investigated in these animal experiments and these rules appear to be associated with some genetic factor. Therefore the relevance of the kinds of languagelike systems that have been claimed to be successfully taught to animals may have very little to do with the normal, innately controlled development of language. Therefore these experiments, though they might provide interesting insights into the cognitive abilities of apes, are orthogonal to the question of the evolutionary continuity of language.

At the theoretical level, it has been argued that there was not enough time for language to have evolved as a distinct property of humans. This issue has been addressed by Pinker and Bloom (1990) in some detail where they argue that there was both enough advantages and enough time for the separate evolution of language to have taken place. If, as appears to be the case, neurological development that can have consequences for the ability to construct symbolic rules in language is under genetic control and, furthermore, if this property of language does not appear to be present in ape language, then it would seem to be not unreasonable to suppose that at least some aspects of language could have evolved recently.

5.5.3. Modularity. The data from dysphasia provide evidence that subjects with this disorder cannot construct specific kinds of abstract rules in their underlying grammars, though they seem to have no problems with other parts of the grammar. The kinds of rules that they have problems with are rules that are hypothesized to constitute a well-defined subset of the innate language faculty. The fact that the specificity of this genetic disorder coincides with the hypothesized properties of the innate language faculty lends support to the existence of this faculty.

6. CONCLUSION

The fact that there appears to be a "natural experiment" in which genetic factors, perhaps even an autosomal dominant gene, are associated with a developmental impairment of language provides an opportunity to gain insights into the biological foundation of language. There is much more to be done. From the point of view of determining the linguistic properties of the disorder, we must extend our study of the family that we have been studying to other properties of language such as relativization and passivization. We must also see if the language deficits in this family are typical of familial language impairment. In addition, the investigation of the linguistic consequences of this disorder must be extended to languages with different properties than English or German so that the invariant properties of this disorder can be determined. The precise pattern of genetic inheritance of this disorder are still to be determined. From the neurological point of view, Plante et al.'s (1991) work to determine the neurological architecture must be continued using more recent three-dimensional imaging. In addition, new MRI techniques can begin to provide insights into the ways in which the neurological processing of language differs between the language-impaired and unimpaired populations. The work on providing a complete and comprehensive understanding of this genetic language disorder is just beginning. It is exciting work because it has the potential of answering some of the most fundamental questions about language.

REFERENCES

Borges-Osorio, M. R. L., & Salzano, F. M. (1985). Language disabilities in three twin pairs and their relatives. *Acta Geneticae Medicae et Gemellologiae (Roma), 34*, 95–100.

Clahsen, H. (1989). The grammatical characterization of developmental dysphasia. *Linguistics, 27*, 897–920.

Cohen, M., Campbell, R., & Yaghmai, F. (1989). Neuropathological abnormalities in developmental dysphasia. *Annals of Neurology, 25,* 567–570.

Crago, M. B., & Gopnik, M. (in press). From families to phenotypes: Research into the genetic basis of specific language impairment. In R. Watkins & M. Rice (Eds.), *New directions in specific language impairment.* Baltimore: Brookes.

Cromer, R. F. (1978). The basis of childhood dysphasia: A linguistic approach. In M. A. Wyke (Ed.), *Developmental dysphasia* (pp. 85–134). New York: Academic Press.

Crystal, D. (1987). *Clinical linguistics.* Baltimore: Edward Arnold.

Fodor, J. (1983). *The modularity of mind.* Cambridge, MA: MIT Press.

Gopnik, M. (1990a). Feature-blind grammar and dysphasia. *Nature, 344,* 715.

Gopnik, M. (1990b). Feature-blindness: A case study. *Language Acquisition, 1*(2), 139–164.

Gopnik, M. (1992, October). *Linguistic properties of genetic language impairment.* Paper presented at the meeting of American Association for the Advancement of Science, San Francisco.

Gopnik, M. (1993). *The absence of obligatory TENSE in subjects with genetic language impairment.* Manuscript submitted for publication.

Gopnik, M., & Crago, M. (1991). Familial aggregation of a developmental language disorder. *Cognition, 39,* 1–50.

Grodzinsky, Y. (1990). *Theoretical perspectives on language deficits.* Cambridge, MA: MIT Press.

Hurst, J. A., Baraitser, M., Auger, E., Graham, F., & Norell, S. (1990). An extended family with an inherited speech disorder. *Developmental Medicine and Child Neurology, 32,* 347–355.

Leonard, L. B. (1989). Language learnability and specific language impairment in children. *Applied Psycholinguistics, 10,* 179–202.

Leonard, L. B., Bortolini, U., Caselli, M. C., McGregor, K. K., & Sabbadini, L. (1992). Morphological deficits in children with specific language impairment: The status of features in the underlying grammar. *Language Acquisition, 2*(2), 151–179.

Marshall, J. C. (1989). The description and interpretation of acquired and developmental reading disorders. In A. M. Galaburda (Ed.), *From reading to neurons.* Cambridge, MA: MIT Press.

Panini. (600 B.C.). *Astadhyayi.*

Pinker, S. (1984). *Language learnability and language development.* Cambridge, MA: Harvard University Press.

Pinker, S., & Bloom, P. (1990). Natural language and natural selection. *Behavioral and Brain Sciences, 13,* 707–784.

Plante, E. (1990). Cerebral configurations among the parents and siblings of language-disordered boys. (Doctoral dissertation, University of Arizona, 1990). *Dissertation Abstracts International, 51,* 8B.

Plante, E., Swisher, L., & Vance, R. (1991). MRI findings in boys with specific language impairment. *Brain and Language, 41,* 52–66.

Samples, J. M., & Lane, V. W. (1985). Genetic possibilities in six siblings with specific language disorders. *ASHA, 27*(12), 27–31.

Tallal, P., Stark, R., Kallman, C., & Mellits, D. (1980). Developmental dysphasia: The relation between acoustic processing deficits and verbal processing. *Neuropsychologia, 18,* 273–284.

Tallal, P., Ross, R., & Curtiss, S. (1989a). Familial aggregation in specific language impairment. *Journal of Speech and Hearing Disorders, 54,* 167–173.

Tallal, P., Ross, R., & Curtiss, S. (1989b). Unexpected sex-ratios in families of language/learning-impaired children. *Neuropsychologia, 27*(7), 987–998.

Tomblin, J. B. (1989). Familial concentration of developmental language impairment. *Journal of Speech and Hearing Disorders, 54,* 287–295.

Tomblin, J. B. (1991). Examining the cause of specific language impairment. *Language, Speech, and Hearing Services in Schools, 22*, 69–74.

Travis, L. (1984). *Parameters and effects of word order variation*. Unpublished doctoral dissertation, MIT, Cambridge.

Udwin, O., & Yule, W. (1983). Imaginative play in language disordered children. *British Journal of Disorders of Communication, 18*, 197–205.

Yamada, J. E. (1990). *Laura: A case for the modularity of language*. Cambridge, MA: MIT Press.

CHAPTER TWELVE

The Relationship Between Language and Social Cognition: Lessons from Autism

Helen Tager-Flusberg
University of Massachusetts

1. THEORETICAL APPROACHES TO LANGUAGE DEVELOPMENT

For the past 20 years developmental psycholinguists have successively explored a number of theoretical approaches to account for the process of language development. Early research, which focused primarily on grammatical development, was motivated primarily by linguistic theory dominated by Chomsky's radical nativism (e.g., Chomsky, 1965). As more developmental psychologists joined the field, the scope of interest in language broadened, initially to include an emphasis on cognitive development—especially in relation to semantic development (e.g., Bates, Benigni, Bretherton, Camaioni, & Volterra, 1979; D. M. Morehead & A. Morehead, 1974; Sinclair, 1973)—deriving in large part from Piagetian theory (Piaget, 1962) and then to social interaction and pragmatics (e.g., Bates, 1976; Bruner, 1975). Very soon these broader perspectives were proposed by some as explanations for how all aspects of language are acquired, including syntax. On the cognitive view, syntactic categories could be reduced to semantic concepts, which, in turn, were built up from developing knowledge about the world (e.g., Sinclair, 1973). On the social-interactionist view, syntactic categories and rules could be discovered in the formats of nonverbal social interaction between the infant and caretaker (e.g., Bruner, 1975; Lock, 1980; Snow, 1979).

A considerable amount of research was stimulated by both the cognitive

359

and social-interactionist theories of language acquisition, however, limitations in their explanatory power and empirical validity were soon recognized. A number of critical reviews appeared (e.g., Bates, Bretherton, Beeghly-Smith, & McNew, 1982; Bates & Snyder, 1982; Cromer, 1988; Shatz, 1982) and currently the proposal that formal aspects of language acquisition can be fully explained by either cognitive or social developments is no longer seriously considered by the majority of researchers. Both the cognitive and social-interactionist theories are reductionist theories, assuming that syntactic categories and rules are isomorphic to cognitive or social constructs. Given the ample evidence that syntax is considerably more abstract and irreducible, and that children acquire structure-dependent rules based on syntactic categories at even the earliest stages of acquisition (e.g., P. Bloom, 1990; Levy, 1988; Valian, 1986), the simplistic position of cognitive and social-interactionist theories has been abandoned. As global explanations of all aspects of language acquisition these theories fail; formal aspects of language are domain specific and depend on some dedicated biological mechanisms (e.g., Curtiss & Yamada, 1981). Nevertheless, both the cognitive and social-interactionist perspectives continue to provide important interpretations for the acquisition of semantic and pragmatic knowledge, respectively.

2. THE SPECIFICITY HYPOTHESIS

In recent years a new version of the relationship between cognition and language, called the *specificity hypothesis*, has been proposed (Gopnik & Meltzoff, 1987b). According to this hypothesis there are important relationships between cognition and language but these relationships are not global in the ways conceived by Piaget (1952, 1962), for example. Instead, Gopnik and Meltzoff argued that there are highly specific relationships between particular conceptual achievements and the content or meanings (rather than formal categories) acquired. Their research focuses exclusively on language/cognition relationships in the one-word stage during which they have found empirical support for their view by looking at the close timing in development of related cognitive and lexical developments. Thus, Gopnik and Meltzoff cited evidence for unique relationships holding between object permanence and the production of words encoding disappearance, between means–end abilities and words encoding success or failure, and between categorization skills and the naming explosion (Gopnik & Meltzoff, 1985, 1986, 1987a). Undoubtedly, this perspective on the important relationships that exist between cognition and language is a productive approach to understanding aspects of lexical and semantic development.

Thus far research on the specificity hypothesis has been limited to investigations of normally developing infants who are at the one-word stage of language acquisition (but see also Cromer, 1968). There are obvious difficulties in looking for evidence of links between language and cognition during the toddler and preschool years when there are too many simultaneous developments in the social, cognitive, and linguistic domains to allow one to identify the kinds of highly specific relationships that Gopnik and Meltzoff considered. Yet the idea that aspects of conceptual development might be strongly linked to particular aspects of language development throughout this period is interesting and important, and clearly one task of developmental psychology is to identify such links.

3. THE ROLE OF ATYPICAL CHILDREN IN STUDYING LANGUAGE/COGNITION

An alternative way of investigating particular relationships between cognition and language is to focus on developmentally disordered children. Within the field of developmental psycholinguistics there has been a rich tradition of using evidence from atypical children to inform our theories of language acquisition (e.g., Curtiss, 1977; Lenneberg, 1967; Tager-Flusberg, in press; Yamada, 1990). Much of this work has provided strong evidence against classic cognitive theories of language acquisition, instead arguing for *dissociations* between cognition and language. Again, however, the emphasis of this body of research has been on global measures of language and cognition. It may nevertheless prove worthwhile to investigate more specific links, in line with the specificity hypothesis, by studying children who have circumscribed deficits in cognition, and looking for related problems in the domain of language.

The goal of this chapter is to pursue this approach by studying children with autism. This pervasive developmental disorder is characterized by developmental delays and deficits in social relatedness, in language and communication, and in repetitive behaviors and lack of imagination (APA, 1987). In recent years researchers have come to identify this syndrome with core deficits in the area of social cognition, specifically in the acquisition of a "theory of mind" (e.g., Baron-Cohen, Leslie, & Frith, 1985; Frith, 1989). This term, derived from Premack and Woodruff (1978), refers to the capacity to understand and employ mental state constructs, especially the role of mental states or propositional attitudes in the causation and explanation of human behavior. This chapter explores the relationship between this specific aspect of social cognition to language by investigating the relationship between deficits in the acquisition of a theory of mind and related deficits in language development in children with autism. Whereas earlier researchers have suggested that in normal children developments in communication and language are indicators of an emerging understanding of intentionality and mental states (e.g., Bretherton, McNew, & Beeghly-Smith, 1981; J. Brown & Dunn, 1991; Shatz, Wellman, & Silber, 1983), here deficits in both the social cognitive and language domains characteristic of autism are used to provide more convincing evidence that there are specific relationships between "theory of mind" and particular aspects of language use.

4. THE AUTISTIC SYNDROME

Autism was first identified by Kanner (1943), though it did not make its way into standard diagnostic manuals until about two decades ago. It is a rare disorder (or spectrum of disorders, see Frith, 1989; Gillberg, 1992) that is typically first manifest during the second or third year of life. It is generally regarded as a behaviorally defined syndrome reflecting underlying neurological impairment due to a wide variety of underlying medical etiologies (Coleman & Gillberg, 1985; Gillberg, 1990). The prominent diagnostic features of the syndrome in the social, linguistic, and cognitive/behavioral domains have come to be known as the "triad of impairments" (cf. Wing & Gould, 1979). It should also be noted that about three quarters of the population of autistic individuals are functionally mentally retarded. Among these, many do not develop any spontaneous or communicative language. Because of these additional problems, which complicate the picture of "pure" autism, studies focusing on more theoretical issues about the syndrome are limited to those autistic children that are higher functioning and not retarded.

Over the years there have been several attempts to identify the core psychological problem in autism that might explain the range of features that characterize this disorder. Most of these theories of autism failed, either because they did not account for some of the areas of dysfunction, or, more significantly, they provided an overly rich interpretation of the deficits and were not able to account for those aspects of psychological functioning that are often spared in autism. In 1985 a new psychological theory of autism was proposed by a group of researchers in London (Baron-Cohen et al., 1985), though it had been foreshadowed by Hobson (1981). These researchers argued that autistic children were specifically impaired in their acquisition of a theory of mind and that this deficit in acquiring a theory of mind could account for the range of social and communicative deficits that are typically found in autistic children (Baron-Cohen, 1988; Frith, 1989).[1]

Research on the normal development of a theory of mind has grown exponentially over the past decade and is currently viewed as one of the most significant aspects of conceptual change during the preschool years (Wellman, 1990). One of the hallmark tests of a theory of mind, defined as understanding that mental states are representational, is the ability to understand false beliefs, which requires the child to grasp the fact that beliefs, as representational states, may conflict with reality. By age 4 normal children have developed this understanding (e.g., Astington, Harris, & Olson, 1988; Butterworth, Harris, Leslie, & Wellman, 1991; Perner, 1991; Wellman, 1990; Whiten, 1990). Using an experimental paradigm devised by Wimmer and Perner (1983), Baron-Cohen and his colleagues tested autistic children's understanding of false beliefs. The task involved introducing a child to two characters in a story. One character, Sally, placed a desired object in one location and then left the scene. While she was gone, the second character, Anne, took the object from the original location and moved it to another location. When Sally returned, the child was asked to predict where she thinks the object is, or where she would look for it. Baron-Cohen et al. found that, in contrast to Down syndrome control children matched on verbal mental age and normal 4-year-olds, most of the autistic children failed to pass the false belief test, even though their level of functioning was well above 4 years of age. Since this initial study, there have been subsequent replications using a variety of tasks and procedures (see Baron-Cohen, 1993), which together confirm the view that autistic children have specific difficulties understanding false beliefs, and other related cognitive, or epistemic states.[2]

Epistemic states require the capacity for metarepresentation; that is,

---

[1]Whereas the theory of mind hypothesis has been able to account for many aspects of the social deficit in autism, and of problems in language and communication, especially in the areas of semantics and pragmatics, not all autistic features can be interpreted within a theory of mind framework. These include the repetitive behaviors or obsessional interests of autistic individuals and their unusual reactions to sensory stimuli. For a more detailed discussion of the limitations of the theory of mind hypothesis of autism, see Rutter (1993).

[2]There are some autistic children who do pass this kind of first-order false belief test, however Baron-Cohen (1989a) found that none could pass a second-order false belief test, which entails an understanding of statements such as "John thinks that Mary does not know where the object is located." Baron-Cohen argued that this suggests that autistic children are very delayed in their acquisition of a theory of mind and never reach the same end point as normal children. However, there is also some recent evidence to suggest that even those autistic children who pass a first-order task do so using different processing strategies than normal children and may therefore be considered somewhat deviant on theory of mind tasks (Riviere et al., 1991, cited in Leslie & Roth, 1993).

an understanding that the mind is a representation of reality (cf. Leslie, 1987; Perner, 1991). According to Leslie (1987; Leslie & Roth, 1993), for example, it is this domain-specific metarepresentational capacity that is impaired in autism, and this impairment accounts not only for their deficits in social and communicative functioning, but also in pretence play and joint attention. At the same time, some mental states, such as simple desires and emotions, do not require a metarepresentational capacity, and therefore they should not be specifically impaired in autism. Recent experimental studies have indeed shown that autistic children do not show deficits in their understanding of these nonrepresentational mental states (Baron-Cohen, 1991; Tan & Harris, 1990).

It is not difficult to see how deficits in understanding cognitive mental states would influence language capacities in autism. For example, autistic children have been shown to have great difficulty understanding sources of knowledge (Leslie & Frith, 1988); they fail to appreciate that different people may have access to different information (Perner, Frith, Leslie, & Leekam, 1989), and cannot engage in deceptive acts or tell lies (Sodian & Frith, 1993). These are all aspects of mental state understanding that have particular relevance for language. These deficits suggest that autistic children may fail to appreciate the fundamental nature of language as a means of communicating new information to other individuals, that language could be a source of gaining knowledge from others, or for providing information to others. Furthermore, effective communication entails taking into account the speaker's knowledge about the listener (e.g., status, knowledge, beliefs), and in turn, the listener must employ similar information to understand the speaker's intentions. Thus Sperber and Wilson (1986) argued that both speakers and listeners must employ a theory of mind to structure their ongoing discourse and therefore we may predict that autistic children will have great difficulty engaging in more complex discourse interactions.

5. LANGUAGE AND COMMUNICATION DEFICITS IN AUTISM

Over the past decade it has become widely recognized that autistic children's primary area of language dysfunction lies in the domain of pragmatics (Fay & Mermelstein, 1982; Paul, 1987; Schopler & Mesibov, 1985; Tager-Flusberg, 1981, 1989). Kanner's original papers on autism contained descriptions of the children's language, especially some of the aberrant features such as echolalia, pronominal reversals, noncommunicative speech, and difficulties with literal and nonliteral meaning (Kanner, 1943, 1946). Other kinds of problems that have been noted in autistic individuals include the absence or paucity of certain speech functions (Ball, 1978; Mermelstein, 1983; Wetherby, 1986), difficulty communicating information (Paul & Cohen, 1984), and problems with speaker/listener relations (Baltaxe, 1977). Autistic individuals also do not respond appropriately to indirect requests that they tend to interpret literally (Paul & Cohen, 1985), and they have great difficulties producing and interpreting more complex narrative discourse (Loveland & Tunali, 1993; Loveland, McEvoy, Tunali, & Kelley, 1990).

All these deficits fit broadly with the view that autistic children's language problems are related to their deficits in theory of mind. It is important to note that autism does not involve across-the board impairments in language. Some domains are quite spared, including both phonology and syntax (Bartolucci & Pierce, 1977; Bartolucci, Pierce, Streiner, & Eppel, 1976; Cantwell, Baker, & Rutter, 1978; Pierce & Bartolucci, 1977; Tager-Flusberg et al., 1990). Moreover, autistic children show similar developmental patterns in the acquisition of a lexicon (Tager-Flusberg et al., 1990) and in the development of word meanings that map onto concrete objects (Tager-Flusberg, 1985, 1986). Thus we see that the overall pattern of language functioning in autistic children is consistent with the hypothesis that their language deficit is related to their deficits in a theory of mind (Baron-Cohen, 1988; Frith, 1989; Tager-Flusberg, 1993).

Yet this picture of language deficit does not illustrate a close and unique relationship between this aspect of social cognition and language that would be demanded by the specificity hypothesis. In the remainder of this chapter we discuss three sets of data that do provide more convincing evidence that there is a precise relationship between mental state understanding and particular aspects of language usage. These analyses include an investigation of the mental state lexicons of autistic children, their communicative competence, and their acquisition of personal pronouns. For each of these analyses we focus not only on what is impaired in these areas of language functioning, but also on what is spared in order to highlight the degree of specificity that obtains between language and theory of mind.

6. LONGITUDINAL STUDY OF LANGUAGE DEVELOPMENT IN AUTISTIC CHILDREN

The data are drawn from a longitudinal study of six autistic boys and a control group of six children with Down syndrome, four boys and two girls, who were matched to the autistic children on age and mean length of utterance (MLU) at the start of the study (Tager-Flusberg et al., 1990).

TABLE 12.1
Subject Characteristics

Child	Age	IQ	MLU	Length of Time Followed (months)	Number of Visits
Autistic					
Stuart	3;4	61	1.17	15	8
Roger	3;9	105	2.31	22	10
Brett	5;8	108	3.74	22	10
Mark	7;7	75	1.46	26	13
Rick	4;7	94	1.73	22	11
Jack	6;9	91	3.03	25	12
Down Syndrome					
Charlie	3;3	46	1.21	13	6
Kate	4;1	65	2.98	12	6
Penny	5;1	63	2.69	15	7
Martin	5;4	47	1.63	24	11
Billy	5;7	49	1.68	25	13
Jerry	6;9	54	2.86	24	11

The children were all between 3 and 6 years of age and had begun using multiword utterances (see Table 12.1 for details). They were visited in their homes for about 1 hour every other month for between 1 and 2 years. During these home visits the children interacted with their mothers and the conversations were audiotaped and videotaped. Verbatim transcripts with rich context notes were prepared from the tapes in a form suitable for computerized analyses. In all, there are over 60 hours of tape from the autistic children and over 50 hours from the Down syndrome children. Although the groups were matched on language level, the autistic children had significantly higher IQ scores, based on a nonverbal measure of their intelligence (Leiter International Performance Scale), thus any deficits that we find in the autistic children's language cannot be related to their intellectual level.

7. MENTAL STATE LEXICONS

In the first analysis we explored the development of autistic children's *use* of mental state language (Tager-Flusberg, 1992). Four different categories of mental state were investigated: *desire, perception, emotion,* and *cognition*. In recent research autistic children have been found to be relatively unimpaired in their understanding of perception. In contrast to their poor performance on belief and other epistemic state tasks, autistic children can do well on direct visual perspective-taking tasks that do not entail a capacity for metarepresentation (Baron-Cohen, 1989c; Dawson & Fernald, 1987; Hobson, 1984; Tan & Harris, 1991). As noted earlier, there is also evidence suggesting that they are not impaired in their understanding of desire (Tan & Harris, 1991) or simple emotions (Baron-Cohen, 1991). This uneven profile of autistic children's understanding of different types of mental states leads to highly specific predictions about their use of these categories of mental state lexical terms. Thus, on the specificity hypothesis we predict that, compared to the Down syndrome children, the autistic children should be less likely to talk about cognitive states or attention, both of which are tied to the development of metarepresentational capacities.

For each category of mental state a set of lexical terms was compiled, based on lists used by previous researchers, and summary word lists drawn from the children's transcripts. A computer program (Systematic Analysis of Language Transcripts, SALT; Miller & Chapman, 1985) was then used to search the transcripts for utterances containing any of these terms. Any incomplete, imitated, or repeated utterance was excluded from further analysis. Table 12.2 lists the different mental state terms used by the children in this study.

The utterances containing lexical terms in the four categories of mental states were then coded according to their use within the conversational context, to distinguish true references to mental state from simple idiomatic, behavioral, descriptive, or conversational uses of the terms

TABLE 12.2
Mental State Terms Used by Autistic and Down Syndrome Subjects

DESIRE	care, want, wish[2]
PERCEPTION	
VISION	look, see, watch
HEARING	hear, listen, loud,[2] noise
TOUCH	cold, dry,[2] feel,[1] hard, hot, hurt, messy,[1] ouch, soak,[2] touch, wet, yucky[1]
SMELL	smell
TASTE	taste,[2] sour,[2] yucky[2]
EMOTION	
BEHAVIOR	cry, hug, kiss, laugh,[2] scream,[2] smile
EMOTION	angry,[1] bad,[2] better,[1] calm, fun, good,[1] happy, hate, like, love, mad,[1] sad, scare, surprise,[1] upset,[2] worry[2]
COGNITION	believe,[1] dream, figure,[1] forget,[1] guess,[1] idea,[1] know, make believe,[2] mean,[1] pretend, remember, think, trick,[1] understand, wonder

[1] Down syndrome children only
[2] Autistic children only

(J. Brown & Dunn, 1991; Shatz et al., 1983). For the desire and cognition terms, actual references to subjective mental states were distinguished from conversational uses (e.g., requests, utterances that mark degree of certainty, direct interaction or clarify previous utterances), or idioms (*I don't know*). For the perception terms, utterances about perception were classified according to the five senses (see Table 12.2), and utterances that called for joint attention rather than perception were categorized separately. Finally, for the category of emotion, true references to emotional states were distinguished from behavior terms (e.g., *cry, laugh*) and dispositions (e.g., *I like that box; A happy face*).

Table 12.3 shows the average frequency, per 1,000 utterances for the actual references to the different mental states in each category. Statistical analyses of these data revealed no significant differences between the groups for mental state reference to desire, emotion, and perception (summing across the five senses). Autistic children were, however, found to make significantly fewer calls for attention [$t (10) = 4.46, p < .001$], and mental state references to cognition [$t (10) = 1.98, p < .05$].

These findings confirm our prediction that autistic children would show a specific impoverishment in their talk about epistemic states. In addition to the overall reduction in the frequency of utterances referring to cognition and attention, Table 12.2 shows that the autistic children used 8 different cognitive terms compared to the 14 different cognitive terms used by the Down syndrome children. For each of the other categories autistic children used as many or more different lexical types than the Down syndrome controls. These findings suggest that, in-

TABLE 12.3
Mean Frequency of Uses of Lexical Terms to Refer to Mental States

	Autistic	Down Syndrome
	M	M
DESIRE	10.14	6.16
PERCEPTION		
Vision	10.95	4.19
Hearing	0.59	0.44
Touch	5.01	2.62
Smell	0.46	0.05
Taste	0.27	0.00
Attention	1.10	10.40[b]
EMOTION	0.56	0.25
COGNITION	0.17	1.66[a]

[a] $p < .05$
[b] $p < .001$

deed, autistic children have a highly specific impairment in their knowledge of mental states, and in their concomitant use of lexical terms referring to epistemic states.

The autistic children in this study were also deficient, compared to the Down syndrome children, in using utterances such as *Look!* or *Watch this Mom!* to call for attention. These findings fit well with accumulating evidence that autistic children are especially impaired in their ability to use nonverbal signals (such as pointing) as cues for joint attention (e.g., Landry & Loveland, 1988; Mundy & Sigman, 1989). Again, we find close parallels between the nonverbal deficit in joint attention, which has been theoretically related to later developments in theory of mind (see Baron-Cohen, 1989b; Leslie & Happe, 1989), and specific functional uses of language to call for attention using perceptual terms.

This analysis of spontaneous speech indicates that there is no across-the-board deficit or development in the acquisition of the language of mental states. On the contrary, these language data from autistic children coupled with the findings from experimental studies of conceptual knowledge in this area, suggest two distinct developmental strands: Desire, emotion, and perception form one strand, which is relatively unimpaired in autism, and attention and cognition form the second strand, which is quite specifically impaired. Consistent with the specificity hypothesis then, we can conclude that in autistic children the paucity of language for epistemic states mirrors an impaired ability to reflect on their own and other people's minds.

8. COMMUNICATIVE COMPETENCE

Autistic children and adults are notoriously difficult to engage in normal conversation. Typically conversations are limited to a small range of topics, revolving around the special obsessive interests of the autistic individual (Paul, 1987). It is generally not easy for a nonautistic listener to participate much in the ongoing discourse or as speaker, to maintain a more neutral socially appropriate topic over many turns. In the second analysis of the data from the longitudinal study we looked at what kinds of impairments and spared abilities autistic children show in their conversational skills, focusing on the ability to maintain an ongoing topic of discourse (Tager-Flusberg & Anderson, 1991). For this analysis we used a coding scheme developed by L. Bloom, Rocissano, and Hood (1976), who found that normal children showed increased ability to respond contingently (i.e., topically related) to their mothers' utterances by adding new relevant information as they became more advanced linguistically (as measured by increases in MLU).

From each child, four samples of spontaneous speech spanning 1 year of the study were selected for this analysis. For each sample MLU was computed using R. Brown's (1973) criteria. The coding scheme for analyzing the child's utterances for communicative competence was a hierarchical one with three levels. At the first level adjacent utterances (those child utterances following immediately after a mother's utterance) were distinguished from nonadjacent and unintelligible utterances. This level provides a measure of turn-taking ability. At the second level, only adjacent utterances were coded for their contingency to the mother's utterance—that is, whether or not the child's utterance was topically related (contingent or noncontingent)—thus maintaining the ongoing discourse topic. At the final level, contingent utterances were coded further to distinguish the different ways in which the child maintained the topic. These were divided into two groups: contingent utterances that did not add new information (including imitation, yes–no responses, responses to test questions, routines, recodes, and self-recodes); and those that did add new information (including expansion—adding to the content of the mother's utterance; self-expansion; alternation—adds new information by opposing content of mother's utterance; expatiation—adds to content of mother's utterance and introduces new related topic).

The analysis of the data revealed no differences between the autistic and Down syndrome children in the proportion of adjacent utterances. Between 70% and 80% of the utterances from the two groups of children were adjacent at all MLU stages. This suggests that there were no differences between the groups in their turn-taking abilities, one basic aspect of communicative competence. Turning now to the data from the second level of the coding scheme we found that autistic children were overall significantly less likely to produce contingent utterances $[F(1, 46) = 5.71, p < .03]$ and more likely to produce noncontingent utterances $[F(1, 46) = 7.4, p < .01]$. These data are presented by MLU stage in Fig. 12.1, which shows that the groups began to diverge in their ability to maintain the topic of discourse after MLU Stage II.

The final level of the coding scheme revealed more specifically what accounts for this interesting difference in communicative competence between the groups. In general, at all MLU stages both Down syndrome and autistic children used more of the categories of contingent discourse that did not add new information (see Table 12.4). Nevertheless, as MLU increased, the Down syndrome children began producing more utterances that added new information, especially expansions. The autistic children, on the other hand, showed no such increase. Instead, they continued to rely on simpler, developmentally less advanced means for communicating with their mothers. Overall, Down syndrome children used significantly more expansions $[F(1, 46) = 6.33, p < .02]$ and expatiations $[F(1, 46) = 5.31, p < .03]$ than the autistic children.

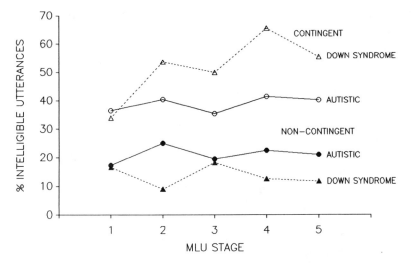

FIG. 12.1.   Distribution of contingent and noncontingent utterances.

The findings from the Down syndrome children parallel those reported for normal children by L. Bloom and her colleagues (1976). As their linguistic abilities increased (as measured by MLU), the Down syndrome children contributed more novel and substantive content to the ongoing discourse, telling their mothers new and more interesting information. Despite the parallel gains in linguistic ability made by the autistic children,

TABLE 12.4
Means for Categories of Contingent Responses for Autistic
and Down Syndrome Children

	Autistic		Down Syndrome	
	M	(s.d.)	M	(s.d.)
No New Information				
Yes/No	12.2*	(10.4)	27.9[b]	(15.5)
Routine	7.9	(6.6)	2.9[b]	(2.7)
Recode	5.3	(2.6)	4.5	(2.4)
Self-recode	4.1	(3.2)	2.9	(2.0)
Wh-response	29.3	(9.9)	14.3[b]	(8.3)
Imitation	28.9	(17.8)	24.8	(19.1)
New Information				
Expansion	7.8	(4.5)	16.6[a]	(10.2)
Self-expansion	2.2	(2.1)	2.3	(1.8)
Alternative	1.9	(2.7)	3.2	(2.1)
Expatiation	0.3	(0.8)	0.7[a]	(0.9)

*% of contingent utterances.
[a]$p < .05$. [b]$p < .01$

they did not show the same developmental changes in the content or style of their conversation. Whereas the autistic children's language became more sophisticated structurally, its substance did not change.

This deficit in the communicative development of autistic children suggests that they do not develop the understanding that they can be a source of new knowledge or information for their mothers. This language problem complements the specific difficulties that autistic children have in understanding sources of knowledge (Leslie & Frith, 1988) or that people may have access to different information (Perner et al., 1989) as measured by cognitive tasks. In contrast, turn-taking ability that does not require an understanding of other minds is not impaired in autistic children. Thus these findings from the study of communicative competence again provide quite strong support for the specificity hypothesis proposed here.

9. PERSONAL PRONOUNS

One striking linguistic error that autistic children are known to make involves the reversal of first- and second-person personal pronouns—calling oneself *you* and the listener *I* (Kanner, 1943). These errors have received a good deal of theoretical attention and widely different interpretations of their significance have been offered in the literature (e.g., Bettelheim, 1967; W. H. Fay, 1971; Oshima-Takane & Benaroya, 1989). Beyond anecdotal evidence and clinical descriptions there are almost no studies of pronoun errors in spontaneous speech and just a handful of studies involving autistic children's performance on structured experimental tasks (Bartak & Rutter, 1974; Hobson, Lee, & Chiat, 1991; Jordan, 1989; Silberg, 1978).

These kinds of pronoun reversal errors are also reported among nonautistic children, including blind children (e.g., Dunlea, 1989), and more rarely among normal children (e.g., Chiat, 1982). The source of these errors is generally considered to be pragmatic. For example, Chiat (1982) argued that reversal errors are evidence for a pragmatic difficulty in understanding shifting reference between the speaker and listener, given that the primarily function of first- and second-person pronouns is to mark these discourse roles. Development of the social-cognitive notion that speaker and listener denote distinct discourse roles entails a fundamental understanding that people have different conceptual perspectives (see also Hobson, 1990). Indirect support for this interpretation comes from Loveland (1984), who found that normal children consistently began using personal pronouns correctly only after they understood that different people have distinct spatial perspectives or points of view. This interpretation fits well with the idea that for the autistic child these linguistic problems with personal pronouns are closely related to conceptual deficits in developing a theory of mind.

To investigate this hypothesis further we analyzed the use of personal pronouns in the transcripts collected from the children in the longitudinal study. Using the entire corpus of transcripts from the autistic and Down syndrome children we extracted all examples of first- and second-person pronouns produced by the children, with the aid of the SALT program. Pronouns used in incomplete, imitated, repeated, or routine utterances were excluded from further analysis. Context, both verbal and nonverbal, was used to code whether a pronoun was used correctly or involved a reversal error.

Across all the subjects we found over 250 reversal errors among the autistic children but not one among the Down syndrome children. These errors represented approximately 13% of all the pronouns used by the autistic children, and some examples taken from each autistic child are shown in Table 12.5. Both first- and second-person errors were made across a range of cases. By the end of the longitudinal study two of the six autistic children no longer made these kinds of errors. These data suggest that indeed pronoun reversal errors are very widespread, perhaps universal, among young autistic children, but they may disappear as the children get older and linguistically or cognitively more advanced.

In every transcript we found autistic children used pronouns correctly alongside the errors they made. Thus autistic children were not always

TABLE 12.5
Examples of Pronoun Reversal Errors by Autistic Children

STUART:	You wet.
	You want candy.
	Errors: 6 Correct: 99
MARK:	Wednesday you sad.
	Errors: 14 Correct: 116
RICK	Hurt yourself.
	I write.
	Stan helped you.
	Errors: 31 Correct: 330
ROGER:	You did a good job.
	You're done.
	Errors: 95 Correct: 275
JACK:	You hit Debbie.
	Are you watching the video?
	Do you wanna go next Thursday?
	Errors: 65 Correct: 248
BRETT:	Help you please.
	I'm wearing glasses.
	You have to go to your father's.
	Errors: 47 Correct: 824

reversing pronouns; clearly there were some contexts in which errors were made, and there were others in which the children were able to use pronouns correctly to denote discourse roles. We investigated a number of possible alternatives to identify the contexts in which the children were most likely to make reversal errors. The clues to explaining when autistic children would reverse pronouns came from a pragmatic analysis of the children's utterances. Errors were concentrated in two main functional categories, which were relatively infrequent and gave the autistic children particular difficulty. One category involved utterances that introduced new information to the ongoing discourse that was about the child or mother. Providing new information in a conversation is difficult for autistic children and an aspect of communicative ability that we have already shown'is impaired. Autistic children are more used to having their mothers tell them information, not the reverse. The second category in which most reversal errors were concentrated involved responses to questions that the mother asked about herself, rather than about the child. Typically mothers asked the children questions about themselves; and only rarely asked questions about other people, especially their mothers. Thus, both these pragmatic contexts are complex for autistic children as they involve speaking about things that they typically listen to. In these contexts negotiating the speaker and listener discourse roles is especially difficult, requiring them to take a different conceptual perspective. Reversal errors are most likely to occur in these situations.

This analysis of the autistic children's pronoun reversal errors provides support for Chiat's pragmatic interpretation and fits well with the specificity hypothesis that language deficits in autism will be closely related to their deficits in understanding minds. Interestingly, we also analyzed the pronouns produced by both the autistic and Down syndrome children for the presence of a very different type of error—an error in case marking. Budwig (1989) showed that at certain stages normal children acquiring English frequently make errors such as *My do it* or *Me cool off*. Because the acquisition of case does not entail theory of mind knowledge, the specificity hypothesis would predict that autistic children should not make these errors more frequently than the Down syndrome controls. In fact there were only 2 such errors produced by two children in the autistic group compared to 28 errors from five of the six Down syndrome children. All other uses of first- and second-person pronouns in nominative, accusative, and possessive case were correct, indicating that the autistic children had no special problems acquiring the case system. This contrast in the infrequent number of case errors and the relatively frequent perspective errors confirms the specificity of the problem that autistic children have in acquiring the pronoun system.

10. CONCLUSIONS

The study of developmentally disordered children has much to contribute to our understanding of language acquisition. Studies of brain-damaged, mentally retarded, and other atypical children have been instrumental in shaping and constraining our theories (cf. Curtiss, 1977; Lenneberg, 1967), particularly by highlighting the important contributions of biological factors in acquisition, and in providing crucial evidence about the limited role played by nonlinguistic cognitive factors (e.g., Cromer, 1991; Yamada, 1990). But thus far, we have used evidence from these various populations of children in very general ways, reflecting perhaps the very global ways that theories are often discussed in the field of language acquisition.

The recent introduction of the specificity hypothesis by Gopnik & Meltzoff (1987b) offered us a more fine-grained analysis of the role that cognitive factors may play in language acquisition, specifically the relationship that holds between particular conceptual achievements and related semantic developments. In this chapter I have argued that a parallel approach can be taken with evidence drawn from one developmentally disordered population, namely, autism. Because of the advances made in our understanding of the underlying social cognitive deficit in this syndrome, autistic children provide a unique opportunity for testing the hypothesis that distinctive circumscribed deficits in social cognition are closely related to particular impairments in language.

This hypothesis was confirmed in the three studies discussed in this chapter. These studies indicated that deficits in the acquisition of knowledge about mental states, or a theory of mind, are specifically linked to narrowly defined deficits in lexical development, in the acquisition of certain aspects of communicative competence, and in the development of pragmatic knowledge about discourse roles. In each case, the linguistic impairment did not spill over into closely related developments that do not entail an understanding of minds.

The studies and interpretation discussed here offer an expanded perspective on the specificity hypothesis. Children acquire a full-fledged, representational theory of mind long after the one-word stage of language acquisition. Thus these studies investigated aspects of language that develop in later stages. Furthermore, theory of mind as an aspect of social cognition is tied not only to semantic development (cf. the study of mental state lexicons), but more importantly to particular aspects of pragmatic development. In turn, the theory of mind hypothesis of autism allows us to define more precisely, and more narrowly, the nature of the pragmatic deficits found in this population.

One question remains: What is the direction of the relationship between language and cognition according to the specificity hypothesis? Gopnik and Meltzoff (1986, 1987b) found that for the particular semantic/conceptual relationships that they investigated, in some children the conceptual developments occurred just prior to the appearance of the related words, whereas in other children the linguistic developments happened first. On the basis of their findings, they suggested that there is a two-way relationship between language and cognition. In this chapter we have looked for parallels between deficits in cognition and deficits in language, thus we do not have the kind of timing data that Gopnik and Meltzoff used to reach their conclusion. Nevertheless, in the case of autism we know that problems in understanding other minds predate the onset of language. Even in prelinguistic communication autistic children show impairments that are theoretically related to later developments in both language and theory of mind (Gomez, Sarria, & Tamarit, 1993). It is likely that in autism the underlying problem is in social cognition and this deficit in acquiring a theory of mind is, in turn, reflected in their language.

It remains to be seen whether high functioning verbal autistic children can use language as means by which they can begin to develop some understanding of mental states. Perhaps some autistic children, those few who pass theory of mind tests later on (see, e.g., Baron-Cohen et al., 1985), learn to use the transparent syntactic forms of propositional attitudes (especially complement constructions) and thereby develop some understanding of mental states. If research bears out this hypothesis we would have an even stronger case for the close and highly specific connection that exists between theory of mind and language.

ACKNOWLEDGMENT

Preparation of this chapter was supported by a grant from the National Institute on Deafness and Other Communication Disorders (1RO1 DC 01234-01).

REFERENCES

American Psychiatric Association (1987). *Diagnostic and statistical manual of mental disorders: DSM IIIR*. Washington, DC: American Psychiatric Association.

Astington, J., Harris, P. L., & Olson, D. (1988). *Developing theories of mind*. Cambridge: Cambridge University Press.

Ball, J. (1978). *A pragmatic analysis of autistic children's language with respect to aphasic and normal language development*. Unpublished doctoral dissertation, Melbourne University.

Baltaxe, C. A. M. (1977). Pragmatic deficits in the language of autistic adolescents. *Journal of Pediatric Psychology, 2*, 176–180.

Baron-Cohen, S. (1988). Social and pragmatic deficits in autism: Cognitive or affective? *Journal of Autism and Developmental Disorders, 18*, 379–402.

Baron-Cohen, S. (1989a). The autistic child's theory of mind: A case of specific developmental delay. *Journal of Child Psychology and Psychiatry, 30*, 285–297.

Baron-Cohen, S. (1989b). Joint attention deficits in autism: Towards a cognitive analysis. *Development and Psychopathology, 1*, 185–189.

Baron-Cohen, S. (1989c). Perceptual role-taking and proto-declarative pointing in autism. *British Journal of Developmental Psychology, 7*, 113–127.

Baron-Cohen, S. (1991). Do people with autism understand what causes emotion? *Child Development, 62*, 385–395.

Baron-Cohen, S. (1993). From attention-goal psychology to belief-desire psychology: The development of a theory of mind and its dysfunction. In S. Baron-Cohen, H. Tager-Flusberg, & D. J. Cohen (Eds.), *Understanding other minds: Perspectives from autism* (pp. 59–82). Oxford: Oxford University Press.

Baron-Cohen, S., Leslie, A., & Frith, U. (1985). Does the autistic child have "theory of mind"? *Cognition, 21*, 37–46.

Bartak, L., & Rutter, M. (1974). The usage of personal pronouns by autistic children. *Journal of Autism and Childhood Schizophrenia, 4*, 217–222.

Bartolucci, G., & Pierce, S. (1977). A preliminary comparison of phonological development in autistic, normal, and mentally retarded subjects. *British Journal of Disorders of Communication, 12*, 137–147.

Bartolucci, G., Pierce, S., Streiner, D., & Eppel, D. (1976). Phonological investigation of verbal autistic and mentally retarded children. *Journal of Autism and Childhood Schizophrenia, 6*, 303–316.

Bates, E. (1976). *Language and context*. New York: Academic Press.

Bates, E., Benigni, L., Bretherton, I., Camaioni, L., & Volterra, V. (1979). *The emergence of symbols: Cognition-communication in infancy*. New York: Academic Press.

Bates, E., Bretherton, I., Beeghly-Smith, M., & McNew, S. (1982). Social bases of language development. In H. W. Reese & L. P. Lipsitt (Eds.), *Advances in child development and behavior* (Vol. 16). New York: Academic Press.

Bates, E., & Snyder, L. (1982). The cognitive hypothesis in language development. In I. Uzgiris & J. McV. Hunt (Eds.), *Research with scales of psychological development in infancy* (pp. 137–161). Urbana-Champaign, IL: University of Illinois Press.

Bettelheim, B. (1967). *The empty fortress*. New York: Free Press.

Bloom, L., Rocissano, L., & Hood, L. (1976). Adult-child discourse: developmental interaction between information processing and linguistic knowledge. *Cognitive Psychology, 8*, 521–552.

Bloom, P. (1990). Syntactic distinctions in child language. *Journal of Child Language, 17*, 343–355.

Bretherton, I., McNew, S., & Beeghly-Smith, M. (1981). Early person knowledge as expressed in verbal and gestural communication: When do infants acquire a "theory of mind"? In M. E. Lamb & L. R. Sherrod (Eds.), *Infant social cognition*. Hillsdale, NJ: Lawrence Erlbaum Associates.

Brown, J., & Dunn, J. (1991). "You can cry mum": The social and developmental implications of talk about internal states. *British Journal of Developmental Psychology, 9*, 237–256.

Brown, R. (1973). *A first language*. Cambridge, MA: Harvard University Press.

Bruner, J. (1975). From communication to language: A psychological perspective. *Cognition, 3*, 255–287.

Budwig, N. (1989). The linguistic marking of agentivity and control in child language. *Journal of Child Language, 16*, 263–284.

Butterworth, B., Harris, P. L., Leslie, A., & Wellman, H. (Eds.). (1991). *Perspectives on the child's theory of mind.* Oxford: Oxford University Press.

Cantwell, D., Baker, & Rutter, M. (1978). A comparative study of infantile autism and specific developmental receptive language disorder: IV: Analysis of syntax and language function. *Journal of Child Psychology and Psychiatry, 19*, 351–362.

Chiat, S. (1982). If I were you and you were me: The analysis of pronouns in a pronoun-reversing child. *Journal of Child Language, 9*, 359–379.

Chomsky, N. (1965). *Syntactic structures.* Cambridge, MA: MIT Press.

Coleman, M., & Gillberg, C. (1985). *The biology of the autistic syndromes.* New York: Praeger.

Cromer, R. (1968). *The development of temporal reference during the acquisition of language.* Unpublished doctoral dissertation, Harvard University.

Cromer, R. (1988). The cognition hypothesis revisited. In F. Kessel (Ed.), *The development of language and language researchers* (pp. 223–248). Hillsdale, NJ: Lawrence Erlbaum Associates.

Cromer, R. (1991). *Language and thought in normal and handicapped children.* Oxford: Blackwell.

Curtiss, S. (1977). *Genie: A psycholinguistic study of a modern day "wild child."* New York: Academic Press.

Curtiss, S., & Yamada, J. (1981). Selectively intact grammatical development in a retarded child. *UCLA Working Papers in Cognitive Linguistics, 3*, 61–91.

Dawson, G., & Fernald, M. (1987). Perspective-taking ability and its relationship to the social behavior of autistic children. *Journal of Autism and Developmental Disorders, 17*, 487–498.

Dunlea, A. (1989). *Vision and the emergence of meaning: Blind and sighted children's early language.* Cambridge: Cambridge University Press.

Fay, D., & Mermelstein, R. (1983). Language in infantile autism. In S. Rosenberg (Ed.), *Handbook of applied psycholinguistics.* New York: Wiley.

Fay, W. H. (1971). On normal and autistic pronouns. *Journal of Speech and Hearing Disorders, 36*, 242–249.

Frith, U. (1989). *Autism: Explaining the enigma.* Oxford: Blackwell.

Gillberg, C. (1990). Autism and pervasive developmental disorders. *Journal of Child Psychology and Psychiatry, 31*, 99–119.

Gillberg, C. (1992). Autism and autistic-like conditions: subclasses among disorders of empathy. *Journal of Child Psychology and Psychiatry, 33*, 813–842.

Gomez, J. C., Sarria, E., & Tamarit, J. (1993). The comparative study of early communication and theories of mind: ontogeny, phylogeny, and pathology. In S. Baron-Cohen, H. Tager-Flusberg, & D. J. Cohen (Eds.), *Understanding other minds: Perspectives from autism* (pp. 397–426). Oxford: Oxford University Press.

Gopnik, A., & Meltzoff, A. (1985). From people to plans to objects: Changes in the meanings of early words and their relation to cognitive development. *Journal of Pragmatics, 9*, 495–512.

Gopnik, A., & Meltzoff, A. (1986). Relations between semantic and cognitive development in the one-word stage: The specificity hypothesis. *Child Development, 57*, 1040–1053.

Gopnik, A., & Meltzoff, A. (1987a). The development of categorization in the second year and its relation to other cognitive and linguistic developments. *Child Development, 58*, 1523–1531.

Gopnik, A., & Meltzoff, A. (1987b). Early semantic developments and their relationship to object permanence, means-end understanding, and categorization. In K. E. Nelson & A. van Kleeck (Eds.), *Children's language* (Vol. 6, pp. 60–69). Hillsdale, NJ: Lawrence Erlbaum Associates.

Hobson, R. P. (1981). The autistic child's concept of persons. In D. Park (Ed.), *Proceedings of the 1981 international conference on autism.* Washington, DC: National Society for Children and Adults with Autism.

Hobson, R. P. (1984). Early childhood autism and the question of egocentrism. *Journal of Autism and Developmental Disorders, 14,* 85–104.

Hobson, R. P. (1990). On the origins of self and the case of autism. *Development and Psychopathology, 2,* 163–181.

Hobson, R. P., Lee, A., & Chiat, S. (1991, April). *Autism and "the self": An experimental study of personal pronoun comprehension and use.* Paper presented at the Biennial Meeting of the Society for Research in Child Development, Seattle, WA.

Jordan, R. (1989). An experimental comparison of the understanding and use of speaker-addressee personal pronouns in autistic children. *British Journal of Disorders of Communication, 24,* 169–179.

Kanner, L. (1943). Autistic disturbances of affective contact. *Nervous Child, 2,* 217–250.

Kanner, L. (1946). Irrelevant and metaphorical language in early childhood autism. *American Journal of Psychiatry, 103,* 242–246.

Landry, S., & Loveland, K. A. (1988). Communication behaviors in autism and developmental language delay. *Journal of Child Psychology and Psychiatry, 29,* 621–634.

Lenneberg, E. (1967). *Biological foundations of language.* New York: Wiley.

Leslie, A. M. (1987). Pretence and representation: The origins of "theory of mind." *Psychological Review, 94,* 412–426.

Leslie, A. M., & Frith, U. (1988). Autistic children's understanding of seeing, knowing, and believing. *British Journal of Developmental Psychology, 4,* 315–324.

Leslie, A. M., & Happe, F. (1989). Autism and ostensive communication: The relevance of metarepresentation. *Development and Psychopathology, 1,* 205–212.

Leslie, A. M., & Roth, D. (1993). What autism teaches us about metarepresentation. In S. Baron-Cohen, H. Tager-Flusberg, & D. J. Cohen (Eds.), *Understanding other minds: Perspectives from autism* (pp. 83–111). Oxford: Oxford University Press.

Levy, Y. (1988). On the early learning of formal grammatical systems: Evidence from studies of the acquisition of gender and countability. *Journal of Child Language, 15,* 179–188.

Lock, A. (Ed.). (1980). *The guided reinvention of language.* London: Academic Press.

Loveland, K. A. (1984). Learning about points of view: Spatial perspective and the acquisition of I/you. *Journal of Child Language, 11,* 535–556.

Loveland, K. A., & Tunali, B. (1993). Understanding other persons: Narrative language in autism. In S. Baron-Cohen, H. Tager-Flusberg, & D. J. Cohen (Eds.), *Understanding other minds: Perspectives from autism* (pp. 247–266). Oxford: Oxford University Press.

Loveland, K. A., McEvoy, R., Tunali, B., & Kelley, M. L. (1990). Narrative story telling in autism and Down's syndrome. *British Journal of Developmental Psychology, 8,* 9–23.

Mermelstein, R. (1983, October). *The relationship between syntactical and pragmatic development in autistic, retarded, and normal children.* Paper presented at the Eighth Annual Boston University Conference on Language Development, Boston.

Miller, J., & Chapman, R. (1985). *Systematic analysis of language transcripts: User's guide.* Madison, WI: University of Wisconsin Language Analysis Laboratory.

Morehead, D. M., & Morehead, A. (1974). From signal to sign: A Piagetian view of thought and language during the first two years. In R. L. Schiefelbusch & L. L. Lloyd (Eds.), *Language perspectives: Acquisition, retardation, and intervention* (pp. 153–190). Baltimore: University Park Press.

Mundy, P., & Sigman, M. (1989). The theoretical implications of joint-attention deficits in autism. *Development and Psychopathology, 1,* 173–183.

Oshima-Takane, Y., & Benaroya, D. (1989). An alternative view of pronominal errors in autistic children. *Journal of Autism and Developmental Disorders, 19,* 73–85.

Paul, R. (1987). Communication. In D. J. Cohen & A. M. Donnellan (Eds.), *Handbook of autism and pervasive developmental disorders* (pp. 61–84). New York: Wiley.

Paul, R., & Cohen, D. J. (1984). Responses to contingent queries in adults with mental retardation and pervasive developmental disorders. *Applied Psycholinguistics, 5,* 349–357.

Paul, R., & Cohen, D. J. (1985). Comprehension of indirect requests in adults with mental retardation and pervasive developmental disorders. *Journal of Speech and Hearing Research, 28,* 475–479.

Perner, J. (1991). *Understanding the representational mind.* Cambridge, MA: Bradford Books, MIT Press.

Perner, J., Frith, U., Leslie, A., & Leekam, S. (1989). Exploration of the autistic child's theory of mind: Knowledge belief and communication. *Child Development, 60,* 689–700.

Piaget, J. (1952). *The origins of intelligence in children.* New York: Norton.

Piaget, J. (1962). *Play, dreams, and imitation in childhood.* New York: Norton.

Pierce, S., & Bartolucci, G. (1977). A syntactic investigation of verbal autistic, mentally retarded, and normal children. *Journal of Autism and Childhood Schizophrenia, 7,* 121–134.

Premack, D., & Woodruff, G. (1978). Does the chimpanzee have a theory of mind? *The Behavioral and Brain Sciences, 1,* 516–526.

Rutter, M. (1993). Thinking and relationships: Mind and brain (some reflections on theory of mind and autism). In S. Baron-Cohen, H. Tager-Flusberg, & D. J. Cohen (Eds.), *Understanding other minds: Perspectives from autism* (pp. 481–504). Oxford: Oxford University Press.

Schopler, E., & Mesibov, G. (1985). *Communication problems in autism.* New York: Plenum.

Shatz, M. (1982). On mechanisms of language acquisition: Can features of the communicative environment account for development? In L. Gleitman & E. Wanner (Eds.), *Language acquisition: The state of the art.* New York: Cambridge University Press.

Shatz, M., Wellman, H., & Silber, R. (1983). The acquisition of mental verbs: a systematic investigation of first references to mental state. *Cognition, 14,* 301–321.

Silberg, J. L. (1978). The development of pronoun usage in the psychotic child. *Journal of Autism and Childhood Schizophrenia, 8,* 413–425.

Sinclair, H. (1973). Language acquisition and cognitive development. In T. E. Moore (Ed.), *Cognitive development and the acquisition of language* (pp. 9–26). New York: Academic Press.

Sodian, B., & Frith, U. (1993). The theory of mind deficit in autism: Evidence from deception. In S. Baron-Cohen, H. Tager-Flusberg, & D. J. Cohen (Eds.), *Understanding other minds: Perspectives from autism* (pp. 158–177). Oxford: Oxford University Press.

Sperber, D., & Wilson, D. (1986). *Relevance: Communication and cognition.* Cambridge, MA: Harvard University Press.

Snow, C. A. (1979). The role of social interaction in language acquisition. In W. A. Collins (Ed.), *Children's language and communication.* Hillsdale, NJ: Lawrence Erlbaum Associates.

Tager-Flusberg, H. (1981). On the nature of linguistic functioning in early infantile autism. *Journal of Autism and Developmental Disorders, 11,* 45–56.

Tager-Flusberg, H. (1985). The conceptual basis for referential word meaning in children with autism. *Child Development, 56,* 1167–1178.

Tager-Flusberg, H. (1986). Constraints on the representation of word meaning: Evidence from autistic and mentally retarded children. In S. A. Kuczaj & M. Barrett (Eds.), *The development of word meaning* (pp. 139–166). New York: Springer-Verlag.

Tager-Flusberg, H. (1989). A psycholinguistic perspective on language development in the autistic child. In G. Dawson (Ed.), *Autism: Nature, diagnosis and treatment* (pp. 92–115). New York: Guilford Press.

Tager-Flusberg, H. (1992). Autistic children's talk about psychological states: Deficits in the early acquisition of a theory of mind. *Child Development, 63,* 161–172.

Tager-Flusberg, H. (1993). What language reveals about the understanding of minds in children with autism. In S. Baron-Cohen, H. Tager-Flusberg, & D. J. Cohen (Eds.), *Understanding other minds: Perspectives from autism* (pp. 138–157). Oxford: Oxford University Press.

Tager-Flusberg, H. (Ed.). (in press). *Constraints on language acquisition: Studies of atypical children.* Hillsdale, NJ: Lawrence Erlbaum Associates.

Tager-Flusberg, H., & Anderson, M. (1991). The development of contingent discourse ability in autistic children. *Journal of Child Psychology and Psychiatry, 32,* 1123–1134.

Tager-Flusberg, H., Calkins, S., Nolin, T., Baumberger, T., Anderson, M., & Chadwick-Dias, A. (1990). A longitudinal study of language acquisition in autistic and Down syndrome children. *Journal of Autism and Developmental Disorders, 20,* 1–21.

Tan, J., & Harris, P. L. (1991). Autistic children understand seeing and wanting. *Development and Psychopathology, 3,* 163–174.

Wellman, H. (1990). *Children's theories of mind.* Cambridge, MA: Bradford Books, MIT Press.

Wetherby, A. (1986). Ontogeny of communicative functions in autism. *Journal of Autism and Developmental Disorders, 16,* 295–316.

Whiten, A. (1990). *Natural theories of mind.* Oxford: Blackwell.

Wimmer, H., & Perner, J. (1983). Beliefs about beliefs: Representation and constraining function of wrong beliefs in young children's understanding of deception. *Cognition, 13,* 103–128.

Wing, L., & Gould, J. (1979). Severe impairments of social interaction and associated abnormalities in children: Epidemiology and classification. *Journal of Autism and Developmental Disorders, 9,* 11–29.

Valian, V. V. (1986). Syntactic categories in the speech of young children. *Developmental Psychology, 22,* 562–579.

Yamada, J. (1990). *Laura: A case for the modularity of language.* Cambridge, MA: Bradford Books, MIT Press.

CHAPTER THIRTEEN

Concluding Chapter: Modularity Reconsidered

Yonata Levy
The Hebrew University
Jerusalem

As I read and reread the chapters of the book, I was aware of two things: First, the chapters speak for themselves and there is no need to reiterate what the authors have so eloquently conveyed in their writings. Second, the issue addressed in all the chapters, whether directly or indirectly, is that of modularity. I have therefore taken the opportunity to reexamine the merit of the evidence that has been brought to bear on the modularity thesis. My concern is chiefly with data from pathology. Within the literature on acquisition, the term *modularity* has been affected by the notion of modules in Chomsky's theory of Government and Binding (GB). The modules of GB are Theta-theory, Case theory, Control, Binding, the Empty Category principle and X-theory. Acquisition data that can be explained in terms of principles governing one of these modules enhance the plausibility of the particular principles, as well as the specific modular organization of language, as stated in this model. More generally, modularity has been used loosely to refer to the presence of formal syntactic knowledge in children that seems independent of meaning considerations. Such studies in normal, as well as in pathological, populations of children address the issue of internal modularity, that is, the modular organization of the language system. For the purpose of illustration, let me mention a few studies in pathology that have looked at specific subsystems within grammar and have argued for or against internal modularity.

Roeper and Seymour (chap. 10) examine barriers on long and short distance binding in a language-impaired child. It is argued that this child knew the binding conditions but had serious difficulties with relative clauses. Similar problems, though less severe, were found in normal children. Gopnik (chap. 11) considers a multigenerational family in which there is a large number of dysphasics, all of whom have a characteristic pattern of deficiency in marking plurality. Gopnik describes the deficit as affecting the Number feature of the AGR[eement] node. She notes other difficulties with features such as Tense and Aspect and possibly Aux, which suggest that, in these patients, grammatical properties of AGR differ from the normal. Our own study (Levy, Amir, & Shalev, 1992) concerned the development of Hebrew morphology in a child with a congenital, left-hemisphere brain lesion. A longitudinal, naturalistic study of the development of Hebrew in this child showed that aspects of morphology were independent of semantics and pragmatics and were clearly more advanced. Tager-Flusberg (chap. 12) studied autism and found connections between a deficient theory of mind in autism and specific problems in the language that related to it. Her data support the contention that distinctive, circumscribed deficits in social cognition are closely related to particular impairments in language. These data support the specificity hypothesis (Gopnik & Meltzoff, 1986), which argues for specific dependencies between cognition and language.

Studies such as these speak to the issue of the internal organization of language. But there is another sense to modularity, that which draws from Fodor's (1983) model and argues for the autonomy of the language faculty within the human mind. It is this latter idea, which I spell with a capital M, Modularity, that is the concern of the present chapter. The question of Modularity is discussed with specific emphasis on language in children with congenital pathologies. Data from these populations have been crucial in arguments supporting the Modularity of language. I review the major findings in this area and conclude that these by-now-famous cases are not instances of Modularity. Consequently, they do not support or detract from the plausibility of Modularity. For the most part, they are simply irrelevant to it. They remain, nevertheless, extremely important because they pose intriguing problems for models of access and use.

The vision of the mind as comprised of relatively seamless, all-purpose central processes, along with a number of distinct, highly specialized, structurally idiosyncratic input modules has been reintroduced into psychology by Fodor (1983). The hypothesis states the following: Whereas major cognitive tasks—such as long-term memory and problem solving—are carried out by nonmodular, neurally scattered, relatively slow central processes, other, primarily input, systems are modular. Modules are characterized by the following cluster of properties: domain specificity, mandatoriness, informational encapsulation, autonomy of computation, speed of operation, lack of access by other systems to intermediate levels of representations, shallow output, neural localization, and susceptibility to characteristic breakdown. Modules are input driven. They are encapsulated from much of the individual's background knowledge. The higher the cognitive process, the less modular it is, because high cognitive functions necessitate interactions between superficially dissimilar domains. Fodor's prime examples of modules are language processing and visual perception.

Being an empirical claim, the Modularity hypothesis defines a research agenda. For example, the aforementioned list of properties defining modules present features that may or may not co-occur as a cluster. Research will show whether these properties are correlated or may, in fact, exist independently of each other. One could ask whether these are necessary features defining Modularity, whether there are logical entailments between them, or if there is more than one sense in which the mind can be thought of as being modular.

Fodor (1985) viewed Modularity as a statement of the separability of perception from cognition. What are the implications of such a distinction for language? Can the linguistic realm be exhaustively represented by the perceptual mechanism of language? Surely it cannot. The language faculty viewed in its multiple functions is more appropriately conceived of as a central system than as an input system. Does this necessarily mean that it is nonmodular (Higgenbotham, 1987)? Clearly, if the defining characteristics of Modularity include all of the features listed by Fodor (1983), then language must be thought of as nonmodular. Yet, there may be other possibilities. For example, although informational encapsulation logically entails domain specificity, the reverse is not true. Thus, although categories and rules that the grammar operates with may be specifically linguistic, they may partially overlap with other domains, or there may be intermediate levels of representations feeding into other domains, or requiring information other than linguistic. If one posits domain specificity, but not informational encapsulation, than Modularity of language in its complexity may be a possibility worth investigating.

Fodor's (1983) claim with regard to language can also be interpreted as referring primarily to the work of the parser. If so, then it becomes akin to the familiar notion of the autonomy of syntax, as argued for by Chomsky (1965) since the advent of generative grammar. Discussions of the Modularity of syntax and the nature of the parser typically bring up problems concerning notions such as reference and logical scope. Can those be made sense of independent of semantic considerations? According to Chomsky (1986), when notions such as reference and scope are used internal to the study of mental representations they are syntactic. Scope and reference become semantic when they are given an extra-mental interpretation. In other words, Chomsky (1986) distinguished between elements of the linguistic system that are mental representations, and their interpretations, which have to do with reality in the world. However, it is not clear how one can adopt this distinction in the case of abstract concepts, which although they have to do with extra-mental reality, there is a semantics associated with them (Macnamara, 1989).

It seems that if one adopts Chomsky's aforementioned distinction between syntax and nonsyntax, namely, if the distinction is between symbol–symbol relationships and symbol–world relationships, without distinguishing types of symbol–symbol systems, then one is left with a division between syntax and pragmatics and essentially without a well-defined domain of semantics. The theoretical gains from such a position have yet to be spelled out. In the context of the present discussion, extending the notion of syntax to include what has hitherto been referred to as the semantics of linguistic entities, obscures the idea of informational encapsulation. It further removes linguistic models from a basic psychological intuition, namely, that one cannot conceive of language comprehension and production independent of meaning.

What exactly is being claimed about the mind when Modularity is invoked? Fodor's model is a processing model that defines types of operations and states constraints on processing information. There are at least two ways in which one can conceive of an instantiation of a processing model—it may be fixed in the mental architecture in such a way that it will be obligatorily triggered by the relevant input, or it may be an operational option that is available to the mind if circumstances favor it. Fodor (1983) seemed to opt for the first possibility: The expectation of localization of functions—from which follows the prediction that in cases of well-defined, localized insults to the brain, there will be a characteristic breakdown—suggests that Fodor considers Modularity as a structural property of the brain. But Modularity can be construed as a description of the ways in which the mind can analyze perceptual input when speed and automaticity are required. It is conceivable that the human mind has the option of working in an informationally encapsulated way, giving priority to domain-specific rules and operations to achieve speed and assure automatic analyzability.

Thus, one may envisage two different "pictures of the mind"—in one the properties that Fodor listed are fixed in the mind's "hardware" and become operative when triggered by the relevant input. In the second picture, Modularity is a processing option that the mind can select. It may be task specific or it may be modality specific or it may depend on the circumstances in which the task is performed. In this case neural specificity will have a different sense than the straightforward anatomical interpretation. For example, it may imply a capacity for reorganization that is specific to certain neural strata and not present in others. These distinctions are relevant to the discussion that I now present.

Finally, does internal modularity, such as has been argued for in the work cited earlier, affect the intriguing question of Modularity? Although internal modularity enhances the plausibility of Modularity, the latter remains essentially an independent issue. Even if the modules of grammar were dependent on each other, this would not prevent the grammatical system as a whole from being domain specific and Modular. However, following the logic of the Specificity Hypothesis (Gopnik & Meltzoff, 1986), if there is enough evidence pointing to specific ties between language and cognition and, in particular, if those can be shown to play a role in syntax, claims of Modularity will become less plausible.

A similar logic obtains when one considers the impact of claims concerning the acquisitional course on Modularity. As it stands, the Modularity thesis makes no claim with regard to development. Yet, clearly, if the developmental course exhibits modular properties from its inception, the plausibility of the Modularity thesis in reference to the mature grammar will be greatly enhanced. For example, if one can show that early linguistic categories do not derive from preexisting cognitive or social communicative categorization and that linguistic rules require domain-specific categories as input, then this is support for Modularity. On the other hand, it is quite possible to conceive of an interactive, nonmodular developmental course that will result in a system that will be ultimately "bootstrapped" into Modularity. Schlesinger's (1982) semantic assimilation model could, in principle, be such a proposal. Schlesinger suggested that the child starts off with a semantic definition of linguistic categories that, through a process of assimilation, became co-extentional with formal grammatical categories. Schlesinger argued that the adult grammatical categories, although formal, maintain a semantic flavor that attests to their origin and remains, in part, responsible for category membership. In other words, the categories never actually become informationally encapsulated. In a series of experiments Schlesinger (1989) and Guberman (1992) presented evidence for the semantics of grammatical categories in adults and in children. But suppose one could show that these semantic connotations and associations are artifacts of the experimental situation and in spontaneous use the mature categories lack these semantic aromas, then we would have a nonmodular acquisitional process that results in domain-specific categories.

Another example is Bloom (chap. 3) who argues that some transitions in language development are the result of the interaction between (a) mapping that is part of linguistic knowledge and (b) cognitive biases. Bloom's example relates to the learning of the count/mass distinction in English. He suggests that learning in this case is a function of the interaction between (a) the linguistic knowledge that count nouns refer to kinds of individuals and (b) a cognitive bias that is responsible for the fact that whole objects will be construed as individuals. Clearly, Bloom's interactive learning mechanism does not preclude the possibility of Modularity of the mature, postacquisition grammar.

In recent years there have been a number of studies arguing for the Modularity of the language faculty. Two such studies concern linguistic isolates, Genie and Chelsea.

Genie is among the better-studied cases of language pathology (Curtiss, 1977, 1979). She suffered a uniquely traumatic experience of social and emotional isolation. From age 20 months to 13;7 Genie was socially isolated. During that time she lived in a severely impoverished environment and did not hear any human speech.

Genie's mental profile was uneven. She had good visual-spatial functions, but impaired verbal short-term memory. Her expressive vocabulary was relatively rich. It included color concepts, numbers, and emotional terms belonging to various levels of category membership. She had no closed-class morphology and essentially no syntax, only stringing of words in ways that generally conveyed the intended sense of the proposition. Here is a sample of Genie's utterances (Curtiss, 1988; numbers are mine):

	Utterance	Gloss
(1)	Applesauce buy store	'Buy applesauce at the store'
(2)	Man motorcycle have	'The man has a motorcycle'
(3)	Genie full stomach	'I have a full stomach'
(4)	Very angry Miss L.V. house	'I was very angry at Miss L.V.'s house'
(5)	Want Curtiss play piano	'I want you to play the piano'
(6)	Father hit Genie cry long time ago	'When father hit me I cried, a long time ago'
(7)	Mama have baby grow up	'Mama has a baby who grew up'

These examples demonstrate inconsistent and often ungrammatical order of constituents, lack of syntactic devices marking clausal relations, and omission of obligatory constituents. But note the semantic transparency of the propositions. Curtiss (1988) remarked that despite such examples, there was evidence that Genie had acquired some syntactic rules. For example, facts concerning subcategorization of verbs seem to have been learnt, order within phrasal categories was preserved, and bound morphology was never attached to the wrong grammatical category. Genie was able to establish and maintain topics in a conversation, but she never used any of the linguistic social conventions such as "Hello," "How do you do?," and so forth.

Chelsea was a hearing-impaired adult who began acquiring her first language in her early thirties (Curtiss, 1988). As a child she was misdiagnosed and therefore received no instruction or training. At age 32 her language was without syntax or morphology.

The following examples are taken from Curtiss (1988; numbers are mine):

(8) The small a the hat
(9) Richard eat peppers hot
(10) Banana the eat
(11) the boat sits water on
(12) Combing hair the boy
(13) The woman is bus the going
(14) The girl is come the ice cream shopping buying the man
(15) Daddy are be were to the work

The unconstrained use of determiners, the unpredictable order among constituents, the ungrammatical use of Aux, and the switch in constituents within NP suggest that Chelsea had no syntax. However, she did have a good knowledge of vocabulary and of situational pragmatics. She acquired words rapidly and steadily. Her lexicon appeared to be organized along normal semantic lines, yet it seemed not to include subcategorization information or logical connectives. Unlike Genie, Chelsea made effective use of fixed phrases and social formulas in conversation.

The cases of Genie and Chelsea, although striking and interesting, are only indirectly related to the issue of Modularity. They raise a question concerning the time limitation on the availability of mechanisms that are crucial for the acquisition of linguistic structure, since both these women learned language at a very late age. If there is indeed a critical age beyond which first language acquisition is doomed to remain structurally deficient, then this indirectly supports the notion of domain specificity in acquisition. But, although both Genie and Chelsea show severe impairments in syntax, neither show completely normal lexical or cognitive functioning, except in selected areas. Furthermore, they both grew up in severe environmental deprivation. Thus, in these cases a variety of features seem to be confounded: severe deficits in syntax, the critical age issue, a deficient cognition, and abnormal environmental conditions. Consequently, these cases are hard to interpret as either supporting or refuting the Modularity thesis.

The literature on congenital pathology includes cases in which there is no confounding between these various factors. These are cases of children with congenital retardation due to various etiologies, who grew up in normal environmental conditions. As expected, these children show very different linguistic and cognitive profiles from those of Genie and Chelsea. One of the groups to be considered here is the William's syndrome children (WMS). WMS is a genetic disorder that affects numerous organic systems. The most common features of WMS are mental retardation, characteristic facial features, and cardiovascular problems. Significantly, clinical reports of WMS children repeatedly mention their extraordinary linguistic abilities.

William's syndrome children have recently been the subject of intensive research ranging over genetic, physiological, and behavioral aspects. In Bellugi, Bihrle, Neville, Doherty, and Jernigan (1992) and Bellugi, Wang, and Jernigan (in press) 10 WMS adolescents were compared to Down syndrome (DNS) subjects. Subjects were matched for age, sex, and mental function on various cognitive and IQ measures. The WMS subjects and the DNS subjects were equally low on IQ tests. Both groups characteristically fail on Piagetian tests of conservation and seriation and on a variety of tests of concept formation and problem solving. The WMS subjects, but not those with DNS, showed a remarkable pattern of dissociation between cognitive and linguistic functions. The WMS subjects scored almost at ceiling on a test of comprehension of passives, negation, and conditionals. They did well on tag questions, on sentence completion, and on metalinguistic tasks that require detection and correction of syntactic anomalies. In spontaneous speech the WMS adolescents used a variety of grammatically complex forms, including passives, conditionals, and relatives. They used morphological markers correctly, including auxiliaries and articles. WMS subjects had an unusually large vocabulary. They used rare words in conversation and give within category, yet rather uncommon, responses. For example, when asked to name as many animals as they can, one child said: "weasel, newt, salamander, chihuahua, ibex, yak" (Bellugi et al., in press, p. 11). Such knowledge of words far exceeds that of normal, unexceptional individuals. WMS narratives exhibited well-formed story grammar and a variety of narrative enrichment devices. The following sentences are illustrative: "Once upon a time, when it was dark at night. . . . Next morning . . . there was no frog to be found. Lo and behold, they find him" (Bellugi et al., 1992, p. 12).

In sum, to use the authors' words: "WMS presents a rare decoupling of language from other cognitive capacities" (Bellugi et al., 1992, p. 22). Another population of children in which there were individual cases of children with exceptional linguistic abilities along with poorly functioning cognition were the retardates. Antony was 6 to 7 years old when he was studied (Curtiss, 1982; Curtiss & Yamada, 1981). Laura (Yamada, 1990) and D.H. (Cromer, in press) were in their adolescent years when they were studied. Both Antony and Laura suffered severe retardation of unknown origin, and D.H. was a spina-bifida child with an arrested hydrocephalus; she too was severely retarded. The children had similar cognitive profiles: extremely poor cognitive performance in contrast with reasonable, and at times exceptional, language use. Of the three children, D.H., who was diagnosed as having the "chatterbox" syndrome, had the most impressive linguistic abilities: Her language was fluent, her topics were varied, and her syntax was flawless. Antony was the youngest and this affected the way he spoke and the things he talked about. Despite quantitative differences, these individuals appear to have similar cognitive profiles, that is, as similar as can be expected in clinical studies. Consider in detail Laura's linguistic abilities, which I believe serve as a good illustration of the kind of empirical findings typically used to argue in favor of Modularity. The data are taken from Yamada's (1990) comprehensive study of Laura.

Laura was age 16 to 18;6 during observation and testing. Standard intelligence tests reflected a striking discrepancy between her performance IQ and her verbal scores. She failed most of the conservation tasks and all of the seriation and classification tasks. Laura's drawings were at the preschool level and were perseverative and stereotypic. Her spatial abilities, her number concept, her performance on classification and categorization tasks, and her hierarchical constructions were all at the level of 3- to 4-year-olds. Her performance on a variety of neuropsychological tests was equally poor: figure-ground perception, Mooney faces, Corsi blocks, Knox cubes, facial recognition test were all way below expected age level. Surprisingly, Laura scored below the level of adequacy on Auditory Memory span and the Digit Span test. Adequate performance on these tests is believed to be prerequisite for language functioning. Note that although Antony, D.H., and Laura present a similar picture in their spontaneous use of language, they differ in their performance on various language tests. For example, whereas D.H. does very well on comprehension tests, Laura does rather poorly on tests of comprehension, but amazingly well on tests of production.

Laura's linguistic production revealed an extensive knowledge of English. Yamada reported that she could correctly produce the following constructions: full and agentless passives, coordination, conjunctions, subordination of all kinds (wh-relative clauses, subject and object relatives, double coreferentials, conjunctions of time and causality, headless relatives), complements with participials, temporal adverbs, modification, strings of adjectives, and elliptical constructions. Laura performed well on sentence repetition tasks. In her repetitions, she corrected errors of syntax. Laura scored at ceiling on the Developmental Scoring Test, which is a production test, but scored very low on the CYCLE-R and the Token Test, both tapping comprehension of syntax. In formal testing of comprehension of morphological forms Laura failed to even approach the level she achieved in spontaneous production. In her spontaneous speech Laura correctly marked agreement on verbs, used appropriately the third person -s, the possessive - 's, and noun plurals. These were correct referentially, as well as morphologically. She had good knowledge of the auxiliary system, including complex auxiliaries and the irregular forms, and formed questions correctly.

Laura's spontaneous utterances indicated that she had correctly sorted out the meanings of many forms and could use them appropriately. She used subject pronouns and correctly marked them for gender, number, and person. Laura's use of gender and person was referentially correct. She used animacy appropriately, used inanimate *it* correctly, and appropriately marked negation and past and future tense. She showed knowledge of semantic relations and had an impressive vocabulary. She often did not know the full meaning of the terms she was using, but knew what kind of word was needed (e.g., a number or a color term). Yamada reported on the use of *before*, *after*, *until*, *if*, and *because* and of temporal adverbials such as *during*, *after*, and *ago*. Laura seemed to know about tenses and about their relatedness to temporal adverbs. Laura was often factually wrong and suffered a severe deficit of world knowledge. Her deficient performance on tests of comprehension was evident with respect to semantics as well. Despite her rich knowledge of words, Laura did poorly on the Peabody Picture Vocabulary Test and was inconsistent in her performance on various semantic aspects in the CYCLE-R. Although Laura made use of some discourse conventions, her conversation was often odd. She often failed to make the necessary logical connection between the preceding utterance and her own. She often did not supply the listener with the necessary information. She failed to respond to questions and introduced topics inappropriately. In short, Laura's use of language as a communicative tool was extremely poor.

The following are some examples of Laura's language. Examples are taken from Yamada (1990; numbers are mine):

(16) There's a car gettin' ticketed, Dad. That's last year at (name of school) when I first went there three tickets were gave out by a police last year.

(17) We're really excited about school starting and I love it myself.

(18) She does paintings, this really good friend of the kids who I went to school with last year, and really loved.

(19) Did you hear about me not going to this school up in Altadena?

(20) They just went to a bar after the movie was over.

(21) I do not have a roomer. My roommate left. Alexandra left.

Not only did Laura have a good vocabulary, but she could also converse about the meaning of words and about synonyms. For example:

(22) J: Can a book be happy?
L: A person can.

(23) J: Can an apple be eaten by a stove?
L: No, apples are eaten by people!

(24) J: Bachelors are married.
L: No, they live alone.

(25) [J. has asked Laura to name as many fruits as she can]
L: pears . . . apples . . . pomegranates

Utterly bizarre, however, were the replicas that Laura produced. These made little pragmatic sense. Yamada wrote that

> Laura's most complex, voluminous output was produced during lengthy stretches of speech that could aptly be termed "spiels." These spiels contained many examples of complex structures that seemed quite normal out of context. However, in context many of the utterances were uninterpretable. Although individual sentences might have been well-formed, connections between utterances were often unclear. The spiels contained many stereotyped or perseverative chunks and phrases, unclear anaphoric references, frequent topic switches, neologisms, and imprecise articulations. There were many false starts and hesitations and the speech was punctuated by unintelligible items. . . . Much of this is reminiscent of the speech of a Wernicke's aphasic. (p. 58)

The spiels are striking in the extent to which they lack cohesion among discourse units that is typically achieved through topic maintenance or semiotic relevance. Yet, one can discern in them structurally well-formed phrases as well as whole sentences.

The existence of such rich and appropriate language alongside factually false, linguistically inaccurate, and socially inept utterances was characteristic of Laura. More often than not, there is structural as well as semantic coherence at the sentence level, whereas at the level of the discourse one often finds inadequate performance.

Laura is indeed a striking case of the fractionation of cognition; on the one hand, there is a deplorably low performance on various cognitive tests and—most importantly—in everyday life, and on the other, an amazing language ability. Should this fractionation be interpreted as support for the Modularity of language, as claimed by Yamada (1990)? Do the cases of Antony, D.H., and the WMS children, who are so similar to Laura, constitute such support?

The purpose of presenting the case of Laura in such detail was to impress the reader with the **impossibility** of separating linguistic aspects from conceptual ones in Laura's language production and comprehension. Although there are a few secondary features, for example various morphological markers, for which it is possible to separate form from meaning, yet for the bulk of the data, such linguistic performance seems to be dependent on a sufficiently rich conceptual system that is capable of subserving such a feat. How else would Laura know how to speak about bars, movies, roommates, and tickets in a sensible way? A similar case can be made for Antony, D.H., and the WMS children.

The moral of these cases seems very different from what has been argued for in the literature. In my view, one cannot conclude from these cases about the status of language as an independent module; it is not just lexical knowledge that is revealed in the way the children use words within sentences, but a whole conceptual network, a putatively nonexistent one, given their severe retardation, that must be involved. One is struck by the exceptional achievements that these retarded individuals are capable of when the vehicle is language; particularly, natural, spontaneous use of language. It seems that these individuals have uniquely preserved abilities that show up only through the use of language. Thus, when the task is linguistic, the necessary conceptual work becomes manageable too and language is produced and comprehended in a remarkable way.

Could there be, then, a separate conceptual system that is uniquely designed to accommodate language? Notice that a semantic system, namely a system that is part of linguistic competence, is not the issue here. Nothing short of a general conceptual network will suffice. Although it is logically possible that the mind has system-specific conceptual networks, still, it seems an ad hoc solution to the problem that these patients pose. Because normal individuals provide no evidence for the existence of a host of conceptual systems, the distinction does not seem sufficiently motivated.

But what if the routes that allow access into the conceptual system were task-specific? If this were the case, we may conclude that in these disabled individuals, the language route is the only one through which the conceptual system may be accessed, though that too may fall short at times. Access for performance of tasks other than linguistic invariably fails and the consequences for the individual are catastrophic.[1]

Are there acquired pathologies that present behavioral patterns that favor explanations in terms of differentially preserved access routes?

---

[1]The WMS children, however, show remarkable abilities in face recognition as well as in language (Bellugi et al., 1992).

The behavioral pattern that characterizes Genie and Chelsea is not unlike patterns observed in patients who have suffered brain damage, yet the behavioral profile of Laura, Antony, WMS patients, and D.H. are rarely encountered as a result of acquired insults. Although patients with neurological deficits often show language impairments in conjunction with preserved cognitive functioning, it is very unusual for spontaneous language to be intact when general cognitive abilities are impaired. The dementias in their earlier phases might perhaps be such cases, but to date there is no detailed study that describes such a state (R. Ostrin, personal communication, December 1992). There have been, however, several descriptions of cases of various pathologies associated with language that are relevant to the previous discussion. The analogy to the present cases is only partial, because these are patients in whom problems of access are identified within the various *linguistic* modalities. Such are the cases reported by Funnell and Allport (1987) and cases of the modality-specific and category-specific aphasias (Shallice, 1988). They are, nevertheless, instructive because the model of the mind they favor includes certain features necessary to account for the aforementioned developmental cases as well.

Funnell and Allport presented an account of two patients with "privileged access," involving transcoding from written to spoken or from spoken to written linguistic forms. One patient is a fluent aphasic who had severe anomia, that is, loss of specific references and its replacement by nonspecific, general purpose terms. The patient had a combined pattern of fluent, anomic speech, with a marked repetition deficit and phonological errors in naming, characteristic of "conduction" aphasia. The second patient was a nonfluent Broca's aphasic whose speech was confined almost exclusively to specific nouns and was devoid of syntactic constructions. Despite their very different pattern of aphasia, amounting to a "double dissociation" with respect to their usage of "specific" and "nonspecific" words, *both* patients were significantly more successful in transcoding specific than nonspecific words in the three tasks used: reading aloud a visually presented word, writing to dictation (first letter only), and oral-to-visual matching. When asked to repeat the same tasks with a set of pronounceable, one-syllable pseudowords and then with single letters and their spoken phonetic counterparts, the patients were completely unable to read these stimuli or to produce them from dictation. Although impairments were discerned, in auditory-to-vocal repetition and in copying written words—that is, in within-modality tasks—all classes of letter-strings were affected, real words were better than nonwords and there was no sign of the superiority of specific over nonspecific word classes that was so marked in the cross-modal tasks. Thus, it seems that in order to transcode from written to spoken or from spoken to written linguistic forms the patients had to encode the referential word meaning. This was not necessary for a within-modal task. In other words, the direct route leading from visual to auditory stores was unavailable. The targets could be reached, though, through the lexicon, provided they were stored there—in other words, if they were real words.

Another case in point is presented by the modality-specific aphasias. Shalice (1988) described those in the following way:

> The essential characteristics are that naming from one modality alone is impaired but there appears to be no agnostic difficulty in that modality. Thus, in optic aphasia . . . the naming of visually presented objects is impaired but objects can be named from touch; the syndrome cannot be a loss of the names of objects. Yet, the patient can identify objects presented visually if identification is assessed, say, by demonstrating use. (p. 292)

For example, patient GJ (Gil et al., 1985) made 38% errors in naming from vision, whereas in naming from touch or indicating use there were no errors at all.

One of the explanations offered for the modality-specific aphasias has been the existence of separable, modality-specific lexicons (Shallice, 1988). The deficits were held to result from impairments in the transmission of information from one lexicon to another, specifically, to the verbal linguistic one. Alternative hypotheses posit a single semantic system, but different routes for the different input modes. Orthogonally, access and degraded store impairments may be distinguished in different patients. However, more empirical work is needed before a satisfactory theoretical account may be attempted. Even more puzzling than the modality-specific aphasias are the impairments in specific semantic categories. Such are Dennis' (1976) patients, who had difficulties in naming body parts, but not in naming other words of comparable frequency; or Goodglass and Kaplan's patient (1972), who made significantly more errors in naming fruits and vegetables than on all other items. Warrington and Shallice (1984) described two patients whose ability to identify by description pictures of inanimate objects was much better than that of identifying living things or foods. Silveri and Gianoti's (1987; reported in Shallice, 1988) patient, LA, was much better in naming on the basis of perceptual definitions than on either metaphorical or functional definitions.

As data accumulated from various patients, it became clear that these deficits can occur as semantic access deficits, as degraded store deficits or as naming deficits. There seem to be patterns of categories that go together and are either selectively impaired or preserved.

How are these cases of modality-specific aphasias and of specific transcoding abilities related to cases such as Laura, Antony, and D.H. and to the WMS children? Whatever the explanation of these domain-specific or category-specific effects, it is clear that the patterns of dissociation point at connections among different types of information, some of which are outside of the semantic system itself. One particular attempt to describe these nonlinguistic attribute domains included action-oriented elements, kinesthetic elements, tactile elements, visual elements and auditory elements, all of which, when intact, can access the verbal linguistic representations (Allport, 1985). The aforementioned domains taken together are, presumably, what we mean by "conceptual system." This is the network that represents meanings and, of course, it is not exclusively linguistic. The previous cases demonstrate that access may depend on the exact nature of the task. For tasks that are semantic, when the target word may be reached through one modality but not through another, one has to assume that the relevant linguistic representation exists and it is processing or access that is at fault.

Of particular relevance to this chapter is the fact that the picture of the mind that emerges from considerations of these cases is one in which there are modality-specific routes leading to a single verbal-semantic system. I suggest that a similar metaphor be used to describe the cases of the congenitally retarded children. The problem that these individuals have involves the routes, or perhaps the keys that open the gates to the different routes. Those seem to be molded to fit task-specificity, rather than modality-specificity. What we see in these patients, is that the entry-point used by the language system in the production and comprehension of spontaneous speech, is the least affected by the pathology. When the mediator is spontaneous use of language the person can make use of his mind, so to speak, whereas the routes or entry points, designed for other tasks are sadly blocked.

In summary, the cases that have been reviewed here suggest a functional organization of the mind, one of the principles of which is that the availability of cognitive resources is conditional on the type of task they are called on to perform. Thus, we assume that there is an intact underlying conceptual system in these individuals, which is unreachable for most tasks, but is accessible by means of language. In this respect the patients discussed here are unlike Down syndrome patients or other retarded individuals in whom there is a general profile of depressed performance with no outstanding abilities. The previous argument will be strengthened if cases of "double dissociation" can be found in which impairment of general cognition is accompanied by linguistic malfunctioning, yet there will be some other symbolic system—drawing or mimicking—that has been spared. Such cases may be found among autistic children or possibly in the rare cases of idiot savants; the latter case still awaits in-depth empirical and theoretical work.

As for the question of the Modularity of language, the cases of Laura, Antony, D.H., and the WMS patients have not brought us any closer to an answer than we were before they were studied. These children's performance is perhaps marginally relevant to the issue of modularity of the parser because of their impressive control of syntax but, crucially, their cognitive and linguistic profiles are not appropriately interpretable as addressing the issue of Fodorian Modularity.

REFERENCES

Allport, D. A. (1985). Distributed memory, modular systems and dysphasia. In S. K. Newman & R. Epstein (Eds.), *Current perspectives in dysphasia* (pp. 32–60). Edinburgh: Churchill Livingstone.

Bellugi, U., Bihrle, A., Neville, H., Doherty, S., & Jernigan, T. (1992). Language, cognition and brain organization in neurodevelopmental disorder. In M. Gunnar & C. Nelson (Eds.), *Developmental behavioral neuroscience: The Minnesota symposia on child psychology* (pp. 22–57). Hillsdale, NJ: Lawrence Erlbaum Associates.

Bellugi, U., Wang, P. P., & Jernigan, T. L. (in press). William's syndrome: An unusual neuropsychological profile. In J. Broman & J. Grafman (Eds.), *Atypical cognitive deficits in developmental disorders: Implications for brain function.* Hillsdale, NJ: Lawrence Erlbaum Associates.

Chomsky, N. (1965). *Aspects of the theory of syntax.* Cambridge, MA: MIT Press.

Chomsky, N. (1986). Some observations on language and language learning: Reply to MacNamara, Arbib and Moore and Furrow. *New Ideas in Psychology, 4*(4), 363–377.

Cromer, R. (in press). A case study of dissociation between language and cognition. In H. Tager-Flusberg (Ed.), *Constraints on language acquisition: Studies of atypical children.* Hillsdale, NJ: Lawrence Erlbaum Associates.

Curtiss, S. (1977). *Genie: A psycholinguistic study of a modern-day "wild-child."* New York: Academic Press.

Curtiss, S. (1979). Genie: Language and cognition. *UCLA Working Papers in Cognitive Linguistics, 1,* 15–62.

Curtiss, S. (1982). Developmental dissociations of language and cognition. In L. Obler & L. Menn (Eds.), *Exceptional language and linguistics* (pp. 285–312). New York: Academic Press.

Curtiss, S. (1988). Abnormal language acquisition and the modularity of language. In F. J. Newmeyer (Ed.), *Linguistics: The Cambridge survey.* Cambridge, MA: Cambridge University Press.

Curtiss, S., & Yamada, J. (1981). Selectively intact grammatical development in a retarded child. *UCLA Working Papers in Cognitive Linguistics, 3,* 61–91.

Dennis, M. (1976). Dissociated naming and locating of body parts after left anterior temporal lobe resection: An experimental case study. *Brain and Language, 3,* 147–163.

Fodor, J. (1983). *The modularity of mind.* Cambridge, MA: MIT Press.

Fodor, J. (1985). Multiple book review of *The modularity of mind. Behavioral and Brain Sciences, 8,* 1–42.

Funnell, E., & Allport, A. (1987). Non-linguistic cognition and word meanings: Neuropsychological exploration of common mechanisms. In A. Allport, D. M. MacKay, W. Prinz, & E. Scheerer (Eds.), *Language perception and production* (pp. 367–400). London: Academic Press.

Gil, R., Plunchon, C., Toullat, G., Michenau, D., Rogez, R., & Levevre, J. P. (1985). Disconnexion viso-verbale (aphasie optique) pour les objects, les images, les couleurs et les visages avec alexie "abstractive." *Neuropsychologia, 23*, 333–349.

Goodglass, H., & Kaplan, E. (1972). *The assessment of aphasia and related disorders.* Philadelphia: Lea & Febiger.

Gopnik, E., & Meltzoff, A. N. (1986). Relations between semantic and cognitive development in the one-word stage: The specificity hypothesis. *Child Development, 57*, 1040–1053.

Guberman, A. (1992). *The development of the verb category in Hebrew child language.* Unpublished doctoral dissertation, Hebrew University, Jerusalem.

Higginbotham, J. (1987). The autonomy of syntax and semantics. In J. L. Garfield (Ed.), *Modularity in knowledge representation and natural-language understanding* (pp. 129–163). Cambridge, MA: MIT Press.

Levy, Y., Amir, N., & Shalev, R. (1992). Linguistic development of a child with a congenital, localised L.H. lesion. *Cognitive Neuropsychology, 9*(1), 1–32.

MacNamara, J. (1989). More about principles and parameters: A reply to Chomsky. *New Ideas in Psychology, 7*(1), 33–40.

Schlesinger, I. M. (1982). *Steps to language.* Hillsdale, NJ: Lawrence Erlbaum Associates.

Schlesinger, I. M. (1989). Instruments as agents. *Journal of Linguistics, 25*, 189–210.

Shallice, T. (1988). *From neuropsychology to mental structure.* Cambridge, MA: Cambridge University Press.

Silveri, M. C., & Gianoti, G. B. (1987). *Interaction between vision and language in category specific semantic impairment for living things.* Unpublished manuscript.

Warrington, E. K., & Shallice, T. (1984). Category specific semantic impairments. *Brain, 107*, 829–853.

Yamada, J. E. (1990). *Laura—A case for the modularity of language.* Cambridge, MA: MIT Press.

Author Index

Language Index

Subject Index